AN INTRODUCTION

AN INTRODUCTION TO
ELVISH

AND TO OTHER TONGUES AND PROPER NAMES AND WRITING SYSTEMS OF
THE THIRD AGE OF THE WESTERN LANDS OF MIDDLE-EARTH
AS SET FORTH IN THE PUBLISHED WRITINGS
OF
PROFESSOR JOHN RONALD REUEL TOLKIEN

Edited and Compiled by
JIM ALLAN
from his own researches and from those of
NINA CARSON, BJÖRN FROMÉN, CHRIS GILSON, ALEXANDRA TARASOVNA
KICENIUK, LAURENCE J. KRIEG, PAULA MARMOR, LISE MENN,
BILL WELDEN, *and others.*

As Authorized by the Mythopoeic Linguistic Fellowship,
a Discussion Group of
the Mythopoeic Society.

BRAN'S head

dedicated to
Richard Plotz

An Introduction to Elvish
copyright 1978 Jim Allen

First published 1978
Reprinted 1983, 1987, 1995,
2001, 2002, 2003

ISBN 0 905220 10 2

Printed at
The Bath Press, Bath

Bran's Head Books
Helios, Glenfinnan, Inverness-shire

Acknowledgments

'Quenya Grammar & Dictionary', 'Sindarin Grammar & Dictionary', 'Other Tongues', 'The Evolution of the Tengwar', and 'Runes' are expansions of material originally published as *A Glossary of the Eldarin Tongues*, copyright © 1972, Canada, by James D. Allan, save as follows:
'Verbs' in the section 'The Structure of Quenya' is largely based on 'Notes Toward a System of Quenya Verb Structure', copyright © 1974, Canada, by Paula Marmor, published in *Tolkien Language Notes* 1.
'On Pronouns in Quenya' by Bill Welden is a revision of the article of the same name published in *Parma Eldalamberon* 3, copyright © 1973, U.S.A, by the Mythopoeic Society, and incorporates material from 'Eldarin Pronouns', copyright © 1974, Canada, by James D. Allan, published in *Tolkien Language Notes* 2.
The comparisons between Welsh and Sindarin scattered throughout 'The Structure of Sindarin' originally appeared as 'Welsh & Sindarin', copyright © 1974, Canada, by James D. Allan, published in *Tolkien Language Notes* 1.
The correspondences with non-Eldarin languages in the dictionaries are largely from 'Mathoms', copyright © 1973, Canada, by Paula Marmor and James D. Allan, published in *Tolkien Language Notes* 1.
'Valinórenna' by Björn Fromén, copyright © 1973, Sweden, by the 'Forodrim', published in *Palantiren* 2.

'English-Quenya/Sindarin Index' is an expansion of 'English Index to the Quenya and Sindarin Sections of A GLOSSARY OF THE ELDARIN TONGUES', copyright © 1973, Canada, by Nina Carson, Alexandra Kiceniuk, and James D. Allan, published in *Tolkien Language Notes* 1.

Much of the material in 'The Giving of Names' originally appeared in the following articles:
'A Categorial List of the Proper Names in the Fiction of J. R. R. Tolkien', 'Comments on Names in the Fiction of J. R. R. Tolkien,' 'The Northern Names', all copyright © 1973, Canada, by James D. Allan, all published in *Tolkien Language Notes* 1.
'Name Giving', copyright © 1974, Canada, by James D. Allan, published in *Tolkien Language Notes* 2.
'The Queer Brandybuck Names' by Jim Allan, copyright © 1973, U.S.A. by the Mythopoeic Society, published in *Parma Eldalamberon* 4.

'Tengwar Fact Sheet Notes' and 'Tengwar Fact Sheet' in the article 'The Tengwar of Fëanor' by Laurence J. Krieg appeared in earlier versions as 'fact sheet guide' and 'Tengwar Fact Sheet', copyright © 1974, U.S.A., by the Mythopoeic Society, published in *Parma Eldalamberon* 4.

'A Survey of Some English-Tengwar Orthographies' by Laurence J. Krieg is reprinted with slight revisions from the article of the same name, copyright © 1974, U.S.A., by the Mythopoeic Society, published in *Parma Eldalamberon* 4.

The following material appears here in revised form by permission of the Mythopoeic Society:
'An Etymological Excursion Among the Shire Folk' by Paula Marmor, copyright © 1971, U.S.A., by the Mythopoeic Society, published in *Mythlore* 7.
Additions and corrections to the above article in a letter by Paula Marmor, copyright © 1972, U.S.A., by the Mythopoeic Society, published in *Mythlore* 8. (This material has been incorporated in the article as here printed.)
'The Wielders of the Three and Other Trees' by Paula Marmor,

ACKNOWLEDGMENTS

copyright © 1972, U.S.A., by the Mythopoeic Society, published in *Mythlore* 8.

'On the Formation of Plurals in Sindarin' by Bill Welden, copyright © 1971, U.S.A., by the Mythopoeic Society, published in *Parma Eldalamberon* 1. The revised version here printed incorporates material from 'Welsh & Sindarin', copyright © 1974, Canada, by James D. Allan, published in *Tolkien Language Notes* 1.

'A Parallel to the Tengwar' by Jim Allan, revised from 'A Source for Tolkien's Tengwar?', copyright © 1972, U.S.A., by the Mythopoeic Society, published in *Parma Eldalamberon* 2.

'Proto-Eldarin Vowels: A Comparative Survey' by Chris Gilson & Bill Welden, copyright © 1977, U.S.A., by the Mythopoeic Society, published in *Parma Eldalamberon* 5.

'The Correct Tengwar and Certar Values' by Jim Allan, revised from 'Corrections to the Tengwar and Certar Values Assigned in Current Editions of *The Lord of the Rings*', copyright © 1977, U.S.A., by the Mythopoeic Society, published in *Parma Eldalamberon* 5.

FOREWORD

IN AN INTERVIEW WITH Henry Resnik (*Niekas* 18, Late Spring, 1967), Tolkien said:

> The real seed was starting when I was quite a child by
> inventing languages, largely to try and capture the
> esthetic mode of the languages I was learning, and I even-
> tually made the discover that language can't exist in a
> void, and if you invent a language yourself you can't cut
> it in half. It had to come alive—so really the languages
> came first and the country after. (p. 41)

But there is little enough pure linguistic material in Tolkien's published writings on the first three ages of Middle-
earth, much less than many of Tolkien's readers desire.

The long-ago world shown forth in *The Hobbit* and *The Lord
of the Rings* is no utopia. Grim horrors and evil doings
abounded then as they do now. Yet it was also a time of
great beauty, when nature had not been so dispoiled by Man,
and when Elves and other speaking races still walked openly
in the world and wrought works of wonder and enchantment.
The books whet the desire of the reader for more of the same.
O! to be able to walk through the ancient streets of old Min
Minas Tirith, to ride through the Wold with the Rohirrim,
to see and handle the skilled and cunning works of Dwarvish
hands, or to wander beneath blossoming *mallorn* branches in
the forest of Lothlórien in the spring! But though the
reader cannot do any of these in body, many are drawn to
come as close as they can to those enchanted times by in some
measure attempting to relive them, or to renew them.
    The publication of *The Lord of the Rings* in 1954, 1955
inspired the foundation of numerous small local Tolkien discussion groups and societies. Others, who did not know of
such groups, worked alone, or with one or two friends,

discussing the histories of the peoples of those days,
devising Hobbit recipes, writing their own stories set in
the same world, making use of the tengwar of certar alphabets, and even investigating the fragments of the old languages of the Elves that appeared in *The Lord of the Rings*.
    Ten years later *The Lord of the Rings* was published in
paperback and became accessible to multitudes who otherwise
would never have known of it. There was an immense increase
in the amount of 'fan activity'. Local groups proliferated,
and a larger number of small publications—'fanzines'—
appeared dealing with Tolkien's works, with the Tolkien
Society of America—founded and managed by New York high
school student Dick Plotz—as a sort of super-group to which
almost everyone belonged. Matters linguistic were not neg-
lected in these publications. Several different tengwar
and certar modes were proposed and argued over; it was discovered that Tolkien's dwarf names could mostly be found in
the Norse Eddas; Bob Foster attempted translations of many
of the Elvish personal names and place names in his *Guide to
Middle-Earth* which was being published in installments in
the fanzine *Niekas*, and sparked linguistic arguments in that
journal's letter column.
    Two fanzines are of special interest: *Glyph* and *Caran-
daith*. *Glyph* was founded in 1969 by Stanley Hoffman and,
after the first two issues, continued in 1970 by Frank Den-
ton. It was unique in being written entirely in tengwar and
certar characters. *Carandaith*'s editor Alpajpuri (Paul Nov-
itsky) had a special interest in the Elvish tongues and cal-
ligraphy, and he wrote articles for his fanzine attempting
to translate and explain the grammar of some of Tolkien's
Elvish, and setting forth his own tengwar mode (see pp. 261-
64 of this book).
    By this time there seemed to be a reasonable number of
people who had acquired a certain basic knowledge of the Elvish tongues, several of them being in regular correspondence
with one another. Also, the Mythopoeic Society, a group
centered in Southern California, interested in fantasy in
general and in the works of Tolkien, C. S. Lewis, and Charles
Williams in particular, had become the second largest of the
Tolkien oriented fan groups, and by far the most active in
publishing. There were in the Mythopoeic Society a few
persons in the Southern California area who had got very much
into Tolkien's languages and into invented language in general, and it seemed that it might be desireable that some
publication appear, under the aegis of the Mythopoeic Society, to provide a central focus for the study of Tolkien's
languages and names and writing systems, and the languages
in the works of C. S. Lewis, and other such tongues found in

published works of other authors, or devised by individuals
for their own amusement. So, in 1971, the Mythopoeic Linguistic Fellowship was founded, and the first issue of its
journal, *Parma Eldalamberon*, appeared. In the following
year I, myself, privately published a short booklet titled
A Glossary of the Eldarin Tongues, with the intention of
providing what could serve, at least, as a firm basis of
disagreement for Quenya, Sindarin, the other languages, and
the writing systems.

In *Parma Eldalamberon* 1, Paula Marmor, the 'Middle-earth
editor', had written:

> One of the first goals of the Mythopoeic Linguistic
> Linguistics Fellowship was and is the publication (or
> preparation for publication) of The Book, a composite
> dictionary, grammar, sourcebook and history of the Elven
> languages, with appendices covering the other tongues of
> Middle-earth, including glossaries of the Anglo-Saxon,
> Frankish, Norse and Celtic names found among the Rohir-
> rim, Dwarves, Woodmen and Hobbits; Adûnaic, Westron,
> Old Mannish and Hobbitish and *their* relationships; the
> evolution of Elven grammar and the interconnections of
> those tongues with the other languages of Middle-earth,
> and so on to the point of an Excedrin headache. This is
> obviously too great a work for one person alone, or for
> a small group of people, and our Dream expanded to a
> Grand Compendium of Tolkienian Trivia, with contributors
> scattered near and far, with conflicting theories neces-
> sitating sections of minority opinions, with mail flying
> from state to state and continent to continent to dispute
> a certain Quenya inflexional ending....

In 1973, as supplies of my own booklet diminished, I began
to think of a revised version. (There were too many errors
that had been pointed out to me—or which I had discovered
myself—to allow a simple reprinting, and much extra material
that I wished to include.) But a new, much expanded version
would not be, as the earlier *Glossary* was, mainly an individual effort. My increased knowledge owed too much to the published work and private correspondence of others, and there
were whole articles by others that should be included. So, I
wrote to Paula Marmor, urging that the MLF get down to serious work on The Book, volunteering to do anything I could to
help in its swift completion. If there were really no way
that she or others involved with *Parma* could see their way
clear to getting ahead with this project, then I would even
be willing to take charge of it myself. Paula wrote back
that she had talked with Bill Welden and others, and the con-
census was that there was little enthusiasm on their part to

getting right down to work at the present time, but lots of enthusiasm for me putting forth my efforts and taking charge of the project, if I wanted to.... I agreed.

I began collecting and organizing material, some of which was circulated in 1973 and 1974 under the title *Tolkien Language Notes* to those involved in the project, and to others whose advice was solicited. In 1974 Bill Welden managed to crack the problem of Proto-Eldarin and circulated his notes on the subject. But work proceeded slowly. In 1975 the Elvish material had been worked into publishable form, along with material on the other languages and much of the material on names, but the manuscript was destroyed in an apartment fire, leaving me with only my initial notes. Then, beginning in September 1975, I found myself involved as one of the editors of *Mythprint*, the bulletin of the Mythopoeic Society (then a fairly large monthly publication) and dropped that only in the spring of 1976 to work as one of the production editors on *Mythlore*, the Mythopoeic Society Journal. Only when my involvement ceased in December 1976 was I finally able to devote full leisure-time activity to this book—save for that taken up by my duties as programmer for a local science-fiction convention in the summer of 1977. (Leisure time?)

As the project drew to a close, it was announced that the long-awaited *Silmarillion* was scheduled for publication the forthcoming autumn. This will have the effect of rendering at least the Elvish sections of this guide obsolete upon publication, and it may be asked why the book was not delayed for another six months or so, to enable such further data as *The Silmarillion* will contain to be incorporated.

First, the incorporation of further data is more likely to take three years than three months, if it is to be done thoroughly and well. But I still regularly receive requests for copies of my out-of-print *Glossary*, indicating a need felt by many Tolkien fans for some sort of commentary and dictionary on Elvish, written by people who know something about it, if only because they have been working at it so long, and have been in communication with one another to share and criticize their individual theories.

Second, a book with is somewhat outdated may actually prove more involving to the reader than one which takes account of all the evidence that the reader also has. We hope that the necessity of comparing the dictionary entries we give and our clever theories (some undoubtedly too clever by half) with the data supplied by *The Silmarillion* will enable you to make your own discoveries as to the correct meanings of words and names, and how different forms are related to each other.

Third, *The Silmarillion* is unlikely to have any effect

on the accuracy (or lack thereof) of the larger portion of
this book which does not deal with the Elvish languages.
So, this volume is offered without presumption, for
whatever you, the reader, may find of worth in its pages. It
is in no sense an authorized publication. We have had some
access to unpublished materials, but our findings from this
have been minor indeed; they were mostly of value in providing addtional confirmation of theories already held. You,
the reader, after absorbing what has been compiled in this
book, should be as fully competent in the areas here covered
as we are, and you are encouraged to participate with us in
further exploration. Comments on any of the material published here are very welcome, and may be sent to the editor,
c/o the publisher, or the the Mythopoeic Linguistic Fellowship, c/o The Mythopoeic Society as given on page 302.

The following works by J. R. R. Tolkien are the main
sources for the material compiled in this volume, and may be
thought of as the corpus or canon:
>   *The Hobbit*, abbreviated 'H';
>   *The Lord of the Rings*, consisting of
>   *The Fellowship of the Rings*, abbreviated '1',
>   *The Two Towers*, abbreviated 'II', and
>   *The Return of the King*, abbreviated 'III';
>   *The Adventures of Tom Bombadil and other verses from
>   the Red Book*, abbreviated 'TB';
>   *The Road Goes Ever On* (music by Donald Swann),
>   abbreviated 'R';
>   'Guide to the Names in *The Lord of the Rings*' in *A
>   Tolkien Compass*, ed. Jared Lobdell (La Salle,
>   Illinois: Open Court, 1975), abbreviated 'G'; and
>   *A Map of Middle-Earth*, designed by J. R. R. Tolkien,
>   C. R. Tolkien, and Pauline Baynes, abbreviated 'MB'.
There are several variant texts for *The Lord of the
Rings*. The text of the first edition, also appearing with a
few misprints in the Ace paperback edition, is here symbolized by α. The earliest version of the revised text is that
which appears in the Ballantine paperback editions, here symbolized by β. (Some corrections of typographical errors were
made in β after the first few printings, and the symbols β_1
and β_2 might be used to cover this if required.) Further
revisions were made for the hardcover editions, most important of which was a reworking of the Index to include translations of some of the names, and annotations to some of the
entries. This is the text of the current Houghton-Mifflin
editions, and of Allen and Unwin edition published before
1969, and is here symbolized by γ. In 1969 Allen and Unwin
issued a one-volume paperback edition that omitted most of
the Appendices and the Index. Tolkien slightly revised

this text further, for example, changing the spellings *Galad-rim* and *Galadon* to *Galadhrim* and *Galadhon*, and introducing a new name of Aragorn's, *Envinyatar*. This same text, combined with the Appendices and Index from γ is found in all print-ings of the Allen and Unwin editions from 1969 onward, and also in the Canadian three-volume Methuen paperback .edition, and is here symbolized by δ. (The text δ is also used for the current Allen and Unwin three volume paperback edition, but with a change of pagination, and the addition of some typographical errors; the symbols δ₁ and δ₂ might be used.) Finally, in 1969, Allen and Unwin produced a one-volume deluxe edition, in which the text was reset. This version is unfortunately replete with typographical errors, but does correct some of the typographical errors of γδ (see the Quenya dictionary entry *Atan). Tolkien also revised the entry 'Star, as emblem' in the Index, ascribing to the Star of Elendil and to the seven stars of Elendil and his captains five points where γδ read 'six'. This text is here symbol-ized by ε.

Chris Gilson has informed me of one further change in the most recent Allen & Unwin printing of the deluxe one-volume edition (see the Sindarin dictionary entry Finarfin), and so we seem to have yet a further revised text, to be symbolized ζ.

The base text used in this book is that of δ, and all page references, save where otherwise stated, are to this version. (These references largely apply to other hardcover three-volume editions, of course.) Variants of the names and words found in other editions are listed also in the dictionary sections, and I believe that all intentional changes have been caught. In some cases we have preferred the form of a word or name found in a text other than δ. Note that a reference like βIII:401 does NOT mean that the reader should refer to page 401 of the Ballantine edition of *The Return of the King*, but to the page(s) in the Ballantine edition corresponding to page 401 of the second edition hard-cover versions of *The Return of the King*.

The first printings of the Pauline Baynes map (MB) had .umerous spellings errors, and they have not even been con-sidered for tabulation. All references to this map are to printings of 1971 or later.

Some portions of this book treat the Elvish languages as true historical tongues of a real people ('Elvish Loan-words in Indo-European: Cultural Implications', by Lise Menn), while in others they are considered as artificial creations invented by Tolkien ('Tolkien's Pronunciation: Some Observations', by Laurence J. Krieg). The editor has not tried to impose a consistent viewpoint here. The

Foreword to the first edition of *The Lord of the Rings* quite
definitely indicates that Tolkien is a translator and adap-
tor working primarily from the Red Book of Westmarch, but
also from records surviving from Gondor, and he states that
his map of part of the Shire 'has been approved as reasonably
correct by those Hobbits that still concern themselves with
ancient history'. In the Foreward to the later editions the
work is presented as a fiction. It is impossible to PROVE
by internal evidence which is the truth. Perhaps in the first
edition Tolkien was using the standard author's pose of pres-
enting an imagined tale as true. But perhaps, rather, in
later editions he falsely declared the work a tale of imagina-
ation to forestall inquiries as to his sources—sources which
he was quite certainly not at liberty to reveal.
    J. E. A. Tyler, in his *The Tolkien Companion* (London:
MacMillan London, 1976, pp. 8-10), insists that the corpus is
indeed compiled from ancient sources that had come into Tolkien's possession. On the other hand, Humphrey Carpenter, in
his *J. R. R. Tolkien: A biography* (London: George Allen &
Unwin, 1977) indicates, with what appears to be full circum-
stantial evidence, that the works are fictional, and that the
languages are invented. But whence springs invention?
Carpenter also tells of a purportedly fictional uncompleted
story by Tolkien called 'The Lost Road' in which

> a professor of history named Alboin (the Lombardic form.
> of 'Ælfwine'), invents languages, or rather, he finds
> that words are transmitted to him, words that seem to be
> fragments or ancient and forgotten languages. Many of
> these words refer to the downfall of Númenor, and the
> story breaks off, unfinished, with Alboin and his son
> setting off on their journey through time towards
> Númenor itself. (HC:171)

    That Tolkien apparently invented the languages is no
PROOF that they are altogether fictional. Their resemblance
to languages of our own day—Finnish and Welsh—and the
resemblances of many of their words to words of other tongues
might be considered a stronger argument. But there is the
generally unpopular—but not impossible—linguistic theory
that land and climate can mold language, so that similar
tongues might be expected to exist today in the lands where
the old Elves dwelt. Or it might be that some of the spirit
and the being of those Elves clings still to the land, as a
ghostly aura of enchantment—in Eregion Legolas could hear
the stones lament the passing of the Noldor (I:297)—and
the languages of Men have not been unaffected.
    Tolkien, for the most part, claimed the languages as
his inventions. He also claimed that '*Hobbit* is an invention' (III:416). Yet the word *hobbit* is to be found in a

nineteenth century list of various kinds of fairies, spirits,
and other supernaturals in *The Denham Tracts: A Collection
of Folklore*, Volume II, by Michael Aislabie Denham (ed.
Dr. James Hardy, London: The Folklore Society, 1895, p. 79).

The Elvish languages are here treated separately with
individual dictionaries for Quenya and Sindarin. It is
usually not too difficult to tell the languages apart by
the style of the words, though forms occasionally occur that
might belong to either language. For example, *Erusén, Fëanor*, *Mardil*, and *Melian* are here listed as Quenya, though
some argue they are Sindarin; and *Fingolfin*, *Nan-tasarion*,
Tasarinan, and *tinúviel* are here listed as Sindarin, though
some argue they are Quenya. (See, perhaps, *The Silmarillion*
for the answer.)

An attempt has been made to give meanings for as many as
possible of the forms cited, with the result that many meanings given, particularly those given for personal names, are
simple guesses. Question marks have been used to indicate
doubt, and could have been used much more frequently than
they have been.

In listing Quenya verb forms, the verb stem is given
first as the main entry, then the meaning of the stem, and
only then the forms actually found containing the stem.

Unless marked as plural, all nouns, adjectives, and
verbs are to be considered singular. The decision as to
whether a form is a noun or an adjective is sometimes rather
arbitrary. A noun may act as an adjective on occasiona, and
an adjective may act as a noun. I have not made, myself, any
distinction between adjectives and participles. Only forms
that Tolkien himself has called participles are so listed.

Nouns are listed in the main entry in the singular form,
save where none occurs and one cannot be easily derived from
the plural form. Such derived forms are marked by a preceding asterisk *. Forms which are found only in compounds in
the published corpus, but which look able to stand alone, are
marked by a preceding dagger †. Where it looks as those a
form would not stand along, a hyphen is placed preceding or
ᵒⁿllowing, depending on whether the form appears as a suffix
or prefix.

Where possible, in a dictionary entry, the word or words
of corresponding meaning in the other Eldarin tongue are
given between slashes / /. These words are sometimes derived
from the same original as the entry word, but sometimes not.
'Cf.' is used to direct the reader to other forms that MAY
have some relationship to the entry word.

Text references do not, usually, list all occurences of
a word or morpheme. Rather, they provide the reader with proof
that the form exists as cited, and, where possible, direct

the reader to the occurence(s) most helpful in establishing
the correct form(s) and meaning(s).

In *The Road Goes Ever On* Tolkien sometimes uses the
macron ˉ rather than the acute accent ´ to indicate long
vowels. In this book the acute accent is used throughout,
save for Proto-Eldarin forms. Tolkien is not consistent in
his use of the diaresis ¨ indicating a vowel to be pronounced. In general I have tried to include it on a form if
Tolkien ever uses it on that form, and to use it on reconstructed forms in parallel cases. But the sign is used by
Tolkien only as a convenience for English readers, to help
them pronounce the words correctly; it corresponds to no
feature of the Elvish spellings of the words, and has been
omitted on all forms in the discussions of Proto-Eldarin.

An examination of the early drafts of *The Lord of the
Rings* preserved in the archives in Marquette State University in Milwaukee reveals that Tolkien originally used *k*
rather than *c* generally in Elvish words and names for the
sound [k] (e.g. *Keleborn*, not *Celeborn*), and only changed to
an imitation of the Classical Latin style of spelling very
late. A few Eldarin forms with *k* are still found in the
corpus, mostly as variants of forms with *c*. The *k* forms are
given in the dictionaries in their proper alphabetical
sequence, but are cross-referenced to the *c* forms which are
the main entries. Where no *c* form occurs in the corpus, one
has been created.

The articles in Proto-Eldarin are not to be take as
final definitive studies, but as preliminary surveys to lay
the groundwork in an area where much more research is needed.

The section 'Personal Names' deals, in intention, with
all personal names not covered in the sections on Quenya,
Sindarin, and the Other Tongues. Place names are treated
only in passing in various parts of this section and elsewhere with no attempt at even the beginning of completeness.
The meanings of most of the non-Elvish place names are either
self-evident, easily found out by looking up the elements
of which they are composed in any good English dictionary, or
are given with additional comment in Tolkien's own 'Guide to
the Names in *The Lord of the Rings*'. A full treatment here
seemed superfluous.

Laurence Krieg's article 'A Survey of Some English-
Tengwar Orthographies' is essentially an examination of various tengwar modes to see what light they shed on orthographic systems in general, but most users of this book will
probably find the article useful rather as a fund of examples
of how various people have written English using the tengwar.

Paula Marmor's 'The Wielders of the Three and Other
Trees' is an essay inspired largely by the mythological

scholarship of Robert Graves, and uses largely the same tech-
niques. It is included here in part because much of the
evidence she presents arises from analyses of names, in part
because it provides a change from the other material, and in
part because her imitiation of Graves' methods and her success with them in very minor points where no such success
can reasonably arise indicates the basic flaw in Graves'
theorizing. He essentially works by creating connexions
between symbols, so that the lines of connexion may then be
followed almost anywhere and almost any kind of meaning can
be attributed to a text. Of course, the essay is not all of
this kind. I leave to the reader the task of distinguishing
the legitimately made points from the parody.

This work owes much to more people than are credited on
the title page. There are the numerous individuals who
pointed out minor slips in my earlier *Glossary*, or who presented new and thought-provoking ideas on the meanings of some
of the words and names. To list all these would be impossible—of some I do not know the names, as their suggestions
were passed on to me. But I thank you all.

Special thanks go to Mike Bazinet whose many and thor-
ough comments on Elvish words and names have influenced a
substantial number of the dictionary entries. Also invaluable were Björn Fromén's suggestions on some of the Elvish
forms, and his corrections on a first draft of the material
on the Northern Names. Then there is Richard Plotz, who
allowed the Mythopoeic Linguistic Fellowship access to Tolkien's correspondence with him. Finally, I here personally
thank Dr. Peter Gratke for his extreme hospitality upon my
visit to the Tolkien manuscript collection at Marquette in
the autumn of 1975.

All royalties on this book are being donated to 'Help
the Aged', as was recommended to us by Christopher Tolkien
whom we asked to name a charity or cause to which his father
would have liked the money to go. 'Help the Aged', according
to Christopher Tolkien's letter in reply, '...was one public
charity about which my father felt keenly and supported consistently.... He sold the desk on which he wrote the Lord of
the Rings to raise money for this organisation.'

'Help the Aged' sponsors subsidized housing and day
centres for the elderly, encourages self-help programs, pub-
lishes a newspaper, *Yours*, dealing with the interests and
problems of the aged, and tried to educate the public on
these problems.

For further information, write 'Help the Age' at 8/10
Denman St., London, England W1A 2AP; or at 179 Main St.,

FOREWORD

White Plains, N.Y. 10601, U.S.A.; or at 350 The Driveway,
Ottawa, Ont., Canada, K1S 3M1.

Jim Allan, Toronto
August, 1977

POSTCRIPT:

Almost a year has passed since I typed the above.
During that time the publisher for whom I had prepared this
book found himself unable to bring it out, and it has been
necessary to find a second publisher. Also, during that
time *The Silmarillion* has appeared, providing—as expected—
a plethora of further data on the Elvish tongues. Unfortunately, time does not permit the incorporation of the new
material into this book with any completeness. So, rather
than attempt a few piecemeal changes here and there, I have
decided it best to leave the text as it is, save that the
note at the end on groups of interest to Tolkien fans has
been brought up to date by the inclusion of three further
groups.
        Generally *The Silmarillion* has supported our interpre-
tations of Eldarin tongues, though we have made mistakes in
some details. Fortunately, Christopher Tolkien has so presented the new information on Elvish in *The Silmarillion*
that the serious user of this book should have no difficulty
in cross-checking our information, and correcting us where
we are wrong in details. It will be found, I believe, that
our discussions of the grammars of Quenya and Sindarin are
still valid in their entirety, and that our theories on the
reconstruction of Proto-Eldarin are vindicated. The single
flaw in the latter is our proposal of a series of 'nasal
stops' to explain a small number of apparent correspondences
which formed a consistent pattern. That pattern was a result
of coincidence.
        As to the material here on the non-Elvish languages,
personal names, and the writing systems—in a couple of cases
The Silmarillion provides information that allows the reader
to make the correct choice between two alternate explanations
give here. Otherwise the discussions are unaffected.
        Those who wish more detail I refer to the pages of cur-
rent and future issues of *Parma Eldalamberon* where the new
Silmarillion information is being fully evaluated.

CONTENTS

List of Charts . . . . xxij

Abbreviations and Symbols xxiv

THE ELDARIN TONGUES

QUENYA GRAMMAR & DICTIONARY By Jim Allan
  The Structure of Quenya
    Origin 3
    Sounds & Spelling 6
    The Noun 12
    The Adjective 18
    The Article 19
    Pronouns 19
    Verbs (With Paula Marmor) 21
    Syntax 22
    On Pronouns in Quenya By Bill Welden 22
  Quenya-English Dictionary 27
  Valinórenna By Björn Fromén 44

SINDARIN GRAMMAR & DICTIONARY By Jim Allan
  The Structure of Sindarin
    Origin 47
    Sounds & Spelling 51
    Consonant Mutation 57
    On the Formation of Plurals in Sindarin By Bill Welden . 62
    The Article 68
    Pronouns 69
    Verbs 69
    Syntax 70
  Sindarin-English Dictionary 71

ENGLISH-QUENYA/SINDARIN ENTRY INDEX By Nina Carson,
    Alexandra Tarasovna Kiceniuk, Jim Allan . . . 91

PROTO-ELDARIN VOWELS: A COMPARATIVE SURVEY By Chris Gilson
    & Bill Welden
    Introduction 107
    Short Vowels 112
    Long Vowels 117
    Diphthongs 121
    Vowel Contraction 123
    Final Syllables 124
    Svarabhakti 125
    Acknowledgments 126

CONTENTS

Vowel Summary Chart By Jim Allan 127

PROTO-ELDARIN CONSONANTS By Jim Allan, Chris Gilson & Bill
    Welden 128
    Before Proto-Eldarin 140

ELVISH LOANWORDS IN INDO-EUROPEAN: CULTURAL IMPLICATIONS
    By Lise Menn 143

THE CALENDAR OF IMLADRIS By Jim Allan 151

TOLKIEN'S PRONUNCIATION: SOME OBSERVATIONS By Laurence J.
    Krieg 152

OTHER TONGUES
By Jim Allan

KHUZDUL 163

THE BLACK SPEECH 166

THE ADÛNAIC LANGUAGES 169

MORE OBSCURE LANGUAGES 173

PERSONAL NAMES

AN ETYMOLOGICAL EXCURSION AMONG THE SHIRE FOLK By Paula
    Marmor 181

THE GIVING OF NAMES By Jim Allan
    The Germanic System of Nomenclature 185
    Elvish Names 188
    Old Rhovanion Names 189
    Hobbit Names 190
    Names of the Rohirrim 212
    Northern Names 220
    The Names of the Early Edain and Old English . . 226
    Hobbit Month Names 227

CONTENTS

WRITING SYSTEMS

THE TENGWAR OF FËANOR By Laurence J. Krieg

How to Learn the Tengwar 231

Tengwar Fact Sheet Notes 233

Shape-Sound Correspondence: A Supplement . . . 239

THE EVOLUTION OF THE TENGWAR By Jim Allan 241

A SURVEY OF SOME ENGLISH-TENGWAR ORTHOGRAPHIES By
Laurence J. Krieg

Orthographic Theories 248

Tengwar Spelling Systems 256

Conclusions 274

A PARALLEL TO THE TENGWAR By Jim Allan 276

THE RUNES By Jim Allan

Old English Runes 280

The *Certar* or *Cirth* 283

THE WIELDERS OF THE THREE AND OTHER TREES
By Paula Marmor 291

List of Charts

Consonant sounds . . . . xxviij

Vowel sounds xxx

Early Quenya consonant sounds 6

Third Age Quenya consonant sounds 7

Quenya vowels 9

Quenya diphthongs 10

Quenya noun declensions 15

Quenya adjective endings 18

Personal pronouns in Quenya as reconstructed by Bill
Welden 25

Sindarin consonant sounds 51

Early Sindarin vowels 52

Third Age Sindarin vowels 52

Sindarin diphthongs 53

The consonants of Sindarin and Welsh 54

The vowels and diphthongs of Sindarin and Welsh . . 55

Lenition in Sindarin 57f

Lenition of initial *g* in Sindarin 59

Nasal mutation in Sindarin 61

Plural vowel shifts in Sindarin 65

Vowel summary chart of Proto-Eldarin vowels and their
reflexes 127

Simplified consonant summary chart of Proto-Eldarin
consonants and their reflexes 128f

Full consonant summary chart of Proto-Eldarin
consonants and their reflexes . 135, 139, 141

The Calendar of Imladris and the French Revolutionary
Calendar 151

Vowel sounds in the LANE system 154

Recurring themes in the genealogy of the Half-elven . 188

The Hobbit month names 227

Tengwar fact sheet 237

The tengwar: theoretic Eldarin values 242

The tengwar: Early Quenya 245

The tengwar: Late Quenya 245

The tengwar: vowels in the northern Westron Mode . . 246

The tengwar: the Mode of Beleriand 247

The tengwar: a mode for Westron & the Black Speech . . 247

CHARTS

Transliteration correspondences for the samples of
    English-tengwar modes   257

Symbols used in the transcription from 'Eärendil was a
    mariner' 271

The Univerfal Alphabet 277

Old English Runes used by Tolkien 282

Angerthas Daeron   284

The evolution of the cirth 286

Abbreviations and Symbols

abl. ablative
acc. accusative
adj. adjective
adv. adverb
Akk. Akkadian
all. allative
Ar. Arabic
Aram. Aramaic
art. article
c. about
cf. compare
compos. compositive
conj. conjunction
Corn. Cornish
CSK Clyde S. Kilby, 'Mythic and Christian Elements in Tolkien', in ed. J. W. Montgomery, *Myth: Allegory: & Gospel* (Minneapolis: Bethany Fellowship, 1974)
Dan. Danish
dat. dative
dim. diminutive
du. dual
Du. Dutch
e.g. for example
Egypt. Egyptian
Eng. English
EW J. R. R. Tolkien, 'English and Welsh', *Angles and Britons: O'Donnell Lectures* (Cardiff: Univ. of Wales Press, 1963)
f and following page
ff and following pages
Finn. Finnish
Fr. French
fut. future
G J. R. R. Tolkien, 'Guide to the Names in *The Lord of the Rings*' in ed. Jared Lobdell, *A Tolkien Compass* (La Salle, Ill.: Open Court, 1975), 153-201
g. pl. group plural
Gael. Gaelic
gen. genitive
Ger. German
Gk. Greek
Gmc. Germanic
GME Robert Foster, *A Guide to Middle-earth* (Baltimore: Mirage Press, 1971; rpt. New

York: Ballantine, 1974)
Goth. Gothic
H *The Hobbit*, page references to standard hardcover editions
HC Humphrey Carpentery, *J. R. R. Tolkien: A biography* (London: Allen & Unwin, 1977)
Hd. Heraldic designs on β post-1973 boxed sets and in 1974 Allen & Unwin Tolkien Calendar
Heb. Hebrew
Hung. Hungarian
I ⎰ Refer respectively to the
II ⎱ three volumes of *The Lord
III ⎰ of the Rings*, page references to the standard three-volume hardcover editions and to the Methuen paperback edition
IE Indo-European
imper. imperative
instr. instrumental
inter. interrogative
interj. interjection
IPA International Phonetic Alphabet
It. Italian
Lat. Latin
len. lenited
loc. locative
M unpublished
M1 map of northwest of Middle-earth at the end of the Third Age, in I and II
M2 map of east Gondor, northwest Mordor, southeast Rohan, in III
MB version of M1 by Pauline Baynes, corrected post-1971 printings
ME Middle English
MFr. Middle French
Mod. Modern
MWel. Middle Welsh
n footnote
n. noun
N J. R. R. Tolkien 'The Nameless Land', *Realities: An Anthology of Verse*, ed. G. S. Tancred (London: Gay & Hancock, 1927),

p. 24
nm. name
neut. neuter
obj. object
OE Old English
OFr. Old French
OHG. Old High German
OIr. Old Irish
ON Old Norse
OWel. Old Welsh
p. page
PE Proto-Eldarin
PEI Proto-Indo-European
Per. Persian
pers. person, personal
Phoen. Phoenician
pl. plural
pl. mult. plural of multitude
post. postposition
pp. pages
prep. preposition
pres. present
prn. pronoun, pronominal
prob. probably
Q Quenya
R *The Road Goes Ever On: A Song Cycle*
rpt. reprinted by
Russ. Russian
s. singular
S Sindarin
S.A. Second Age
Scot. Scottish
Sem. Semitic
Skt. Sanskrit
suff. suffix
Syr. Syriac
Sw. Swedish
T.A. Third Age
TB *The Adventures of Tom Bombadil and other verses from the Red Book*
TS Clyde S. Kilby, *Tolkien and "The Silmarillion"* (Wheaton, Ill.: Harold Shaw Publishers, 1976)

Univ. University of
v. verb
viz. that is, namely
VLat. Vulgar Latin
Wel. Welsh

α text of first hardcover editions and Ace paperback edition
β text of Ballantine edition
γ text of Houghton Mifflin second edition and of pre-1969 Allen & Unwin second edition
δ text of post-1968 Allen & Unwin three volume second edition and of Methuen paperback
ε text of post-1968 deluxe Allen & Unwin one volume second edition

1st first person
2nd second person
3rd third person

* unattested, hypothetical
** (used to indicate an intentionally incorrect constructed form)
† found only as part of a compound
+ plus (used to separate parts of a compound form in its etymology)
→ produces
← derives from
> produced by regular historical development
< is descended from, derived from
= equals (used in 'Proto-Eldarin Vowels' to indicate that the following form is cognate with the form[s] under discussion; the formulation of the actual reconstruction is sometimes left to the ingenuity of the reader)
?, ??? uncertain, possibly
ł tengwar or certar

PRONUNCIATION SYMBOLS

The symbols used to indicate pronunciation are mostly taken from the International Phonetic Alphabet, and are used according to the directions of the International Phonetic Association. The only major deviations are: 1) y, rather than j, is used for the initial vowel sound in *yet, you*; 2) accordingly, ɥ, rather than y, is used for the first vowel sound in Fr. *lune*, Ger. *über*; 3) α is most conveniently used to indicate a central low vowel, its normal IPA value as the unrounded low back vowel (Cardinal 4 unrounded) being indicated by ɑ. This re-assignment of values is one not uncommon in American linguistics.

Consonants:

The following are used to represent sounds approximately the same as their normal English values: b, d, f, h, k, m, n, p, t, v, w, z.

As to other consonant symbols:

β a sound like v, but made with both lips, as with *b* in Sp. *haber*, rather than with the lower lip against the upper teeth, as in Eng. *have*.

ç a voiceless spirant y; a weak version is often heard in *huge* [çu:dʒ]; the sound of *ch* in Germ *eoht*, *licht*. May be roughly described as having a sound halfway between ∫ and x.

dʒ the sound represented by *j* and *dg* in *judge*, and by *g* in *gem*.

ð the voiced *th* sound in *thy*, *breathe*; cf. θ. This symbol was used in Old English for both [θ] and [ð].

Φ a sound like f, but made with both lips, and so the voiceless counterpart to β.

g represents only the 'hard' sound in *get*, *rag*. For the sounds of *g* in *gem*, *rouge*, see dʒ and ʒ.

ʒ the sound of *g* in *rouge*, the sound of *s* in *pleasure*.

γ a sound like g, but spirant: that is, the back of the tongue does not quite make contact with the roof of the mouth, allowing air to buzz through. This is the voiced version of x.

h used to indicate ASPIRATION (a moment of non-voicing between the release of a voiceless stop and the beginning of voice in the pronunciation of the following vowel). Compare the *p*'s in *pat* [pʰæt] and *spat* [spæt]. We do not know to what degree voicless consonants in Elvish may have had some amount of aspiration. Normal English aspiration has not been transribed by Krieg on page 158. The Khuzdul sounds *kh* and

th were probably more strongly aspirated than are English appirated *k* and *t*.

l̴ in the Eldarin tongues this indicates an *l* with a resonance of about ε

l̦ a somewhat palatalized *l*, that is, one with a resonance close to ı. This is shown only in the pronunciations given for Quenya and Sindarin.

ɫ a velarized *l*, that is one pronounced with the back of the tongue raised toward the velum. This occurs normally in English adjoining *o* and *u*. Velarized *l*'s did not normally occur in the Eldarin tongues. The normal initial *l* in American English has some degree of velarization. On page 158 only unusual velarization is recorded.

l̥ voiceless *l*, as in *please* compared with *lease*.

ɬ the Welsh voiceless *ll*, made by pronouncing a voiceless *l* with the tongue held closely enough against the roof of the mouth that the air hisses as it is forced out to one side; a spirant voiceless *l*.

ʎ a palatal *l* made with the tongue against the palate, having a sound very similar to *ly*.

ŋ the sound spelt *ng* in *singe:* ['sıŋəʲ] and *n* in *finger* ['fıŋəʲ] and *sink* [sıŋk].

ɲ a palatal *n* often heard in English for *ny*, *ni*, as in *canyon*, *opinion*. This is the Spanish *ñ* and the French *gn*.

ʔ the glottal stop, often heard in English in expressions like *uh-oh* [ˈʔʌˌʔoʊ] or between vowels in emphatic pronunciations, as *triumphant* [tˌaɪˈʔʌmfənt]. Might be described in imprecise language as a sort of light grunt in the throat.

ʾ a variant writing of **ʔ**, used especially in transcriptions of Semitic words and names.

ʿ used in roman letter transcriptions of Semitic words and names to represent a voiced spirant gargling sound between ɣ and ɦ. The official IPA symbol is ʕ.

r a tongue-trilled (rolled) *r*, as in Scottish dialect, or Spanish *rr*. It was probably sometimes realized as ɾ.

ɾ an *r*-sound made with a single tap or flap of the tongue, rather than with many taps to make a trill. Occurs in many varieties of English as a variant of the /r/ phoneme (*three* [θɾiː], *very* [ˈvɛrɪ]) or the /t/ phoneme (*water* [ˈwɑɾəʲ], *butter* [ˈbʌɾəʲ]).

ɹ used here to cover the various spirant and approximant allophones of the normal untrilled English *r*.

ʴ used here where ɹ is pronounced in some varieties of English but omitted in others.

ɹ̥ a voiceless version of ɹ. Can be approximated by pronouncing h + ɹ. This is the normal sound for voiceless *r* in languages that have it, but variant realizations do occur. In the Eldarin tongues it may have sometimes been trilled like its voiced counterpart, resulting in ɾ̥.

ʀ 'uvular *r*', a trilled *r* sound made at the back of the throat. It is a normal *r* sound in

French and German.

s always represents the voiceless sound in *sister*, never a z sound as in *was*, *reside*.

ʃ the English *sh* sound, as in *shush* [ʃʌʃ], *mission* [ˈmɪʃən].

tʃ the English *ch* sound, as in *church* [tʃoˑʲtʃ], *catch* [kʰætʃ].

θ the voiceless *th* sound in *thigh*; cf. ð.

þ this symbol is traditionally used instead of θ in reconstructions of Germanic forms; it was used in Old English for both [θ] and [ð].

ʍ voiceless *w*, as in *which* rather than *witch* for those varieties of English that still make this distinction. Can be approximated by pronouncing h + w, and attempting to meld them together as one sound.

ɥ an approximant (weak) version of ɣ; pronounce w, but with lips spread and apart.

x the velar spirant, the *ch* sound of Eng. *echhh!*, Scot. *loch*, Ger. *ach*, *doch*. Place the back of the tongue against the velum as if to pronounce k, then open slightly and allow air to hiss through.

x̣ indicates the pronunciation x in Eldarin speech, but h in the speech of Gondor.

χ this symbol is often used in place of x in historical linguistics to avoid confusing the sound [x] with written *x* [ks]. So used here for Proto-Eldarin. In IPA it indicates an uvular x.

y as *y* in Eng. *yacht*, *young*.

Most of these consonant symbols appear in the chart at the head of the facing page which indicates the relationship of the sounds they represent to one another. Sounds made using the lower lip as an organ of articulation are LABIALS. Sounds made with the tongue as an organ of articulation may be called LINGUALS. Sounds made or associated with the glottis in the back of the throat are classified as GLOTTAL.

Labial sounds made using both lips as organs of articulation

PRONUNCIATION SYMBOLS

	LABIAL		LINGUAL			GLOTTAL
	Bilabial	Labio-dental	Dental and Alveolar	Palatal	Velar	
Stop........	p b	(ꞯ) (6)	t d	c ɟ .	k g	ʔ
Nasal.......	m	ɱ	n	ɲ	ŋ	
Spirant.....	ɸ β	f v	θ ð ∣ s z ∣ ʒ ɹ ∣ɬ̠ɮ̠	ç j	x ɣ	h ɦ
Approximant.	β	ʋ	ð z ɹ ∣ l̠	y ʎ̠	ɰ	
Flap, Tap...	(ρ)	(ɲ)	ɾ l̠			
Trill.......	(ρ)		r			

w *is a Labial-velar spirant or approximant in which* β *is articulated simultaneously with its velar counterpart:* γ͡β *or* ɰ͡β.
ʍ *is the voiceless counterpart to* w: x͡ɸ.
ʃ ʒ *are the voiceless and voiced Palato-Alveolar spirants, made with the tongue against both the alveolar ridge and palate.*
tʃ d͡ʒ *are combinations of* t + ʃ d + ʒ.

are BILABIALS. Those using the lower lip against the teeth are LABIO-
DENTALS.
     Sounds made with the front of the tongue against the teeth are
classified as DENTAL; those made with the front of the tongue against
the alveolar ridge (upper gums) as ALVEOLAR. (This distinction is
meaningful in some languages.) Sounds made with the front of the tongue
against the hard palate behind the alveolar ridge are called PALATAL.
Sounds made with the back of the tongue against the velum (soft palate)
are called VELAR. Further distinctions are often needed in respect to
tongue sounds, but the listing of three place of articulation here given
is sufficient for this study.
     Sounds in which the organs or articulation touch, close off the
airstream completely, and then release it with a sort of pop or thud are
called STOPS (or PLOSIVES).
     Sounds made in the same way as the stops, but with the air directed
through the nose during the time of closure between the organs of articulation in the mouth are called NASALS.
     If the organs of articulation do not touch but come closely enough
together that the airstream hisses or buzzes as it passes through, the
sounds are called SPIRANTS (or FRICATIVES). The flexibility of the front
of the tongue allows it to direct the airstream in more than one manner,
hence there are a variety of dental and alveolar spirants.
     If the organs of articulation are opened apart still further so that
there is no friction (hissing or buzzing) heard, the sound is called an
APPROXIMANT. Approximants are closely related to vowels; indeed, the
approximants [ɥ], [w], [y], and [ŭ] (this last = [ỹβ͡]) are called SEMI-
VOWELS, and are only non-syllabic versions of the vowels [ɯ], [u], [i],
and [y].
     If the airstream in a spriant or approximant is directed sidways
(laterally) across the tongue a LATERAL is produced. These are the l-
sounds, and are marked on the chart by + indicating laterality.
     Where two symbols appear in a box, the first is voiceless and the
second voiced. Where a voicless equivalent to a voiced sound is rare
a symbol for only the voiced sound has been devised. The diacrtic ॰

may be used to indicate a voiceless counterpart when needed: ņ, ļ, ŗ, ň̥.
The difference between spirant and approximant is only one of degree
of openness of the organs of articulation, and so a single symbol may be
sufficient for both. Where greater discrimination is required diacritics
indicating 'more open' may be used to indicate an approximant (e.g. β̞ or
β˅ = approximant β), or diactrics signifying 'closer' may be used to
indicate a spirant (e.g. β̝ or β^ = spirant β).
Parentheses in the table enclose symbols not specifically endorsed
by the IPA representing sounds of rare occurrence.

Consonants written double are to be pronounced double:
tt as in *heat too*, not *he too*;
mm as in *I'm made*, not *I made*;
nn as in *kindness* ['kaïnnɛs], not *highness* ['haïnɛs];
ll as in *I'll like*, not *I like*;
ff as in *sheaf for*, not *she for*;
and so forth.

Vowels

a the Italian *a*, halfway between
ɑ and æ.

ɑ as *a* in *father*, *ah*

æ as *a* in *pan*, *last*.

e as *a* in *fate* [feït], as *e* in
weigh [we·ï], but pure, without
the ι glide.

ə the 'obscure' mid-central vowel
written as *a* in *about*, *e* in
ailment, *o* in *confess*. In
Proto-Indo-European ə₁, ə₂,
ə₃, are used respectively to
indicate three so-called
laryngal consonants.

ɔ a sound related to 3 as e is to
ɛ.

ɛ as *e* in *men*, *bed*, *were* [wɛ̆ʲ].

3 as *i* in *bird*, *u* in *fur*, *ea* in
learn, especially when the *r*
is not pronounced.

i as *i* in *machine*, *ee* in *feet*.

ɨ as *i* in *get'im* ['gɨtɨm] for
get him; cf. *get'em* ['gɛtəm]
for *get them*.

ι as *i* in *fit*, *did*. The symbol
ɪ is sometimes used instead.

o as *o* in *note* [noŏt], *dough*
[doŏ], but pure, without the o
glide.

ŏ see ø.

ø as *eu* in Fr. *feu*, as ŏ (or oŏ)
in Ger. *Göthe* (*Goethe*). Round
the lips as for o and pronounce
e. The symbol ŏ is used here
in historical reconstruction.

ɔ as *o* in *for*, *au* in *caught*. In
the Old English pronunciations
given the sound is somewhat
lower, closer to ɒ.

ɒ as *o* in *not*, *long*, *box*. In
Sindarin it should be pronounced with more lip-rounding
than in English.

u as *u* in *brute*, *oo* in *school*.

ü see ɥ.

ʊ as *u* in *pull*, *oo* in *foot*. The
symbol ᴜ is sometimes used
instead.

ʌ as *u* in *cut*, the first *o* in
colour.

ɯ spread the lips as for i and
pronounce u.

ɥ as *u* in Fr. *duc*, *ü* in Ger.
grün. Round the lips as for
u and pronounce i. The sound
i was generally substituted in
the speech of Gondor. The
symbol ü is used here in historical reconstruction.

The vowels appears in the usual arragement on the chart on the
following page. The irregular quadralateral represents the mouth cavity
above the tongue, and the position of each vowel on the chart indicates

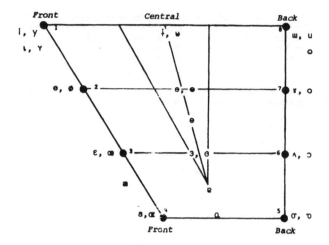

the theoretical highest point on the tongue when it is pronounced. If
the front of the tongue is highest the vowel is called a FRONT VOWEL,
if the back part of the tongue is highest it is called a BACK VOWEL, and
if the middle of the tongue is highest it is called a CENTRAL VOWEL.
Vowels made with a large amount of of tongue raising are said to be HIGH
or CLOSE. Vowels made with a small amount of tongue raising are said to
be LOW or OPEN.

For most positions on the chart a pair of symbols is given, the
first indicating pronunciation with lips spread, and the second pronunciation with lips rounded. For certain rare sounds or ones seldom need-
ing to be distinguished from other sounds the IPA provides no symbol.
Thus there are no rounded counterparts given for ə, æ, or ɑ, and no
unrounded counterpart given for ɒ.

In Laurence Krieg's transcriptions on page 158 small arrows are
used to further pin down vowel sounds, using the concept of this chart.
Thus ɪᵛ indicates a sound between ɪ and e, but closer to ɪ; oᐱ indicates
a sound between o and ɔ, but closer to o; ɒ‹ indicates a rounded sound
close to ɑ.

Normal long vowels are indicated by a modified colon (ː). Short
vowels are unmarked. If an intermediate length is to be shown a half-
length mark (·) can be used. For example: bit [bɪt], bid [bɪ·d], beat
[bi·t], bead [biːd]. Extra-long vowels can be indicated with (ːː).
(In Laurence Krieg's transcriptions (·) is used for normally long vowels
and (ː) for extra-long vowels.)

Diphthongs

Diphthongs occur when the tongue moves from one position to another
during pronunciation of a vowel. They are written by showing first the
vowel where the diphthong begins, and then the sound on which it ends or,
at least, that towards which it is moving. In this book the second element in a diphthong, the glide vowel, is usually marked by ˘ to indicate
it is not to be given separate vocalic pronunciation. Laurence Krieg, in
his transcriptions, uses ˘ only where the glide is particularly short.

Where the glide is almost inaudible a raised letter is used. Where a diphthong combination occurs that is unusual in English he uses a tie, e.g. ͡ɔ. Otherwise the glide vowel is unmarked. Pronunciation given for the diphthongs of Quenya and Sindarin can only be approximate. The diphthongs appearing in the Eldarin tongues follow, with a few additional ones from English also.

aĭ   as *i* in *high*, *lie*, as *y* in *rye*.

a·ɛ̆   similar to aĭ. Pronounce a and glide into ɛ.

aŏ   as *ou* in *rout*, *house*.

a·ŏ   as *ou* in *loud*, *ow* in *now*.

eĭ   as *ey* in *grey*, *a* in *lady*. *make*.

ɛ̆   as *ea* in *bear*, *ai* in *fair*, especially when the *r* is not pronounced.

ɛŏ   Pronounce ɛ and glide into o.

ɔĭ   as *oy* in *boy*, *oi* in *noise*.

ʊ·ɛ̆   similar to ɔĭ. Pronounce ʊ and glide into ɛ.

oŏ   as *o* in *go*, *home*.

uĭ   similar to *ui* in *ruin*; glide the two sounds together without a break.

u·ĭ   similar to *ui* in *pursuing*; glide the two sounds together without a break.

Stress

The primary stress is indicated by ' at the beginning of the stressed syllable. A secondary stress is indicated by ₁. In Eldarin words with two primary stresses the second is the stronger.

Other Signs

~ over a vowel or consonant indicates nasalization, that is, the diversion of the airstream in part through the nose. when passed through a consonant it indicates velarization, that is, the raising of the back of the tongue to produce an *o* or *u* resonance.

, signifies palatalization, that is, the raising of the front of the tongue to produce a strong *e* or *i* resonance. Thus ļ is a strongly palatalized *l*, closer to *ly* than the weaker |; ç is a palatalized *r*.

. is used in transcriptions of Semitic words and names to mark certain emphatic (pharyngalized) consonants.

‾ is used in transcriptions of Hebrew words to mark that the stop under which it appears is to be pronounced as a corresponding spirant: t̲ = θ, k̲ = x.

A variety of alevolar consonants are produced by bending back the tip of the tongue. They are called RETROFLEX consonants, and are marked by extending the stem of the character downward: ţ, ḑ, ɳ, ɽ, ʂ, etc.

‿ beneath a consonant indicates it is syllabic: *whittling* ['ʍɪtļ₁ɪŋ], ' *happen* ['hæpn̩].

‾ beneath a consonant (or occasionally above) indicates labialization, that is, pronunciation of the consonant with lips rounded.

THE
ELDARIN
TONGUES

QUENYA GRAMMAR & DICTIONARY

Jim Allan

In part derived from articles by Bill Welden and Paula Marmor as credited. Modern language comparisons in the dictionary are mostly compiled by Paula Marmor.

THE STRUCTURE OF QUENYA

ORIGIN

The name *Quenya* is itself Quenya and seems to mean
simply 'Speech'. Quenya was originally a tongue of Eldamar·
'Elvenhome', beyond the Sea in the West, derived mainly from
the language—or languages—of the West-elves who had come
there from Middle-earth. In Eldamar the speech of the West-
elves changed, but not so quickly or so drastically as did the
speech of those West-elves who remained in Middle-earth and
became the Sindar, the Grey-elves. Quenya was therefore more
ARCHAIC than the Sindarin tongue, that is, it retained more
features of their common original. Quenya also adopted some
words from the language of the Valar, such as *miruvóre*, and
perhaps also from other tongues of the Far West.
      In Eldamar the West-elves increased their skills and
knowledge and became known as High Elves, and their language
became richer and fuller than that of their kindred in
Middle-earth. Quenya was brought to Middle-earth by the Noldor, who returned in exile to regain from Melkor, the Great
Enemy, the three Silmarils that he had stolen. But the Noldor were only a few among the numerous Grey-elves, and many

3

were slain in the war against the Dark Power. Thus the Noldor
more and more used Sindarin as their everyday speech, even
among themselves. They even translated their own names from
the Quenya speech to the Sindarin tongue, as Q *Altáriel to S
Galadriel. Quenya remained in use only as a tongue of learning and lore and poetry.

Towards the end of the First Age the Eldar of Middle-
earth took as allies those Men called Atani in Quenya—the
first of the races of Men to reach the west of Middle-earth;
and so the tongues of the Eldar became known among Men. The
Atani esteemed the High-elven Quenya above all other tongues,
and when, at the beginning of the Second Age, the star-shaped
island of Elenna was given to them for their home, they named
the kingdom they founded there in the Quenya tongue as Númenóre or Númenor 'Westernesse'. Places within Númenor were
also named in Quenya: Andúnië, a region in the west of Númenor; Meneltarma, a mountain in the midst of the land. And,
until the reign of Ar-Adûnakhôr, the kings of Númenor took
names of Quenya form. So also did the lords of Andúnië until
the final destruction.

After the fall of Númenor, in the Third Age, Quenya was
kept in use for the royal names in the realms of Arnor and
Gondor, and also, in Gondor at least, by others of the royal
kindred. The leaders of the Corsairs of Umbar who were descended from the royal line of Gondor also bore Quenya names.
But in the North, when Arnor became divided into three separate realms, the kings of these realms ceased to take names
in the Quenya tongue, using names of Sindarin form instead.
In Gondor, when the line of kings failed, the use of High-
elven names ceased also; for the Ruling Stewards of Gondor
have names of Sindarin form or, occasionally, of mixed Sindarin and Quenya form.

Faramir, the name of the second son of Denethor (last of
the Ruling Stewards of Gondor), seems to be pure Quenya, however. To be sure, in αIII:406n Tolkien writes, 'The names of
other lords of the Dúnedain, such as Aragorn, Denethor, Faramir, are of Sindarin form....' But in Sindarin original m
becomes v following a vowel—cf. Aravir; and so we would
expect **Faravir as the correct form if the name is indeed
pure Sindarin. Similarly we would expect **Borovir instead
of Boromir. Tolkien corrects this error in his rewording of
the note in βγδεIII:406n: 'Most of the names of the other men
and women of the Dúnedain, such as Aragorn, Denethor, Gilraen
are of Sindarin form.... Some few are of mixed form, as
Boromir.'

When Aragorn, chieftain of the Rangers of the North,
gained the throne of Gondor and refounded Arnor, he revived
the old tradition of using royal names of Quenya form, taking
the name Elessar 'Elfstone', as had been prophecied, and

giving to himself and his descendants the surname *Telcontar*
'Strider'. His son and heir bore the Sindarin name *Eldarion*.
Ancient learning was revived again among Men in that time of
peace, and doubtless knowledge of Quenya again spread somewhat. But by that time all of the exiled Noldor had crossed
again to the other side, and many of the Sindar with them, so
that it is doubtful that any native speaker of Quenya
remained in Middle-earth.

To some extent Quenya, in Middle-earth, would have
assumed different forms among different groups of speakers.
We are told that for '*lv*, not for *lw*, many speakers, especially Elves, used *lb*' (III:399). Native speakers of Westron
usually pronounced Q *ty* as English *ch* [tʃ] (III:392 *TY*) and
often pronounced Q *hy* and Q *h* in the combinations *iht* and *eht*
as English *sh* [ʃ] rather than [ç] (III:392 *Y*). Differences
in the use of words undoubtedly also existed between different groups.

In Tolkien's reading of the poem 'Namárië' on the record
albums *J. R. R. TOLKIEN reads and sings his THE HOBBIT and The
Fellowship of the Ring* and *J. R. R. Tolkien reads and sings his
THE LORD OF THE RINGS: The Two Towers: The Return of the King*
(New York: Caedmon Records, No. TC 1477 and No. TC 1478,
1975) variants are found from the version published. The
second and third lines of the poem differ as follows:

Published Version	*Recorded Versions*
Yéni únótimë ve rámar aldaron!	Inyar únóti nar ve rámar aldaron!
Yéni ve lintë yuldar avánier	Inyar ve lintë yulmar vánier

The form *nar* is to be explained as the plural of *ná* 'is' and
so to be translated 'are': '*Inyar* are uncountable as...'
The recorded versions also have *Calacilyo* instead of *Calaciryo*. Part of a Quenya poem appears on page 76 of Humphrey
Carpenter's *J. R. R. Tolkien: A biography* in a form of the
language differing from that in the published *Lord of the
Rings*. In the Appendix of Tolkien's *The Father Christmas
Letters* (ed. Baillie Tolkien, London: George Allen & Unwin;
New York: Houghton Mifflin; Toronto: Methuen Publications;
1976) a sentence of a language called Arctic appears, which
seems to be related to Quenya. The variants of the records
and these other fragments are of interest, but pending further information are best not taken as correct examples of
standard Quenya of the Third Age. Accordingly, forms found
in them are not included in the Quenya dictionary.

Of the languages spoken in Middle-earth of today Quenya
bears most resemblance to Finnish. Finnish was one of the
languages with which Tolkien fell in love. Of learning it
he said, 'It was like discovering a wine-cellar filled with

bottles of amazing wine of a kind and flavour never tasted
before. It quite intoxicated me' (HC:59). In 1955, in the
paper 'English and Welsh', Tolkien spoke of the aesthetic
pleasure given him by different tongues. After relating how
Gothic first took him by storm through a simple vocabulary
list, he continued: 'I have, in this particular sense, studied ("tasted" would be better) other languages since. Of all
save one among them the most overwhelming pleasure was provided by Finnish, and I have never quite got over it' (EW:
38).

SOUNDS & SPELLING

Consonants

The consonantal system of Early Quenya is indicated by
the arrangement of the tengwar of Fëanor, and is given below
in chart form using letters and symbols of the International
Phonetic Alphabet. Where Tolkien's spelling of the sound
differs, it follows in small italics in parentheses.

	Labial	Dental/Alveolar	Palatal	Velar	Labialized Velar
Voiceless Stop:	p	t	ty	k(c)	kw(qu)
Nasal:	m	n	ny	ŋ(ng, n)	ŋw(ngw)
Nasal + Voiced Stop:	mb	nd	ndy	ŋg(ng)	ŋgw(ngw)
Voiceless Spirant:	f	θ(th) ʝ(hr) s	ç(hy)	x(h)	ʍ(hw)
Voiced Spirant/Approximant:	v	ɹ(r) z	y		w
Other Sounds:	{	r ry			
		rd			
		ɬ(hl)		h	
		l	ly		
		ld			

Though *rdy* and *ldy* do not occur in the extant corpus
they may have occurred in the language, and if so should also
be included in the chart. The sound [ŋ] is, of course, written *n* in the combinations *nc*, *ng*, *nqu*.

The sounds fall into a fairly regular pattern, the only
holes being the lack of the voiced counterparts of [θ] and
[x], namely [ð] and [ɣ] or [ɰ]. The dental/alveolar spirant/
approximant sounds are very numerous

The sounds [ɹ] and [z] did not occur initially as their
letter names *óre* and *áze* indicate, nor did the nasal + voiced
stop combinations occur initially. The sound [ŋ] occurred
only initially or preceding [k] or [g] medially.

By the Third Age the pattern of the Quenya consonantal
sounds had changed so that it could be charted as follows:

	Labial	Dental-Alveolar	Palatal	Velar	Labialized Velar
Voiceless Stop:	p	t	ty	k(c)	kw(qu)
Nasal:	m	n	ny	ŋ(n)	
Nasal + Voiced Stop:	mb	nd	ndy	ng(ng)	ngw(ngw)
Voiceless Spirant:	f	s	ç(hy, h)	x(h)	ʍ(hw)
Voiced Spirant/Approximate:	v		y		w
Other Sounds:		ɹ(hr)			
		r	ry		
		rd			
		l	ly	h	
		ld			

By the Third Age [θ] and [s] had fallen together as [s]; and [z], [ɹ], and [r] had fallen together as [r]. This has greatly simplified the dental/alveolar series. Original *hl* [ɬ] was normally pronounced [l] and so generally fell together with it. Initial [ŋ] became [n], even when part of the initial combination [ŋw], and since medial [ŋw] had not existed in any case—in both Early and Third Age Quenya [ŋ] was found medially only before [k] and [g]—the combination [ŋw] was not found anywhere in Third Age Quenya.

Original [x] had become [h] initially and medially, save in the original combination [xt]. Tolkien writes this combination as *ht*, and tells us that it 'has the sound of *cht* as in German *echt*, *acht*' (III:391 *E*), these German words being pronounced respectively [εçt] and [ɑxt]. We are to understand then, following the pattern of German, that the sound [ç] occurs in the Quenya combinations written *eht* and *iht* (see III:392 *Y*), while [x] is found in the combinations written *aht*, *oht*, and *uht*.

Initial [w] became [v], falling together with original [v], but as medial [w] still occurred in some internal environments independent of [kw] and [gw] (see *Elwe, vanwa*) it is still listed in the chart.

(The changes from Early Quenya to Third Age Quenya discussed here are taken from Tolkien's discussion of the Fëanorean letter names III:400f).

The charts are not to be understood as giving the phonemes of Quenya. Our information on the language is not quite sufficient to give sure results in that area. But some speculation is possible.

The sound [ty] should probably be analyzed as a combination of two phonemes, /t/ and /y/. Similarly [kw] would be taken to be a combination of two phonemes, /k/ and /w/; and [ndy] and [ŋgw] would be combinations of three phonemes, and so with other sounds written as combinations. (This is further discussed on pages 10-12.)

The sounds [x] and [ç] are best considered allophones of
a phoneme /ç/, written ⅄ (hy) initially and ⅄ (h) before t,
not to be confused with the phoneme /h/ which contrasts with
it initially (hyarmen vs. harma).
   The sound [ŋ] can be considered an allophone of /n/
used before /k/ and /g/.
   The sounds [b], [d], and [g] are probably to be listed
as phonemes in their own right, though very limited in the
environments in which they occur: /b/ only following /m/, /d/
only following /n/, /r/, and /l/, and /g/ only following /n/
(with /ng/ normally realized as [ng]). The combination mv is
not found in the extant corpus. If it does not occur at all
in normal Third Age Quenya it might be best to take [b] not
as a full phoneme, but as an allophone of /v/ found following
/m/. That is, /mv/ would be realized as [mb]. (In the discussion of Proto-Eldarin Consonants it is demonstrated that
Q v not derived from initial EQ w derives from PE b, as does
Q b.) The combination mw is also found lacking in the extant
corpus, so it would also be possible, though less likely,
that [b] could be classed as an allophone of /w/ used following /m/. But it is impossible that [b], [v], and [w] are all
allophones of the same phoneme, for /v/ and /w/ contrast
following /l/ (omentielvo vs. Elwe). Of pertinence to this
discussion is Tolkien's remark 'that, 'For lv, not for lw,
many speakers, especially Elves, used lb' (III:399). This
provides a second indication that lv and lw contrast in
Quenya, and also lends support to an attempt to connect [b]
with [v].
   Another way of classifying phonemes in Quenya would be
to give [ŋ] full phoneme value as /ŋ/, and to introduce a
phoneme that might be written /ʮ/, realized as [b] following
/m/; as [d] following /n/, /r/, and /l/; and as [g] following /ŋ/.

   All words in the extant corpus of Quenya end either in
a vowel or in one of the dental/alveolar consonants l, r, n,
and more rarely t and s. (In Finnish also these are the
only allowable final consonants.) Final t is found only on
three forms where it indicates duality: laituvalmet 'we will
praise (them???) both', máryat 'hands-her-two', and met 'us-
two'. Final s is found only on the name Arciryas and on the
form utúvienyes 'I have found it'.
   These same consonants, with the exception of r, and the
consonant m, are the only consonants found doubled: ll, nn,
tt, ss, mm. That rr does not appear might be considered an
accident of the small number of words available (like the
non-appearance of 'the combinations ts, ps, ks(x), that were
favoured in Quenya' [III:400]). But Fíriel 'Mortal-woman' is
best explained as from *fír- 'mortal' (cf. S firith 'fading')
+ -riel 'woman' (as in *Altáriel, Quenya for S Galadriel).

8

Similarly, *Míriel* 'Jewel-woman'. If *rr* were allowed in Quenya we would expect to find **Firriel* and **Mirriel*.

The combination *nd* reduces to *d* or, more rarely, *n* following *l*, *n*, or *r* (*vala* + *ndil* → *Valandil*; *cirya* + *ndil* → *Ciryandil*; *menel* + *ndil* → *Meneldil*; *Aman* + *ndil* → *Amandil*; *elen* + *ndil* → *Elendil*; *mar* + *ndil* → *Mardil*; *minar* + *ndil* → *Minardil*; *ëar* + *ndil* → *Eärnil*). The reason for *nd* sometimes becoming *n* rather than *d* is not apparent.

The combination *n* + *s* simplifies to *ss* (*elen* + †*sar* → *Elessar*).

We never find *m* following *n*, *ng*, or *nc*, but *w* is very common (with *ncw* being written as *nqu* in Tolkien's transcriptions). The commonness of the noun and adjective endings *-ma* and *-me* following vowels and the consonants *l* and *r* causes the non-appearance of *m* following *n*, *ng*, and *nc* to be especially noticeable. It has been assumed in the dictionary, therefore, that *-ma* and *-me* became *-wa* and *-we* following *n*, *ng*, and *nc*. This can be explained partly by DISSIMILATION, the change of one of two similar or identical sounds away from the other to difference it. (Compare the not uncommon juvenile mispronunciation of *chimney* as *chimley*, and the difficulty in repeating quickly any tongue-twister based on the repetition of the same or similar sounds.) That is, *m* is dissimilated from the nasal *n*, *ng*, and *nc* by the loss of its nasality, and becomes *w*. It might also be that simple *gm* and *cm* became *ngw* and *ncw* (written *nqu*) by a sort of metathesis of nasality.

Following *l* both *m* and *w* occur (*silme* vs. *Elwe*). In *Elwe* it is possible that the *w* belongs to the root rather than the ending (that is, that we have *elw* + *e*, not *el* + *me*), or that we have simplification of a larger consonant cluster (that is, *Elwe* < *Elnwe* or *Elgwe* or *Elque* or *Elhwe*), or that following *l* either the *-me* variant or the *-we* variant could be used (probably on the basis of a false analogy with forms with *lw* where the *w* did belong to the root or is the remains of a longer cluster).

Vowels

The vowels in Quenya may be arranged as follows using the letters and symbols of the International Phonetic Alphabet, and Tolkien's transcriptions in small italics in parentheses:

i *(i)*, iː *(í)*	u *(u)*, uː *(ú)*
eː *(é)*	oː *(ó)*
ɛ *(e)*	ɔ *(o)*

aː *(a)*, aː *(á)*

This very regular vowel system is matched by a balanced series of diphthongs, front vowels with a *u*-glide, back vowels with an *i*-glide, and the central vowel *a* with both:

iu	*ui*
eu	*oi*
au, ai	

The most common vowel is *a*. The least common is *u*. The others fall between.

Original long vowels are normally shortened when they fall into a closed syllable, that is, one ending in a consonant. For example, the root NÁR 'red fire' appears in open syllables in *Nárië* 'Fiery' and *Anárion* with a long *á*, but in closed syllables in *Anar* 'Sun' and *Anardil* with a short *a*. Also, *Númenóre* with a long *ó*, but *Númenor* with a short *o*. Exceptions to this rule are *Erusén*, *palantír* (but we find the name *Tar-Palantir* with short *i*), and *yén*. It may be that the long vowel retained its length in closed stressed monosyllables, and sometimes also in compounds formed from them when they fall in the final syllable of the compound.

Original long vowels are normally shortened when they fall in a completely unstressed syllable. (For rules of stress see III:394.) Thus, *En'dóre* with long *ó* in the stressed syllable, but *'Endo'renna* with short *o* in an entirely unstressed syllable.

Diphthongs seem to follow the same rules, shortening by resolving themselves into a single vowel. The sole example is the shortening of *laure* 'golden colour' to *lore-* in the compound *'lindelo'rendor* 'singing-golden-land'.

Final vowels 'had nearly all formerly been long vowels (or they would have disappeared)' (R:61).

The final vowel of a word sometimes disappears when the following word begins with a vowel and there is a close connection between them, thus *lúmenn' omentielvo* 'on the hour of our meeting' instead of **lúmenna omentielvo*; and *tenn' Ambar-metta* 'unto the ending of the world' instead of **tenna Ambar-metta*.

Problems in Pronunciation

Quenya contains two series to sounds which Tolkien refers to as the 'palatal series' and the 'labialized' series. It is necessary to determine whether sounds in these series parallel to single sounds in other series are here single sounds or sound combinations. For example, does *ny* represent a simple combination of dental or alveolar nasal

+ palatal approximate [ny], or does it represent a single
sound: a palatal nasal [ɲ], or a palatalized dental or alveolar nasal [nʸ]?
To begin with the labialized velars: Tolkien calls *qu*
'a combination' (III:392 *QU*). Also, in the word *nuquerna*
the first element *nu-* derives from the root *NDŪ 'down, descend' as in *númen* 'west', with reference to the going down
of the sun. The shortening of the vowel in *nuquerna* can only
be explained by assuming that *qu* represents two sounds [kw],
and not a single sound, a labialized *k*, [k] or [kʷ]. We can
similarly take *ŋgw* as [ŋgw], not [ŋǧ] or [ŋgʷ]. But *hw*,
which Tolkien says is 'a voiceless *w*, as in English *white* (in
northern pronunciation)' (III:392 *W*) we may take as a single
sound [ʍ], not [hw] or [ʍʍ]. And *w* alone is, of course, simple [w].
For the palatal series evidence can be found from an
examination of the stress patterns and the vowel lengths in
words where the sounds occur. For *ly* there is the word
hiruvalye which would be stressed *hi'ruva₁lye* if *ly* were a
simple palatal lateral [ʎ] or strongly palatalized dental or
alveolar lateral [lʸ] or [ļ]. But Tolkien indicates it is
to be stressed *'hiru'valye* (R:58) which shows that *ly* cannot
represent a single sound. For *ny* we can use the root NÉN
water which preserves its long *é* in an open syllable in
Nénimë 'Wet', but has a short *e* in *Nenya* 'Water-one' indicating it has fallen into a closed syllable, so that *ny* stands
for two sounds. Similarly *ry* in *Narya* must indicate [ry],
not a single sound [ɟ] or [rʸ], for the root NÁR contains a
long *á* as shown by the month name *Nárië* and the personal
name *Anárion*. And this also holds for *ry* in *ómaryo* which
would be stressed *'óma₁ryo* if the *ry* were a single sound, but
which Tolkien indicates is stressed ₁ó'maryo (R:58).
It would seem then that we can make the rule that the
sounds of the palatal series in Quenya are double sounds in
all cases. But, there is an exception, in *máryat*. If *ry*
represents two sounds then we would normally expect to divide
máryat into syllables as *már·yat*; but if we do this we find
a long *á* in a non-final closed syllable, which Quenya does
not allow. So we must divide the word as *má·ryat*. It would
appear that syllable division in such cases follows etymology. In *Narya* the word is thought of as *nár* + *ya*, and so
divided into syllables, and *á* becomes *a* in a closed syllable.
But in *máryat* the word is thought of as *má* 'hand' + *rya* 'her'
+ *t* 'two', it is divided into syllables as *má·ryat*, and *á*,
being in an open syllable, remains long. In the recordings
of 'Namárië' Tolkien pronounces *máryat* as ['marʃat] in the
spoken version and as ['maːrɛt] in the sung version.
To summarize, the palatal combinations *ny*, *ry*, *ly*, and
probably *ty* represent double sounds. But unlike other such

combinations they may be treated as a single consonant for syllable division when the etymology suggests it. In the pronunciation given in the Quenya dictionary *ny*, *ry*, and *ly* have been given respectively as [ny], [ry], and [ly] or (after *e* or *i*) [ly] as the best way of indicating an acceptable pronunciation, but these may have often been realized as [ɲy], [ɕy], and [ʎy], or something similar: or even as [ɲɲ], [ɕɕ], and [ʎʎ]. Or, to go in the other direction, they may have been realized sometimes as [nl], [rl], and [ll]. Free variations of this kind are heard throughout Tolkien's recitation and singing of 'Namárië'.

It is not certain whether *n* in *ng* and *nc/nq* is always intended to represent [ŋ] rather than [n], particularly when the *ng* or *nc/nq* derives from an original *n* + *g* or *n* + *c/q*. In both the recitation and singing of 'Namárië' Tolkien pronounces the *nq* of *enquantuva* as [nk], not [ŋk]. But in the tengwar writing of the poem we find ᴄᴐᴰ which must stand for [ŋkw] and not for [nkw], which would be written ᴛᴐᴐᴄᴈ. So the pronunciation in the recording is quite likely an error on Tolkien's part, caused by a hasty reading of the text and Tolkien's knowledge that *en-* in *enquantuva* is indeed an independent morpheme meaning 'again'—as in *envinyatar* 'renewer'. Accordingly, [ŋ] is used throughout the pronunciations in the dictionaries before [g] and [k]. But one must also recognize the possibility that, as in English, either [ŋ] or [n] is sometimes correct. For example, *income* may be pronounced either as ['ɪŋkʌm] or ['ɪnkʌm].

In his recitation of 'Namárië' Tolkien represents *a* by [a] in almost every case. In his singing of 'Namárië' he uses [ɑ]. For the pronunciations given in the Quenya dictionary [a] has been used. This choice was made because the spoken version of 'Namárië' contains less provable errors in pronunciation than the sung version. Also, [a] alone is not a normal English sound, while [ɑ] is. To achieve [a] instead of [ɑ] or [æ] would have required for Tolkien some effort which he would certainly not have made if [a] was incorrect. As to the sung version, there his concentration would have been more on the singing and the tune, and so it is not surprising that instead of [a] Tolkien let settle for the more normal English sound of [ɑ].

THE NOUN

Structure

The Quenya noun (and adjective) normally contains a root and ending. For example, from the root FANA 'veil' with no ending comes *fana*, a word applied to the 'veils' or 'raiment' in which the Valar presented themselves to physical eyes; but from FANA and the ending *-ya* comes *fanya* '(white) cloud'. *Cala-* (in *Calacirya*)—presumably from a root CALA—appears without an ending with the meaning 'light'. With the ending *-ma* comes *calma* 'lamp'. It is not clear to what extent these endings still have special meanings in Third Age Quenya.

It is not always possible to distinguish between root and ending. For example, is *téma* to be derived from a root *TÉ plus the ending *-ma*, or from a root *TÉM? However, by isolating roots by word comparison it is possible to prove that the following are genuine Quenya endings:

-*da*, in *Elda* (see *el-*), *alda* (see †*alta*), **yulda* (see *yulma*)
-*de*, in **marde* (see *mar-*, -*mar*), **Quende* (see *Quenya*)
-*do*, in *ando* 'gate' (see *anto* 'mouth'—assuming *an-* here basically has to do with some kind of 'opening')
-*ië*, (see dictionary entry)
-*ma/-wa*, (see dictionary entry)
-*me/-we*, (see dictionary entry)
-*na*, in †*morna* (???)
-*ne*, in *andúnë* (see *NDÚ)
-*ta*, in †*alta* (see *alda*), **certa* 'cut character' (see *Cermië* 'Harvest, i.e, Cutting')
-*to*, in *anto* (see -*do* above)
-*ya*, (see dictionary entry)

Possibly we should also include -*co* (accepting a connexion between *tinco* 'metal' and *TIN 'spark, sparkle') and -*en* (in *elen*).

The root + ending or the root alone may make up the STEM of a Quenya noun. The vowels in the endings would originally have been long in most cases; it is still convenient to so represent them in giving stems as they remain long in certain environments. For example, from a root *ÓR 'high' (as in *Pelóri*, *oromardi*) and the ending -*ne*(-*né*) comes the stem *orné-* 'tree' written †*orne* when uninflected (as in *ornemalin*). Case endings are added to the stem, with the vowel normally remaining long in an open syllable (save when entirely unstressed), hence the genitive plural of multitude †*ornélion* (in *malinornélion*).

The Noun Declension

There is no distinction made in form between nominative and accusative in Third Age Quenya; but other distinctions of case are indicated by inflexional markers suffixed to the noun stem. From an examination of inflected singular and plural forms it is possible to compile a fairly complete chart of the Quenya noun inflexions, as given on the facing page. Two separate declensions are given, but the only real differences are in the nominative/accusative and genitive plurals.

Quenya uses two different plural forms, a regular plural form indicated by -r or -i in the nominative and accusative case, and a plural of multitude indicated by -li which is used when it is a matter of a large number of whatever is being talked of. Quenya also possessed a dual, as indicated by the dual pronouns ending in -t and by *Aldúya* 'Two trees - one' compared to *Aldëa* (from *alda* + *ya*) 'Tree-one'. But further published information on the dual is needed for any further discussion.

The nominative and accusative case take their regular plural forms in either -r (for the first declension) or -i (for the second declension). In the first declension are found nouns whose singulars (nominative and accusative) end in a (*tehta*, pl. *tehtar*), o (*Noldo*, pl. *Noldor*), and *ië* (*enquië*, pl. *enquier*). In the second declension are found nouns whose singular (nominative and accusative) end in a consonant (*Silmaril*, pl. *Silmarilli*; *yén*, pl. *yéni*; *palantír*, pl. *palantíri*) or in a consonant + e (*lasse*, pl. *lassi*). Note, however, the plural form *tyeller*, the singular of which is most easily reconstructed as **tyelle*, indicating some nouns ending in a consonant + e belong to the first declension. We have no examples of plurals for nouns whose singulars end in i (*†tári*) or u (*Eru*). The nominative and accusative case are used for the subject of a verb (*Varda...ortanë* 'Varda...uplifted'), for the object of a verb (*yulma...enquantuva* 'cup...will refill'), and when governed by a preposition (*ve fanyar* 'like clouds').

The genitive singular is indicated by the addition of -o to the nominative and accusative singular (*cirya*, gen. *ciryo*; *Varda*, gen. *Vardo*; *Oiolosse*, gen. *Oiolosséo*; *†tári*, gen. *†tário*; **Altáriel*, gen. *Altariello*). The expected final combination *ao* is simplified to o (*Vardo*, not ***Vardao*). Similarly single o rather than double *oo* would be found with o-stems (*Noldo*, gen. **Noldo*, not ***Noldóo*), and probably -io, not -iëo, with nouns ending in *ië* in the nominative and accusative (*hísië*, gen. **hísio*, not ***hísiëo*).

The genitive plural is indicated by the addition of -on to the nominative and accusative plural (**aldar*, gen. *aldaron*; *eleni*, gen. *elenion*; *Silmarilli*, gen. *Silmarillion*).

The gentive is used to indicate possession (*rámar aldaron*

QUENYA

QUENYA NOUN DECLENSIONS

The noun stem is indicated by a standard face, case markers and
plural markers by script. Stress has also been indicated. Blanks in
the chart indicate where a form cannot reasonably be reconstructed from
published information.
NA = 'nominative and accusative'; G = 'genitive'; I = 'instrumental'; C = 'compositive'; Al = 'allative'; Lc = 'locative'; Ab = 'ablative'.

1ST DECLENSION

aldá- 'tree'

NA	s.	'alda	pl.	'aldaⲛ	pl. mult. 'alda₁ℓⲓ
G		'aldo		'alda₁ⲛon	₁al'dáℓⲓ₁on
I		'alda₁ⲛen			
C		'alda₁va			
Al		₁al'danna		₁al'dannaⲛ	'alda'ℓⲓnnaⲛ
Lc		₁al'daⳚⳚe		₁al'daⳚⳚen	'alda'ⳚⳚen
Ab		₁al'daℓℓo			

2ND DECLENSION

lassé- 'leaf'

NA	s.	'lasse	pl.	'lassⲓ	pl. mult. 'lasse₁ℓⲓ
G		'lassë₁o		'lassⲓ'on	₁las'séℓⲓ₁on
I		'lasse₁ⲛen			
C		'lasse₁va			
Al		₁las'senna		₁las'sennaⲛ	'lasse'ℓⲓnnaⲛ
Lc		₁las'seⳚⳚe		₁las'seⳚⳚen	'lasse'ℓⲓⳚⳚen
Ab		₁las'seℓℓo			

elen- 'star'

NA	s.	'elen	pl.	'elen₁ⲓ	pl. mult. e'lelℓⲓ
G		'elen₁o		e'lenⲓ₁on	e'lelℓⲓ₁on
I		e'lenⲛen			
C					
Al		e'lenⲛa		e'lennaⲛ	'elel'ℓⲓnnaⲛ
Lc		e'lesⳚe		e'lesⳚen	'elel'ℓⲓⳚⳚen
Ab		e'lelℓo			

'wings of trees'; *Vardo tellumar* 'Varda's domes'). It also
appears used as a subjective genitive (*ómaryo...lírinen* 'her
voice's...song-in'; *lírinen airetário* 'in song of holy-queen'

15

[R:59]; *Altariello nainië* 'Galadriel's lament'); it appears
as an explicative genitive (*Calaciryo míri* 'Lightcleft's jewels'; *lúmenn' omentielvo* 'on the hour of our meeting' [I:
90]); and is used as well in a separative sense (*Varda Oiolosséo...ortanë* 'Varda from Everwhite...has uplifted'). In
the name *Silmarillion* a plural genitive is used as a singular substantive: literally meaning 'of the Silmarils', it
must be understood as a title of a literary work 'story of
the Silmarils' or something similar.

The published corpus provides one definite example of
the genitive plural of multitude, *malinornélion* 'of many
golden trees'. The form *vanimálion* is probably a second.
The long vowel of the stem is preserved in an open syllable
on which the main stress of the form falls.

In *Altariello*, *Silmarilli*, and *Silmarillion* the final *l*
of the stem is doubled when the plural and genitive case
markers are suffixed. This might be taken to indicate that
the final *l* in these words represents an earlier *ll*,
preserved only intervocalically. But *Silmaril* probably represents an earlier *Silmazil* from *Silima + sil* (see p. 132f
for *s > z > r*). And in the noun *Silima* and in the verb *síla*
'shine(s)' only a single *l* occurs. So the root is SIL with a
single *l*, The *l* may double intervocalically in certain stress
patterns, or the second *l* may be the remains of a stem ending.
There will, in such words, be no distinction between the regular plural and plural of multitude in the NA and G cases.

The instrumental case is marked by *-nen* in the singular.
It occurs on the forms *lírinen* and *súrinen* which Tolkien
translates respectively as 'in song' and 'in the wind'. The
contexts show that 'in' here has to do with manner and agent
rather than with place. The leaves are blown by the wind.
The stars tremble because of Varda's song. There are no published examples of any instrumental plural forms.

The only published example of the *-va* case marker is on
the form *miruvóreva* in the phrase *yuldar...lisse-miruvóreva*
'draughts...of sweet-mead'. Here *-va* indicates that the noun
to which it is attached comprises the substance from which
something is COMPOSED. Accordingly, the case marked by *-va*
may be labelled the COMPOSITIVE case pending further data
demonstrating other uses.

The singular case markers *-nna*, *-sse*, and *-llo* indicate
respectively three directive cases: an allative case indicating direction towards; a locative case indicating place
where; and an ablative case indicating away from. That is,
they respectively answer the questions whither?, where?, and
whence?

The allative ending -*nna* is to be normally translated
'to' or 'toward(s)', but also 'on' in the sense of 'onto, upon'. The singular appears in *Endorenna utúlien* 'to Middle-
earth I am come' and (with loss of final vowel) in *síla
lúmenn' omentielvo* 'shines on [the] hour of our meeting'.
The name *Elenna* may be an allative form used as a proper
name, but might also be analyzed as the root ELEN (already
expanded from simple EL) plus the noun ending -*na*. The
preposition *tenna* 'unto, until' (as in *tenn' Ambar-metta*
'unto the ending of the world'), however, is certainly in
origin the allative form of a noun.
    There is no example of a simple plural allative. But,
one allative plural of multitude form does appear: *falmalinnar* 'upon many foaming waves', indicating that the allative
marker -*nna* pluralizes with -*r*.
    In Finnish there is an ilative case with the basic mean-
ing 'into', marked by a lengthing of the final vowel of the
noun stem and adding -*n*. Finnish also has an essive case
with the basic meaning 'in, on, at', marked by the ending
-*na/-nä*.
    The locative ending -*sse* is to be normally translated
'in, at, on'. The singular appears in *Lóriendesse* 'in
Lórien' (R:58). The month names *Víressë* and *Lótessë* might be
explained as original locative forms. If so, then it would
appear that the locative could indicate place in time as well
as space.
    The only example of the simple plural locative is the
relative pronoun form *yassen* 'in which', marked by Tolkien as
plural (R:58). This does indicate the locative marker -*sse*
pluralizes with -*n*.
    In Finnish there is an inessive case with the basic mean-
ing 'within', marked by the ending -*ssa/-ssä*.
    The ablative ending -*llo* is to be normally translated
'from, out of'. The singular appears in *sindanóriello* 'out
of a grey country', in *Et Eärello* 'Out of the Great Sea', and
in *Rómello* '(one) from the East'.
    There are no examples of plural forms in the ablative.
    In Finnish the ablative is indicated by the ending -*lta/
-ltä*. There are also Finnish case endings -*lla/-llä* and -*lle*
which respectively mark the adessive case (basic meaning 'in,
on') and the allative case (basic meaning 'to, onto').
    The nominative and accusative forms of the ablative *Eär
Eärello* and *Rómello* are †*Eären* and *rómen*, indicating an
assimilation of *n* before *ll*. That is, †*Eären* + *llo* →
Eärenllo → *Eärelllo* → *Eärello*, and the same for *rómen* + *llo*.
Assimilation of *n* before *s* is indicated by *Elessar*, from *elen*
+ †*sar* (cf. S *sarn*), and so the locatives of †*Eären* and

rómen would be the forms **Eäresse* and **rómesse*. The declension of *elen* in the chart on page 15 has been given to show the found and postulated assimilations of *n* in the declension of stems ending with that consonant. In the chart it is postulated that *n* would also assimilate before the *-li* marker of the plural of multitude, producing the forms **elelli*, **elellion*, etc., instead of ***elenli*, ***elenlion*, etc. Predicting the most probable form for the singular compositive case is more difficult. There are three possibilities: **elenva* with no assimilation of *n*; **eleva* (contracted from a theoretic ***elevva*) with complete assimilation of *ñ*; and **elemba* with partial assimilation of *n* and *v* represented by *b*.

We have no examples to show to what extent stems ending in *l* or *r* may, or may not, have assimilated their final consonants to the following case marker. Would, for example, the ablative of *palantír* be **palantirlo*, **palantillo*, or even something like **palantiriilo*?

THE ADJECTIVE

The only adjective found in both singular and plural forms is *laurëa*, plural *laurië*. But this is sufficient to indicate that Quenya adjectives generally show number. Adjectives modifying singular nouns are found ending in *a* (*halla*, *†morna*, *sindarinwa*, *vanwa*), in *e* (*lisse*, *losse*), and in a consonant (*alcarin*). Adjectives modifying plural nouns are found ending in *e* (*lintë*, *ilyë*) and *i* (*luini*). The following represent the apparent singular and plural correspondences:

SINGULAR	PLURAL
-a	-e
-e	-i
-ëa	-ië
-consonant	*-consonant* + i

It is probable that in Early Quenya *-i* was the universal plural marker, and adjectives ending in the singular in *-a*, *-e*, and *-ëa* respectively, in the plural ended in *-ai*, *-ei*, and *-ëai*. By the Third Age final long vowels had been shortened, and the evidence of the adjectives indicates that final *-ai* fell together with final *-é*, both becoming *-e*, and final *-ei* fell together with final *-í*, both becoming *-i* by the Third Age. Final *-ëai* would become *-ié* (the original *e* being raised to *i* by dissimilation), which became *-ië*.

The adjective ending *-imë* appears to be both singular and

plural. In 'Namárië' *únótimë* modifies the plural noun *yéni*, but Tolkien does not mark it as a plural form in his very literal translation in R:58. And the ending appears on the month names *Nénimë*, *Súlimë*, *Urimë*, and *Hísimë* where a singular meaning would be expected. Cf. the corresponding S *-ui*.

THE ARTICLE

Quenya has only a definite article, *i*, corresponding to English 'the'. It is used generally as in English. It is not used before a noun modified by a genitive: *Elen síla lúmenn' omentielvo*, translated by Tolkien 'A Star shines on the hour of our meeting.' But if we render *omentielvo* by the English possessive case, instead of by a phrase governed by the preposition *of*, we get 'A star shines on our meeting's hour'—not very good English, but sufficent to indicate why the article is not necessary in the Quenya sentence. The article is also lacking in *Sinome maruvan ar Hildinyar tenn' Ambar-metta*, which Tolkien renders 'In this place will I abide, and my heirs, unto the ending of the world.' But the capitalizing of *Ambar* indicates it is a proper name in Quenya, and so explains the lack.

The form *mí* is translated by Tolkien as 'in the', and and so must be taken as incorporating the article. Compare similar absorbed forms of the article in other languages, e.g. French *du* 'of the' (*de* 'of' + *le* 'the'), *au* 'at the' (*à* 'at' + *le* 'the').

PRONOUNS

A full discussion of personal pronouns and an attempt to construct the complete personal pronoun system follows in a separate article on page 22. It will be sufficient here to note forms actually found:

1st Person: *-n* 'I'; *-nye* 'I'; *nin* 'for me'; *-nya* 'my'; *-lvo* 'of our' (inclusive); *-lme* 'we' (exclusive); *-lmo* 'of our' (exclusive); *met* 'us both' (exclusive).

2nd Person: *elyë*, *-lyë* 'thou'.

3rd Person masculine: none found.

3rd Person feminine: *-rya* 'her' (possessive); *-ryo* 'of her' (possessive).

3rd Person neuter: *-s* 'it'.

3rd Person dual: *te, -t* 'them both'

Sources for these forms may be found by consulting the Quenya dictionary and the article beginning page 22.

That Elves distinguished between masculine and feminine pronouns is indicated by Tolkien's note that 'Elves (and Hobbits) always refer to the Sun as She' (I:176n). It is not certain that they used a neuter, and it may be that what is here called the neuter is, in fact, the masculine.

INCLUSIVE, applied to the 1st person plural pronouns, means that both the speaker and the person spoken to are included in the 'we', 'us', or 'our'. EXCLUSIVE means that the person spoken to is not included in the 'we', 'us', or 'our'. The inclusive forms are marked by *v*, the exclusive by *m*.

In αI:90 'of our meeting' is rendered *omentielmo*, in the earliest printings of β and in γδε it is rendered as *omentielvo*, and in all but the earliest printings of β it is rendered *omentilmo*. On this, Dick Plotz, founder of the Tolkien Society of America, has written (MP 10:1, 3):

> The original version was *Elen síla lúmenn' omentielmo,* which means, literally, 'A star shines on the hour of our (my, his, her, NOT your) meeting.' Tolkien, on reflection, changed this to *omentielvo,* 'of our (my, your, possibly his, her) meeting.' This was[,] of course, a proper change, and this is how it appeared in the earliest printings of the Ballantine edition. I, however, saw it as an obvious error, and prevailed upon Ballantine to CORRECT it! The "correction" introduced another error, since *omentilmo,* as far as I know, means nothing at all. Now they won't change it back, because it's too expensive. But *omentielvo* is correct. Sorry to have messed everyone up.

The use of the exclusive form in *laituvalmet* 'we will praise them both.' has also been questioned'. But here no particular second person is being addressed, and the exclusive may have been the normal form in those circumstances.

It is possible that *te, -t* are not only 3rd person forms, but are used for all persons, and best translated literally simply as 'both'.

The only example of a relative pronoun is the locative plural form *yassen* 'in which'. The nominative and accusative singular is listed in the dictionary as **ya,* but there are other possibilities: **yan, *yán, *yas, *yás,* etc.

QUENYA

Verbs

The following discussion is partially based on Paula Marmor's 'Notes towards a System of Quenya Verb Structure', circulated to those involved with the compilation of this book.

The Quenya verb system is far from clear. We cannot even be sure that it is a tense system, not an aspect system. However, a viewpoint must be chosen, that of a tense system seems best from the point of view of the general reader, and there is nothing in the date to argue against it.

The present tense is indicated by *-a* (*caita mornië* 'darkness falls', *elen síla* 'a star shines'; *lantar lassi* 'leaves fall', *tintilar i eleni* 'the stars twinkle'). The present singular is also used as the imperative (*laita* 'praise!, give praise!').

The past is indicated by *-e*. This alone is attached to the stem for the simple past tense (*Elentári ortanë* 'Star-queen lifted up', *lumbulë undulávë* '(heavy) shadow down-licked'; *yéni...vánier* 'long years...passed away'). Tolkien writes that '*ortane* is a past tense and refers to events in the far past' (R:60). Paula Marmor has, accordingly, suggested that *ortanë* and *undulávë*, marked by *-e* alone, belong to an HISTORICAL PAST TENSE, while *vánier*, marked by *-ie*, is the regular past tense. But one must also face the possibility of verb stems ending in *-i*.

The perfect tense, indicating action completed, is marked by *-ie* and by a prefixed reduplication of the stem vowel (*yéni...avánier* 'long years...have passed away'; *utú-lien* 'I am come'; *utúvienyes* 'I have found it').

The future is indicated by *-uva* (*Man...enquantuva* 'Who ...will refill?', *elyë hiruva* 'even thou wilt find'; *hiruvalyë* 'thou wilt find'; *maruvan* 'I will dwell').

Paula Marmor suggests that it 'is possible that the modal suffix *-uva* "shall, will" contains the present indicator *-a*, and that the corresponding past "should, would" should be presented by a form *-uvë, *-uvië; thus *maruven, *maruvien "I would dwell".'

As indicated by the examples above, verbs agree with their subjects in number. All examples found in the text with an independant plural subject—that is, do not have suffixed to them a plural pronoun—pluralize by addition of *r*.

Forms of the personal pronouns may be suffixed to the verbs. For the first person is found *-n* (*utúlien* 'I am come', *maruvan* 'I will dwell') and the longer form *-nye* (*utúvienyes* 'I have found it'); and also the plural exclusive first person suffix -*lme* (*laituvalmet* 'we will praise them both'). For the second person is found -*lyë* (*hiruvalyë* 'thou wilt find'). As seen from the examples, further shortened forms of the pronouns may be further suffixed as objects of the verbs.

Quenya also possessed a subjunctive. But the only form found is *nai* 'be it that, maybe', from *ná* 'is' + *i* (R: 60).

SYNTAX

To judge from Tolkien's arrangement of 'Namárië' 'into clearer and more normal style' (R:58f), the normal word order of Quenya is as follows:

Subject modifier(s) + subject + verb + object + verb modifier(s)

Following *yassen* the positions of subject and verb are inverted.

Genitive forms and adjectives usually precede the form they govern, but follow when connected by sense to other matter which follows. There is no instance of two adjectives, or a genitive and an adjective, preceding the governed noun in immediate sequence. This may be an accident of the material available. But we do have the odd—to English sensibilities—arrangement *Vardo nu luini tellumar* 'Varda's under blue domes' where * *nu Vardo luini tellumar* 'under Varda's blue domes' would be the normal English word order. The Quenya word order seems designed to avoid the placing of the genitive form *Vardo* between a preposition and its object.

As indicated by the unchanged text of 'Namárië', a great amount of freedom was allowed in word order as would be expected in such a highly inflected language.

ON PRONOUNS IN QUENYA

BY BILL WELDEN

with slight additions and revisions by Jim Allan

THERE ARE MANY EXAMPLES of pieces of different declensions of pronouns in Quenya which hint at a complex system in the language. This article will attempt to construct a system

from which the examples we have could be formed.[1]
An obvious place to start is with the pair *hiruva-lye*
and *elye hiruva* 'thou wilt find' (R:59) where the latter is
considered emphatic—'even thou wilt find'. In an earlier
stage of the language the former would have been two words:
*hiruvā elyē, and over time the two coalesced.
We can assume that during the time when the former was
still two words a reversal of the verb and its pronomininal
subject indicated special emphasis on the pronoun. The more
common and natural order gave rise to the verbal ending,
while the less natural form remained two words. We have as
our only certain nominative pronoun: *elye* 'thou.'

Other well-founded examples have to do with possessive
forms.[2] After removing genitive endings (*-o*), we have four
examples: *omentie-lva* 'our meeting' (I:90), *óma-rya* 'her
voice' (I:394;R:58f.), *má-rya-t* 'her two hands' (I:394;R:
58f.), and *hild-i-nya-r* 'my (pl.) heirs' (III:245). Thus, it
would seem that pronoun endings are of the form CCV, where
CC is a consonant cluster and V is a vowel. Reconstructing
these possessive pronouns in parallel with *-lye*, *elye* we get
three probable possessive pronouns: **elva* 'our', **erya* 'her',
and **enya* 'my'. Since these possessive forms are adjectives,
they must agree in number with the nouns they modify. The
plural forms add *r* to the singular form. Thus *hildinyar* consists of a plural form of the noun, *†hildi*, plus a pluralized
form of the possessive pronoun, *(e)nyar*. The singular would
be **hildenya* 'my heir'. This would also appear as **enya
hilde*, to be pluralized as either **enyar hildi* or **enye
hildi* (from earlier **enyai hildí*), depending on whether the
possessive pronouns followed the noun or adjective pattern
of pluralization when used independantly.
A fifth possessive pronoun form is **elma*, from *omen-
tielma* (in α the form *omentielmo* appears instead of *omentielvo*). Both **elva* and **elma* are 1st personal plural forms,
the difference being that **elva* is inclusive and **elma*
exclusive. (See p. 20.)
Now consider the word *utúvienyes* 'I have found it' (III:
250).[3] This will have both a subject ('I') and an object

---

[1] If you'll look closely, you'll see that throughout the course of
this discussion I never make a definite statement. It's safer that way.
I think, however—pending further authoritative information—that we
should establish 'accepted' hypothetical forms for pronouns and things.
If you like **este* better than **elte*, say so, and we'll vote on it.

[2] I use the term POSSESSIVE rather than GENITIVE here mainly to
avoid confusion when forms like *ómaryo* 'of her voice' are considered. In
addition, the pronominal genitive bears little resemblance to the mormal
genitive.

[3] Cf. Gk. εὕρηκα ⟨heúrēka⟩ 'I have found it, "Eureka"'.

('it') marker. If the subject marker follows the pattern of
the other examples, we can divide the word *utúvie-nye-s*,
where *-nye* is the 1st person pronoun nominative 'I'. We
reconstruct the independant form as **enye* 'I'. Thus it would
appear that the nominative forms end in *-e* and their corresponding possessives end in *-a*. We construct the following
nominative forms of pronouns: **erye* 'she', **elve* and **elme*
'we', and construct the possessive form **elya* 'thy'.

The two examples *maruva-n* 'I will abide' and *utúlie-n*
'I am come' (III:245) show a shortened form of the first person subject marker **enye*. This form would be used when the
marker is the last element in the word. Quite possibly
other markers follow the same pattern, but there are no
examples. The second person reverential(?) marker *elye*, at
least, does not.[4]

The form *laituvalmet* (III:231) must, from its context,
and from comparison with other forms, be translated something
like 'we will praise them'. We can divide this into *laituva-
lme-t*, where our subject marker is the first person plural
exclusive **elme*. The object marker *-t* is paralleled by the
object marker *-s* in *utúvie-nye-s*. From *má-rya-t* 'hands-her-
two' and *me-t* 'us-two' we know that *-t* is generally a sign
of duality. Accordingly we are better to render *laituva-
-lme-t* as 'we will praise them both', or even, 'we will
praise both', if *-t* in fact does not necessarily indicate a
the third person in particular. However, as our one example
shows that it is used as a third person dual accusative
pronoun, we will consider only that use in the discussion.

A nominative form meaning 'they both' will also most
likely contain a *t*. The only possibilities, thanks to the
restrictive Quenya phonology, are **elte*, **ente*, **erte*, **etye*,
*ehte, and **ette*. Any one of these could be correct, but
looking at the other plural nominative **elve/*elme*, the first
possibility seems the best choice; so we have **elte* 'they
both'. The corresponding possessive would be **elta*.

Similarly, we would expect an *s* in the nominative for
'it', and so would construct **esye* in parallel with **enye*,
*erye, *elye*. But original *sy* became *hy* in Quenya (III:392f.
y), and so we arrive at **ehye* 'it'. The possessive form
would be **ehya* 'its'. Support for this reconstruction can
be found in Sindarin. Q *hy* corresponds to S *h*, and we find
the Sindarin third person plural neuter pronoun *hain*, and
also the plural demonstrative pronoun *hin*.

From 'Namárië' we have *me-t* 'us two'. The accusative
form of **elme* is then †*me*. For **elve* we reconstruct the

---

[4] As in *hiruvalye*. It may be that **maruvanye* and **hiruval* are grammatical alternatives to the ones which appear. The long form *hiruvalye*
may be chosen to fit the metre of the poem.

QUENYA

	Singular	Dual	Plural
NOMINATIVE	1. *enye *'I'* 2. elye *'thou'* 3. {*erye *'she'* / ?*ehye *'it'*	3. ?*elte *'they both'*	1. *elve *'we'* *elme
POSSESSIVE or genitive	1. *enya *'my'* 2. *elya *'thy'* 3. {*erya *'her'* / ?*ehya *'it'*	3. ?*elta *'their (both)'*	1. *elva *'our'* *elma
ACCUSATIVE	1. †ni *'me'* 2. *li *'thee'* 3. {*ri *'her'* / ?*si *'it'*	1. *vet *'us both'* met 3. te *'them both'*	1. *ve *'us'* †me
DATIVE	1. nin *'for me'* 2. *lin *'for thee'* 3. {*rin *'for her'* / ?*sin *'for it'*	3. *ten *'for them both'*	1. *ven *'for us'* *men

parallel forms *vet and *ve. The -e ending is also found on the dual accusative form '(them) both'. If we assume that nin is ni-n 'for me'[5] where ni is the accusative form of *enye, we have a singular accusative form. This gives nine accusative forms in all: †ni 'me', *li 'thee', *ri 'her', *si 'it', *vet and met 'us both', te '(them) both', and *ve and †me 'us'.

If we assume, as we did to get †ni, that the dative is formed by adding -n to the accusative form, we have seven dative pronouns, for it is not clear how -n would have been added to *vet and met.

All of the forms discussed here are shown in the above table.

---

[5] Not a bad assumption when you consider that an is 'for' and prepositions generally take the accusative as in imbe met 'between us two' (I:394;R:58f.).

A

a [a] interj. O! / S. a/ III:231,
259. (Eng. O!, ah!)

aha ['aha] n. 1. rage. 2. the letter
ɑ, also called harma. III:401. (Skt.
ahas 'distress'.)

ai [ai̯] interj. ah!, alas! / S. ai/
I:394;R:58f,61.

†aire ['ai̯rɛ] adj. holy. I:394;R:58f.
(Gk. hieros 'holy'.)

airetári ['ai̯rɛ'taːri] adj. holy and
queenly. I:394;R:58f.

aiya ['ai̯ya] n. (ai + ya) holy one ???
II:329;III:192. Cf. †aire.

alcar ['alkar] n. glory. / S. aglar/
R:65.

alcarin ['alka,rin] adj. glorious.
III:318,324;R:65.

alda ['alda] n. (gen. pl. aldaron ['al-
da,rɔn]) 1. tree. / S. galadh, †ga-
lad, †thorn, -orn/ 2. the letter ᠊.
I:394;III:391,401;R:58f,65. Cf. †alta.
(Eng. alder, akin to many tree names;
Gk. aldaino·'nourish, make to grow'.)

Aldalómë ['alda'loːmɛ] nm. place 'Tree-
shadow'. II:72.

Aldamir ['alda,mir] nm. pers. 'Tree-
jewel'. III:319,367.

Aldarion [,al'dari,ɔn] nm. pers. 'Tree-
---'. III:315,330n.

aldaron, see alda.

Aldëa ['aldɛ,a] n. (alda + ya) 'Tree-
one', the fourth day of the Númenorean
week, called Trewsday in the Shire.
Corresponds to Aldúya in the Eldarin
week. / S. Orgaladh/ III:388f.

aldû- [,al'duː-] n. du. the two trees,
referring to Laurelin and Telperion
that once gave light to the land of the
Valar. / S. †galadhad/ III:388f.

Aldúya [,al'duːya] n. 'Two-trees one',
the fourth day of the Eldarin week.
Corresponds to Aldëa in the Númenorean
week. / S. Orgaladhad/ III:388.

†alta ['alta] n. tree. / S. †galad,
galadh, †thorn/ See *Altáriel. Cf.
alda.

*Altáriel [,al'taːri,ɛl] nm. pers. (gen.
Altariello ['alta,ri'ɛllɔ]) 'Tree-
woman'. / S.Galadriel/ R:58.

Aman ['aman] nm. place 'Blessed' ???
III:317;G:79. Cf. Manwe. (Ar. aman
'safety'.)

Amandil [a'mandiḷ] nm. pers. 'Friend
of Aman' or 'Lover of Aman'. III:
315f.

ambar ['ambar] n. (< MBAR) world.
III:245f. (Amharic amba 'mountain'.)

ambar-metta ['ambar'mɛtta] n. 'world-
ending', ending of the world. III:
245f.

Ambarona [,am'barɔ,na] nm. place May
contain ambar 'world'. II:72.

ampa ['ampa] n. 1. hook. 2. the letter
ɑ. III:401. (Lat. ampla 'handle',
amplexus 'encircling'.)

an [an] conj. for. I:394;R:58f.

†Anar, Anár- ['anar, a'naːr-] n. (< NÁR)
Sun. / S. Anor, Anór-/ III:388f;
Anárion III:317.

Anardil [a'nardiḷ] nm. pers. 'Sun-
friend' or 'Sun-lover'. III:318.

Anárion [a'naːri,ɔn] nm. pers. 'Sun-
---'. III:317.

Anarya [a'narya] n. 'Sun one', the
second day of both the Eldarin and Númenorean weeks, called Sunday in the
Shire. / S. Oranor/ III:388f.

anca ['aŋka] n. 1. jaws. / S. carach/
2. the letter ɑ. III:401. Cf. S.
Orthanc. (Skt. aṅkas 'bend, hook'; Gk.
ankos 'bend, hollow'.)

ancalima [,aŋ'kali,ma] either n. (and +
cali + ma) great light; or v. imper.
s. (an + calim + a) give light! Cf.
andave, anna, cal(a)-, Calimmacil, S.
an(n)-. II:329;III:192. Cf. Anca-
Tímë, Ancalimon.

Ancalimë [,aŋ'kali,mɛ] nm. pers. 'Wo-
man of Great Light' ???; 'Light-giver'
??? See discussion under ancalima.
III:315. Also cf. Ancalimon.

Ancalimon [,aŋ'kali,mɔn] nm. pers.
'One of Great Light' ???; 'Light-
giver' ??? See discussion under ancalima. III:315. Also cf. Ancalimë.

andave ['anda,vɛ] adv. greatly. III:
231. Cf. S. an(n)-.

ando ['andɔ] n. 1. gate. / S. annon/
2. the letter ρ. III:401. Cf. anto.

27

andū- [ˌan'duː-] adj. (contains *NDŪ)
1. of the sunset. 2. west, western.
/ S. annú-/ I:290;III:437.

andūnë [ˌan'duːnɛ] n. 1. sunset. 2.
west. /·S. annūn/ I:394;III:394;R:
58f. See *NDŪ, númen.

Andūnië [ˌan'duːni̯ɛ] nm. place (andūnë
+ ië) 'Westering'. III:316,323n.

Andūril [ˌan'duːril̯] nm. obj. (andú +
sil) 'Flame of the West'. I:123,290;
III:437.

anga ['aŋga] n. 1. iron. / S. ᵗang/
2. the letter cꞯ. III:401.

Angamaitë ['aŋga'mai̯tɛ] nm. pers.
'Iron-handed' ??? III:328. Cf. má-,
morimaite, Telemaitë. α misspells as
'Angomaitë'.

anna ['anna] n. 1. gift. 2. the letter
cꞯ. III:401. Cf. S₁ ónen. (Finn. anti
'gift', annan 'I give'.)

Antani, see *Atan.

anto ['antɔ] n. 1. mouth. 2. the letter ᵬ. III:401·. Cf. ando. (Skt.
ánta 'edge, end, limit, interior', akin
to Eng. end; Gk. antron Lat. antrum
'cave, grotto, cavern'.)

ar [ar] conj. and. / S. a/ I:394;III:
245f;R:58f.

aranion, see asëa aranion.

Arantar [a'rantar] nm. pers. 'Royal-
one' ??? III:318. See S. aran.

Arciryas [ˌar'kiryas] nm. pers. ----.
III:330. Cf. cirya, S. ar(a)-.

arda ['arda] n. 1. region, realm. / S.
ᵗarth/ 2. the letter y. III:401;R:66.
Cf. S. ar(a)-. (Du. aarde, Ger. Erde
'earth'; OE geard 'yard, garden, pad-
dock'; OIr. āird 'direction'.)

áre ['aːrɛ] n. (earlier áze ['aːzɛ]) 1.
sunlight. 2. the older name of the
letter ᵹ, later called esse. III:401.
(Gk. arγos 'white, bright, shining';
Lat. aurora 'dawn'; Sem. ᵓWR 'light'.)

áre nuquerna ['aːrɛ nuk'werna] n. the
older name of the letter ᵹ, later
called esse nuquerna. III:401.

Artamir ['arta,mir] nm. pers. May contain *mír 'jewel'. III:329. Cf. S.
ar(a)-.

asëa aranion ['asɛˌa a'rani,ɔn] n.
(Valinorean origin) kingsfoil, a plant
with long sweet-smelling leaves. / S.
athelas/ I:210;III:141. Cf. S. aran.
(Lat. asarum 'hazelwort'.)

*asta ['asta] n. (pl. astar) month.
III:386. (Skt. ásta 'home': used of
astrological houses; Gk. astron, Lat.
astrum 'star'.)

at- [at-] adj. two, double. / S. ad-,
-ad/ See atendëa. Cf. -t, te.

*Atan ['atan] n. (pl. Atani ['ata,ni])
Man: Atani being the name given especially to the 'Fathers of Men', the
people of the Three Houses of the Elf-
friends who came into the west of Middle-earth in the First Age, to the
shores of the Great Sea, and aided the
Eldar against the Dark Power of the
North. / S. adan/ Plural form misspelt as 'Antani' in βγδIII:406. III:
314,406.

Atanamir [a'tana,mir] nm. pers. 'Jewel-
of-Men' ??? III:315. Used in error
for Atanatar in αIII:366;R:318.

Atanatar [a'tana,tar] nm. pers. 'King-
of-Men' ??? III:319.

Atani, see *Atan.

atendëa [a'tɛndɛˌa] n. (at + endëa)
'double-middle', leap year, in which
two enderi 'middle-days' were substituted for the loëndë (Midsummer Day),
hence the name. It occurred every
fourth year except the last of a century. αIII:386.

Aulë ['aɔ̃lɛ] nm. pers. (May be of Valinorean origin.) ----. γδ misspell it
once as 'Aluë'. III:415.

aurë ['aɔ̃rɛ] n. day(light). / S. ca-
lan/ αIII:385n. Cf. ré, úre, S. aur,
or-. (Lat. aurora 'dawn'; Sem. ᵓWR
'light'.)

avánier, see ván-.

áze, see áre.

C

cait- ['kai̯t-] v. stem to lie. —
caita ['kai̯ta] v. pres. s. lie(s).
I:394;R:58f.

cal(a)- ['kal(a)-] n. light. / S.
*cal(a)-, *calad/ I:394;III:430;R:
58f. (Lat. calor 'heat'.)

Calacirya [ˌkala'kirya] nm. place (gen.
Calaciryo [ˌkala'kiryɔ]) 'Light-
cleft'. Spelt 'Kalakirya' R:59. I:
394;R:58f,62.

*Calaciryan(de) ['kala,kir'yandɛ, ˌkala-
'kiryan] nm. place 'Light-cleft
land'. Anglicized as 'Calacirian'

I:248;R:62. *Text spelling is* Kalakir-
yan(de) R:62.

Calimehtar ['kali'meçtar] *nm. pers.*
'Light----'. III:319. *Cf.* Telumehtar.

Calimmacil [ka'limma'kił] *nm. pers.* (cal
+ in *or* calim + macil) 'Light----'.
III:330. *Cf.* ancalima.

calma ['kalma] *n.* 1. lamp. / S. *ca-
lar/ 2. the letter ɕf. III:399,401.

Calmacil ['kalma˛kił] *nm. pers.* (cal +
macil *or* calma + cil) 'Light----' *or*
'Lamp-man'. III"315,318.

calmatéma ['kalma'te:ma] *n.* 'k-series',
*containing the velar consonants and
consonant combinations, such as* c [k],
g, ch [x], gh, ng [ŋ], ng [ŋg], nc
[ŋk], *and* h. III:398.

*carne ['karnɛ] *adj.* (*pl.* ᵗcarni ['kar-
ni]) red. / S. caran, car-/ II:87.
(Gk. *kermes,* root of Eng. *carmine,
crimson.*)

Carnimírië ['karni'mi:ri˛ɛ] *nm. applied
to a rowan tree* (carni + mír + ië)
'Red-jewelled', *referring to red berries.* II:87.

Castamir ['kasta'mir] *nm. pers. May
contain* *mír 'jewel'. III:319.

Cemendur [kɛ'mɛndur] *nm. pers.* ----.
III:318. *See* -ndur, ᵗtur.

Cermië ['kermi˛ɛ] *n.* 'Cutting', *the seventh month* (July), *called Afterlithe in
the Shire.* / S. Cerveth/ III:388.

*certa ['kerta] *n.* (*pl.* certar) rune,
*that is, an angular letˌter sign primar-
ily intended for carving or scratching
into rock or wood.* / S. ᵗcerth/ III:
395. *Cf.* cirya, S. cair, cirith. (ME
caract 'mark' < Gk. *kharaktēr* 'mark,
sign' < Gk. *kharassein* 'to engrave';
Lat. *cerdo* 'craftsman'; Gael. *certh*
'mark, sign'.)

-cil [-kił] *n.* person, -er, -or ???
See -dacil, ᵗmacil, tarcil.

cirya ['cirya] *n.* (*gen.* ciryo ['ciryɔ])
1. cleft, ravine. / S. cirith/ 2.
ship. / S. cair/ I:394;III:430;R:58,
62; *names in the line of the 'Ship-
kings'* III:318. *Cf.* *certa. (Lat.
carina 'keel'.)

Ciryaher ['kirya˛her] *nm. pers.* 'Ship-
lord'. α *has* 'Ciryahir'. III:318.

Ciryandil [˛kir'yandił] *nm. pers.*
'Ship-friend' *or* 'Ship-lover'. III:
318.

Ciryatan ['kirya˛tan] *nm. pers.* 'Ship-
man' ??? III:315.

coirë ['kɔïrɛ] *n.* 1. stirring. 2. the
last of the six seasons in the Calendar
of Imladris, lasting 54 days. / S.
echuir/ III:386. *Cf.* S. cuio.

*colindo [kɔ'lindɔ] *n.* (*pl.* ᵗcolindor
[kɔ'lindɔr]) bearer. III:231.

cor- ['kɔr-] *n.* round, circle. / S.
ᵗcor/ III:385. (Hung. *kör* 'circle';
Lat. *corona* 'crown, circlet'.)

coranar ['kɔra˛nar] *n.* 'sun-round',
that is, a solar year. III:385.

corma ['kɔrma] *n.* ring. / S. ᵗcor/
III:231,390. (Lat. *corona* 'crown,
circlet'.)

*cormacolindo ['kɔrma˛kɔ'lindɔ] *n.* (*pl.*
cormacolindor ['kɔrma˛kɔ'lindɔ])
ring-bearer. III:231.

Cormarë ['kɔrma˛rɛ] *n.* (corma + rë)
'Ring-day', *an annual festival celeb-
rating the destruction of the One Ring.*
III:390.

D

-dacil [-da˛kił] *n.* (*Initial form' would
be either* *lacil *or* *nacil, *depending
on whether it derives from a PE form*
*dacil *or* *ndacil.) victor. / S.
ᵗdegil/ *See* Hyarmendacil, Rómendacil,
Umbardacil.

-dil, *see* -ndil.

-dómë, *see* lómë.

-dóre, -dor, *see* -ndóre, -ndor.

-dur, *see* -ndur.

E

ëar ['ɛar] *n.* sea. / S. aear/ R:65.
(OE *ēa* 'water, stream, river'.)

ᵗEären ['ɛa˛rɛn] *n.* (Great) Sea, Ocean.
/ S. aearon/ III:388. — Eärello
[˛ɛa'rɛłłɔ] *abl.* from the Great Sea.
III:245.

Eärendil [˛ɛa'rɛndił] *nm. pers.*
'Ocean-friend' *or* 'Ocean-lover', *the
name of the Morning Star (I:249) and
Evening Star (III:314), that is, the
planet Venus.* I:249,380. (OE *Earendel,* glossed as 'brightness', and
apparently the name of a very bright
star or constellation, usually identified as Venus or Orion.)

Eärendur [‚ɛa'rɛndur] nm. pers. 'Ocean-
---'. III:318. See -ndur, †tur.

Eärenya [‚ɛa'rɛnya] n. 'Great-Sea One',
the sixth day of the Númenorean week,
called Mersday in the Shire. / S. Or-
aearon/ III:388f.

Eärnil [ɛ'arnil̨] nm. pers. 'Sea-friend'
or 'Sea-lover' ??? III:318f.

Eärnur [ɛ'arnur] nm. pers. 'Sea----'.
III:245.

EL [ɛl̨] root 1. star. / S. el-/ 2.
(west-)elf. R:65. See Elda, elen,
elen-, Elessar, menel, S. êl. (Heb.
'ēl, a name of God, traditionally
translated 'God'; Akk. ilu(m) 'god',
written in cuneiform with a sign whose
primary meaning is 'star'.)

Elda ['el̨da] n. (el + da) (pl. Eldar)
'Star----', one of the People of the
Stars, a West-elf. Usually rendered
simply as Elf. / S. edhel/ III:405f,
415f;G:163,198.

Eldacar ['ɛl̨da‚kar] nm. pers. 'Elf----'
or 'Star----'. III:318. Cf. Valacar.

Eldamar ['ɛl̨da‚mar] nm. place 'Elf-
home', rendered 'Elvenhome'. I:318.

Eldar, see Elda.

Eldarion [‚ɛl̨'dari‚on] nm. pers. 'Elf-
---'. III:343f.

elen ['ɛlɛn] n. (pl. eleni ['ɛlɛ‚ni];
pl. gen. elenion [ɛ'lɛni‚on]) star.
/ S. êl, gil/ I:90;II:329;III:192,388;
R:65; Elendil III:421. (Corn. elven
'spark'.)

elen- [ɛ'lɛn-] n. (west-)elf. Elendil
III:421.

Elendil [ɛ'lɛndil̨] nm. pers. 'Star-
lover' or 'Elf-friend'. III:421.

Elendilmir ['ɛlɛn'dil̨mir] nm. obj.
'Elendil-jewel', glosses as 'the Star
of Elendil'. III:323.

Elendur [ɛ'lɛndur] nm. pers. 'Star----'
or 'Elf----'. III:318. See -ndur,
†tur.

eleni, see elen.

elenion, see elen.

Elenna [ɛ'lɛnna] nm. place 'Star----',
glossed as Land of the Star. III:315,
328.

Elentári ['ɛlɛn'ta:ri] nm. pers. 'Star-
queen'. / S. Elbereth/ I:394;III:394,
421;R:58f,66.

Elenya [ɛ'lɛnya] n. 'Star-one', the

first day of both the Eldarin and Númenorean weeks, called Sterday in the
Shire. / S. Orgilion/ III:388f.

Elessar [ɛ'lɛssar] nm. pers. (elen +
sar) 'Elfstone'. I:391;III:139,406.

Elwe ['ɛl̨we] nm. pers. (May be Valinor-
ian or archaic.) 'Star----' or 'Elf-
---' ??? Hd.

elyë ['ɛl̨yɛ] pers. prn. 2nd s. even
thou. / S le/ I:394;R:58f. Cf. -lyë,
†-nye, †-lme.

en- [ɛn-] adv. again, re-. enquantuva
I:394;R:58f; Envinyatar δɛIII:139.

end(e)- ['ɛnd(ɛ)-] adj. middle. III:
386,393; atendëa aIII:386. (Gk. endo
'within'.)

†tendëa ['ɛndɛ‚a] n. middle. See atendëa.

*enderë ['ɛndɛ‚rɛ] n. (ende + rē) (pl.
enderi ['ɛndɛ‚ri]) middle-day. In
the Calendar of Imladris three enderi
were inserted between the seasons yávië
and quellë and doubled every twelfth
year. In the Númenorean calendar two
enderi were substituted for the loëndë
(Midsummer's Day) every fourth year
except the last year of a century.
III:386.

Endóre [‚ɛn'do:rɛ] n. (end + n̨dóre)
Middle-earth. / S. Ennor/ III:393.
— Endorenna ['ɛndɔ'rɛnna] all. to
Middle-earth. III:245f.

enquantuva, see quant-.

enquië ['ɛŋkwi‚ɛ] n. (pl. enquier ['ɛŋ-
kwi‚er]) week. III:385.

envinyatar [‚ɛn'vinya‚tar] n. (en +
vinya + tar) renewer. δɛIII:139.

Eressëa [ɛ'rɛssɛ‚a] nm. place
'Lonely Isle'. R:62. Cf. Eru, S.
er(e)-.

Eru ['ɛru] n. 'the One', God. III:317;
R:66;GME:88. Cf. Eressëa, S. er(e)-.

Erusén ['ɛru‚se:n] n. pl. 'Children
of God', apparently referring to Men
and Elves. R:66.

esse ['ɛssɛ] n. 1. name. 2. the letter ʒ, earlier known as áre. III:401.
(Lat. esse 'to be'; Per. esm 'name'.)

esse nuquerna ['ɛssɛ nu'kwerna] n. the
letter ʒ, earlier known as áre nuquerna. III:401.

et [ɛt] either adv. 'out', or prep.
'out of' taking the abl. case. / S.
*e(t)-/ III:245f.

F

fal- ['fal-] *n.* foam ???, foaming wave ??? I:394;III:325;R:58f. *Cf.* falas-, *falma, S. †falas.

falas- [fa'las-] *n.* coast, strand. / S. †falas/ III:325.

Falastur [fa'lastur] *nm. pers.* 'Coast-lord', *rendered* 'Lord of the Coasts'. III:325.

*falma ['falma] *n.* foaming wave. — ***falmali** ['falma‚li] *pl. mult.* (many) foaming waves. — **falmalinnar** ['falma'linnar] *all. pl. mult.* on/ upon the (many) foaming waves. I:394; R:58f. (OE *fām* 'foam'; OIr. *fulumain* 'turning, rolling'.)

FANA ['fana] *root* veil. R:66. (Goth., OE *fana* 'bit of cloth, patch, banner.')

fana ['fana] *n.* (< FANA) (*pl.* fanar) the radiant form or body in which a Vala embodied and clothed itself to present itself 'to physical eyes. / S. fân, fan-/ R:66. (Gk. *phanos* 'bright', *phanein* 'to show', whence Eng. *phantom, fantasy,* etc.)

fanya ['fanya] *n.* (FANA + ya) (*pl.* fanyar) (white) cloud. / S. fân, fan-/ I:394;R:58f,66.

Faramir ['fara‚mir] *nm. pers.* '---- jewel'. III:329.

†farne ['farnɛ] *adj. ???* ----. II:87.

fëa- [fɛa-] *n.* spirit. *See* Fëanor.

Fëanor ['fɛa‚nɔr] *nm. pers. rendered* 'Spirit of Fire'. *Cf.* NÁR; *but the* o *in this form is puzzling.* III:394; CSK:127.

Finwe ['finwɛ] *nm. pers.* ----. Hd. *Cf.* S. fin-‚ -fin.

Fíriel [fi:ri‚ɛl] *nm. pers.* (fír + riel) 'Mortal-woman'. TB:8. *Cf.* S. firith.

for- ['fɔr-] *adj.* right-hand direction, right. III:401. *Cf.* S. for(o)-. (Dan. *ventre,* Sw. *vänster* 'left': *see* hyar-.)

formen ['fɔrmɛn] *n.* (for + men) 1. north, *that is the* 'right-hand region' *with reference to the sun's daily journey westward.* / S. forod/ 2. the letter **b.** III:401.

H

halla ['halla] *adj.* tall. / S. hal-/ — *n.* the letter **l.** III:401n.

haranyë [ha'ranyɛ] *n.* the last year of a century. III:386.

harma ['harma] *n.* 1. treasure. 2. the older name of the letter **d,** later called aha. III:401.

-her [-‚her] *n.* lord. / S. *hîr, †tur/ See* Ciryaher, Ondoher, Ostoher. α has '-hir'. (Ger. *Herr,* Finn. *herra* 'lord, gentleman, sir, Mister'.)

*hilde ['hiḻdɛ] *n.* (*pl.* †hildi ['hiḻdi]) heir. — Hildinyar [‚hiḻ'dinyar] *n. pl. + pers. prn. adj. s.* (hildi + nya + r) my Heirs. III:245f.

hir- ['hir-] *v. stem* to find. —hiruva ['hiru‚va] *v. fut. s.* will find. — hiruvalyë [‚hiru'valyɛ] *v. fut. 2nd s.* thou wilt find. I:394;R:58f.

-hir, *see* -her.

hísië ['hi:si‚ɛ] *n.* mist. / S. †hith/ I:394;R:58f.

Hísimë ['hi:si‚mɛ] *n.* 'Misty', the eleventh month (November), called *Blotmath* in the Shire. / S. Hithui/ III:386.

hrívë ['ʒi:vɛ] *n.* 1. winter. 2. the fifth of the six seasons in the Calendar of Imladris, lasting 72 days. / S. rhîw/ III:386,389. (Gk. *rhígos* 'cold, frost'; Fr. *hiver* 'winter'.)

hwesta ['ʍɛsta] *n.* 1. breeze. 2. the letter **d.** III:401.

hwesta sindarinwa ['ʍɛsta ‚sinda'rinwa] *n.* the letter **d,** Grey-elven hw. III: 401.

hyar- ['çar-] *adj.* left-hand direction, left. III:401. *Cf.* S. har(a)-. (Dan. *højre,* Sw. *höger* 'right': *see* for-.)

hyarmen ['çarmɛn] *n.* 1. south, *that is, the* 'left-hand region' *with reference to the sun's daily journey westward.* / S. harad/ 2. the letter **λ.** III: 401.

Hyarmendacil [‚çar'mɛnda‚kiḻ] *nm. pers.* 'South-victor'. III:325.

I

i [i] art. the. / S. e(n), i-/ I:394; R:58f. (Wel. yr, y 'the'.)

-ië [-i,ɛ] n. suff. (pl. -ier [-i,er]) 'thing' of..., belonging to..., connected with.... See Andúnië, Carnímirië, Cermië, enquië, hísië, mornië, nainië, namárië, Nárië, ᵗnórië, quellië, Yavannië, yávië.

Ilmarin ['ilma,rin] nm. place ----. I: 247f,389.

*ilya ['ilya] adj. (pl. ilyë ['ilyɛ]) each ???, all of ???; pl. all. I:394; R:58f.

imbë ['imbɛ] prep. between. I:394;R: 58f. (OE ymbe 'around, about'.)

-imë [-i,mɛ] adj. suff. both s. & pl. -able, -y, etc. / S. -ui/ See Hísimë, Nénimë, ᵗnótimë, Súlimë, únótimë, Úrimë. (May be, in origin, a form of -me used after long syllables terminating in a consonant.)

-in [-in] adj. suff. -ious, -en, etc. / S. -en/ See alcarin, ᵗmalin.

Isil ['isil] n. Moon. / S. Ithil/ III:392.

Isildur [i'sildur] nm. pers. 'Moon----'. III:318. Cf. -ndur, ᵗtur.

Isilya [i'silya] n. 'Moon-one', the third day of both the Eldarin and Númenorean weeks, called Monday in the Shire. / S. Orithil/ III:388f.

*Istar ['istar] n. (pl. Istari ['ista,ri]) Wizard. III:365f.

K

Kalakirya, see Calacirya.

Kalakiryan(de), see *Calaciryan(de).

L

lairë ['laɪrɛ] n. 1. summer. 2. the second of the six seasons in the Calendar of Imladris, lasting 72 days. / S. laer/ III:385f,389.

lait- ['laɪt-] v. stem to praise. — **laita** ['laɪta] v. imper. praise! — **laituvalmet** ['laɪtu'valmɛt] v. fut. 1st pl. + pers. prn. 3rd??? du. acc. (lait + uva + lme + t) we will praise

(them???) both. III:231. (Lat. laetus 'joyful, glad'.)

lambe ['lambɛ] n. 1. tongue. / S. *lam(m)???, naith/ 2. the letter ϲ·. III:401. (Lat. lambere 'to lick'.)

lant- ['lant-] v. stem to fall. — lantar ['lantar] v. pres. pl. fall (pl.). I:394;R:58f.

lanta ['lanta] n. fall. III:386.

lasse ['lassɛ] n. (pl. lassi ['lassi]) leaf. / S. las(s)/ I:394;III:386;R: 58f. (Goth. laufs, Russ. list 'leaf'.)

lasse-lanta ['lassɛ'lanta] n. 'leaf-fall', the fourth of the six seasons in the Calendar of Imladris, lasting 54 days. Also called quellë. / S. narbeleth/ III:386.

lasselanta ['lassɛ'lanta] n. 'leaf-fall', the latter part of autumn and the beginning of winter. Also called quellë. III:389.

Lassemista ['lassɛ'mista] nm. applied to a rowan tree 'Grey-leaved'??? II:87.

lassi, see lasse.

laure ['laɒrɛ] n. (Resolves to ᵗlore [lɔ'rɛ] when the diphthong au is unstressed in a compound.) golden colour. II:70;R:62; See laurëa, lindelorendor.

laurëa ['laɒrɛ,a] adj. (pl. laurië ['laɒri,ɛ]) golden (coloured), like gold. / S. glor-, -lor/ I:394;R:58f, 62.

Laurelin ['laɒrɛ,lin] nm. tree 'Golden-song' or 'Singing-gold' ??? III:314n.

Laurelindórenan ['laɒrɛ,lin'do:rɛ,nan] nm. place (laure + lindë + ndóre + nan) 'Golden-singing-land-valley', rendered 'Land of the Valley of Singing Gold'. II:70.

laurië, see laurëa.

ᵗláv- ['laɪv-] v. stem to lick. — undulávë ['undu'laːvɛ] v. past s. (undu + láv + e) licked down (s.). I:394; R:58f. (Lat. lavāre 'to wash', whence Eng. lave and lava.)

-le [-lɛ] adj. great. / S. -on/ See lumbulë, ᵗtumbale, li-, -li.

leuca ['lɛɒka] n. snake. / S. lyg/ III:393. (Eng. lug, a large marine worm found in sea sand.)

li-, -li [li] adv. & indicator of pl.

mult. many. *See* falmalinnar, ornélion, Taureli**lómëa**, van**īmál**ion, -le.

†**lin(de)** ['lin(dɛ)] *n??? adj???* song,
singing. / S. lin(n)-/ *See* Laurelin-
dorenan, lindelorendor. *Cf.* líri.

lindelorendor ['lindɛlɔ'rɛndɔr] *n.*
(linde + laure + ndor) singing-golden-
.land. II:70.

*****linta** ['linta] *adj.* (*pl.* linte ['lintɛ])
swift. / S. bre-/ I:394;R:58f.

*****líri** ['liːri] *n.* song. — **lírinen**
['liːri,nɛn] *instr.* in/by (the) song.
I:394;R:58f. *Cf.* †lin(de). (Eng.
lyric, lyre.)

lisse ['lissɛ] *adj.* sweet. I:394;R:
58f.

*****lisse-miruvóre** ['lissɛ,miru'voːrɛ] *n.*
sweet mead, sweet nectar. — **lisse-
miruvóreva** ['lissɛ,miru'voːrɛ,va]
compos. (composed) of sweet mead/
nectar. I:394;R:58f,61.

-llo [-llɔ] *abl.* indicator from, of.
/ S. o/ *See* Eärello, Rómello, sindanóriello.

*****-lma** [-lma] *pers. prn. adj. 1st pl.*
exclusive (-lmo [-lmɔ] *when terminating
a gen. compound.*) our (of me and him/
her/it/them). -lmo *is used in error
for* -lvo *in* αI:90 *and in all but the
earliest printings of the corresponding
passage in* β. *See letter by R. Plotz,
p. 20. Cf.* †-lme, *-lva, met, †-nya,
-rya.

†**-lme** [-lmɛ] *pers. prn. 1st pl.* exclusive
we (I and he/she/it/they). See laituvalmet. *Cf.* *-lma, *-lva, -lyë, -n,
-nye.

LO [lɔ] root growing, springing up.
See loa, loëndë, S. *Gwathló, Ringló.

loa ['lɔa] *n.* 1. growth. 2. year
(*conceived as a cycle of growth*). III:
285.

loëndë [lɔ'ɛndɛ] *n.* (lo**á** + endë) 'year-
middle', the middle (183rd) day of the
year in the Númenorean calendar.
Called *Mid-year's Day* in the Shire.
III:386f,390.

lómë ['loːmɛ] *n.* (< PE *dōmē; in compounds following n (and presumably r
and l) the form -dómë* [-'doːmɛ] *is
used with the original initial d preserved.*) 1. shadow, gloom. / S. *dū/
2. night. / S. fuin/ II:72;αIII:385n.
Cf. lumbulë, tindómë, undómë.

†**lómëa** ['loːmɛ,a] *adj.* shadowed, gloomy.

/ S. du-/ II:70;III:409.

Lómëanor [,lo:'mɛa,nor] *nm. place*
'Gloomyland'. II:70;III:409.

†**lore-,** *see* laure.

*****Lóriende** ['loːri'ɛndɛ] *nm. place*
'Dreaming-land' ??? / S. Lórien(n)/
— **Lóriendesse** ['loːri,ɛn'dɛssɛ] *loc.*
in Lórien (Dreaming-land???). II:72;
R:58f.

losse ['lɔssɛ] *n.* (*gen.* lossëo ['lɔssɛ,ɔ]) (fallen) snow. / S. loss/
— *adj.* snow-white. / S. glos(s),
-los(s)/ I:394;R:59,61.

*****lóte** ['loːtɛ] *n.* flower, blossom.
/ S. loth-, -loth/ *See* Lótessë. (Gk.
lōtos 'lotus'.)

Lótessë [,lo:'tɛssɛ] *n.* (< *loc.* of
lóte ???) 'In-flower', the fifth
month (May), called *Thrimidge* in the
Shire. / S. Lothron/ III:388.

*****luinë** ['luĩnɛ] *adj.* (*pl.* luini ['luĩni])
blue. / S. luin/ R:394;R:58f.

lumbulë ['lumbu,lɛ] *n.* (heavy) shadow,
darkness. / S. *dū/ I:394;R:58f.
Cf. lómë, tumbale.

*****lúmë** ['luːmɛ] *n.* hour. — *lúmenna
[,lu:'mɛnna] *all.* (lúmenn' [,lu:'mɛnn]
*when closely connected to a following
word beginning with a vowel.*) on the
hour. I:90.

lúva ['luːva] *n.* bow. III:398.

*****-lva** [-lva] *pers. prn. adj. 1st pl.*
inclusive (-lvo [-lvɔ] *when terminating a gen. compound.*) our (of me and
you). -lmo *is used in error for* -lvo
in αI:90 *and in all but the earliest
printings of the corresponding passage
in* β. *See letter by R. Plotz, p. 20.
Cf.* *-lma, †-lme, met, †-nya, -rya.

-lyë [-lyɛ] *pers. prn. 2nd s.* thou. I:
394;R:58f. *Cf.* elyë, †-lme, -n, †-nye,
S. le.

M

má- ['maː-] *n.* hand. — **máryat** ['maː-
ryat] *n. stem + pers. prn. adj. 3rd
fem. s. + du. suff.* (má + rya + t) her
two hands. I:394;R:58f.

-ma [-ma] *n & adj. suff.* (*pl.* -mar)
(*Takes the form* -wa [-wa] (*pl.* -war)
*aften n, c, and q (cwa being transcribe
as qua).*) *Found chiefly on nouns
representing made objects and objects
easily seen as being discrete and*

individual. See nouns: calma, corma, *falma, harma, †óma, parma, *ráma, †tarma, *telluma, téma, *tengwa, yulma; *adjectives:* sindarinwa, vanwa. *Forms ending in* -ima: ancallima, sillima, *vanima. In some cases the* m *or* w *may belong to the stem. Cf.* -me.

†macar ['makar] *n.* swordsman. / S. *magor/ I:91;III:391. (Lat. *machaera,* ON mækir 'sword'.)

†macil ['makil] *n.* ----. / S. *megil/ See Calimmacil, Narmacil.

Maia ['maïa] *n.* (*Possibly not Quenya.*) One of a race also called 'the people of the Valar', apparently a sort of lesser Valar. *'...Melian the Maia who filled the silence of Arda before the dawn with her voice.'* CSK:129. *Cf.* III:314. (Gk. *Maia* 'Grandmother', a minor goddess, mother of Hermes; Lat. *Māia,* goddess of the month of May.)

-maitë [-'maïtɛ] *adj???* -handed ??? *See* Angamaitë, morimaitë, Telemmaitë, má-.

†malin ['malin] *adj.* golden. / S. ¬al-, †mallen/· II:70. *Cf.* malta. (Wel *mál* 'gold', *melyn* 'yellow'.)

*malinorne ['mali'norne] *n.* (malin + orne) (*pl. mult. gen.* malinornélion ['mali,nor'ne:li,on]) 'golden-tree', *a kind of tree found only in Laurelin-dórenan, characterized by smooth, silver-grey bark, yellow blossoms, and leaves which turned gold in autumn, but did not fall until spring. Also called* ornemalin. / S. *mallorn/ I:394;II:70.

malinornélion, 'of many golden trees'. *See* *malinorne.

malta ['malta] *n.* 1. gold. 2. the letter ᴍ. III:401. (Wel. *mál* 'gold'.)

man [man] *inter. prn.* who? I:394;R: 58f.

Manwe ['manwɛ] *nm. pers.* ----. R:60f, 66. *Cf.* Aman. (Wel. *Manawydan,* sea god who gave his name to the Isle of Man.)

mar- [mar-] *v. stem* (< *MBAR) to abide. — maruvan ['maru,van] *v. fut. 1st s.* (mar + uva + n) I will abide. III: 245.

-mar [-mar] *n.* (< *MBAR) home, dwelling. / S. bar(a)-, -bar, -mar/ *See* Eldamar, Valimar. (Finn. *maa* 'land'.)

*marde ['mardɛ] *n.* (mbar + de) (*pl.* †mardi ['mardi]) hall. / S. -rond/ I:394;R:58f. *Cf.* S. barad.

Mardil ['mardil] *nm. pers.* (mbar + ídil) 'Home-friend' *or* 'Home-lover'. I:319.

maruvan, *see* mar-.

máryat, *see* má-.

*MBAR [mbar] *root* dwelling. *See* ambar, mar-, -mar, *marde, S. `bar(a)-, -bar, barad, -mar.

-me [-mɛ] *n & adj. suff.* (*Takes the form* -we [-wɛ] *after* n, c, *and* g *(cwe being transcribed as* que*).) Found chiefly on nouns representing abstractions and characteristics of objects and people. See nouns:* Finwe, lómë, Manwe, nwalme, Oromë, silme, tindómë, tinwe, undómë, ungwe, unque; *adjectives:* voronwë. *Also cf.* -imë. *In some cases the* m. *or* w/u *may belong to the noun stem. Cf.* -ma.

*Melcor ['mɛlkɔr] *nm. pers.* (*May be Valinorean*) ----. *Text spelling is* 'Melkor'. CSK:136. (Phoen. *Melqart* 'King (of the) City', the god of Tyre.)

†melda ['mɛlda] *n.* friend ??? / S. mellon ???/ α *reads* '-malda'. I:367.

Melian ['mɛlian] *nm. pers.* (*May be Valinorean or Sindarin*) ----. III: 314.

Melkor, *see* *Melcor.

†men [mɛn] *n.* region, direction. / S. men-/ R:64.

menel ['mɛnɛl] *n.* (men + el) 'region-starry', (high) heaven, heaven on high, firmament, the region of the stars. the sky. / S. menel/ R:64; G:190.

Meneldil [mɛ'nɛldil] *nm. pers.* 'Heaven-friend' *or* 'Heaven-lover'. III:318.

Meneldur [mɛ'nɛldur] *nm. pers.*· 'Heaven---'. III:315. *See* -ndur, †tur.

Menelmacar ['mɛnɛl'macar] *nm. pers.* 'Heaven-swordsman', *rendered* 'Şwordsman of the Sky'. *Refers to the constellation Orion. Also called* Telumehtar. / S. Menelvagor/ I:91;III: 391.

Meneltarma ['mɛnɛl'tarma] *nm. place* 'Heaven-hill' ??? III:315.

Menelya [mɛ'nɛlya] *n.* 'Heaven-one', *the fifth day of both the Eldarin and Númenorean weeks, called Hevensday or Hensday in the Shire.* / S. Ormenel/ III:388f.

met [mɛt] *pers. prn. 1st du. exclusive*

acc. (me + t ???) us two (myself & him/her/it). I:394;R:58f. *Cf.* *-lma, †-lme, -t, te.

metta ['mɛtta] n. ending. III:245. *Cf.* S. *medui, †methed.

mettarë ['mɛtta,rɛ] n. (metta + rë) 'ending-day', the final day of the year in the Númenorean calendar, corresponding to 1 Yule in the Shire. III:386f.

mí [miː] prep. in the. *Misspelt 'mi'* I:394. *Misspelt* ꝏ (= mé) in tengwar R:57. R:58f.

Minalcar [mi'nalkar] nm. pers. ----. III:318. *Cf.* alcar, Valacar, †macar, S. min-¹, min-².

Minardil [mi'nardil] nm. pers. '---- friend' or '----lover'. III:319. *Cf.* S. min-¹, min-².

Minastan [mi'nastan] nm. pers. ----. III:319. *Cf.* *Atan, S. -dan, minas.

Minastir [mi'nastir] nm. pers. 'Tower-watch(ing)' ??? III:315. *See* TIR, S. minas.

Minyatur ['minya,tur] nm. pers. (min+ya + tur) 'First-lord' ???. *This was the royal name taken by Elros, the FIRST KING of Númenor.* III:315. *See* †tur, S. min-¹.

*míre, -mir ['miːrɛ, -mir] n. (pl. míri ['miːri]) 1. jewel. 2. (metaphorically) star. / S mîr/ I:394;R:58f; *Elendilmir* III:394. (Lat. *mīrus* 'wonderful', whence the star name *Mira*.)

Míriel ['miːri,ɛl] nm. pers. (míré + riel) 'Jewel-woman'. III:315.

miruvóre ['miru'voːrɛ] n. (< *Valinorean*) the drink of the Valar, believed to be made from the honey of the undying flowers in the garden of Yavanna, thus a kind of mead, but clear and transparent. *Corresponds to the* νέκταρ *(nectar) of Classical Mythology.* / S. miruvor/ — miruvóreva ['miru'voːrɛ,va] compos. (composed) of the divine mead. R:61.

†mista ['mista] n??? adj??? grey ??? II:87.

morimaite ['mori'maitɛ] adj. (mori + maite) black-handed ??? III:257. *Cf.* morna, mornië, Angamaitë, Telemmaitë, S. mor-. *morn.

morimaite-sincahonda, *see* morimaite and sincahonda.

†morna ['morna] adj. black. / S. *morn, mor-/ II:72;III:409. (Gk. *mauros*

'black', whence Eng. *Moor*.)

mornië ['morni,ɛ] n. darkness. I:394; R:58f. *Cf.* †morna.

N

-n [-n] pers. prn. 1st s. I. / S. -n, im/ *See* maruvan, utulien. *Cf.* †-nye, and *-nya, nin, S. anim.

*na- ['na-] v. stem to be. — ná [naː] v. pres. s. (na + a) is, are (s.). — nai [nai] v. precative s. (ná + i) be it that, may it be that, maybe. I: 394;R:58ff.

nainië ['naini,ɛ] n. lament. R:65. (Lat. *nēnia* 'dirge'.)

namárië [na'maːri'ɛ] interj. farewell. I:394;R:58f.

†nan [nan] n. valley. / S. nan/ *See* Laurelindorénan. (Gallic *nanto*, Wel. nant 'valley'.)

NÁR [naːr] root having to do with fire, red flame, and the sun. / S. nar-, naur, nór-/ *See* Anar, Anardil, Anárion, Anarya, Nárië, Narmacil, Narquelië, Narsil, Narinye, Narya. (Ar. & Per. nar 'fire'.)

Nárië ['naːri,ɛ] n. 'Sunny', the sixth month (June), called *Forelithe* in the Shire. / S. Nórui/ III:388.

Narmacil ['narma,kil] nm. pers. 'Fire/Sun----'. III:318.

Narquelië [,nar'kwɛli,ɛ] n. 'Sun-waning', the tenth month (October), called *Winterfilth* in the Shire. / S. Narbeleth/ III:388,390; *Narbeleth* III: 386.

Narsil ['narsil] nm. obj. 'red flame - white flame', rendered 'Red and White Flame'. III:438.

Narvinyë [,nar'vinyɛ] n. 'New-sun', the first month (January), called *Afteryule* in the Shire. / S. Narwain/ III:388.

Narya ['narya] nm. obj. 'Sun-one'. III:310.

-nde [-ndɛ] n. land, region. / S. -n(n)/ *See* *Calaciryan(de).

-ndil [-ndil] n. (Resolves to -dil [-dil] or (once) -nil [-nil] following r, l, and n.) -friend, -lover. *See* Amandil, Anardil, Ciryandil, Eärendil, Eärnil, Elendil, Mardil, Meneldil, Minardil,

Ornendil, Siriondil, Valandil.

-ndóre, -ndor [-n'do:rɛ, -ndɔr] n. (*Resolves to* -dóre, -dor [-'do:rɛ, -dɔr] *or* -nóre, -nor [-'no:rɛ, -nɔr] *following* r, l, *and* n.) land, country, earth. / S. dor, -nor/ *See* Endóre, Laurelindórenan, lindelorendor, Númenóre, Númenor, Valinóre, Valinor.

***NDÚ** [ndu:] *root* down, descend. *See* andú-, andúnë, nu, númen, nuquerna, undómë, und(u)-, untúpa, S. annú-, annún, dún.

-ndur [-ndur] n. (*Resolves to* -dur [-dur] *or* (*once*) -nur [-nur] *following* r, l, *and* n.) *Perhaps related to* †tur 'lord'. *See* Cemendur, Eärendur, Eärnur, Elendur, Isildur, Meneldur, Pelendur, Valandur.

NÉN [ne:n] *root* water. *See* Nénimë, Nenya, S. nen, Bruinen, Carnen, Nínui.

-nen [-nɛn] *instr.* indicator by means of, in. *See* lírinen, súrinen.

Nénimë ['ne:ni,mɛ] n. 'Wet, Watery', the second month (February), called Solmath in the Shire. / S. Nínui/ III:338.

Nenya ['nɛnya] nm. obj. 'Water-one'. III:308.

ngoldo, *see* Noldo.

ngwalme, *see* nwalme.

-nil, *see* -ndil.

nin [nin] pers. prn. 1st s. dat. me-for, for me. / S. anim/ I:394,R:58f. *Cf.* -n, *-nya, †-nye, S. nin.

-nna [-nna] all. indicator (pl. -nnar) (-nn' [-nn] *when closely connected with a following word beginning with a vowel.*) to, upon, on. / S. na/ *See* Endorenna, falmalinnar, lumenn', tenn'. (Finn. -n 'into', -na, -nä 'at'.)

Noldo ['nɔldɔ] n. (*earlier* *Ngoldo, ngoldo* ['ŋɔldɔ]) (pl. Noldor ['nɔldɔr]) a member of the Noldor, one of the kindreds of the Eldar, perhaps the same as that called 'Deep-elves'. — noldo the letter ca. ¨H:178;I:89;III:392,395, 401; High Elves III:424. αßIII:401 reads 'ŋoldo' instead of 'ngoldo'.

-nóre, -nor, *see* -ndóre, -ndor.

***nórië** ['no:ri,ɛ] n. (ndóré + 1ë) country. / S. dor, -nor/ — †nórielló ['no:ri'ɛɬlɔ] abl. out of a country. I:394;R:58f.

nostari ['nɔsta,ri] ??? ----. III:259.

Cf. -tar.

†nót- [no:t-] having to do with counting, numbering. *See* †nótimë, únótimë. (Eng. note.)

†nótimë ['no:ti,mɛ] adj. s & pl. countable. I:394;R:58f.

nu [nu] prep. (< *NDÚ) under, beneath. / S. *di(n)/ I:394;R:58f.

númen ['nu:mɛn] n. (ndú + men) 1. west, that is, the 'region of descending' with reference to the sun's daily journey. 2. the letter m. III:401. *Cf.* andú-, andúne.

Númenóre, Númenor ['nu:mɛ'no:rɛ, 'nu:mɛ-,nɔr] nm. place (númen + ndóre or ndor) 'West-land', rendered 'Westernesse'. III:315,317,406;G:195.

nuquerna [nuk'werna] adj. (ndú + querna) reversed. III:401.

-nur, *see* -ndur.

nwalme ['nwalmɛ] n. (earlier ngwalme ['ŋwalmɛ]) 1. torment. 2. the letter ca. III:401. ß misspells ngwalme as 'ywalme'.

***-nya** [-nya] pers. prn. adj. 1st s. (-nyar *when terminating a pl. form*) my. Hildinyar III:245. *Cf.* -n, †-ɾ.ye, nin, *-lma, *-lva, †-rya.

†-nye [-nyɛ] pers. prn. 1st. s. I. / S. -n, im/ utúvienyes III:250. *Cf.* -n, and nin, *-nya, †-lme, -lyë.

O

-o [-ɔ] gen. indicator (-on [-ɔn] *when terminating a pl. form*) of, from. aldaron, Calaciryo, Oiolosseo, omáryo, Vardo I:394;R:58f; omentielvo I:90; Silmarillion III:314; Altariello R:58; tärio R:59. *Cf.* S. o. (Wel. o 'from, of'.)

Ohtar ['ɔxtar] nm. pers. ----. I:257.

oi(o)- ['ɔï(ɔ)-] adv. ever, everlastingly. / S. ui-/ R:61. (Gk. aei, ON ei, Eng. aye 'ever'.)

oialë ['ɔïɔ,lɛ] adv. ever, everlastingly, for ever. I:394;R:58f.

Oiolosse ['ɔïɔ'lɔssɛ] nm. place (gen. Oiolosseo ['ɔïɔ'lɔssɛ,ɔ]) 'Ever-snow-white', rendered 'Everwhite'. / S. Uilos(s)/ I:394;R:58f,61f.

Olórin [ɔ'lo:rin] nm. pers. (< Valinorean ???) ----. II:279.

†óma ['o:ma] n. voice. — ómaryo
[,o:'maryɔ] n. + pers. prn. adj. 3rd
fem. s. + gen. indicator (óma + ryá +
o) of her voice. I:394;R:58f.

†omentie [ɔ'mɛnti,ɛ] n. meeting. —
omentielvo ['ɔmɛn,ti'ɛlvɔ] n. + pers.
prn. adj. 1st pl. inclusive + gen.
indicator (omentie + lvá + o) of our
(your & my) meeting. — omentielmo
['ɔmɛn,ti'ɛlmɔ] n. + pers. prn. adj.
1st pl. exclusive + gen. indicator
(omentie + lmá + o) of our (my & his/
her/its/their) meeting. The exclusive
form omentielmo was wrongly used in α.
The correct inclusive form omentielvo
was used in the earliest printings of
β and in γδε, but in later and current
printings of β the form has been
mis-corrected again to 'omentilmo'. I:
90; letter by R. Plotz MP 10:1, 3. Cf.
S. govannen.

†ondo ['ɔndɔ] n. stone ??? / S. †gond,
gond(o)- ???/ III:319.

Ondoher ['ɔndɔ,her] nm. pers. 'Stone-
lord' ??? α has 'Ondohir'. III:319.

or(o)- ['ɔr(ɔ)-] adj./adv. (< RÓ) high,
lofty. I:394;R:58f. Cf. TÁR.

óre, -or ['o:rɛ, -ɔr] n. 1. heart
(inner mind), spirit. / S. †úr/ 2.
the letter ɒ. III:401.

†orne ['ɔrnɛ] n. (pl. mult. gen. †orné-
lion [,ɔr'ne:li,ɔn]) tree. / S.
†horn, -orn, †galad, galadh/ II:70.

ornemalin [,ɔr'nɛma,lin] n. 'golden-
tree', a kind of tree found only in
Laurlindórenan, characterized by
smooth, silver-grey bark, yellow blossoms, and leaves which turned gold in
autumn, but did not fall until spring.
Also called *malinorne. / S. mallorn/
I:349;II:70.

Ornendil [,ɔr'nɛndil] nm. pers. 'Tree-
friend' or 'Tree-lover'. III:327.

oro-, see or(o)-.

Orofarne ['ɔrɔ'farnɛ] nm. applied to a
rowan tree 'High----'. II:87.

*oromarde ['ɔrɔ'mardɛ] n. (pl. oromardi
['ɔrɔ'mardi]) high-hall, lofty hall.
I:394;R:58f.

Oromë ['ɔrɔ,mɛ] nm. pers. ----. / S.
Araw/ III:113,319n,346,394.

ortan- ['ɔrtan-] v. stem to lift up,
uplift. — ortane ['ɔrta,nɛ] v. past
s. lifted up, uplifted (s.). I:394;R:
58f. Cf. or(o)-, †tánique.

†osto ['ɔstɔ] n. fortress, citadel ???
/ S. †ost, os(t)- ???/ III:318.

Ostoher ['ɔstɔ,her] nm. pers. 'Fortress-lord' ??? α has 'Ostohir'. III:
318.

P

palan- [palan-] adj./adv. abroad, far
and wide, afar. R:64f. (Wel. pell
'far'.)

palantir [pa'lantir] adj. farsighted.
III:315.

palantír [pa'lanti:r] n. (pl. palantíri
['palan'ti:ri]) 'far-seer', 'that which
looks afar', one of a number of seeing
stones, globes of dark crystal made by
the Noldor, by means of which the
users could view events far off in time
and space and converse in thought with
one another. II:202f;III:439.

parma [parma] n. 1. book. 2. the letter ᵽ. III:401.

parmatéma ['parma'te:ma] n. 'p-series',
containing the labial consonants and
consonant combinations, such as p, b,
f, v, m, mb, mp, w, and hw. III:398.

*pele ['pɛlɛ] n. fence ??? / S. pel-
???/ See Pelendur. (OFr. pel, Eng.
pale 'stake, fence, border', < Lat.
pālus 'stake'.)

Pelendur [pɛ'lɛndur] nm. pers. 'Fence-
----'. III:319. See -ndur, †tur.

pella ['pɛlla] post. beyond (the borders of). I:394;R:58f. Cf. *pele.

Pelóri [pɛ'lo:ri] nm. place 'Fence-
mountains' ???, glossed as the Mountain
Wall. I:248;R:58f,61. See *pele,
or(o)-, S. orod.

Q

quant- ['kwant-] v. stem to fill. —
enquantuva [,ɛŋ'kwantu,va] v. fut. s.
(en + quant + uva) will refill (s.).
I:394:R:58f. (Lat. quantum 'how
much?', whence Eng. quantity.)

†quelië ['kwɛli,ɛ] n. waning. / S.
*peleth/ III:368. Cf. quellë.

quellë ['kwɛllɛ] n. 1. 'fading', the
latter part of autuman and the beginning of winter. Also called
lasselanta. 2. 'fading', the fourth of
the six seasons in the Calendar of
Imladris, lasting 54 days. Also called
lasse-lanta. III:385f,389. Cf. †quellë

*Quende ['kwɛndɛ] n. (pl. Quendi ['kwɛn-di]) 'Speaker', that is, an Elf. III: 415. Cf. Quenya, S. pedo.

Quenya ['kwɛnya] n. 'Speech', one of the tongues of Eldamar, the oldest written language, the birth-tongue of the exiled Noldor, and used by them still for ceremony and poetry when they returned to Middle-earth. III:405f. Cf. *Quende, S. pedo.

†querna ['kwerna] adj. turned ??? III: 401.

quesse ['kwɛssɛ] n. 1. feather. 2. the letter ꞯ. III:401.

quessetéma ['kwɛssɛ'teːma] n. 'kw-series', containing labio-velar consonants and velar-labial combinations, such as qu [kw], gw, chw [xw], ghw, hw, w, ngw [ŋw], ngw [ŋgw], and nqu [ŋkw]. III:398.

R

*ráma ['raːma] n. (pl. rámar) wing. I: 394;R:58f. (Lat. rāmus 'branch'.)

ré, -rë [reː, -rɛ] n. (pl. *rí, -rí [riː, -ri]) day, reckoned from sunset to sunset. / S. aur/ III:385; See Cormarë, enderi, Ringarë.

rembe ['rɛmbɛ] n. mesh. / S. rem(m)/ Misspelt 'rembre' in γб. III:393.

*rí, -ri, see ré, -rë.

-riel [-ri,ɛl] n. woman. / S. -riel/ See *Altáriel, Fíriel, Míriel.

-riën [-ri,ɛn] ??? May be the feminine of -rion. See Silmariën, Telperiën.

-ril, -rilli, -rillion, see †sil.

†ringa ['riŋga] adj. cold. / S. †ring/ See Ringarë, S. Ethring, Ringló.

Ringu̯ë ['riŋga,rɛ] n. 'Cold-time', the twelfth month (December), called Fore-yule in the Shire. / S. Girithron/ III:388.

-rion [-ri,ɔn] ??? ----. See Aldarion, Anárion, Eldarion, Súrion, Telperion, Vinyarion. In some of the above the r probably belongs to the stem, or is a pl. indicator, and an ending -ion or a pl..gen. construction is involved.

*RÓ [roː] root up, rise. See or(o)-rómen, S. rhu-, rhûn, amrûn, ro-, Rodyn. (Skt. ruh 'ascend'.)

rómen ['roːmɛn] n. (ró + men) 1. east, that is, the 'region of rising' with

reference to the sun's daily journey. / S. rhûn, amrûn/ 2. the letter ɣ. III:401. — Rómello [,roː'mɛllɔ] abl. (one) from the East. R:59.

Rómendacil [,roː'mɛnda,kil] nm. pers. 'East-victor'. III:324.

Rúmil ['ruːmil] nm. pers. ----. III: 395. Cf. S. Rúmil.

-rya [-rya] pers. prn. adj. 3rd fem. s. (-ryo [-ryɔ] when terminating a gen. compound.) her. máryat, ómaryo I: 394;R:58f. Cf. *-lma, *-lva, †-nya.

S

-s [-s] pers. prn. 3rd neut. s. acc. it (acc.). utúvienyes III:250.

Sangahyando ['saŋga'çandɔ] nm. pers. ----. α reads 'Sangahyanda'. III: 328.

†sar [sar] n. stone. / S. sarn/ Elessar I:391;III:139,406.

†sén [seːn] n. pl. children. Erusén R: 66.

sí [siː] adv. now. I:394;R:58-60. Cf. S. sí.

†sil [sil] n. (pl. *silli ['silli], pl. gen. *sillion ['silli,ɔn]) white flame. (When following a vowel as part of a compound it takes the forms -ril, pl. -rilli, pl. gen. -rillion.) -ril/ Andúril I:290;III:437; Narsil III:438; silmaril, Silmarilli, Silmarillion III:313f. Cf. síl-, Sillma, silme. (Gk. selas 'flash, blaze, torch'; Gael. reul 'star'.)

síl- [siːl-] v. stem to shine. — síla ['siːla] v. pres. s. shine(s). I:90. Cf. †sil, Silima, silme.

Silima ['sili,ma] n. a crystal substance that Fëanor devised and alone could make. R:65. Cf. †sil, síl-, silme, Silmariën, silmaril, S. silliv-ren.

Silmariën [,sil'mari,ɛn] nm. pers. 'Silima----' ???, 'Shining----' ??? III:316.

silmaril ['silma,ril] n. (Silíma + sil) (pl. silmarilli ['silma'rilli], silmarillion ['silma'rilli,ɔn]) 'Silima-flame', a kind of jewel which Fëanor made from Silima and filled with the light of the Two Trees. III:313f;R: 65.

Silmarillion ['silma'rilli,ɔn] nm. book

'Of the Silmarils'. III:314.

silme ['silmɛ] n. 1. starlight. 2. the letter Ꝇ. ɣ reads 'silma'. III:401. Cf. †sil, síl-, Silima.

silme nuquerna ['silmɛ nuk'werna] n. the letter ၅. III:401.

sincahonda ['siŋka'hᴐnda] ??? ----. III:252. Cf. †sinda.

†sinda ['sinda] adj. grey. / S. mith-, *mithren/ I:394;R:58f.

*Sinda ['sinda] n. (pl. Sindar) 'Grey (-one)', Grey-elf. III:363,405f.

*sindanórië ['sinda'noːri,ɛ] n. grey-country. — sindanóriello ['sinda'noː-ri'ɛllᴐ] abl. from/out of a grey country. I:394;R:58f.

Sindarin ['sinda,rin] n. 'Grey', the Grey-elven language. III:405;R:63;G: 155,165.

sindarinwa ['sinda'rinwa] adj. Grey-elven. III:401.

sinome ['sinᴐ,mɛ] adv. in this place. / S. sí/ III:245f.

Siriondil ['siri'ᴐndil] nm. pers. 'Stream----friend' ??? or Stream---- lover' ??? III:318. See S. †sîr.

-sse [-ssɛ] loc. indicator (pl. -ssen [-ssɛn]) in. See Lóriendesse, yassen. (Finn. -ssa, -ssä 'within, in'.)

súle ['suːlɛ] n. (earlier thúle [θuːlɛ]) 1. spirit. 2. (archaic ???) wind. / S. súl, †gwae/ 3. the letter ᚻ. III:401; see Súlimë. Cf. *súri. (OHG seula 'soul, spirit', Eng. soul; Finn. tuuli 'wind'.)

Súlimë ['suːli,mɛ] n. 'Windy', the third month (March), called Rethe in the Shire. / S. Gwaeron/ III:388.

*súri ['suːri] n. wind. / S. súl, †gwae †gwae/ — súrinen ['suːri,nɛn] instr. in/by the (the) wind. I:394;R:58f. Cf. súle. (Skt. sri 'flow, blow'.)

Súrion ['suːri,ᴐn] nm. pers. 'Wind- ---'. III:315.

T

-t [-t] du. indicator / pers. prn. du. acc. both, two. / S. -ad/ See máryat, met, laituvalmet. Cf. at-, te. (Finn. -t, nominative pl. indicator.)

†tánique ['taːnik,wɛ] adj. high-white. R:61. Cf. ortan-, *TÁR, S. nim-.

Táníquetil [,ta:'nikwɛ,til] nm. place 'High-white-peak'. R:61.

*TÁR [taːr] root 1. high. 2. royal. See Meneltarma, Tar-, tarcil, †tári, tárienna, Tarmenel, Tárion, †tarma.

Tar- ['tar-] n. (< *TÁR) King-, Queen-. / S. ar(a)-/ III:315ff. Cf. S. *taur². -tar [-tar] n. (pl. -tari [-ta,ri]) one who --. doer, --er. See Arantar, Atanatar, envinyatar, Istar, Tarostar, telcontar, Telumehtar. In some of these the t may belong to the stem, and in some '-tar' may derive instead from *TÁR.

Tarannon [ta'rannᴐn] nm. pers. ----. III:318. Cf. *TÁR, anna.

*tarcil ['tarkil] n. (tár + cil) 'high-man'. 'king-man'. Used in Westron for one of Númenorean descent, who are called 'the High' (II:287) and 'Kings of Men' (I:13;III:22,84,344). / S. dúnadan/ Text spelling is 'tarkil'. ɣᴐ̈ɛIII:409. Cf. S. Targon.

Tarciryan [,tar'kiryan] nm. pers. 'King-ship----' ???? III:318.

†tári ['taːri] n. (gen. †tário ['taːri,ᴐ]) queen. / S. bereth/, I: 394;III:421;R:58f,66; -tário R:59.

tárienna ['taːri'ɛnna] adv. (tár + ie + nna ???) highly, to the heights ??? III:231.

Tárion ['taːri,ᴐn] n. 'High----', the last day of both the Eldarin and Númenorian weeks, called Highday in the Shire. Also called Valanya. / S. Rodyn/ III:388f.

†tarma ['tarma] n. (tár + ma) hill ??? mount ??? III:315. Cf. S. *torn.

Tarmenel ['tarmɛ,nɛl] n. (tár + menel) 'High-heaven', rendered 'Over-heaven'. I:309;II:204;G:190.

Tarondor [ta'rᴐndᴐr] nm. pers. ----. III:318. Cf. *TÁR, †ondo, -ndor.

Tarostar [ta'rᴐstar] nm. pers. ----. III:318. Cf. *TÁR, †osto, -tar.

†taure ['taŏrɛ] n. forest. / S. taur¹/ III:409.

taurëa ['taŏrɛ,a] adj. forested. III: 409.

taurelilómëa ['taŏrɛ,li'loːmɛ,a] n. (taure + li + lómëa) forestmany-shadowed. ɑ reads 'Taurililómëa'. III:409.

Tauremorna ['taŏrɛ'mɔrna] nm. place
'Black-forest'. II:72.

Tauremornalómë ['taŏrɛ,mɔrna'loːmɛ] nm.
place 'Forest-(of)-black-shadow'. II:
72.

te [tɛ] pers. prn. (3rd???) du. acc.
(them ???) both. III:231. Cf. at-,
-t.

tehta ['tɛçta] n. (pl. tehtar) mark,
referring especially to the signs and
points used as adjuncts to the Fëanorian writing system to represent vowels,
doubling of consonants, etc. / S.
*talth/ III:397,399. (Finn. tehdä
'make'; Goth. tiuha 'I draw'; Du. tee-
kenen 'to draw'; Sw. tecknen 'mark,
sign'; OE tācn 'mark, sign', whence
Eng. token.)

telco ['tɛḷkɔ] n. stem. III:398.

telcontar [,tɛl'kɔntar] n. strider.
III:139.

Telemmaitë ['tɛlɛm'maĭtɛ] nm. pers.
'----handed' ??? III:315. Cf. Angamaitë, morimaite, Telemnar.

Telemnar [tɛ'lɛmnar] nm. pers. '----
sun' ??? III:319. Cf. Telemmaitë,
*NÁR.

*telluma ['tɛḷlu,ma] n. (pl. tellumar)
dome, vault. I:394;R:58f.

telpe- [tɛḷpɛ-] n. (variant of tyelpe-)
silver. / S. celeb/ See Telperiën,
Telperion, †tyelpe.

Telperiën [,tɛḷ'pɛri,ɛn] nm. pers.
'Silver----'. III:315. Cf. Telperion.

Telperion [,tɛḷ'pɛri,ɔn] nm. tree
'Silver----'. II:252;III:250;βγδɛIII:
314. Cf. Telperiën.

Telumehtar ['tɛlu'mɛçtar] nm. pers.
----. Refers to the constellation
Orior Also called Menelmacar. III:
391.

téma ['teːma] n. (pl. témar) series.
III:397f.

*tengwa ['tɛŋ'gwa] n. (pl. tengwar) let-
ter, character: / S. *tēw/ III:395.

*tenna ['tɛnna] prep. (tenn' ['tɛnn] when
closely connected to a following word
beginning with a vowel.) unto, until.
III:245f. Cf. -nna.

thúle, see súle.

*tië ['tiɛ] n. (pl. tier ['tier]) road,
path. I:394;R:58f. (Finn. tie 'road,
way, path'.)

†til [tiḷ] n. peak (of a mountain).
/ S. *tĭl, †ras(s)/ Tániquetil R:61.

*TIN [tin] root 1. spark, sparkle. 2.
(metaphorically) star. / S. gil, *tĭn/
See tinco, tindómë, Tintalle, tintil-,
tinwe, S. ithĭldin. (Fr. étincelie
'spark, sparkle', whence Eng. tinsel.)

tinco ['tiŋkɔ] n. 1. metal. 2. the
letter ρ. III:401.

tincotéma ['tiŋkɔ'teːma] n. 't-series',
containing the dental/alveolar consonants and consonant combinations, such
as t, d, th [θ], dh [ð], s, z, n, nd,
nt, l, lh/hl, ld, r, hr/rh, and rd.
III:398.

tindómë [,tin'doːmɛ] n. (tin + dómë)
'star-shadow', that is, twilight, usually morning twilight, called morrowdim in the Shire. / S. uial, minuial/
III:389. Cf. undomë.

Tintallë [,tin'tallɛ] nm. pers. 'She-
that-causes-sparkling', 'She-that-
kindles-lights', '(Star-) Kindler'.
/ S. Gilthoniel/ I:394;III:428;R:58f,
61. (ME tyndan 'to kindle'.)

tintil- ['tintil-] v. stem to sparkle,
glitter, twinkle, tremble. —
tintilar ['tinti,lar] v. pres. pl.
sparkle, glitter, twinkle, tremble
(pl.). I:394;R:58f,61.

tinwe ['tinwɛ] n. 1. spark. 2. star.
/ S. gil, *tĭn/ R:61.

TIR [tir] root looking, watching. / S.
TIR/ R:65. See Minastir, palantir,
palantír, Tirion, S. *tĭriel, *tĭriel,
tiro.

Tirion ['tiri,ɔn] nm. place 'Great-
watchtower'. R:65.

tuilë ['tuĭlɛ] n. 1. spring. 2. the
first of the six seasons in the Calendar of Imladris, lasting 54 days. / S.
ethuil/ III:386,389.

tuilerë ['tuĭlɛ,rɛ] n. (tuilë + ré)
'spring-day', a day marking the vernal
equinox, inserted between the third
and fourth months in Stewards' Reckoning. III:387.

†túl- ['tuːl-] v. stem to come. —
utúlien [u'tuːli,ɛn] v. perf. 1st s. I
am come. III:245.

†tumbale ['tumba,lɛ] n. deep valley.
/ S. Imlad/ III:409. Cf. -le, S.
*tum(m).

tumbalemorna ['tumba,lɛ'mɔrna] n. Llack deep valley. III:409.

tumbaletaurëa ['tumba,lɛ'taŏrɛ,a] n. forested deep valley. III:409.

†**túp-** ['tuːp-] v. stem to cover, roof. — **untúpa** [,un'tuːpa] v. pres. s. (und + túp + a) down-roof(s), cover(s) (s.). I:394;R:58f. (Finn. tupa 'cottage'.)

†**tur** [tur] n. lord. / S. †**tur**, *hîr/ III:325. Perhaps related to -ndur.

Turambar [tu'rambar] nm. pers. 'Lord-(of the)-world'. III:318.

†**túv-** ['tuːv-] v. stem to find. — *utúvien [u'tuːvi,ɛn] v. perf. 1st s. I have found. — utúvienyes [u'tuːvi-'ɛnyɛs] v. perf. 1st s. + pers. prn. 3rd neut. s. acc. (utúvien(ye) + s) I have found it. III:250.

*tyelle ['tyɛḷlɛ] n. (pl. tyeller ['tyɛḷ-ler]) grade. III:397.

†**tyelpe** ['tyɛḷpɛ] n. (also telpe-) silver. / S. celeb/ III:398. Cf. Telperion.

tyelpetéma ['tyɛḷpɛ'teːma] n. 'ty-series', containing the palatal consonants and dental/alveolar-palatal consonant combinations, such as ty, dy, (or ch [ʧ], j [ʤ],) sh [ʃ], zh [ʒ], ny, ndy (or nj [nʤ]), nty, ly, ry, hy [ç], and y. III:398.

U

ú- ['uː-] adv. not. / S. ú-/ únótimë I:394;R:58f. (ON u- 'un-'.)

umbar ['umbar] n. 1. fate. / S. amarth/ 2. the letter ⱳ. III:401. The place name Umbar is not related. III:407.

Umbardacil [,um'barda,kiḷ] nm. pers. (Umbar (place name of unknown origin) + -dacil) 'Umbar-victor'. III:328f,407.

undómë [,un'doːmɛ] n. (und + dómë) 'descending shadow', that is, twilight, usually evening twilight, called even-dim in the Shire. / S. ulal, aduial/ III:389. Cf. tindómë.

Undómiel [,un'doːmi,ɛḷ] n. (undómë + el) 'Evening-star', 'Evenstar'. I:239.

und(u)- [und(u)-] adj./adv. (< *NDÚ) down, descending. undulávë, untúpa I:394;R:58f.

undulávë, see †láv-.

ungwe ['uŋgwɛ] n. 1. spider's web. 2.

the letter ⱳ. III:401. Cf. S. ungol.

únótimë [,uː'noːti,mɛ] adj. s. & pl. (ú + nótimë) uncountable, numberless, innumerable. I:394;R:58f. Mispelt 'únótime' in yŏɛIII:393. I:394;III:393;R:58f.

unque ['uŋkwɛ] n. 1. a hollow. 2. the letter ⱴ. III:401.

untúpa, see †túp-

úre ['uːrɛ] n. 1. heat. 2. the letter ⱱ. αß read 'úr'. III:401. Cf. aure. (Sem. 'WR 'light', Heb. 'úr 'flame'.)

Úrimë ['uːri,mɛ] n. 'Hot', the eighth month (August), called Wedmath in the Shire. / S. Úrui/ yŏɛ read 'Urimë'. III:388.

utúlien, see †túl-.

utúvienyes, see †túv-.

-uva [-u,va] fut. indicator will. I:394;R:58f.

V

-va [-va] compos. indicator (composed) of. miruvóreva I:394;R:58f.

Vala ['vala] n. (pl. Valar) Angelic Power, one of a race of powerful spiritual beings. / S. *Balan/ — vala, the letter ⱱ. II:269;III:113,319,388,401;R:62. (Skt. bala 'might, power, strength, force'; Lat. valens 'powerful, strong', valēre 'to be strong'; Finn. valto 'power'; ON vala 'prophetess'; Finn. valo 'light', valari 'shining ones'.)

Valacar ['vala,kar] nm. pers. 'Vala----'. III:318f. Cf. Eldacar.

Valandil [va'landiḷ] nm. pers. 'Vala-friend' or 'Vala-lover'. III:318.

Valandur [va'landur] nm. pers. 'Vala----'. III:318. See -ndur, †tur.

Valanya [va'lanya] n. 'Vala-one', the last day of both the Eldarin and Númenorean weeks, called Highday in the Shire. Also called Tárion. / S. Orbelain/ III:288f.

Valar, see Vala.

Valimar, Valmar ['vali,mar, 'valmar] nm. place 'Valar-home', 'Dwelling-of-the-Valar'. R:62.

Valinóre, Valinor ['vali'noːrɛ, 'vali,nor] nm. place 'Valar-land', 'Land-of-the-Valar'. R:62.

Valmar, *see* Valimar.

ván- [vaːn-] *v. stem* to pass (away).
— **vánier** ['vaːni‚er] *v. past pl.*
passed (away) *(pl.).* αI:394;R:58.
— **avánier** [a'vaːni‚er] *v. perf. pl.*
have passed (away) *(pl.).* βγδεI:394;R:
58f. *Cf.* vani-, vanwa. (Lat. *vānēs-*
cere 'disappear, pass away', *whence Fr.*
vanir and Eng. vanish.)

vani- [vani-] *adj???* departed, passing
away ??? *See* ván-, vanimálion, vanimar, vanimelda, Vanimeldë, vanwa, S.
gwanûr.

vanimálion ['vani'maːli‚ɔn] *perhaps n.*
pl. mult. gen. of a noun *vanima, *and*
means something like 'of the many
departed'. III:259. *Cf.* vanimar.

vanimar ['vani‚mar] *perhaps a v. pres.*
pl. meaning 'are gone', *or a n. s.*
meaning 'vanished home', *or a n. pl.*
meaning 'departed ones'. III:259.

vanimelda ['vani'mɛlda] *n.* absent
friend ???, departing friend ???
α *reads* 'vanimalda'. I:367.

Vanimeldë ['vani'mɛlde] *nm. pers.*
'Departing----' ??? α *reads* 'Vani-
maldë'. III:315.

vanwa ['vanwa] *adj.* lost. I:394;R:58f.

varda ['varda] *adj.* exalted. R:61.
(Skt. *vara* 'best, choicest, most excellent'.)

Varda ['varda] *nm. pers. (gen.* Vardo
['vardɔ]) 'The Exalted'. *Elbereth*
III:421;R:61. (Skt. *vara* 'best,
choicest, most excellent'; PIE **wert-*
'to turn', *whence Gmc.* *wérþanan 'to
become', *past s.* *wárþ, *pl.* *wurðun,
whence OE Wyrd, *OHG* Wurt, *ON* Urðr, *a*
goddess of Fate; PIE *verto 'to turn',
whence ON varða 'guard', *Eng.* ward.)

Vardamir ['varda‚mir] *nm. pers.*
'Exalted-jewel' *or* 'Jewel-of-Varda'.
III:315.

ve [vɛ] *prep.* as. I:394;R:58f.

vilya [vilya] *n. (earlier* wilya
['wilya]) 1. air, sky. 2. the letter
tr. III:401.

Vilya ['vilya] *nm. obj.* 'Air-one',
'Sky-one'. III:308;401.

†**vinya** [vinya] *n??? adj???* newness
???, new ??? *See* envinyatar, Vinyarion, †vinyë.

Vinyarion [‚vin'yari‚ɔn] *nm. pers.*
'New----' ??? III:319.

†**vinyë** ['vinyɛ] *adj.* new. / S. *gwain/
See Narvinyë. *Cf.* †vinya.

Viressë [‚viː'rɛssɛ] *n.* the fourth
month (April), called Astron in the
Shire. / S. Gwirith/ III:388.

voron- [vorɔn-] *n??? adj???* steadfastness *or* steadfast. / S. bor(o)-
???, -born ???/ *See* Vorondil,
voronwë. (ON *var* 'plighted faith',
Vör, goddess of same.)

Vorondil [vɔ'rɔndil] *nm. pers.* 'Steadfast-friend' *or* 'Lover-of-Steadfast-
ness'. III:319.

voronwë [vɔ'rɔnwɛ] *adj.* steadfast.
III:319.

W

-wa, *see* -ma.

-we, *see* -me.

wilya, *see* vilya.

Y

***ya** [ya] *relative prn.* which. —
***yasse** ['yassɛ] *all. (pl.* yassen
['yassɛn]) in which, wherein. I:394;
R:58f. (Skt. *ya* 'who, which, that'.)

-ya [-ya] *n. suff. (pl.* -yar) associ-
ated with --, -one. *See* aiya, Aldëa,
Aldúya, Anarya, Eärenya, Elenya, fanya,
Isilya, Menelya, Narya, Nenya, Quenya,
Valanya, vilya, Vilya.

yanta ['yanta] *n.* 1. bridge. 2. the
letter λ. III:401.

yassen, *see* *ya.

Yavanna [ya'vanna] *nm. pers. or place*
'Fruit-gift' ??? R:61. *Cf.* Yavannië,
yávië, anna.

Yavannië [ya'vanni‚ɛ] *n.* 'Fruit-giving'
???, the ninth month (September),
called Halimath in the Shire. / S.
Ivanneth/ III:388. *Cf.* Yavanna,
yávië. (Skt. *yava* 'grain'.)

yávië ['yaːvi‚ɛ] *n.* 1. autumn, harvest. 2. the third of the six seasons
in the Calendar of Imladris, lasting 54
days. / S. Iavas/ III:386,389. *Cf.*
Yavanna, Yavannië. (Skt. *yava*
'grain'.)

yáviérë ['yaːvi'eːrɛ] *n. (*yávië + ré)
'autumn-day', a day marking the autumnal equinox, inserted between the

ninth and tenth months in Stewards' Reckoning. III:387.

yé [ye:] *interj.* lo! III:250.

yén [ye:n] *n.* (*pl.* **yéni** ['ye:ni]) a period of 144 solar years, *rendered* 'long year'. I:394;III:385,393n;R:58f. (Gk. *aion*, Eng. *aeon, eon.*)

†**yesta** ['yɛsta] *n.* beginning ??? III:386. *Cf.* **metta**. (Ger. *erste* 'first'.)

yestarë ['yɛsta,rɛ] *n.* (yesta + ré)

'beginning-day' ???, the first day of the years in the Númenorean calendar, corresponding to *2 Yule* in the Shire. III:386f,390n.

****yulda** ['yulda] *n.* (*pl.* **yuldar**) draught (of beverage). I:394;R:58f. *Cf.* **yulma**.

yulma ['yulma] *n.* cup. I:394;R:58f. *Cf.* ****yulda**. (Finn. *juoma* 'drink, beverage'.)

[The following Quenya poem with bibliographical note and translation was first presented by Björn Fromén in Palantiren 2 (June 1973), this being the journal of the 'Forodrim', a Tolkien oriented group based in Stockholm, Sweden. Fromén's Swedish was translated into English for me by David Strecker, and the English translation that appears here is partly based on this, partly on an ultra-literal English translation of the Quenya with which Björn kindly provided me, and partly on my own feelings for what is required in English. The translation has been approved by Björn. —J.A.]

Valinórenna

A nainië órenyo arano
envinya súlenyasse i mornië.
Ai nwalmi úquénimë hísiëtilion
    unquiciryassen!
Ai anga nin umbarya, carnenáreva!
ve vilyo lintë fanyar oialë
Endórendilië nin avánië,
ar láva órenya lumbulë lómëavalo.
Sí falmar caituvar únótimë imbë met,
    a Elentinwë!
ar vanwa ná Laurëanórië
yasse nu aldar maltava aquantier
    vilya lindinyar.
Man nin envinya silmë elenion?
ar man anarya laurë nin enanuva?
Ú tári Lóriendëo...ú elyë, Vilyatur!
An súrinen Númello nin utúlië.
Tintallëo laurelindë lisse-ómëa:
nai falas hiruvan i ciryaron
yasse hwestannar vanuva Eärëo
órenyo nwalmë úrima; sí tië hiruvan
    Valinórenna!

Sinomë oioquellë nin alantië,
cala nin ú ná mi mardi Endórëo.
A Nenyo tári...a Undómiel Eldaron...
nu menel alcarin te entiruvan
Andúnëo? umbárya nin untúpa orotar...
Ai! palan ú ná metta Eldaloaron! —
Namárië, Eldatan! ú maruvan
    sí nu túpalva,
an elyë tuluva! Nai Vardo eleni
ilyë lúmenn' enomentielvo siluvar!
Namárië...sí tië hiruvan
    Valinórenna!

To Valinor - Celebrían's Farewell to Elrond

is reconstructed after a preserved fragment from the Fourth Age (*Docum. Apocryph. Sodalit. Daeron IX*). The poem is written in High Elvish (Quenya) and is thought to constitute a separated fragment of the so-called *Telcontarion*, an epic that deals with King Eldarion's ancestors. (With regard to the fragment's historical background, see I:239; II:323. 368.)

    The manuscript, in which this fragment was recovered, is unfortunately rather badly worn. A good many words and forms have therefore had to be constructed on the basis of Elvish material that the *Red Book's* translator/adaptor presented in *The Return of the King* and *The Road Goes Ever On*. Here follows a free translation of the poem:

> Thy bitter lament, O my beloved,
> deepens the darkness in my spirit.
> Ah! torments unspeakable in the hollow dens
>   of the Misty Mountains!
> Ah! the weapon of my doom, red and fiery iron!
> Like the swift clouds of the air, for ever,
> my joy in Middle-earth has passed from me,
> and the Dark Angel's shadow licks at my soul.
> Now must the swells of countless waves lie between us,
>   O Star-descended!
> and lost to me is the Golden Land,
> where, beneath the golden trees, I filled
>   the air with my songs.
> Who will renew the light of the stars for me?
> and who will bring back to me the gold of the sun?
> Not the Lady of Lórien...not even thou, Vilya's master!
> For, in the western wind has come to me
> Tintallë's sweet-voiced golden song—
> Let me find the ships' strand,
> where, in breezes from the Sea, the burning torment
>   of my soul may pass away; now I will find
>   a path to Valinor.
>
> Here an eternal autumn has fallen around me:
> for me there is no light in the halls of Middle-earth.
> O Nenya's Queen...O Fvenstar of the Elves...
> shall I ever again behold those two in the glory of
> a sunset? A Higher Power hides their fate from me.
> Ah! no longer distant is the ending of the Elven-years!
> Farewell, Half-elven! Though I may no longer tarry
>   here beneath our roof,
> yet thou must soon come after me! May all the stars of
> Varda shine on the hour of our reunion!
> Farewell...now I will find a path
>   to Valinor!

                            —*Findegil Mellonath Daeron*
                              (Björn Fromén)

SINDARIN GRAMMAR & DICTIONARY

Jim Allan

Includes material by Bill Welden as credited. Modern language comparisons in the dictionary are mostly compiled by Paula Marmor.

THE STRUCTURE OF SINDARIN

ORIGIN

The name *Sindarin* is from the Quenya tongue, and is the
name given in that language to the speech of the Grey-elves,
those West-elves who did not cross over the Great Sea to the
Undying Lands in the First Age, but remained in Middle-
earth, in the land of Beleriand, west of the Blue Mountains.
The name contains the Quenya word *Sindar* 'Greys', the Quenya
name for the Grey-elves, and so can be translated 'Grey-
elven'. Quenya and Sindarin are related; but, with the
changefulness of mortal lands, Sindarin had departed more
widely from their common original.

When the Noldor came back to Middle-earth in exile from
the Undying Lands, and dwelt among the nore numerous Sindar,
they also took their tongue as their own, and even changed
their names into it. Thus *Altáriel* became *Galadriel*

Sindarin was known and used by the Edain, the first
kindreds of Men to come into the West of Middle-earth in the
Elder Days. The crossed the Blue Mountains into Beleriand
and fought beside the Eldar (both Noldor and Sindar) against
the power of Morgoth in the wars for the Great Jewels, and
the Eldar taught them much. All the early Edain names in *The*

SINDARIN

Lord of the Rings are of Sindarin form, save for *Eärendil* which is Quenya.

In the Second Age, after the destruction of most of Beleriand, some of the Sindar founded kingdoms in the east: Eregion, Lothlórien, the forest realm of Greenwood the Great. In all but Eregion most of the subjects in these kingdoms were of the East-elven kind, but they to some extent took up Sindarin beside, or in place of, their own tongues. For example, in the Third Age in Lothlórien Sindarin was spoken, though most of its inhabitants were of the Silvan race (III: 405n). But it was spoken with an accent strong enough to lead Frodo to think it no Sindarin at all, but a Silvan tongue (αI:374). Sindarin also continued among Men as a learned tongue, especially among the Men of Númenor.

Spoken, as it was, among many divers folk, Sindarin had developed into different dialects by the end of the Third Age. In *The Lord of the Rings* we have as an example of Early Sindarin the inscription on the West-gate of Moria which Frodo cannot make out. Frodo's knowledge of Sindarin would derive from Bilbo, and would probably be mostly of the sort spoken in Imladris (Rivendell) and by the Wandering Companies of High Elves,—a variety much influenced by Quenya, the original tongue of the High Elves (R:64). Many Quenya words had been adopted in this dialect. The Elven hymns to Elbereth are in this kind of Sindarin.

Another sort would be that of Lothlórien, spoken with a strong Silvan accent, and doubtless also containing Silvan words.

Still another would be that of the Dúnedain of Gondor, for even at the end of the Third Age there were many who could speak the Sindarin tongue in some fashion (II:267). In Gondor Sindarin *ch* [x] had weakened to [h], save when final or before *t*, and Tolkien has transcribed some of the names used by Men of Gondor using *h* instead of *ch* to show this. Sindarin vocalic *y* was in Gondor usually pronounced like *i*, that is, as [i] or [ɪ], rather than as [y].

Sindarin names were much used by the Dúnedain. In the North, after the breaking of Arnor into three kingdoms, the Kings of Arthedain, and later the Chieftains of the Dúnedain of the North, took names of Sindarin form. Indeed, save for the Royal Names of Gondor, and the earliest royal names of Arnor, almost all Dúnedain names are Sindarin. Place names also appear in Sindarin when not in the Common Speech. When the the Men of Gondor give praise to Frodo and Samwise for their success in destroying the Ring, they speak in the Sindarin tongue, and even render the Hobbits' names into Sindarin, as *Daur* and **Perhael* (the last lenited after *a* to *Berhael*) (III:231).

Of the languages spoken in Middle-earth today Sindarin
bears the most resemblance to Welsh, far closer than that
of Quenya to Finnish. Tolkien writes of the beauty he found
in Welsh:

> Most English speaking people, for instance, will
> admit that *cellar door* is 'beautiful', especially if
> disassociated from its sense (and from its spelling).
> More beautiful than, say *sky*, and far more beautiful
> than *beautiful*. Well then, in Welsh for me *cellar doors*
> are extraordinarily frequent, and moving to the higher
> dimension, the words in which there is pleasure in the
> contemplation of the association of form and sense are
> abundant. (EW:36f)

He relates how he found this kind of pleasure in other
tongues, Greek, then Gothic, then Finnish, and continues:

> But all the time there had been another call—bound
> to win in the end, through long baulked by sheer lack of
> opportunity. I heard it coming out of the west. It
> struck me in the names on coal-trucks; and drawing
> nearer, it flickered past on station-signs, a flash of
> strange spelling and a hint of a language old and yet
> alive; even in an *adeiladwyd 1887*, ill-cut on a stone
> slab, it pierced my linguistic heart. 'Late Modern
> Welsh' (bad Welsh to some). Nothing more than an 'it
> was built', though it marked the end of a long story from
> daub and wattle in some archaic village to a sombre
> chapel under the dark hills. (EW:38)

> If I were pressed to give any example of a feature of
> this style, not only as an observable feature but as a
> source of pleasure to myself, I should mention the fond-
> ness for nasal consonants, especially the much-favoured
> *n*, and the frequency with which word patterns are made
> with the soft and less sonorous *w* and the voiced spirants
> *f* [= [v]] and *dd* [= [ð]] contrasted with the nasals:
> *nant, meddiant, afon, llawenydd, cenfigen, gwanwyn,
> gwenyn, crafanc*, to set down a few at random. A very char-
> acteristic word is *gogoniant* 'glory'. (EW:40)

> If I may once more refer to my work, *The Lord of the
> Rings*, in evidence: the names of persons and places in
> this story were mainly composed on patterns deliberately
> modelled on those of Welsh (closely similar but not identi-
> cal). This element in the tale has given perhaps more
> pleasure to more readers than anything else in it. (EW:41n)

Some Welsh words and names have similar meanings to
words and names in Sindarin. In both languages *a* means 'Ah!'
or 'O!'. Welsh *amar* 'wound', *amarch* 'dishonour', *amorth*

D

'misfortune, curse' recall Sindarin *amarth* 'doom, impending fate'. The supernatural huntsman of Welsh folklore, Arawn, called Head of Annwn, recalls *Araw*, the Sindarin name for the huntsman of the Valar, who of course dwells in the west, the Sindarin word for 'west' being *annûn*. Compare Welsh *du* 'black' with Sindarin *dúath* 'shadows', and Welsh *mâl* 'gold' with Sindarin *mal-* 'gold'. In Welsh the definite article often appears as *y*, and in Sindarin it is often *i*.

The following are Welsh words close or identical to Sindarin words or parts of words. Their Welsh meanings are given:

adan 'birds', *adain* 'wing', *ai* 'is it?', *an* 'our', *annuun* 'disunited', *ar* 'on', *arth* 'bear', *awr* 'time' (see S *aur*), *balc* 'mistake' (see S *Balchoth*), *barahir* 'long bread', *baran* 'fury, wrath', *ben* 'top', *bran* 'crow', *calan* 'first day', *calen* 'whetstone', *caer* 'castle', *caran* 'crane', *carn* 'cairn', *certh* 'certain', *curin* 'rainstorm', *daeron* 'countries', *dagr* 'dagger' (see S †*dagor*), *dan* under', *derw* 'oak' (see S *Derufin*, *Drúadan*), *dil* 'honeycomb', *dir* 'certain', *dôl* 'meadow', *dôr* 'door', *drud* 'brave, fierce' (see S *Druadan*), *dur* 'steel', *dûm* 'judgement, doom', *dwn* 'dun, dusky', *dwyn* 'to take' (see S *duin*), *dŵr* 'water', *dyn* 'man', *emyn* 'hymn', *en* 'in, at', *ennyn* 'to inflame', *ffwyn* 'foin' (see S *fuin*), *gawr* 'shout' or lenited form of *cawr* 'giant', *gelyn* 'enemy', *glas* green, blue, grey', *gor-* 'over-, sur-', *hael* 'generous', *hawdd* 'easy', *hen* 'old', *hi* 'she, her', *hin* 'weather', *hir* 'long', *hu* 'so', *iâr* 'hen', *iau* 'younger', *llad* 'grace, gift', *llaer* 'moon', *llain* 'sword blade', *llas* 'was killed', *lle* 'instead of', *llaith* 'death' (see S *Amlaith*), *llaw* 'hand', *llith* 'lesson', *llond* 'fulness', *Llun* 'Monday', *llwyn* 'grove, bush', *llyg* 'shrew', *llyn* 'lake', *llwng* 'damp' (see S *Mablung*), *mab* 'son', *melyn* 'yellow', *min* 'edge', *mae* 'is', *mir* 'seas', *môr* 'sea, ocean', *mor* 'so, as', *morgais* 'mortgage', *na* 'no, not', *morwyn* 'maid', *nant* 'brook', *nâr* 'lord', *nawr* 'now', *nef* 'heaven', *nen* 'heaven, ceiling', *nog* 'than', *ost* 'host', *pant* 'valley', *parth* 'part', *pêl* 'ball', *pin* 'pine', *pinoedd* 'pines', *rhandir* 'allotment, region', *rhath* 'mound', *rhiw* 'hill', *rhooh* 'grunt', *rhod* 'wheel', *rhos* 'moor, plain', *rhu-* 'roar', *Rhûn* a common personal name, *sarn* 'causeway', *si* 'murmur', *Sul* 'Sunday', *taith* 'death', *tir* 'land, earth', *tirion* 'sod, country', *tûm* 'tomb', *-waith* (having to do with time), *yrch* 'roebucks'.

It is interesting that *iar-* means 'old' in Sindarin and *iâr* means 'a hen' in Welsh; but *hen* means 'old' in Welsh.

Further comparisons between Sindarin and Welsh will be given when appropriate.

SINDARIN

SOUNDS & SPELLING

Consonants

The consonantal system of Early Sindarin is indicated by the arrangment of the early Certhas Daeron, and is given below in chart form using letters and symbols of the International Phonetic Alphabet. Where Tolkien's spelling of the sounds differs, it follows in small italics in parentheses.

	Labial	Dental/ Alveolar	Velar
Voiceless Stop:	p	t	k(c)
Voiced Stop:	b	d	g
Nasal:	m	n	ŋ(ng, n)
Voiceless Spirant:	f(f, ph)	θ(th) s	x(ch)
Voiced Spirant:	v(v, -f)	ð(dh)	ɣ(gh)
Nasalized Voiced Spirant:	ṽ(mh)		
Voiceless Approximant:	ʍ(hw)	ɹ(rh) ɭ(lh)	ʍ(hw)
Voiced Approximant:	w	l y(i) w	
Trill:		r	
Breath:			h

The sound [ŋ] is written *ng* by Tolkien when it occurs finally, and *n* when it occurs in the combinations [ŋk] *nc* and [ŋg] *ng*. The sound [f] is witten *ph* by Tolkien when it occurs finally or is related to or derived from *p* (III:392 *PH*). The sound [v] is written *f* by Tolkien when it occurs finally (III:391 *F*).

As will be discussed below under 'Lenition', the sound [ṽ] is in origin an variant of [m]. It is possible that a better representation of the sound might be [β̃]. Nasalized spirants normally cause nasalization of either the preceding or following vowel. So in Sindarin, which otherwise had neither nasalized vowels nor nasalized spirants or approximants, [ṽ] was anomalous, and by the Third Age had lost all its nasalization and so fell together with regular [v]. That is, original [b] and [m] in certain positions, as given below under 'Lenition', were opened to spirants, to be symbolized respectively as [β] and [β̃]. In Early Sindarin these bilabials had become the labio-dentals [v] and [ṽ], and by the Third Age—at least in the variety of Sindarin given by Tolkien—had fallen together as [v].

The sound [ɣ] *gh* was lost entirely by the Third Age in the varieties of Sindarin given by Tolkien. In some cases, paralleling Welsh, it may have survived as the final -*i* or *e* of a diphthong.

The consonant sounds of standard Third Age Sindarin are, then, as given in the above chart, with the omission of [ṽ] and [ɣ] (*mh* and *gh*).

SINDARIN

Vowels

The vowels of Early Sindarin may be charted as follows:

i̇, *ü*   *u*

e, *ö*   *o*

a

The vowels *ü* and *ö* represent versions of *i* and *e* pronounced with lip rounding. In standard Third Age Sindarin *ö* had generally become unrounded, and so fell together with *e*, but sometimes remained rounded and fell together with *ü*, which Tolkien writes as *y*. Compare the two plural forms of *orod*: *ered* and *eryd*, indication of an earlier *oröd*.

For Third Age Sindarin we have more complete information on the pronuncation of the vowels, permitting the creation of a more complete chart incorporating long vowels. The symbols of the International Phonetic Alphabet are used with Tolkien's transcription in small italics in parentheses.

i:*(i)*, i::*(í)*; ɥ*(y/ü)*   u:*(ú)*, u::*(û)*

ι*(i)*   o*(u)*

ɛ*(e)*, ɛ:*(é)*, ɛ::*(ê)*   ʊ*(o)*, ʊ:*(ó)*, ʊ::*(ô)*

ɑ*(a)*, ɑ:*(á)*, ɑ::*(â)*

The only occurrence of a long vocalic *y* in the extant corpus is in *lŷg* in αIII:393. But in βγδε this is changed to *lyg* with a short vowel. So, as there is no trustworthy evi-evidence for either *ý* or *ŷ*, these are not included in the above chart.

Long *é/ê*, *á/â*, *ó/ô* have the same quality as their corresponding short vowels 'being derived in comparatively recent times from them' (III:393). Older *ē* had changed to *í/i*, older *ā* had changed to *au/o* and rarely *ó* (this rare *ó* from *ā* falling together with the new *ó/ô* from *o*), and older *ō* had changed to *ú/u* (see p. 118ff).

The changing of the originally short vowels to long vowels occurred especially (if not only) in singly closed stressed monosyllables, and were, in the Third Age, of more than normal length, as Tolkien indicates by his use of the circumflex. Occasionally these specially lengthened vowels were retained in compounds made from these words, as in *amrûn*, *annûn*, *gwanûr*, *Udûn*. (See p. 118 for listing of such words and complete discussion.) In what circumstances the new *é*, *á*, *ó*, of normal length would arise is not clear. They were probably very rare. Indeed, *é* and *á* do not appear in the extant corpus. Long vowels are rarer than in Quenya, sometimes lacking where Quenya would lead us to expect them (e.g. Q *Víressë*/S *Gwirith*). The pairs *Nínui* 'Wet'/*Nindalf* 'Wetwang', *Anórien* 'Sunlending'/*Anor* 'Son' show that, as in Quenya, long vowels are normally shortened when they fall in closed syllables. But long *í* occurs in closed syllables in *Círdan*, *Dírhael*, and *Curunír*, so the rule is not without its exceptions.

Sindarin has developed what can be considered a series of -*i*/-*e* diphthongs as follows:

$$í, î \qquad\qquad\qquad ui$$
$$ei \qquad\qquad oe$$
$$ai$$
$$au$$

The diphthongs *ae*, *oe*, *ui* are called 'long diphthongs' (R: 63), and arise principally from diphthongs in the proto-language or VC or VV combinations. The diphthong *ae* corresponds to Q *ai*, and *ui* corresponds to both Q *oi* and *ui*. (See p. 122.) *Ei* is a short diphthong arising from mutation of original *e* or *a*. (See p. 115 and discussion under 'Lenition' below.) *Ai* is the form taken by *ei* falling in final syllables and monosyllables (cf. *teithant* but *andaith*) and is also a short diphthong. *Ai* also arises from mutation of *ae* (cf. *Gwaeron* but *Gwaihir*). In Modern Welsh *ei* changes to *ai* in a final syllable, save when followed by a double consonant or an originally doubled consonant, or in a few other exceptional cases.

Sindarin also has an *au* diphthong, written by Tolkien as *aw* when final following English spelling conventions, though this practice was often found in tengwar spelling too (III:394). In Welsh, British *ō* (< *ā*) became *aw* in stressed syllables and *o* in unstressed syllables. In Medieval Welsh we thus find *marchawc* 'knight', but *marchogyon* 'knights', as the stress was on the last syllable, and so in *marchawc* original *ō* is stressed, but in *marchogyon* it is not. Later the stress in Welsh was removed from the final syllable to the second-last syllable, and *aw* became *o* everywhere save in words of one syllable. Thus British *Cara'tācos* > Medieval Welsh *Cara'dawg* > Modern Welsh *Ca'radog*. Something similar happens with *au* in Sindarin. Compare *aur* 'day' with *or-* in *Oranor* 'Sunday'; *naur* 'fire' with *Anor* 'Sun', *Nórui* 'Sunny', *Anórien* 'Sunlending'; *iaur* 'old' with *Ioreth*. The difference between Welsh and Sindarin is that long *ō* sometimes appears in the latter. The *a* in *Narwain* and *Iarwain* is a result of the original *ā* becoming *ā* in a closed syllable before the change of *ā* to *ō* to *au/o/ō*. (See p. 119 The diphthongs *eu* and *iu* found in Quenya had disappeared in Sindarin, mostly becoming *y* (III:393).

Sindarin & Welsh

Following is a listing of the consonants and pertinent consonant clusters of Sindarin, in alphabetical order, with a corresponding list for Welsh beneath. Parentheses indicate a combination not regularly found.

SINDARIN: b c ch d dh f g h hw i l lh ll m   mn n ng (ngh) (nh) nn p
WELSH: b c ch d dd ff g h chw i l   ll   m mh   n ng ngh   nh nn p

SINDARIN: ph r rh rr s ss t th v w
WELSH: ph r rh rr s ss t th f w

As indicated, Wel. *f* corresponds to S *v* (having the value [v]), and Wel. *ff* corresponds to S *f* (having the value [f]). Both Wel. *dd* and S *dh* represent [ð]. In medieval spelling *v/u* and *f* are indeed sometimes used instead of the modern *f* and *ff*, and occasionally *dh* is used for *dd* in late seventeenth century spellings.

The pronunciation of Welsh *chw* as [xw] is a comparatively recent phenomenon; the original pronounciation was a voiceless *w* [ʍ] as in Sindarin, and the spelling *hw* often appears in medieval texts.

Welsh has a simple voiced appoximant *l* [l] as in English, spelt *l* in modern Welsh; a lengthened voiced approximant *l* [ll], also spelt *l* in modern Welsh; and a voiceless spirant *l* [ɬ], spelt *ll* in modern Welsh. But in medieval Welsh, *ll* was used for both double [ll] and voiceless [ɬ]— with a ligature *ỻ* sometimes used for [ɬ] to distinguish the sounds. In late seventheenth century texts the spelling *lh* is sometimes used for the voiceless *l* [ɬ] as in Tolkien's Sindarin spelling.

The Sindarin voiceless *l* is not to be pronounced quite as the Welsh voiceless *l*. Tolkien states he uses *l* to represent 'more or less the sound of English initial *l*, as in *let*', that is the normal voiced lateral approximant [l]. He goes on to say that 'LH represents this sound when voiceless' (III:392 *L*), indicating a voiceless lateral approximant [l̥], somewhat as in *clean* [kl̥iːn], not the Welsh voiceless lateral spirant [ɬ].

In modern Welsh spelling a long *m* is written as simple *m*, but in medieval texts the doubling is commonly shown by the writing *mm*.

With these variant spellings taken into account it can be seen that Sindarin and Welsh match almost perfectly in their consonants. Sindarin lacks only the voiceless nasals *mh*, *nh*, *ngh* [m̥, n̥, ŋ̊]; though these may have occurred rarely as realizations of *m + h*, *n + h*, *ng* [ŋ] *+ h*; cf. *Calenhad*,

SINDARIN

Fanghorn.
Another sort of difference is that in both Welsh and Sindarin original initial *sl* and *sr* and become, respectively, voiceless *ll/lh* and *rh*; but, in Welsh ordinary initial *l* and *r* also became *ll* and *rh*. Accordingly, in Welsh *l* and *r* are never found initially save in loanwords or in lenition position, while in Sindarin initial *l* and *r* are very common.

The following list compares the vowels and diphthongs of Sindarin and Welsh:

SINDARIN: a ae ai au/aw e ei   i (iw) o oe   u ui y
WELSH: a ae ai au aw e ei eu ew ey i iw o oe oi ou ow w wy u y yw

Sindarin has fewer diphthongs than Welsh. Also, in Sindarin as transcribed by Tolkien *au* and *aw* are only graphic variants for the same sound, but in Welsh they indicated different pronunciations. In Sindarin *iw* occurred (as in *tîw*), though it was not counted as a diphthong. But it could not have differed greatly in pronunciation from Welsh *iw*. Sindarin probably also had *ew* and *ow* combinations. (In the dictionary the suggested singular given for *tîw* is **têw*.)

Sindarin also writes one fewer vowels than Welsh. As indicated, Welsh vocalic *w* corresponds to S *u* (both pronounced [o] when short and [uː] when long), and Welsh *u* corresponds to S vocalic *y* (*ü*) (both pronounced [ɥ]). Welsh vocalic *y* has no corresponding vowel in Sindarin. Its original sound is between [ɨ] and [ɯ], but it is also used in Modern Welsh for [ʌ] as in English *but* [bʌt].

Tolkien's transcription of Sindarin somewhat hides the similarity between Sindarin and Welsh, as he, quite naturally, does not follow Welsh practice when this conflicts with English usage. He uses *dh* (not *dd*), *f* (not *ff*), *v* (not *f*, save for final [v]), *lh* (not *ll*), *u* (not *w*), and *y* for [ɥ] (not *u*) following Old English and Classical Latin spelling.

Problems in Pronunciation

Tolkien informs us that in Sindarin the combination *ng* [ŋg] 'remained unchanged except initially and finally where it became the simple nasal (as in English *sing*)' (III:393), that is, it simplified to [ŋ]. He repeats this in other words: '*Ng* represents the same sounds as E. *ng*; that in *sing* finally and initially as in *nguruthos* (Vol. II, p. 339); otherwise as in *finger*' (R:63). Taken exactly as he writes it we must interpret the combination *ngb* in *Angband* and *Angbor* as [ŋgb] and the combination *ngm* in *Angmar* as [ŋgm]. But clusters of this sort are not otherwise found, and I have taken the liberty of giving the pronunciations [ŋb] and [ŋm] in the dictionary, as they seem to me much more likely.

SINDARIN

In his discussion of stress Tolkien remarks: 'Note that
Sindarin *dh*, *th*, *ch* are single consonants and represent single
letters in the original scripts' (III:394). But he
remarks elsewhere that he has used *ph* in this transcriptions
'in the middle of a few words where it represents a long *ff*
(from *pp*) as in *Ephel* "outer fence"' (III:392 *PH*). If *Ephel*
represents [ˈɛffɛl], then should not the parallel *Echor* and
Ethir represent [ˈɛxxɔr] and [ˈɛθθir] rather than [ˈɛxɔr] and
[ˈɛθir]? Tolkien may have realized he had overstated the
case, as he later wrote that 'consonants represented by *h*
added as a "spirantal" sign (*ch*, *th*, *ph*, *dh*) are *normally*
single sounds [emphasis mine]' (R:63). The implication is
that usually the diagraphs will indicate a single sound, but
on occasion a double sound.

The names *Araphant* and *Araphor* contain a medial *ph*,
apparently indicating a long *ff*. They would derive from
Aran-pant and *Aran-por*, becoming with assimilation of the *n*
Arappant and *Arappor*, and then *Araffant* and *Araffor*, spelt
by Tolkien, *Araphant* and *Araphor*. Similarly *Arathorn* will
be from *Aran-torn*, and will actually stand for *Araththorn*.
But what of the stress? It is on the first syllable in
'Arador, *'Aragorn*, *'Aragost*, *'Aranarth*, *'Aranuir*, *'Araval*,
'Aravir, and *'Aravorn* according to Tolkien's guidelines (III:
394), but, as indicated below under 'CONSONANT MUTATION' the
medial consonants in these names must also represent an
original double consonat: *dd*, *gg*, *nn*, *vv*. If these have
simplified, may not also *ff*, *thth*, and *chch* have simplified
in a parallel case? In Welsh also *pp*, *tt*, and *cc* become
f(ph), *th*, and *ch*, and there they count as one consonant for
purpose of stress. This would have been decisive, if not
for the form *Arassuil*, with a double voiceless spirant
clearly shown. With this and Tolkien's remark that medial
ph represents a long *ff* it seemed most likely that in these
names *ph* and *th* do represent doubled consonants. This has
accordingly been indicated in the dictionary, and they have
been stressed on the second syllable, rather than on the
first (e.g. *A'rassuil*, *A'rathorn*). The decision was not
made with confidence.

As for other cases, I have accordingly rendered intervocalic *ph* by [ff] throughout. Intervocalic *th* and *ch* I have
had to guess at, and the pronunciations given are the result
of this guessing. The user should be aware of the lack of
evidence in these instances.

Tolkien tells us that in Third Age Sindarin *'mb* became
m in all cases, but still counted as a long consonant for
purposes of stress..., and is thus written *mm* in all cases
where otherwise the stress might be in doubt' (III:393).
This can be interpreted that *mm* indicates the word is to be

stressed as though there were a double *m*, but only one *m* is
pronounced. But Tolkien also says that 'All consonants written double are meant to be so pronounced' (R:63), and in his
reading of 'A Elbereth' he clearly pronounces the *mm* in
galadhremmin as double. Accordingly, *mm* is always rendered
[mm] in the pronunciations given in the dictionary.

CONSONANT MUTATION

Lenition

LENITION means 'softening', and refers to the loosening
and slackening of the pronunciation of a consonant, so that
it becomes more vocalic. Voiceless consonants may be lenited
('softened') to voiced consonants; stops may be lenited
('softened') to spirants; and spirants may be lenited
('softened') to approximants.

In both Sindarin and Welsh a very similar process of
lenition occurs. The environment for lenition is, generally
speaking, between vowels, or between a vowel and a sonant.
(Sonants are consonants that may be syllabic: *l*, *r*, *m*, *n*, *ŋ*).
Not all consonants subject to lenition in a language may
lenit in the same environment. Stress may be involved, and
so, unfortunately, may analogy.

In both Sindarin and Welsh the voiceless stops (*p,t,c*)
lenit to the corresponding voiced stops (*b*, *d*, *g*) in lenition
position.

> *p → b*: S *peleth/Narbeleth*
>   Lat. *populus* 'people'/Wel. *pobyl*
>
> *t → d*: Q *Altáriel*/S *Galadriel*; S *TIR/palan-díriel*;
>   S *talf/Nindalf*; Q *tinwe*/S *ithildin*
>   Lat. *latro* 'ladder'/Wel. *lleidr*
>
> *c → g*: Q *alcar*/S *aglar*; S *certhas/angerthas*;
>   S *calad/Gil-galad*; Q *leuca*/S *lyg*
>   Lat. *placitum* 'principle'/Wel. *plegyd*

In Welsh the voiceless liquids *ll* and *rh* lenit to *l* and
r. We have no example for S *lh*, but *rh* can be seen to lenit
to *r* in the pair *rhûn/amrûn*.

In Old Welsh the voiced stops (*b*, *d*, *g*) lenited to the
corresponding voiced spirants (β, δ, γ). Later β became *v*
and γ disappeared. (In Welsh *v* is written as *f*, and δ as
dd.) Thus the Welsh lenition of voiced stops developed to:
b → f [v], *d → dd* [δ], and *g → ∅*. The same pattern sometimes
appears in Sindarin.

b → v: S _Beleg/A_$rveleg$ (but S *_belain/Orbelain_)

~ f: Lat. _liber_ 'book'/Wel. _llyfr_

d → dh: S _dol/Fanuidhol_; Q $alda$/S $galadh$ (but S _dol/Nardol_)

dd: Lat. _fides_ 'faith'/Wel. _ffydd_

g → θ: S _Gondor/Harondor_ (but S †_gon/Argonath_; S _gil/_
Orgilion; S _Guldur/morgul_)

θ: Lat. _flagellum_ 'whip'/Wel. _ffrewyl_

Reasons for the lack of consistency in the lenition óf the voiced stops are not apparent from the published examples.

In both Welsh and Sindarin _m_ lenits to _v_ (spelt _f_ in Welsh.

_m_ → _v_: S *_medui/Arvedui_; Q _Silima_/S _silivren_

_f_: Lat. _columna_ 'column'/Wel. _colofn_

In Welsh original British _s_ usually becáme _h_ as in _Sabrīna_, the Latin name for the river Severn taken from British, compared to Welsh _Hafren_. But in Irish, and in Sindarin, _s_ only becomes _h_ in lenition position.

_s_ → _h_: S _Sirannon/Duhirion_

A lenition of _n_ to _dh_ (parallel to that of _m_ to _v_) is found, but only between a vowel and _r_, as in _Caradhras_ from _caran_ + _rass_ (III:391 _DH_).

_B_, _d_, and _g_ are not subject to lenition in the combinations _mb_, _nd_, and _ng_ [ŋg]. These have their own independant development as given in III:393. Similarly, _p_, _t_, and _c_ do not undergo lenition when in the combinations _mp_, _nt_, and _nc_ [ŋk] when these combinations are final. Cf. _Celebrant_ but _Mithrandir_.

The unlenited _c_ in _Ancalagon_ is puzzling. (Might it be the result of something like *_anc_ + *_calagon_?)

In Welsh it is found that lenition of an initial consonant often occurs after a closely connected preceding word with a suitable ending, or which once had a suitable ending. In Sindarin this also occurs, as indicated by the only definite example, in the accepted corpus: _Daur a Berhael_ 'Frodo and Samwise' (III:231). _Samwise_ means 'half-wise' (III:414), but 'half' appears as _per-_ in Sindarin in _perian_ 'halfling' and _Peredhil_ 'Half-elven', so _Berhael_ must be an initially lenited form of *_Perhael_.   Two more examples appear in a variant version of the Moria West-gate inscription:

ENNYN ÐURIN ARAN VÓRIA: PEÐO MELLON A MINNO:

(HC, plate 12, facing p. 179). The published version is _Ennyn Durin Aran Moria: pedo mellon a minno_ (I:318), with no initial lenition of *Durin* to *Ðurin*—*Ð* is the capital of *ð*—, and *Moria* to *Voria*.

Another variant form showing lenition occurs in a page of an early draft of material later published in Book IV, Ch. 8, 'The Stairs of Cirith Ungol', printed on the September page of *The Lord of the Rings 1977 Calendar* (London: Allen & Unwin, 1976). There *Morghul* appears instead of the *Morgul* of the published version, showing lenition of *g* to *gh* [γ].

In Welsh *gw* lenits to *w*. This can be considered as merely a special case of the ordinary lenition of *g* to *ø*, but its origin is, in most cases, the reverse. Original *w* remained unchanged in lenition position, but initially it was strenghtened to *gw*. (Phonetically, a strong *w* can be written [γ̂β], and a strengthening of the velar element produces [ᵍγ̂β], further strengthened to [gγ̂β], that is [gw].) So Lat. *versus* 'against' became *gwers* in Welsh. (Lat. *v* was pronounced [w].) This same process is found in other languages, and even goes a step farther in Romance languages. Compare English *William* (> Gmc. *willio* + *helma*) with the French form *Guillaume*, where the original *w* is not pronounced at all, surviving only in the traditional spelling as a silent *u*.)

The same thing happened in Sindarin. *W* by itself is found only in lenition position, and *gw* only initially, where it correspons to Q *v* (from earlier *w*), as in Q. *Víressë*/S *Gwirith*; Q *vanwa*/S *gwanûr*.

In pre-Sindarin *g* would have occurred only before a vowel, *l*, or *w*. Its disappearance in lenition position while unlenited *w* became *gw* gave the following lenition pattern:

$$g \rightarrow ø$$
$$gw \rightarrow w$$
$$gl \rightarrow l$$
$$lh \rightarrow l$$
$$l \rightarrow l$$

By analogy with *w* corresponding to initial *gw*, and *l* corresponding often to original initial *gl*, a *g-* was often prefixed to original initial *l* which did not derive from *gl*. This was the augmentative *g*, which strengthened the meaning of the word. An original **loss* 'snow-white', corresponding to Q *losse*, became *glos(s)* 'dazzling-white' with prefixing of the augmentative *g* (R:62).

Nasal Mutation

In Sindarin *n* + another consonant sometimes results in assimilation of the *n* producing a double consonant, which in turn may mutate. This is most clearly seen in the

formation of names beginning with *Ara-*.
Tolkien states that 'the King of Fornost again claimed lordship over the whole of Arnor, and took names with the prefix *ar(a)* in token of this' (III:318n). An examination of the names revels that there are, in fact, two prefixes: *ar-* and *ara(n)-*.

The shorter prefix *ar-* is used when the second element of the name contains two syllables, as in *Argeleb*, *Argonui*, *Arvegil*, and *Arveleg*. These names show regular initial lenition of the second element following the prefixed *ar-*: *ar + celeb → Argeleb*; *ar + beleg → Arveleg*.

The long prefix appears as *aran-* in *Aranarth* 'King-(of the)-realm'. (*Arth* appears also in *Arthedain* 'Realm-(of the)-Edain'.) Similarly, *Aranuir* is probably *aran + uir*. But in forms were the second element is a consonant the *n* assimilates with it, and so is not found in the final form: hence the writing *ara(n)-* used here. The presence of this *(n)* is indicated by Tolkien's spelling *ph* in *Araphant* and *Araphor*. Tolkien tells us that he uses *ph* 'in the middle of a few words where it represents a long *ff* (from *pp*) as in *Ephel* 'outer fence' (III:392 *PH*). Thus it appears that *ara(n) + pant → *Arappant* realized as *Araphant*, and *ara(n) + por → *Arappor* realized as *Araphor*. Similarly, *ara(n) + torn → *Arattorn* realized as *Arathorn*, and *ara(n) + suil → *Arassuil*. *Arahad* and *Arahael* may indicate *n + h → hh* realized as *h*. But *n + c* would certainly produce *cc* realized as *ch*, which Tolkien sometimes transcribes as simple *h*, as in the name of Aragorn's horse *Roheryn* 'Horse-(of the)-wood', from †*roch + eryn* (see III:391 *H*).

Assuming the same pattern for the voiced stops, we would take *Arador* as a realization of **Araddor* from *ara(n) + dor*. (It cannot be from *ara(n) + tor*, for that would give **Arathor*.) The double consonant has reduced to a single one, but remains protected from lenition. *Araglas*, *Aragorn*, and *Aragost* would be realizations of **Aragglas*, **Araggorn*, **Araggost* from *ara(n) + glas*, *ara(n) + gorn*, *ara(n) + gost*.

This leaves only the forms *Araval*, *Aravir*, and *Aravorn*. The second elements are best considered to have begun with initial *m*. So *(n) + m → mm*, which reduces to *m* and then lenits to *v*. The initial elements of the second elements are unlikely to be *b*, as we would expect *(n) + b → bb* realized as *b*.

Note that *n* does not always cause nasal mutation. *Palan + tiriel → palan-diriel* (with lenition of *t* to *d*), not ***palathiril*. *Len + bas → lembas* (with only partial assimilation of *n*), not ***lebas*. On the other hand, some cases where we don't find the expected lenition of a voiced stop may be because the stop represents a double voiced stops arising from nasal mutation: for example, S *pedo* 'speak!',

SINDARIN

may come from an earlier *peddo* in which the *dd* represents
(n)d. Certainly, we find *nd* in the Quenya word *Quendi*
'Speakers'. Similarly, S *Udûn* probably derives from the
root *NDU*, and so may represent an earlier *Uddûn*. Stress
may have been a major factor in determining whether nasal
mutation or lenition resulted from *n* + consonant. Pending
the revelation of such rules it seems necessary to distinguish between *n* and *(n)*.

A form of the nasal mutation occurs initially, also,
when a word is preceded by another ending in *(n)*. A plural
form of the article 'the' can be reconstructed as *i(n)* from
aerlinn in Edhil (R:62£) 'hymn of the Elves', *Ernil i Pheriannath* 'Prince (of) the Halflings' (III:41,80;R:67; see *Periannath* III:408), and *i thiw hin* 'these signs' (I:319; see *Tîw*
III:395). (For this last, an earlier version of the Moria
West-gate inscription reads *i-ndîw thin* [HC: plate 12 facing
p. 179].) The preposition *na* may well be *na(n)*, in which
case *na-chaered* will represent *naccaered* from *na(n)* + *cae-
red*. And *na vedui* 'at last' will represent *nammedui* rather
than *na* + *medui* with initial lenition of *m* to *v*.

However, this initial nasal mutation does not follow
the same pattern as internal nasal mutation in respect to
the voiced stops. We find *i(n)* *gaurhoth* realized as *i
ngaurhoth* (I:312), not ** *i-gaurhoth*. Similarly we find the
forms *di'nguruthos* (II:339) and *di-nguruthos* (R:64), apparently realizations of *di(n)* *guruthos*; we don't find **di-
guruthos*. A singular form of the article 'the' is *e(n)*, as
in *Dor-en-Ernil* (M2) 'Land-(of)-the-Prince' and *Conin en
Annûn* (III:231) 'Heroes(?) (of) the West'. When preceding
an initial *d* we find *nd*, not plain *d* from *dd*, in *Taur e-
Ndaedelos* 'Forest (of) the Great Fear' (III:412), which will
represent *taur* + *e(n)* + *daedelos*. Following this pattern,
(n) + initial *b* will produce *mb*, not *b* representing *bb*.

To summarize:

(n) + *p* → *ph*
(n) + *t* → *th*
(n) + *c* → *ch/h*
(n) + *s* → *ss*
(n) + *h* → *h*
(n) + *m* → *v*
(n) + *b* → initial *mb*, medial *b*
(n) + *d* → initial *nd*, medial *d*
(n) + *g* → initial *ng*, medial *g*

No examples occur of *(n)* + *n*, *(n)* + *r*, *(n)* + *l*, *n* + *f*, or *(n)*
+ *th*, unless *Caradhras* is to be taken as from *cara(n)* + *rass*
rather than *caran* + *rass*.

SINDARIN

The nasal mutation in Sindarin is very different from
that in Welsh, where *(n)* + *p*, *(n)* + *t*, and *(n)* + *k* produce
corresponding voiceless nasals written *mh*, *nh*, and *ngh*; and
(n) + *b*, *(n)* + *d*, and *(n)* + *g* produce the corresponding
voiced nasals written *m*, *n*, and *ng*. However, in Breton an
initial change of voiceless stop to voiceless spirant is
found in some cases after a word originally ending in *n*.
But Welsh does have the change of original *pp* to *ph* or *f*
(written *ff*), of original *tt* to *th*, and original *kk* (*cc*) to
ch. And assimilation of *n* to the following consonant,
producing a doubled consonant, is a universal rule in the
Semitic languages, and not uncommon to some degree in many
others. For example, Eng. *illegal* from Lat. *illēgālis* from
in + *lēgālis*; Eng. *immature* from Lat. *immatūrus* from *in* +
maturus; Eng. *impatient* from Lat. *impatientem* from *in* + *pati-
entem*.

ON THE FORMATION OF PLURALS IN SINDARIN

by Bill Welden
(with slight revisions and additions by Jim Allan)

In Pre-Sindarin there were at least three plural markers: -*at* signifying two of something; -*(i)ath* signifying all
of something; and a more general suffix -*ī* representing more
than one of something. The two former, probably as common as
the latter, remained merely suffixes, while the latter, -*ī*,
caused the vowels in the word to which it was attached to
shift towards *i*, a form of vowel assimilation. Then the
suffix -*ī* was shortened to -*i*, and eventually vanished altogether. Thus the singular form *Adan* 'Man', from earlier
*Atan, which would pluralize as **Atanī*, changing in standard
Third Age Sindarin to *Edain* 'Men'.
This phenomenon is frequent in Germanic languages, where
it is termed UMLAUT, and in Celtic languages where it is
called VOWEL AFFECTION. In Welsh, as a method of pluralizing, this mostly derives from old -*o*- stems in British.
British **bard-o-s* became Welsh *bard* 'bard'. The nominative
plural would have been **bardī* (from earlier **bardoi*); in
Welsh the -*ī* caused the *a* of the stem to shift to *ei*, and
then was lost, hence the form *beird* 'bards'. In Modern
Welsh this method of pluralization has been extended to all
classes of stems by analogy. In English it is the plural
in *s* that has become generally established by analogy, and
plurals of vowel affection are found in only a few instances:
man/men, *woman/women*, *mouse/mice*, *louse/lice*, *tooth/teeth*,
foot/feet. In German plurals of this kind are very common,
and the change of vowel sound is indicated by marking the

vowel of the singular form with a dieresis (¨) (originally a
small superscript *e*): *Mann* 'man', pl. *Männer*; *Maus* 'mouse',
pl. *Mäuse*; *Zahn* 'tooth', pl. *Zähne*; *Fuß* 'foot', pl. *Füße*;
Koch 'cook', pl. *Köche*; *Dorf* 'village', pl. *Dörfer*; *Strunk*
'stump', pl. *Strünke*.

The position most strongly affected by the original *-i*
was, of course, the syllable immediately preceding, and the
vowel shifts in this position were most complex.

> *a → ai*:   *Adan*, pl. *Edain*; *perian(n)*, pl. *periain(n)*;
>   *aran*, pl. *erain*. In Welsh also *a* is affected to
>   *ai* in words ending in a double consonant, or which
>   earlier did so, as *dafad* 'sheep', pl. *defaid*.
>   Otherwise it becomes *ei*, as *march* 'horse', pl.
>   *meirch*. In some rare cases it becomes *y*.

> *e → i*:   *certh*, pl. *cirth*; *galen*, pl. *gelin*. In Welsh
>   *e* is affected to *y*, as *cerdd* 'song', pl. *cyrdd*.

> *o → y*:   *orod*, pl. *ered*, *eryd*; *amon*, pl. *emyn*; †*Onod*,
>   → *e*:   pl. *Enyd*, but *Ened* in *Enedwaith*; *orch*, pl.
>   *yrch*. In Early Sindarin *o* was affected to *ö*, which
>   in Third Age Quenya had sometimes become *e* and
>   sometimes vocalic *y* (*ü*). It may be of significance
>   that the shift to *e* is found only and universally
>   in place names in the extant corpus. In Welsh also
>   *o* is affected to *y*, as *esgob* 'bishop', pl. *esgyb*.

The other vowels in Sindarin are *i*, *u*, and *y/ü*. We
would expect *i* not be be affected, but to remain *i*. It does
so in Welsh. Since *y/ü* is halfway between *u* and *i*, the most
obvious shift for *u* would be to *y/ü*. Indeed, Tolkien says
of the Sindarin vocalic *y*: 'It was partly a modification of
o and *u*' (III:393). It has been shown above that the *y* vowel
arises from *o* by the pluralizing *i*-affection, and it seems
straightforward to assume that *u* also shifts to *y* in the same
circumstances. The Welsh vocalic *w*, which corresponds to S
u, shifts to *y* in the plural. The only vowel left in doubt,
then, is *y*. But, since there are no other vowels between *y*
and *i*, the only vowel to which it can shift, as with *e*, is *i*.
So:

> *i → i*
> *u → y*
> *y → i*

The diphthongs will be treated in two groups: those that
end in *i* (*ai*, *ei*, *ui*), and those which do not (*ae*, *oe*, *au/
aw*).

According to one line of reasoning the *i* on the end of
ai, *ei*, and *ui* would protect the preceding vowel from mutation. This seems to be the case with *ui*: we find *luin* is

singular in *Mindolluin*, but plural in *Ered Luin* 'Blue Mountains', and the adjectival ending -*ui* marks a singular form
in *Arvedui* 'Last-king', but a plural form in *Ered Lithui*
'Ashen Mountains'.

Medieval Wel. *ei* became *ai* in Modern Welsh in a final
syllable or in a monosyllable, save when followed by a double
consonant or an originally doubled consonant (and in a few
exceptional cases). The same rule, or one very similar, is
indicated for Sindarin by the element *teith-* 'mark', which
shows *ei* in *teithant* 'drew', but *ai* in *andaith* 'long mark'.
So, it would appear that if we can find a plural for either
of these two, we will quite probably have the plural for
both. Affection to *í* is found in *Círdan* 'Shipwright'. That
cir- can be considered a plural form can be shown by turning
the translation round: 'shipwright' means 'ship-builder',
that is, a 'builder of ships', not a 'builder of a ship'.
The singular 'ship' appears as *cair* in the place name *Cair
Andros* 'Ship (of) Longfoam'. We can construct the uncompounded form of the plural as *cîr*, with the normal specially
long vowel found in singly closed stressed monosyllables in
Sindarin. This shift can be arrived at logically also, for
since *e* shifts to *i*, then the diphthong *ei* would shift to *ii*,
which is identical to a long *i*, that is, *í* or *î*.

The question raised by this explanation is, of course,
why *ui* is unaffected by the shift? A possible explanation is
that *u* and *i* were so far apart that it required a greater
amount of effort to pronounce this diphthong, and this effort
is what kept the vowel from shifting. So here are three more
shifts:

$$ui \rightarrow ui$$
$$ei \rightarrow í$$
$$ai \rightarrow î$$

The only example of a shift that we have for the remain-
ing diphthongs is that of *ae* to *ai* in *Gwacron* contrasted to
Gwaihir 'Windlord'. Reversal of this translation gives
'Lord-(of)-winds', indicating plurality.

It would seem natural that *oe* would shift to *oi* parallel
to the shift of *ae* to *ai*. Unfortunately *oi* is not a diphthong in Sindarin. Therefore, either the *o* would shift forward to form the diphthong *ei*, or it would shift upward to
form the diphthong *ui*. Sindarin *ui* corresponds to Quenya *oi*
(Q *Oiolosse*/S *Uilos*) which lends support for this second
hypotheses. Also, in Welsh *oe* shifts to *wy*, which is the
diphthong most closely corresponding to Sindarin *ui*. So a
shift of *oe* to *ui* seems more likely than a shift to *ei*.

Au might shift to either *ai* or *ý/ŷ*. But it seems that
the final vowel would shift forward first, and *y* is not described by Tolkien as being a variant of *au*. So, if there is

a shift, that to *ai* seems the better choice. However, in Welsh neither *au* nor *aw* undergo *i*-affection, and this seems most likely for Sindarin also. (This shift and the proced-are, it must be stressed, entirely hypothetical, and are included here only to complete the list.)

So, another three shifts:

ae → *ai*:   †*gwae*, pl. †*gwai*
oe → *ui*
au → *au*

The following chart shows the shifts graphically. Long vowels are not marked, and those which are circled do not change.

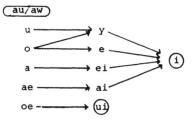

The second vowel from the end of the word is not so strongly affected. It appears to shift uniformly to *e*, except in the case of *i* which remains *i*, as in *perian*, pl. *periain*. We have no examples with *u*, nor any clear examples with diphthongs. (On *celerdain* and *Hithaiglin* see below.)

The third vowel from the end, it would seem, does not undergo any mutation. (There are only a few examples of this, and none of them are conclusive; but it seems reasonable that vowels far away from the original ending would not be affected, and they are not affected in Welsh.)

When analyzing words which may be compounds, as two or three syllable words may be, there is a danger of incorrectly allocating plurals to the components. *Celerdain* 'lamp-wrights' could be the plural of *calar-dan* or of *celeir-dan*, where *celeir-* is the plural of *calar-*. (The plural of uncompounded *calar* would, of course, be *celair*.) The formation *celeirdan* is preferable, since otherwise we have to find another explanation for *e* rather than *a* in the first syllable of *celerdain*. Also, as was argued with *Círdan*, the first element in such compounds is probably plural: a lamp-wright is a 'maker of lamps', not a 'maker of a lamp'.

The combination *aea*, as in *aear*, would pluralize as *eair* according to the guidelines given. However in Welsh *aea* pluralizes as *ey*, and if Sindarin follows a par.llel

development, then *aea* will pluralize to *ei*, so that the
plural of *aear* 'sea' will be **eir*, possibly realized as **air*,
following the regular change of *ei* to *ai* in final syllables.

Note that we have no certain evidence of *í*-affection of
long vowels. *Gwanûr* can be identified as a plural form in
the phrase *Haudh in Gwanûr* because *in* is the form of the
article used with plural nouns. (The plural form *Gwanûr* is
most likely derived from PE **wanôrí*; the corresponding singular **wanôrê* would also probably result in S *Gwanûr*, so there
would be no difference between the singular and plural. The
Quenya forms would be singular **vanôre* or **vanor*, pl.
*vanôri; cf. Q *van-, ôre*.) But the plural form *tîw* quite
probably has the singular **têw*, with the *e* of its Quenya cognate **tengwa*, though a singular **taiw* (from earlier **teiw*) is
also possible.

Examples of *í*-affection can be found in some forms outside the singular/plural pairs, for example: *aglar* 'glory',
eglerio 'glorify!' (perhaps simplified from earlier **eglei-*
rio); *aigl-* in *aiglos*, *Hithaiglin* appearing as *egl-* in *Egla-*
dil; S *-degil* (see *Findegil*) compared with Q *-dacil* (see
Hyarmendacil, Rômendacil, Umbardacil); S *-vegil* (see *Arvegil,*
Malvegil) compared with Q *-macil* (see *Calimmacil, Narmacil*).

In Welsh many nouns and adjectives pluralize by addition
of an ending rather than by vowel mutation. Various endings
are used, including *-eu, -au, -iau, -i, -ydd, -oedd, -ed,*
-ion, and *-on*.

The extant corpus of Sindarin contains a few plurals in
-in: *elin* 'stars', *Hithaiglin* 'Misty Mountains', and possibly
Cerin 'Rings(?)'. The plural form *elin* is either from the
root EL 'star' + *in*; or a normal *í*-affection plural of an
earlier singular form **elen* (cf. Q *elen* 'star') which fell
into disuse in favour of *êl*. That this second explanation is
the correct one is indicated by the group plural form *elenath*
which contains the original singular **elen*. The singular of
†*aiglin* might be something like **aigal*, or possibly **aiglen*.
In any case, the singular *aiglos* indicates that *ai* in †*aiglin*
does not arise from *í*-affection. If *cerin* in *Cerin Amroth*
does mean 'rings', it may be the plural of **côr, cor-* 'ring'.
But a singular **coren* is also possible. See also *Conin*.

An original genitive plural ending *-on*, still found regularly in Quenya, appears in some Sindarin names: *Dorthonion,*
Nanduhirion, Galathilion, Orgilion. Accordingly *-ion* has
been given as a genitive plural ending in the dictionary, and
forms found with it have been identified as genitive plurals.
But in Third Age Quenya the ending *-ion* may have lost is genitive sense, and indicate only plurality, or, alternatively,
it may have become a simple adjectival suffix. This *-ion* is

to be distinguished from -*ion* cognate with the Quenya ending
-*ion* found in Q *Anárion*.
The ending -*on* in *Caras Galadhon* 'City of Trees (?)' may
also represent a genitive plural ending.

The plural ending -*(i)ath* (originally a collective noun
suffix) is used as a group plural embracing all things of the
same name, or those associated in some special arrangement or
organization. It appears as -*ath* when pluralizing polysyllables (*periannath, ennorath, Argonath*) and long monosyllables,
that is, monosyllables containing a long vowel or ending in
an originally doubled consonant (*dúath, pinnath, sammath*).
It appears as -*iath* when pluralizing short monosyllables,
that is, those ending in a short vowel + consonant (*Doriath*).
The names *Osgiliath* 'Citadel of the Stars' and *Minhiriath*
'Regions of the Streams' are not exceptions to this rule,
since the ending -*iath* pluralizes only the second element of
each compound, not the entire word. *Osgiliath* is *os(t)* +
giliath. A form **Osgilath* would mean 'the Citadel-stars'.
Similarly, in *Argonath* the total word is pluralized so that
it translates as 'The Royal Stones'. **Argoniath* would mean
'King of the Stones'.
The effect of this ending can best be rendered in English
by the use of 'the'. But in Sindarin both the article and
the group plural ending can be used together, as in *Ernil i
Pheriannath* 'Prince of the Halflings'.

Dual endings -*ad* and -*u*/-*w* are also found. See *Orgaladhad* 'Day-(of)-Two-trees' (compared with *Orgaladh* 'Tree-
day'), and *lhaw* '(two) ears'.

Adjectives pluralize in the same way as the nouns and
agree in number with the nouns they modify. As with the
nouns, *ui* does not change, hence *Mindolluin* 'Blue-hill-
tower', and *Ered Luin* 'Blue Mountains'. The adjectival suffix -*ui* also shows no change: *Arvedui* 'Last-king', *Ered
Lithui* 'Ashen Mountains'. But in such forms it may be that
the vowel in the second-last syllable undergoes the regular
change; that is, the plural of *fanui* may be **fenui*, the
plural of †*gonui* may be **genui*.
Adjectives do not take the group plural ending. When
modifying a noun in the group plural, they take on the normal
plural form. For example, *galadhremmin ennorath*, not
*galadhremmenath ennorath (the singular would be **galadhremmen Ennor*); *Pinnath Gelin*, not *Pinnath *Galenath* (the singular would be **Pin Galen*).

Sindarin also has two gentilic endings -*(h)oth* and -*rim*,
to be translated as '-people, -folk, -men'. The use of a
plural form of the article in *i ngaurhoth* indicates that
-*(h)oth*, at least, is, or can be, plural.

THE ARTICLE

The forms taken by the definite article 'the' in Sindarin are confusingly various, and evidence from unpublished material does not seem to be in agreement with that in the published material. If Sindarin nouns varied in gender, then the form of the article may have varied in agreement. But ignoring this possibility, and taking only evidence appearing in the published material, it is possible to lay out a coherent system of rules.

The definite article appears as *e(n)* with a singular noun, save when it is the direct object of a verb, in which case the definite article appears as *i-*. The definite article appears as *i(n)* with a plural noun.

The only example of the singular accusative *i-* in the extant corpus is in the clause *Ónen i-Estel Edain* 'I gave Hope to the Dúnedain' (III:342).

Before a vowel *e(n)* and *i(n)* are realized as *en* and *in*: *Conin en Annûn* 'Heroes(?) (of) the West' (III:231); *Dor-en-Ernil* 'Land-(of)-the-Prince' (M2); *aerlinn in Edhil* 'hymn (of) the Elves' (R:62ℓ).

Before a voiceless stop nasal mutation occurs, with *e(n)* and *i(n)* realized as *e* and *i*, and the voiceless stop being replaced by the corresponding voiceless spirant: for *Periain, Cuio i Pheriain anann!* 'Live the Halflings long!' (III:231); for *Periannath, Aglar'ni Pheriannath!* (short for *Aglar an i Pheriannath!*) 'Glory to the Halflings' (III:231), and *Ernil i Pheriannath* 'Prince (of) the Halflings' (III:41,80;R:67); for *tîw, i thiw hin* 'these signs' (I:319).

Before a voiced stop *e(n)* and *i(n)* may be realized as *en* and *in*: *Haudh in Gwanûr* 'Monument (of) the Departed-spirits (?)' (III:335). But more often the *(n)* is prefixed to the following voiced stop: *Taur e-Ndaedelos* 'Forest (of) the Great-fear' (III:412); *Naur dan i ngaurhoth* 'Fire --- of the demon-folk' (I:312). That is, 'the West' would be written as *en Dûn* or *e-Ndûn*, 'the tower' would be written as *en barad* or *e-mbarad*, and 'the star' would be written as *en gil* [ɛn 'gɪl] or *e-ngil* ['ɛŋɪl] (the hyphens being optional).

Refer to page 51 for a complete discussion of the nasal mutation in Sindarin.

The definite article is often omitted in Sindarin where it would be expected in English.

SINDARIN

PRONOUNS

Here follows a listing of the few personal pronoun forms found in the published corpus:

1st Person: *-n* 'I'; *im* 'I'; *nin* 'me'; *anim* 'for me, for myself'.

2nd Person reverential: *le* 'to thee' (borrowed from Quenya; see Q *elyë, -lyë* 'thou' and R:64f).

3rd Person neuter(?): *hain* 'them'; the expected singular is **han* 'it'.

A demonstrative pronoun or pronominal adjective *hin* 'these' is found as well. The probable singular would be **hen* 'this'.

VERBS

All the verbal forms in the extant published corpus are given below:

Imperative: *cuio* 'live!', *daro* 'halt!', *edro* 'open!', *eglerio* 'praise', *lasto* '(???)!'; *minno* 'enter!', *noro* 'go(?)!, move(?)!, hurry(?)!', *pedo* 'speak!, say!', *tiro* 'look towards!, watch over!'.

Present:

s.   *penna* 'slant(s)-down, slanting fall(s)'.
s. 1st   *nallon* 'I cry'.
participle   **tiriel* 'gazing', *palan-diriel* 'gazing afar'.

Past:

s.   *echant* 'made', *teithant* 'drew'.
s. 1st   *-chebin* 'I have kept', *ónen* 'I gave'.
participle   **tíriel* '(after) having gazed', *palan-díriel* '(after) having gazed afar'.

Future:

s. 1st   *linnathon* 'I will sing, I will chant'.

The first person singular can be indicated using a first person verb form with the *-n* termination as appear in the above tabulation, or by using a standard singular verb form and the 1st person singular pronoun *im*, as in *Im Narvi hain echant* 'I Narvi made them' (I:318).

This chart does not make a distinction between past and perfect, though such quite probably existed in Sindarin.

SINDARIN

SYNTAX

Adjectives normally follow the noun they modify. The genitive or possessive is indicated by placing the genitival noun in adjectival position after the primary noun. Thus: *Ennyn Durin Aran Moria* 'Doors (of) Durin King (of) Moria' (I:322f;R:67), *Ernil i Pheriannath* 'Prince (of) the Half-lings' (III:41,80;R:67), *Fennas nogothrim* 'gateway (of) dwarf-folk' (I:320;R:67). A certain ambiguity exists in compounds. Frodo glosses the Sindarin name *Gil-galad* as 'Star-light' (I:203), but Tolkien elsewhere translates it 'Star of bright light' (R:65). Tolkien translates the name *Fanuilos* as 'bright (angelic) figure ever white (as snow)' (R:66 col. 2), but elsewhere says that Elbereth was given this name when she appeared to the Elves visiting the *palantír* of the Tower Hills in a vision 'as a majestic figure, shining white, standing upon the mountain *Oiolosse* (S. *Uilos*)' (R:66 col. 1), so it would appear that it might also be translated as 'bright (angelic) figure of (Mount) Everwhite'.

Standard word order seems to be subject + verb + object. The clause *Ónen i-Estel Edain* 'I gave Hope to the Dúnedain' (III:342) indicates that an indirect object follows the direct object, just the opposite of English practise. In English, if we wished to avoid using the word 'to', we would have to translate the clause as 'I gave the Dúnedain Hope'.

A

a [ɑ] interj. O! / Q. a/ Appears as
'O' in aII:338f. I:250;ßγδεII:338f;R:
65f. (Eng. O!, ah!)

conj. and. / Q. ar/ I:318f.

ad-, -ad [ɑd] adj. & du. indicator two.
/ Q. at-, -t/ See aduial, Orgaladhad.

adan ['ɑdɑn] n. (pl. edain ['ɛdaɪ̈n])
Man: Edain being the name given especially to the 'Fathers of Men', the
people of the Three Houses of the Elf-
friends, who came into the west of Middle-earth in the First Age, to the
shores of the Great Sea, and aided the
Edhil against the Dark Power of the
North. / Q. *Atan/ I:245;III:314,342,
406. (Sp. Adan, form taken by Heb.
'Ādām 'Man'.)

Adorn ['ɑdɒrn] nm. river ----. III:
346,350.

aduial ['adu·ɪ̈,ɑl] n. (ad + uial)
'second-twilight', that is, evening
twilight, called evendim in the Shire.
/ Q. undómë/ III:389.

aear ['a·ɛ̈ar] n. sea. / Q. ëar/ I:
250;R:63ff.

aearon ['a·ɛa,rɒn] n. great sea, ocean,
wide and sundering sea. / Q. †Eären/
I:250;R:64f. Mispelt 'aeron' R:63.

†aer [a·ɛ̈r] adj. holy. / Q. †aire/ See
aerlinn.

aerlinn ['a·ɛ̈rlɪnn] n. (aer + linn)
hymn. R:62ℓ.

aglar ['ɑglɑr] n. glory. / Q. alcar/
I:250;R:64f. (Gk. aglaia 'splendour',
aglaos 'bright'.) Cf. eglerio.

aglar'ni [,ɑg'lɑrnɪ] contracted form of
aglar an i 'glory to the'. III:231.

Aglarond [,ɑg'lɑrɒnd] nm. place (aglar +
rond) 'Glory-hall', glossed as 'Glittering Caves'. II:154,205.

ai [aɪ̈] interj. 1. hail! 2. woe!
alas! / Q. ai/ I:222,344.

†aiglin ['aɪ̈glɪn] n. pl. peaks. See
Hithaiglin. Cf. aiglos, Egladil.

aiglos ['aɪ̈glɒs] n. (aigl + los)
icicle. I:256;III:437. Cf. †aiglin,
Egladil.

alfirin ['ɑlfɪ;rɪn] n. a golden field
flower. III:151.

alph [ɑlf] n. swan. III:392. (OHG
albiz, ON elptr, OE ælfitu 'swan'.)

amarth ['ɑmɑrθ] n. doom, impending
fate. / Q. umbar/ III:317;G:183.
(Lat. amarus 'harsh, bitter'; Gk. amar-
tia 'failure, error, sin'; Wel. amar
'wound', amarch 'dishonour', amorth
'misfortune, curse'.)

Amlaith ['ɑmlaɪ̈θ] nm. pers. ----. III:
318.

ammen ['ɑmmɛn] ??? ----. I:304,312,
320.

amon ['ɑmɒn] n. (pl. emyn ['ɛmɥn]) hill,
mount. I:410,416;III:317,378;G:183.

Amroth ['ɑmrɒθ] nm. pers. (< Silvan)
----. III:405n.

amrûn ['ɑmruːn] n. (am + rhûn ???) 1.
sunrise. 2. east. / Q. rómen/ III:
394,401.

an [ɑn] prep. to. / Q. -nna, -nn'/ I:
304,312. See aglar'ni, anim, na.

an(n)- ['ɑn(n)-] adj. long. III:43,335,
393,397,400. — and- ['ɑnd-] form used
preceding r. III:393. Cf. Q. andave.

-an(n) [-ɑn(n)] n. (older -and [-ɑnd])
land. / Q. -nde/ III:393. See -n(n),
Beleriand, Rochand, Rohan(n), Cardo-
lan(n).

anann ['ɑnɑnn] adv. (an + ann ???) long.
III:231.

Anborn ['ɑnbɒrn] nm. pers. 'Tall----'
???, 'Long----' ??? II:283. Cf.
an(n)-, -born.

Ancalagon [,ɑŋ'kɑlɑ,gɒn] nm. dragon (Perhaps not normal Sindarin.) ----. I:
70. Cf. Q. anca.

and-, see an(n)-.

-and, see -an(n).

andaith ['ɑndaɪ̈θ] n. (an(n) + taith)
'long mark', an acute accent used to
indicate long vowels. III:400.

Andrast ['ɑndrɑst] nm. place 'Long----'.
MB.

Andros ['ɑndrɒs] nm. place 'Long-foam'.
III:393.

Anduin ['ɑndu·ɪ̈n] nm. river 'Long-river',
usually rendered, 'the Great River'. I:
61,355.

Anfalas ['anfa,las] nm. place 'Long-coast', rendered 'Langstrand'. III:43.

†ang [aŋ] n. iron. / Q. anga/ I:14, 206.

Angband ['aŋband] nm. place 'Iron----'. I:206.

Angbor ['aŋbɔr] nm. pers. 'Iron----'. III:151. Cf. bor(o)-, Poros.

angerthas [,aŋ'gerθas] n. (an(n) + cer-thas) long rune rows, that is, long runic alphabet. III:397.

Angmar ['aŋmar] nm. place 'Iron-home'. III:320.

angren ['aŋgrɛn] adj. (ang + ren) iron. II:76,III:197,205;G:187.

Angrenost ['aŋgrɛ,nɔst] nm. place 'Iron-fortress', rendered 'Isengard' in archaic Common Speech. II:76;G:187.

anim ['anɪm] pers. prn. 1st s. dat. (an + im ???) for me, for myself. / Q. nin/ III:342. Cf. im, -n, nin.

ann-thennath ['ann'θɛnnaθ] n. gr. pl. long----, a mode of Elvish song. I: 205.

annon ['annɔn] n. (pl. ennyn ['ɛnnɥn]) door, gate. / Q. ando/ I:314,318f, 320;II:244,R:67.

annú- [,an'nu:-] adj. west, western, of the sunset. / Q. andú-/ I:257. See annûn, dûn, Q. *NDÚ.

Annúminas [,an'nu:mɪ,nas] nm place. 'Western-tower'. I:257.

annûn ['annu:n] n. sunset, west. / Q. andúnë/ II:282;III:394,401. See annú-, dûn, Q. *NDÚ. (Wel. Annwn, an otherwordly realm, ruled by Arawn: see Araw.)

Anor, Anór- ['anɔr, a'nɔ:r-] n. Sun. / Q. †Anar, Anár-/ I:257,III:19,77, 243,388. Cf. naur.

Anórien(n) [a'nɔ:rɪ,ɛn(n)] nm. place 'Land-of-the-Sun', rendered 'Sunlend-ing' in Rohirric. III:19,77,393.

ar(a)- [ar(a)-] n. king, lord. / Q. Tar-/ III:318,330. See aran. Cf. Q. Artamir.

Arador ['ara,dɔr] nm. pers. 'King-of-the-Land'. III:318.

Araglas [a'raglas] nm. pers. 'King-leaf' ??? III:318.

Aragorn ['ara,gɔrn] nm. pers. 'King-tree' ??? III:318. See -horn, -orn.

Aragost ['ara,gɔst] nm. pers. 'King----'. III:318.

Arahad ['ara,had] nm. pers. 'King----'. III:318. Cf. Calenhad.

Arahael ['ara,ha·ĕl] nm. pers. 'Wise-king'. III:318. See †hael.

aran ['aran] n. (pl. erain ['ɛraɪn]) king, lord. I:318f;III:273;R:67. See ar(a)-, ernil, Q. asëa aranion, Aran-tar.

Aranarth ['ara,narθ] nm. pers. (aran + arth) 'King-of-the-Realm'. III:318.

Aranuir ['ara,nu·ɪr] nm. pers. 'King----'. III:318.

Araphant [a'raffant] nm. pers. (aran + pant) 'Full-king'.

Araphor [a'raffɔr] nm. pers. (aran + por) 'King----'. III:318. Cf. Poros.

Arassuil [a'rassu·ɪl] nm. pers. (aran + suil) 'King----'. III:318.

Arathorn [a'raθθɔrn] nm. pers. (aran + torn) 'King-of-the-Hill'. III:318.

Araval ['ara,val] nm. pers. 'Golden-king'. III:318. See mal-.

Aravir ['ara,vir] nm. pers. 'King-jewel'. III:318. See mîr.

Aravorn ['ara,vɔrn] nm. pers. 'Black-king'. III:318. See *morn.

Araw ['ara·ŏ] nm. pers. ----. / Q. Oromë/ III:27,319n. (Wel. Arawn, a supernatural being, ruler of Annwn [see annûn], pictured as a huntsman.)

Argeleb ['argɛ,lɛb] nm. pers. (ar(á) + celeb) 'Silver-king'. III:318.

Argonath ['argɔ,naθ] nm. place (ar(á) + gon + ath) 'The Royal Stones', the name of 'the Pillars of the Kings', two enormous sculpted figures of Isildur and Anárion on either side of the Anduin at the northern frontire of Gondor. I:409;R:67.

Argonui ['argɔ,nu·ɪ] nm. pers. (ar(á) + gonui) 'Stoney-king'. III:318.

Arnen ['arnɛn] nm. place 'Royal-water' ??? III:22,247.

Arnor ['arnɔr] nm. place (ar(á) + nor) 'Royal-land'. I:256,III:320.

†arth [arθ] n. region, realm. / Q. arda/ See Aranarth, Arthedain, Calen-ardhon. (Eng. earth.)

Arthedain ['arθɛ,daɪn] nm. place 'Realm-of-the-Edain'. III:330.

Arvedui ['ɑrvɛˌduˑĩ] nm. pers. (ar(á) + medui) 'Last-king'. III:330.

Arvegil ['ɑrvɛˌgɪl] nm. pers. (ar(á) + megil) 'King----'. III:318.

Arveleg ['ɑrvɛˌlɛg] nm. pers. (ar(á) + beleg) 'King----'. III:318.

Arvernien(n) [ˌɑr'vɛrnɪˌɛn(n)] nm. place ----. I:246.

Arwen ['ɑrwɛn] nm. pers. 'Royal----' ??? I:239. Cf. Morwen, Ivorwen.

Asfaloth ['ɑsfɑˌlɒθ] nm. horse '---- flower' ??? I:225.

-ath, -iath [-ɑθ, -ɪˌɑθ] gr. pl. indicator, embracing all things of the same name, or those associated in some particular arrangement or organization. The form -ath is used with polysyllables and long monosyllables; the form -ath is used with short monosyllables. I:257;R:66f.

athelas ['ɑθɛˌlɑs] n. (athe + las(s)) kingsfoil, a healing herb. / Q. asëa aranion/ III:141. (OE æðele 'noble, high-born'.)

athrad ['ɑθrɑd] n. ford. G:190.

aur, or- [ɑˑŏr, ɒr-] n. day, reckoned from sunset to sunset. / Q. ré/ aIII:385n;III:388f. Cf. Q. aurë. (Lat. aurora 'dawn'; Sem. 'WR 'light'.)

B

*balan ['bɑlɑn] n. (pl.ᵗbelain ['bɛlaĩn]) angelic power, one of a race of powerful spiritual beings. / Q. Vala/ III:388. (Skt. bala 'power'.)

Balchoth ['bɑlᶄɒθ]´ nm. people '---- men'. III:333f.

Balrog ['bɑlrɒg] n. a fiery demon. I:344f. (OE bealu 'harm', whence Eng. bale; wrēgan 'stir up'.) Cf. *balan, torog.

bar(a)-, -bar ['bɑr(ɑ)-, -bɑr] n. home, land. / Q. *MBAR, -mar/ See Barahir, barad, Gondobar, -mar.

barad ['bɑrɑd] n. (pl. beraid ['bɛraĩd]) tower. I:309;III:378.

Barahir ['bɑrɑˌhir] nm. pers. 'Lord-of-the-Land' ??? III:314.

baran ['bɑrɑn] adj. golden brown, yellow-brown, brown. III:416;G:179.

Baranduin [bɑ'rɑnduˑĩn] nm. river 'Golden-brown river', 'the long gold-brown

river'. III:416;G:178f.

Baranor ['bɑrɑˌnɒr] nm. pers. ----. III:33. See bar(a)-, baran, -nor.

ᵗ**bas** [bɑs] n. bread. lembas III:438.

Bel [bɛl] nm. bay ----. TB:8,36.

ᵗ**belain,** see *balan.

Belecthor [bɛ'lɛkθɒr] nm. pers. ----. Contains beleg. III:319.

beleg ['bɛlɛg] n. (len. veleg) ----. Beleg III:318. See Arveleg, Belecthor, Belegorn, Belegost.

Belegorn ['bɛlɛˌgɒrn] nm. pers. '---- tree' ??? III:319.

Belegost ['bɛlɛˌgɒst] nm. place '---- fortress' ??? III:352.

Beleriand [bɛ'lɛrɪˌɑnd] nm. place '---- land'. III:393. (Belerion, oldest known name for what is now Cornwall.)

-beleth, see *peleth.

Belfalas ['bɛlfɑˌlɑs] nm. bay '---- coast'. III:22.

Ben-adar ['bɛn'ɑdɑr] nm. pers. glossed as '(and) fatherless'. I:278.

beraid, see barad.

Beregond ['bɛrɛˌgɒnd] nm. pers. '---- stone' ??? III:33.

Beren ['bɛrɛn] nm. pers. ----. I:205.

bereth ['bɛrɛθ] n. 1. queen. / Q. ᵗtári/ 2. (original meaning) spouse. I:250;R:63f,66.

Bergil ['bɛrgɪl] nm. pers. '----star'. III:41.

Berhael, see *Perhael.

Berúthiel [bɛ'ruːθɪˌɛl] nm. pers. ----. I:325.

beth [bɛθ] ??? ----. I:320.

Bladorthin [blɑ'dɒrθɪn] nm. pers. ----. H:243. Cf. Thingol.

bor(o)-, -bor ['bɒr(ɒ)-, -bɒr] n??? adj??? steadfastness ??? steadfast ??? / Q. voron- ???/ See Angbor, Borgil, Boromir, -born.

Borgil ['bɒrgɪl] n. 'Steadfast-star' ???, the star Aldebaran. I:91.

-born [-bɒrn] n??? adj??? steadfastness ??? steadfast ??? / Q. voron-???/ See Anborn, bor(o)-, -bor.

Boromir ['bɒrɒˌmir] nm. pers. (bor(o) + Q. mír) 'Steadfast-jewel' ??? III:406.

Brandir ['brandir] nm. place ----.
I:389;G:194.

bre- [brɛ-] adj. quick (lively). II:
86;G:172. (Fr. bref 'short'.)

Bregalad ['brɛgɑ,lad] nm. pers. 'Quick
(lively) Tree', rendered 'Quickbeam' in
archaic Common Speech. Quickbeam is
another name for the rowan tree. II:
86;G:172.

†brethil ['brɛθɪl] n. (bre + íthil ???)
'quick (lively) moon' ???, birch. Fimbrethil III:423. Translated 'beech' in
III:409. But in the name Nimbrethil I:
246 the element nim- 'white' better fits
with the translation 'birch'.

*brui-, or *bruin- ['bru·ĭ-, 'bru·ĭn-]
adj. loud. I:212. (Fr. bruit
'noise', bruire 'make noise'.)

Bruinen ['bru·ĭnɛn] nm. river 'Loudwater'. I:212. Misspelt 'Buinen' in
αI:212.

C

cair [kaĭr] n. (pl. *cîr, cîr- [ki:r,
ki:r-]) ship. / Q cirya/ I:253,III:
335n. (Lat. carina 'keel'.)

*cal(a)- ['kɑl(ɑ)-] n. light. / Q.
cal(a)-/ See *calad, calan, *calar,
†calen. (Lat. calor 'heat'.)

*calad ['kɑlad] n. (len. galad) bright
light. / Q. cal(a)-/ I:203;R:65.

calan ['kɑlan] n. day(light). / Q.
aurë/ αIII:385n.

*calar ['kɑlar] n. (pl. *celair
['kɛlaĭr]) lamp. / Q. calma/ See
*celeirdan. (Lat. calor 'heat'.)

Calembel [kɑ'lɛmbɛl] nm. place (calen +
pel or bel) 'Light----' ??? III:63.

†calen ['kɑlɛn] adj??? of light ???,
bright ??? See Calembel, Calenardhon,
Calenhad, *cal(a)-, *calad, calan,
*calar.

Calenardhon ['kɑlɛ'narðon] nm. place
(calen + arth + on ???; -ardhon < PE
*ardān > Q arda ???) 'Great-bright-
region' ??? 'Bright-region' ??? II:
287.

Calenhad [kɑ'lɛnhad] nm. place 'Light-
---' ??? III:19. Cf. Arahad.

car- [kar-] adj. red. / Q. *carne/
III:353. Cf. caran.

carach ['karax] n. jaws. ' Q. anca/
III:197;G:187f. (Gk. kharakɪ s 'cut

in, notched as a saw'.)

Càradhras [kɑ'raðras] nm. place (caran
+ ras(s)) 'Red-peak', rendered 'Redhorn'. III:391.

caran ['karan] adj. red. / Q. *carne/
III:391. Cf. car-. (Gk. kermes,
whence Eng. carmine, crimson; Gael.
cear 'red'.)

caras ['karas] n. (< Silvan) city. I:
368;III:430;βγδεIII:405n. (Wel. caer
'town, fortress'.)

Carchost ['karĸost] nm. place 'Red-
tooth' ??? III:176

Cardolan(n) ['kardo,lan(n)] nm. place
(car + dol + an(n)) 'Red-hill-
country'. III:320f.

carn ['karn] n??? ----. I:157.

Carnen ['karnɛn] nm. river 'Redwater'.
III:353.

cel- ['kɛl-] adj. running. III:353.
(Lat. celer 'swift'; Gk. kelado 'roar,
murmur, esp. of water'.)

*celair, see *calar.

Celduin ['kɛlduĭn] nm. river 'Running-
river', rendered 'River Running'. III:
353.

celeb ['kɛlɛb] n. (len. geleb) silver.
/ Q. †tyelpe, telpe-/ I:296;III:391;
G:191. (Lat. chalybs 'steel'.)

Celebdil [kɛ'lɛbdɪl] nm. place (celeb +
tîl) 'Silvertine'. I:296;G:191.

Celeborn ['kɛlɛ,born] nm. pers.
'Silver-tree'. I:369.

Celebrant [kɛ'lɛbrant] nm. river
'Silver-course', rendered 'Silverlode'
in archaic Common Speech. III:430;
G:191.

Celebrían ['kɛlɛb'ri:an] nm. pers.
'Silver----'. I:391.

Celebrimbor ['kɛlɛb'rɪmbor] nm. pers.
'Silver----'. I:266,318.

Celebrindal ['kɛlɛb'rɪndal] nm. pers.
'Silver----'. III:314.

Celebrindor ['kɛlɛb'rɪndor] nm. pers.
'Silver----'. III:318.

Celepharn [kɛ'lɛffarn] nm. pers. (celeb
+ sarn) 'Silver-stone'. III:318.

*celeirdan [kɛ'leĭrdan] n. (celair +
-dan) (pl celerdain [kɛ'lerdaĭn])
lampwright. II:40,435.

celerdain, see *celeirdan.

Celos ['kɛlɒs] nm. river (cel + los(s) ???) 'Running-snow' ??? But, cf. Poros. Spelt 'Kelos' in M2.

cerin ['kɛrɪn] n. pl??? (s. could be *côr, *coren, *cêr, *ceren, etc.) circles ??? mound ??? I:364f. Cf. *côr, cor-, certh, Cerveth, Echor.

certh [kerθ] n. (pl. cirth [kirθ]) rune, that is, an angular letter sign primarily intended for carving or scratching into rock or wood. / Q. *certa/ Cf. cair, cirith, Q. cirya. III:395,397,401-04. (Gael. certh 'mark, sign'.)

certhas ['kerθas] n. rune-rows, runic alphabet. III:397,401.

Cerveth ['kɛrvɛθ] n. 'Cutting', the seventh month (July, called Afterlithe in the Shire. / Q. Cermië/ III:388.

-chaered [-'x̣a·ɛ̆red] n. remote distance, lands remote. — na-chaered ['na'x̣a·ɛ̆red] to a remote distance, to lands remote. I:250;R:63f.

-chebin [-'x̣ɛbɪn] v. past 1st s. I have kept. — ú-chebin ['uː'x̣ɛbɪn] v. past 1st s. negative I have not kept, I have kept no... III:342. (OE cēpan 'keep'.)

-chost [-x̣ɒst] n. tooth ??? III:176.

*cîr, cîr-, see cair.

Círdan ['kiːrdan] nm. pers. (cîr + -dan) 'Shipwright'. I:253;III:310,319.

Ciril ['kɪrɪl̩] nm. river ----. III:63, 151. Spelt 'Kiril' in TB:8;M2.

Cirion ['kɪrɪ,ɒn] nm. pers. ----. III: 319.

cirith ['kɪrɪθ] n. cleft, narrow passage CUT through earth or rock, pass. / Q. cirya/ II:244,342;III:430;G:181. Spelt 'Kirith' in M2. Cf. cair, certh, Q. *certa.

cirth, see certh.

conin ['kɒnɪn] n. pl. heroes ???, saviours ??? III:231.

*côr, cor- [kɒːr, kɒr-] n. ring. / Q. corma, cor-/ See Cormallen, Echor. (Hung. kör 'circle'; Lat. corona 'crown, circlet'.)

Cormallen [,kɒr'mallɛn] nm. place 'Golden-ring'. III:235.

*craban ['kraban] n. (pl. crebain ['krɛbaɪn]) a variety of crow. I:298f. (OE crawan 'to crow'; OHG hraban, ON hrafn, OE hræfn 'raven'.)

crebain, see *craban.

cuio ['ku·ɪɒ] v. imper. live! III:231. Cf. echuir.

Curunír ['koro,niːr] nm. pers. 'Man-of-Skill', 'Wizard', rendered 'Saruman' in archaic Common Speech. II:90,157; III:365. (Skt. gurúḥ 'heavy; one having much knowledge', borrowed into English as guru.)

D

*daedelos ['da·ɛ̆dɛ,lɒs] n. great fear. III:412.

daer [da·ɛ̆r] n??? adj??? ----. Lond Daer MB.

Daeron ['da·ɛ̆rɒn] nm. pers. ----. III: 397.

†dagor ['dagɒr] n. battle. See Dagorlad. Cf. †degil.

Dagorlad [da'gɒrlad] nm. place 'Battle Plain'. M2.

Damrod ['damrɒd] nm. pers. ----. II: 267. Cf. Finrod, Nogrod, Rodyn.

-dain, see -dan.

dan [dan] ??? ----. I:312.

-dan [ːdan] n. (pl. -dain [-daɪn]; unlenited forms may be tan and tain.) —maker, -wright. See Círdan, *Celairdan.

daro ['darɒ] v. imper. halt! I:356.

daur[1] [da·ɒ̆r] adj??? Used to render Frodo (< OE frōd 'wise' ???) into Sindarin. III:231.

-daur, see taur[1].

†degil ['dɛgɪl̩] n. victor. / Q. -dacil/ See Findegil. Cf. †dagor.

Denethor ['dɛnɛ,θɒr] nm. pers. ----. III:319.

Derufin ['dɛro,fɪn] nm. pers. '----hair'. III:319.

Dervorin ['dɛrvɒ,rɪn] nm. pers. ----. III:43. Cf. bor(o)-, -bor, mor-.

-dhol, see dol.

*di(n) [dɪ(n)] prep. beneath, under, overwhelmed by. / Q. nu/ See di'nguruthos, di-nguruthos.

-dil, see *tîl.

dîn [diːn] n. silence. III:19. See dínen. (Finn. tynni 'quiet'.)

dínen ['diːnɛn] *adj.* silent. III:100.

di'nguruthos, di-nguruthos [dɪ'ŋɔrɔˌθɒs] (di(n) + guruthos ???) beneath death-horror, overwhelmed by dread of death. II:339;R:63f.

Díor ['dɪɒr] *nm. pers.* ----. I:206.

-dir, see TIR.

Dírhael ['diːrhaˑɛ̃ɫ] *nm. pers.* '---- wise'. III:337.

-diriel, see *tiriel.

-díriel, see *tíriel.

dol [dɒl] *n.* (*len.* dhol [ðɒl]) head, hill, mount. I:263,296;II:194;III:22.

dor [dɒr] *n.* (*g. pl.* doriath ['dɒrɪˌaθ]) land, country. / Q. -ndóre, -ndor, nórië/ II:35;III:314. See Arador, Dor-en-Ernil, Doriath, Dorthonion, Dor-winion, Eriador, Gondor, Harondor, Mordor, Neldor, Neldoreth, -nor.

-dor, see *taur², *tor- for -dor forms not listed under dor above.

Dor-en-Ernil ['dɒˌrɛ'nɛrnɪɫ] *nm. place* 'Land-(of)-the-Prince'. M2.

Doriath ['dɒrɪˌaθ] *nm. place* (*g. pl.* of dor) 'The Lands'. III:314.

Dorthonion [ˌdɒr'θɒnɪˌɒn] *nm. place* 'Land-(of)-Pines' ??? II:72.

Dorwinion [ˌdɒr'wɪnɪˌɒn] *nm. place* 'Land----'. H:190,192. (Eng. wine.)

drú-, dru- [druː-, drɔ-] *adj.* wild ??? Used of a race of squat men who had formerly lived throughout the vales of the White Mountains, and whom the Rohirrim called Woses or Púkel-men. See Druadan, Drúadan, Drúwaith.

Druadan, Drúadan ['drɔɑˌdan, 'druːɑˌdan] *nm. place* 'Wild Man' ??? Druadan III: 104ff,431;M2. Drúadan III:254,374,407; αβIIₗ.405. Misspelt 'Drúdan' γδεIII: 405.

Drúwaith ['druːwaˑɛ̃θ] *nm. place* 'Land-(of)-Wild Men' ???, rendered 'Púkel-land' in Rohirric. MB.

*dū, du- [duːː, dɔ-] *n.* (*g. pl.* dúath ['duːaθ]) shadow. / Q. lómë, lumbulë/ — du- *adj.* overshadowed, dim. / Q. lómëa/ II:244;G:182. Cf. dúm, dúr, dur-, Nanduhirion. Dúath misspelt 'Duath' in M1,M2. (Wel. du 'black'; Egypt. Duat, the Underworld'.)

dúath, see *dū, du-.

Duhirion ['dɒhɪrɪˌɒn] *nm. place* (du + sîr+ion) dim (overshadowed) rill.

G:182.

dui- ['duˑɪ-] *adj.* (< CE DUI 'flow (in volume'.) flowing. G:179. Cf. Dui-lin, duin, Finduilas, Thranduil.

Duilin ['duˑɪlɪn] *nm. pers.* May contain either dui- 'flowing' or duil (see Thranduil) + lin(n) 'song'. III:43.

duin [duˑɪn] *n.* (< CE duinë < DUI) (large) river. III:416;G:178f.

Duinhir ['duˑɪnhir] *nm. pers.* 'River-lord'. III:43.

dūm [duːːm] *n???* *adj???* Perhaps related to *dū, du- and derived from CE *dōmē (whence Q lómë), thus having to do with shadow and darkness. I:157.

dūn, dún- [duːːn, duːn-] *n.* west. / Q. númen, andú-, andúnë/ I:245;III:401, 403. Cf. annûn, Q. *NDÛ.

Dúnadan ['duːnɑˌdan] *n.* (*pl.* Dúnedain ['duːnɛˌdaˑɪn]) 'West-man', 'Man of the West', 'Númenorean'. / Q. *tarcil/ I:13,245.

Dúnedain, see Dúnadan.

dūr, dur- [duːːr; dur-, dɔr-] *adj.* dark. I:309;III:205,412. Cf. *dū, du-, dūm. (Wel. du 'black'.)

-dur, see †tūr.

Durthang ['durθaŋ] *nm. place* 'Dark----'. III:205. Cf. Orthanc, Thangorodrim.

E

e-, see e(n), i-.

e(n)-, i- [ɛ(n), ɪ-] *art.* (with a plural noun: i(n) [ɪ(n)]) the. / Q. i/ For a discussion of the various forms of the article and its effects on the word following refer to p. 68. e- III:412. en III:231;M2. i- III:342. i I:312, 319;III:41,80,231;R:67. in III:335;R: 62ℓ. (Wel. yr, y 'the'.)

echant ['ɛx̃ant] *v. past s.* made. I: 318f.

echor ['ɛx̃x̃ɒr] *n.* (et (see Q. et) + côr) outer ring. Rammas Echor III:22, 435. Cf. ephel, ethir.

echuir ['ɛx̃x̃uˑɪr] *n.* 1. stirring. 2. the last of the six seasons in the Calendar of Imladris, lasting 54 days. / Q. coirë/ III:386. Cf. cuio.

Ecthelion [ˌɛk'θɛlɪˌɒn] *nm. pers.* ----. III:319.

edain, *see* **adan.**

edhel ['ɛðɛ̜] *n.* (*pl.* **edhil** ['ɛðɪ̜]) elf, probably applied specifically to the West-elves. / Q. Elda/ R:63ℓ;G: 191; Peredhil III:314; Edhellond MB.

edhellen [ɛ'ðɛ̜lɛn] *adj.* elven, elvish. I:320.

Edhellond [ɛ'ðɛ̜lɒnd] *nm. place* 'Elf-haven'. MB.

edhil, *see* **edhel.**

edraith ['ɛdraïθ] *n. pl???* ----. I: 394,312. Cf. edro, Q. et.

edro ['ɛdrɒ] *v. imper.* open! I:320f. Cf. edraith, Q. et.

Egalmoth [ɛ'galmɒθ] *nm. pers.* ----. III:319. Cf. Elmoth.

egladil ['ɛgla͕dɪ̜] *n.* (**aigla** + **tîl ???**) angle. I:361. Cf. †aiglin, aiglos.

eglerio [͕ɛg'lɛrɪ͕ɒ] *v. imper.* (aglar + io) give praise!, glorify! / Q. laita/ III:231.

†eithel ['eïθɛ̜] *n.* spring (of water), source. I:212;III:412;G:187.

êl, el- [e::̜, ɛl-] *n.* (*pl.* **elin** ['ɛlɪn]; *g. pl.* **elenath** ['ɛlɛ͕naθ]) star. / Q. elen, EL/ I:250;R:63ff,67.

elanor ['ɛla͕nɒr] *n.* (**êl** + **anor**) sun-star, a small star-shaped golden flower that grew on Cerin Amroth in Lothló-rien. I:365;III:306.

Elbereth ['ɛl̜bɛ͕rɛθ] *nm. pers.* 'Star-queen'. / Q. Elentári/ I:89;III:421; R:66.

elenath, *see* **êl, el-.**

elin, *see* **êl, el-.**

Elladan ['ɛl̜la͕dan] *nm. pers.* (**êl** + adan ???) 'Star-man' ??? I:239.

Elmoth ['ɛl̜mɒθ] *nm. place* 'Star----'. CSK:129. Cf. Egalmoth.

Elrohir ['ɛl̜rɒ͕χ̜ir] *nm. pers.* 'Star-horselord'. I:239.

Elrond ['ɛlrɒnd] *nm. pers.* 'Star-hall'. H:61;III:314.

Elros ['ɛl̜rɒs] *nm. pers.* 'Star-foam'. III:314f.

Elwing ['ɛl̜wɪŋ] *nm. pers.* 'Star----'. I:206.

emyn, *see* **amon.**

en, *see* **e(n), i-**

-en [-ɛn] *adj. suff.* (*pl.* **-in** [-ɪn])

-en, -ish, -y, etc. / Q. **-in/** See †cal̲e̲n̲, díne̲n̲, edhelle̲n̲, gale̲n̲, govanne̲n̲, lamme̲n̲, losse̲n̲, †malle̲n̲, †pele̲n̲, *remme̲n̲. Cf. -re̲n̲.

Enedhwaith, Enedwaith [ɛ'nɛðwaïθ, ɛ'nɛdwaïθ] *nm. place* 'Ents-land' Enedh-MB; Ened- III:370;M1. See †Onod.

Ennor ['ɛnnɒr] *n.* (*g. pl.* **ennorath** ['ɛnnɒ͕raθ]) Middle-earth; *g. pl.* the middle-lands, that is, the group of central lands making up Middle-earth. / Q. Endóre/ I:250;III:393;R:63f.

ennorath, *see* **Ennor.**

ennyn, *see* **annon.**

Enyd, *see* **†Onod.**

ephel ['ɛffɛ̜] *n.* (et (see Q. et) + pel) outer fence. III:392. Misspelt 'Ephal' γδIII:434. Cf. echor, ethir.

er(e)-̂, [er-, ɛr(ɛ)-] *adj.* lonely, lone. III:353. Cf. Erebor, Erui, Q. Eressëa, Eru.

Eradan ['ɛra͕dan] *nm. pers.* 'Lone-man' ??? III:319.

erain, *see* **aran.**

Erebor ['ɛrɛ͕bɒr] *nm. place* (er(e) + bor or por; or ereb + or) glossed as 'the Lonely Mountain'. III:353. See er(e)-, or(o)-.

ered, *see* **orod.**

Eredluin [ɛ'rɛdlu͕ïn] *nm. place* 'Blue Mountains'. R:60. Elsewhere spelt 'Ered Luin' ['ɛrɛd'lu͕ïn] III:357,363; M1.

Eregion [ɛ'rɛgɪ͕ɒn] *nm. place* 'Holly-region', rendered 'Hollin', short for 'Hollin-land' in archaic Common Speech. I:296;G:187.

Erelas ['ɛrɛ͕las] *nm. place* 'Lone-leaf' ??? III:19.

Erestor [ɛ'rɛstɒr] *nm. pers.* ----. I: 253. Cf. *tôr.

Eriador [ɛ'rɪa͕dɒr] *nm. place* '----land'. III:319.

ernil ['ɛrnɪ̜] *n.* (diminutive of aran ???) prince. III:41,80;R:67.

Erui ['ɛru͕ï] *nm. river* 'Lone'. It flows from the mountains to Anduin as a single stream with no tributaries. III:151;M2.

eryd, *see* **orod.**

eryn ['ɛrʉn] *n.* wood (forest). III: 375;MB.

Esgalduin [ˌɛsˈɡɑldu·ɪn] *nm. river '----river'. Called 'the enchanted river', which may translate the Sindarin name.* I:206.

Esgaroth [ˈɛsɡɑˌrɒθ] *nm. place Called 'Lake-town' in Common Speech, which may be a translation.* H:205;I:38;MH;M1.

estel [ˈɛstɛl̩] *n. hope.* III:338,342.

ethir [ˈɛθθir] *n. (et (see Q. et) + sîr) outflow.* III:431. *Cf.* echor, ephel.

Ethring [ˈɛθrɪŋ] *nm. place 'Ford-cold' ???* See **athrad** and **Ringló**. *The place is located where a road crosses the river Ringló.* M2.

ethuil [ˈɛθθu·ɪl̩] *n.* 1. *spring.* 2. *the first of the six seasons in the Calendar of Imladris, lasting 54 days.* / Q. tuilë/ III:386.

F

†**falas** [ˈfɑlɑs] *n. coast, strand.* / Q. falas-/ III:43,429.

†**fân, fan-** [fɑːn, fɑn-] *n.* (< CE FANA *'veil'*) 1. *cloud (floating as a veil over a blue sky or the sun or moon, or resting on hills.* / Q. fanya/ 2. *the radiant form or body in which a Balan embodied and clothed itself to present itself to physical eyes.* / Q. fana/ I:250;R:64,66. (Goth., OE *fana* 'bit of cloth, patch, banner'; Gk. *phanos* 'bright', *phanein* 'to show', whence Eng. *phantom, fantasy*, etc.)

†**fang** [fɑŋ] *n. beard.* II:67;III:409.

Fangorn, Fanghorn [ˈfɑŋɡɒrn, ˈfɑŋhɒrn] *nm. pers. 'Beard-(of)-Tree, rendered 'Treebeard' in Common Speech.* II:67; III:409.

fanui [ˈfɑnu·ɪ] *adj. cloudy.* I:296;R:66.

Fanuidhol [fɑˈnu·ɪðɒl] *nm. place (fanui + dol) 'Cloudyhead'.* I:296.

Fanuilos [fɑˈnu·ɪlɒs] *nm. pers. (fân + ui + glos(ɸ); and fân + Uilos) 'Bright-(angelic)-Figure - Ever - White (-as-Snow)', with the secondary meaning 'Bright-(angelic)-Figure - (of) - (Mount) - Everwhite'; rendered 'Snow-white' in Common Speech.* I:88,250;R:63f,66.

Felagund [ˈfɛlɑˌɡɒnd] *nm. pers.* ----. III:322n,363,406. *Cf.* **Gundabad**.

fen(n) [fɛn(n)] *n. door.* III:99,127,432.

fennas [ˈfɛnnɑs] *n. gateway.* I:320; R:67.

fim- [fɪm-] *adj. (possibly the form taken by fin- before b.) slim, slender.* III:409

Fimbrethil [ˈfɪmbrɛˌθɪl̩] *nm. pers. 'Slim-birch'.* III:423;G:175. *Translated 'slender-beech'* III:409.

fin-, -fin [fɪn] *n. hair. Possibly also adj. slim, slender. See* **fim-**. *See* **Derufin, Finarfin, Findegil, Finduilas, Fingolfin, Finrod**.

Finarfin [fɪˈnɑrfɪn] *nm. pers. 'Hair-king-hair' ??? In most recent printing of* ɛIII:406. *Spelt 'Finarphir' in earlier printings of* ɛ *and in* βγδ.

Findegil [ˈfɪndɛˌɡɪl̩] *nm pers. 'Hair-victor'.* βγδɛI:24.

Finduilas [ˌfɪnˈdu·ɪlɑs] *nm. pers. 'Slender-flowing-leafage' ??? 'Locks-(of)-flowing-leafage' ???* III:239. *See* **fin-**.

fing [fɪŋ] *n. lock of hair.* II:78;G:169.

Finglas [ˈfɪŋɡlɑs] *nm. pers. 'Lock of hair - (of) - leaf', rendered 'Leaflock'.* II:78;G:169.

Fingolfin [ˌfɪŋˈɡɒlfɪn] *nm. pers.* ----. Hd. *See* **fin-, -fin, Golasgil, Legolas, Thingol, fing**.

Finrod [ˈfɪnrɒd] *nm. pers.* ----. I:89; III:363,406,416. *See* **fin-, Damrod, Nogrod, Rodyn**.

firith [ˈfɪrɪθ] *n.* 1. *fading.* 2. *the fourth of the six seasons in the Calendar of Imladris, lasting 54 days. Also called narbeleth.* / Q. quellë/ III:386. *Cf.* Q. **Firiel**.

Fladrif [ˈflɑdrɪv] *nm. pers. (fla + drif or flad + rif ???) 'Bark-(of)-Skin', rendered 'Skinbark'.* II:78; G:169,173f.

for(o)- [fɒr(ɒ)-] *adj. north, northern.* / Q. formen/ *See* **Forlindon, Forlond, Fornost, Forochel, forod, *foron-**.

Forlindon [ˌfɒrˈlɪndɒn] *nm. place 'North-----'.* M1.

Forlond [ˈfɒrlɒnd] *nm. place 'North-haven'.* III:331;M1. *Misspelt 'Forland' on some versions of M1.*

Fornost [ˈfɒrnɒst] *nm. place (forǿn + ost) 'North-city', rendered 'Norbury' in Common Speech as derived from an older 'North-burg'.* I:18;III:273,432;

G:190.

Forochel ['fɔrɒ'x̣ɛl̦] nm. place 'North-
----'. III:321.

forod ['fɔrɒd] n. north. / Q. formen/
III:401. Cf. for(o)-, *foron-.

Forodwaith [fɒ'rɒdwaï̃θ] nm. place 'Nor
'North-land.'. III:321;M1.

***foron-** ['fɔrɒn-] adj. north, northern.
/ Q. formen/ This form is proposed to
account for Fornost on the model of
ar(a)- and aran.

fuin [fuⁱ̃n] n. night. / Q. lomë/
aIII:385n.

G

gal- [gɑl-] adj. green. See ⁺galad,
galadh, galen. Cf. Egalmoth, Galdor,
Galion.

⁺galad ['gɑlɑd] n. tree. / Q. ⁺alta,
alda, ⁺orne/ II:86;G:172. Cf. galadh.

-galad, see *calad.

galadh ['gɑlɑð] n. tree. / Q. alda,
⁺alta, ⁺orne/ I:250;III:391;R:64f.
Cf. ⁺galad.

Galadhon ['gɑlɑ͵ðɒn] nm. place (< Silvan) 'Tree----'. I:368;III:405.
Spelt 'Galadon' throughout aβγ and
this spelling retained accidently in
the Appendices and Index of δε and in
δεIII:404-05. Misspelt 'Galador' in
βIII:506n.

***galadhremmen** ['gɑlɑð'rɛmmɛn] adj. (pl.
galadhremmin ['gɑlɑð͵rɛmmɪn]) tree-
woven, tree-tangled. I:250;III:393;R:
64.

Galadhrim [gɑ'lɑðrɪm] nm. people 'Tree-
people'. I:355,368;III:423. Spelt
'Galadrim' throughout aβγ and this
spelling retained accidently in the
Appendices and Index of δε.

Galadon, see Galadhon.

Galadriel [gɑ'lɑdrɪ͵ɛl̦] nm. pers.
'Tree-woman'. / Q. *Altáriel/ I:368;
R:58.

Galadrim, see Galadhrim.

Galathilion ['gɑlɑ'θɪlɪ͵ɒn] nm. tree
(galadh + íthil + ion ???) 'Tree-(of)-
Moons' ??? Pictured as bearing cres-
cent moons. I:318f,III:250; Tree III:
440.

Galdor ['gɑldɒr] nm. pers. 'Green-lord'
??? 'Tree-lord' ??? I:253.

galen ['gɑlɛn] adj. (pl. gelin ['gɛlɪn])
green. I:411;III:43,375; Pinnath Gelin
III:435. (Gk. kalainos 'greenish-
blue'.)

galenas ['gɑlɛ͵nɑs] n. a plant named
'westmansweed' in Gondor and 'pipeweed'
or 'leaf' in the North where it was
used for smoking in pipes; probably a
variety of Nicotiana. I:17f;III:146.

Galion ['gɑlɪ͵ɒn] nm. pers. 'Green-
---' ??? H:193f.

***gaur, gor-** [gɑˑör, gɒr-] n??? adj???
demon ??? I:312. See gorgor, Gorthad.

***gaurhoth** ['gɑˑörhɒθ] nm. people demon-
folk' ??? I:312.

Gebir ['gɛbir] nm. place ----. This
might be lenited from *Cebir, which
would be related to -chebin and might
mean 'Keepers'. I:384.

-geleb, see celeb

gelin, see galen.

gil [gɪl̦] n. (pl. gen. ⁺gillon ['gɪlɪ-
͵ɒn]; giliath ['gɪlɪ͵aθ]) 1. bright
spark. 2. star. / Q. tinwe/ I:203;
III:388;R:63f,65.

Gildor ['gɪl̦dɒr] nm. pers. 'Star-lord'.
I:89.

Gil-galad ['gɪl̦'gɑlɑd] nm. pers. (gil +
calad) 'Star - (of) - Bright Light',
'Starlight'. I:203;R:65.

⁺giliath, see gil.

⁺gilion, see gil.

Gilraen ['gɪl̦rɑˑɛn] nm. pers. 'Star-
----'. III:337ff; βγδεIII:406.

Gilrain ['gɪl̦rɑïn] nm. river 'Star-
----'. III:151;TB:8;M2.

Gilthoniel [͵gɪl̦'θɒnɪ͵ɛl̦] nm. pers.
'Star-kindleɾ'. / Q. Tintallë/ I:250;
II:339;R:63f.

Girion ['gɪrɪ͵ɒn] nm. pers. ----. H:
261.

Girithron [gɪ'rɪθrɒn] n. the twelfth
month (December), called Foreyule in the
Shire. / Q. Ringarë/ III:388.

Glamdring ['glɑmdrɪŋ] nm. obj. 'Foe-
hammer'. H:62.

Glanduin ['glɑnduˑɪn] nm. river '----
river'. Called 'Swanfleet' (OE flēot
'water, sea, river') in Common Speech,
and so glan- might mean 'swan', but see
alph. III:263,319. Misspelt 'Glandin'
in some printings of M1 and wrongly
applied to the upper reaches of the

River Isen. *Absent on most versions of* Ml.

glor-, -lor [glɒr-, -lɒr] *adj.* golden (coloured), like gold. / Q. laurëa/ *See* Glorfindel, Inglorien, Mallor.

Glorfindel [‚glɒr'fɪndɛḷ] *nm. pers.* 'Golden-hair----'. I:222ff.

glos(s) [glɒs(s)] *adj.* (*augmentative* g + loss) (*len.* los(s) [lɒs(s)]) dazzling white, white (as snow). / Q. losse/ R:62,66. (MHG *glos*, Du. *gloos* 'gleaming'; Eng. *gloss*.)

Golasgil [gɒ'lɑsgɪḷ] *nm. pers.* '---- star'. III:43. *Cf.* Fingolfin, Legolas, Thingol.

gon-, -gon [gɒn] *n.* (*len.* on) stone. *See* Argonath, Gondor. Harondor. *Cf.* †gond, gond(o)-.

†gond, gond(o)- ['gɒnd, gɒnd(ɒ)-] *n???* stone ??? / Q. †ondo ???/ *See* gon-, -gon, Beregond, Gondobar, Gondolin.

Gondobar ['gɒndɒ‚bɑr] *nm. place* 'Stone-land' ??? N.

Gondolin ['gɒndɒ‚lɪn] *nm. place* 'Stone-paths' ???, 'Stone-singing' ??? H:62;I:256;III:314.

Gondor ['gɒndɒr] *nm. place* 'Stone-land', *rendered* 'Stoning-land' *in a Rohirric song in Common Speech, for Rohirric* 'Staning (land)'. III:124;G:192.

†gonui ['gɒnu·ɪ] *adj.* stoney. III:318.

gor-, *see* *gaur.

gorgor ['gɒrgɒr] *adj.* haunted. II:244.

Gorgoroth ['gɒrgɒ‚rɒθ] *nm. place* 'Demon-folk' ??? I:417.

Gorthad ['gɒrθad] *nm. place* 'Haunted----' ??? III:321.

govannen [gɒ'vannɛn] *adj.* met. I:222. *Cf.* Q. †omentië.

gul-, -gul [gɒl] *n.* sorcery. I:258. (Per. *gul* 'fraud, deception'; Eng. *gull* 'trick, deceive'.)

Guldur ['gɒldur] *n.* (gul + tur *or* dûr) 'Sorcery-lord', *rendered* 'Necromancer' *in Common Speech, or* 'Dark-sorcery'. I:263.

Gundabad ['gɒndɑ‚bad] *nm. place* ----. H:293;III:355;MH;Ml. *Cf.* Felagund.

*guruthos ['gɒrɒ‚θɒs] *n.* death-horror, dread of death. II:339;R:63f.

†gwae [gwɑ·ɛ̃] *n.* (*pl.* †gwai [gwaɪ̃])

wind. / Q. súle, *súri/ I:275;III: 388.

Gwaeron ['gwɑ·ɛrɒn] *n.* 'Windy', the third month (March), called *Rethe* in the Shire. / Q. Sulimë/ III:388.

†gwai, *see* †gwae.

Gwaihir ['gwaɪhir] *nm. pers.* 'Windslord', *rendered* 'Windlord'. I:275; III:226.

*gwain [gwaɪn] *adj.* (*len.* wain [waɪn]) new. / Q. †vinyë/ *See* Narwain.

gwanûr ['gwɑnu::r] *n. pl.* departed spirits ??? III:335. *Cf.* Q. vani-vanwa, óre.

†gwath [gwɑθ] *adj.* grey. / Q. †mista/ *See* *Gwathló.

Gwathló ['gwɑθlɒ:] *nm. river* 'Greyflood'. Ml. *Text spelling is* 'Gwathlo', *but cf.* Ringló *where the acute accent is also omitted on the maps. Cf.* Q. LO.

Gwirith ['gwɪrɪθ] *n.* the fourth month (April), called *Astron* in the Shire. / Q. Viressë/ III:388.

H

-had [-had] *n.* ----. *See* Arahad, Calenhad.

Hador ['hadɒr] *nm. pers.* ----. I:284; II:287;III:314.

†hael ['ha·ɛ̃ḷ] *adj.* wise. III:231.

hain, *see* *han.

†hal [hal] *adj???* tall ??? / Q. halla ???/ *See* Halbarad, Haldir, Hallas.

Halbarad ['halba‚rad] *nm. pers.* 'Talltower' ??? III:47ff.

Haldir ['haldir] *nm. pers.* (hal + tir) 'Tall-sight' ??? I:357ff.

Hallas ['hallas] *nm. pers.* 'Tall-leaf' ??? III:319.

*han [han] *pers. prn. 3rd neuter???* acc. *s.* (*pl.* hain [haɪn]) it (*acc.*) ???; *pl.* them. / Q. -s ???/ I:318f. *Cf.* *hen.

har(a)- [har(a)-] *adj.* south, southern'. / Q. hyarmen/ *See* harad, Harlindon, Harlond, Harnen, Harondor.

harad ['harad] *n.* south. / Q. hyarmen/ III:393,401. *Cf.* har(a)-.

Haradrim [ha'radrɪm] *nm. people* 'South-people', *rendered* 'Southrons' *in Common Speech.* III:114,121.

Haradwaith [ha'radwaïθ] nm. *place* 'South-land', *rendered* 'Sutherland' *in Common Speech.* III:325;M1.

Harlindon [‚har'lındvn] nm. *place* 'South----'. M1.

Harlond ['harlvnd] nm. *place* 'South-haven'. III:331;M1.

Harnen ['harnɛn] nm. *river* 'South-water'. III:325.

Harondor [ha'rvndvr] nm. *place* (har(á) + Gondor) 'South-Stoneland'. M1.

haudh [ha·vð] n. mound ??? monument ??? III:335. (ON *haugr* '(burial) mound, hill', *whence Eng.* -how, -howe, -hoe.)

*hen [hɛn] *dem. prn. adj.* (pl. hin [hın]) this; *pl.* these. I:318f. *Cf.* *han.

hen(n) [hɛn(n)] n. eye, (eye)sight. I: 410,416. *Cf.* henneth.

henneth ['hɛnnɛθ] n. window. II:282. *Cf.* hen(n).

Herion ['hɛrı‚vn] nm. pers. ----. III: 319. *Cf.* Q. -her.

hí [hı] ??? ----. I:320.

hin, *see* *hen.

*hîr, hir-, -hir [hi::r, hir-, -hir] n. lord. / Q. -her/ I:275;III:345. *Cf.* Barahir, Duinhir, Elrohir, Gwaihir, Hirgon, Hirluîn, †Rohir, Rohirrîm.

-hir, *see* *hîr, hir- *and* *sîr, sir-.

Hirgon ['hirgvn] nm. pers. 'Lord-stone'. III:72.

-hiriath, *see* *sîr, sir-.

Hirluin ['hirlu·ın] nm. pers. 'Lord-blue'. III:43.

hith- [hıθ-] n. mist. / Q. hísiё/ III:438

Hithaiglin [hıθ'aïglın] nm. *place* 'Mist-peaks', *rendered* 'Misty Mountains' *in Common Speech.* M1.

hithlain ['hıθlaïn] n. mist-thread, *fibre used in making Elvish ropes.* I: 387f;III:438.

Hithoel ['hıθv·ё̣] nm. *lake* 'Mist----'. I:384,410.

Hithui ['hıθu·ï] n. 'Misty', *the eleventh month (November), called Blotmath in the Shire.* / Q. Hísimё/ III:388.

hollen ['hvllɛn] adj. closed. III:99, 127.

---

†horn, -orn [hvrn, -vrn] n. (pl. *hyrn, -yrn [hyrn, -yrn]) tree. / Q. †orne, alda, †alta/ *That the unlenited form of -orn is *horn is suggested by the form* 'Fanghorn', III:409, *but* *gorn *or* *orn *are also possible; cf.* Aragorn. I:356;III:409.

-hoth, -oth [-hv̄θ, -v̄θ] n. -people, -men. R:62. *Cf.* Balchoth, *gaurhoth, Gorgoroth, Lossoth, Nargothrond, nogothrim.

hu- [hv-] adj. speaking, voiced. *See* Huorn.

Huor ['hv̄vr] nm. pers. ----. III:314.

Huorn ['hv̄vrn] n. 'Voiced-tree', *name given to Ents who have gone tree-ish but are still able to speak with other Ents.* II:70.

Húrin ['hu:rın] nm. pers. ----. I:284; III:121,406n. *Misspelt* 'Húnri' *in* βIII: 406n.

I

i, ĩ-, *see* e(n).

-ian(n) [-ı‚an(n)] n. -one ??? person.??? *See* Melian, Perian(n).

Iarwain ['yarwaïn] nm. pers. (iaur + -wain) 'Oldest', *rendered* 'Forn' *(ON forn 'ancient') by the Dwarves and* 'Orald' *(OE* oreald 'very old') by Northern Men. I:278.

-iath, *see* -ath.

iaur, iar-, ior- [ya·ŏr, yar-, yvr-] adj. old. I:278;III:136; Drúwaith Iaur MB. (Eng. yore < OE gēara 'formerly, long ago'.)

iavas ['yavas] n. 1. autumn. 2. *the third of the six seasons in the Calendar of Imladris, lasting 54 days.* / Q. yáviё/ III:386. *Cf.* Ivanneth, Q. Yavanna. (Skt. yava 'grain'.)

Idril ['ıdrı̣] nm. pers. ----. III: 314.

-iel [-ı‚ɛ̣] adj. suff. -ing, -like. *See* Lothíriel, míriel, -thoniel, *tiriel, *tíriel.

-ien [-ı‚ɛn] suff. ----. *See* Inglórien, Lúthien.

-ien(n) [-ı‚ɛn(n)] n. (-ie (see Q. -iё) + -n(n)) land of, land connected with. *See* Anórien(n), Arvernien(n), Ithilien(n), Lórien(n), Lothlórien(n).

im [ım] pers. prn. 1st s. I. / Q. -n,

†-nye/   I:318f.   *Cf.* -n and anim, nin.

imlad ['ɩmlad] *n.* deep valley, deep
dale, glen.   / Q. †tumbale/   II:303;
III:412,433;G:156,190.

Imladris [,ɩm'ladrɩs] *nm.* *place* (imlad +
-ris(t)) 'Deep Valley (of the) Cleft',
rendered 'Rivendell' *in Common Speech.*
I:259;III:412,433;G:156,190.

Imloth ['ɩmlɒθ] *nm.* *place* ----.   III:
142,244.   *Cf.* imlad, loth-, -loth.

in,   *see* e(n), i-.

Inglorien [,ɩŋ'glɒrɩ,ɛn] *nm.* *pers.*
'---gold---'.   I:89.

-ion [-ɩ,ɒn] *suff.* *from at least two
different sources. On some names it
appears to be,derived from a genitive
plural, and may still have this meaning, and is in this book accordingly
identified as GEN. PL. On some names
it must have a singular meaning, and
is possibly cognate with* -ion *in Q.*
Anárion. *See* Cirion, Dorthonion, Dor-
winion, Duhirion, Ecthelion, Eregion,
Galathilion, Galion, †gilion, Girion,
Herion, Nanduhirion, Orgilion, †tasa-
rion, †thonion.

Ioreth ['yɒrɛθ] *nm.* *pers.* 'Old----'.
III:136. *See* iaur, iar-, ior.

Iorlas ['yɒrlas] *nm.* *pers.* 'Old-leaf'
??? III:42. *See* iaur, iar-, ior-.

Ithil ['ɩθɩl] *n.* Moon. / Q. Isil/
III:392.

ithildin [ɩ'θɩ̣ldɩn] *n.* (ithil + tîn)
'moon-star', *rendered* 'starmoon'; *a
substance made by the Elves from* mithril. *It reflected only starlight and
moonlight, and that only when touched
by one who spoke the proper words.* I:
318,331.

Ithilien(n) [ɩ'θɩlɩ,ɛn(n)] *nm.* *place*
'Land-of-the-Moon'. II:258;III:393.

Ivanneth [ɩ'vannɛθ] *n.* 'Fruit-giving'
???, *the ninth month (September),
called* Halimath *in the Shire.* / Q.
Yavannië/ III:388. *Cf.* iavas, Q.
Yavanna.

Ivorwen [ɩ'vɒrwɛn] *nm.* *pers.* ----.
III:338. *Cf.* Arwen, Morwen.

K

Kelos,   *see* Celos.

Kiril,   *see* Ciril.

Kirith,   *see* cirith.

L

-lad [-lad] *n.* plain. II:244; *Dagorlad* M1,M2; *Lithlad* II:244. *Cf.* imlad.
(ON *làð* 'landed possession'; Dan. *fæl-
led* 'village common'.)

laer [la·ɛr] *n.* 1. summer. 2. the
second of the six seasons in the Calendar of Imladris, lasting 72 days.
/ Q. lairë/ III:386.

-lain [-laɩn] *n.* thread. *hithlain*
III:438. (Gk. *linon* 'flaxen cord';
Ger. *lein,* Eng. *line.)*

*lam(m) [lam(m)] *n.* tongue ??? / Q.
lambe ???/ *See* lammen.

Lamedon ['lamɛ,dɒn] *nm.* *place* ----.
III:43. *Cf.* Lindon.

lammen ['lammɛn] *adj???* spoken ???
I:320. *See* *lam(m).

Landroval ['landrɒ,val] *nm.* *pers.*
----. III:226.

las(s) [las(s)] *n.* leaf. / Q. lasse/
III:375;G:169. (Goth. *laufs,* Russ.
list 'leaf'.)

lasgalen ['lasga,lɛn] *n???* *adj???*
(las(s) + galen) green leaf, green
leafage; *or* green-leaved, of green
leaves. III:375.

lasto ['lastɒ] *v.* *imper.* Perhaps a
synonym of edro 'open'. I:320.

le [lɛ] *pers. prn. s. 2nd dat.* reverential (< Q.) to thee. (I:250;R:63-
65) *Cf.* Q. elye, -lye.

Lebennin [lɛ'bennɩn] *nm.* *place* '----
waters'; *perhaps* 'Five-waters', *as
the land contained* 'five swift
streams'. III:36. (Heb. place name
Ləbānôn [Lebanon], a mountain range
in Palestine.)

lebethron [lɛ'bɛθrɒn] *n.* a tree
beloved of the woodwrights of Gondor.
II:303;III:245.

Lefnui ['lɛfnu·ɩ] *nm.* river ----.
III:347;M1,M2.

Legolas ['lɛgɒ,las] *nm.* *pers.* The
epithet 'Greenleaf' given Legolas may
be a translation of the name. III:
106. *Cf.* galen, Golasgil, las(s),
Thingol.

lembas ['lɛmbas] *n.* (len + bas) 'waybread', *a sweet-tasting extremely
concentrated food in the form of very
thin meal cakes.* I:385f;III:438.

len- [lɛn-] n. (pl. lin- [lɩn-]) way.
III:151,438.

lhaw [laˑɔ̃] n. du. ears, hearing. I:
410.

Lhûn [l̩uːn] nm. river ----. Rendered
in Common Speech (=Anglicized) as
'Lune'. III:412;M1. (Eng. river name
Lune, of a river in Lancashire and a
river in the North Riding of Yorkshire;
of unknown meaning.)

lim [lɩm] adv. forward, onward ???
faster ??? I:225.

lin(n)- [lɩn(n)-] stem having to do
with song. / Q. †lind(e)/ I:250;III:
342;R:63f.

Lindir ['lɩndir] nm. pers. (lin(ǹ) +
tîr ???) 'Song-sight' ??? I:249.

Lindon ['lɩndɒn] nm. place 'Song----'
??? III:319-20.

Linhir ['lɩnhir] nm. place (lin (pl. of
len-) + sîr) 'Ways-(through the)-
stream' ???, referring to the fords.
III:151.

linnathon ['lɩnna͵θɒn] v. fut. s. 1st
I will chant, sing. I:250;R:63f.

linnod ['lɩnnɒd] n. verse ??? III:
342.

lith [lɩθ] n. ash. G:178. (Gael.
liath 'grey'.)

lithui ['lɩθuˑĩ] adj. ashen, ashy, of
ash-grey hue. Ered Lithui I:431;R:66;
G:178.

Lithlad ['lɩθlad] nm. place 'Ash-
plain'. II:244.

lond [lɒnd] n. haven, harbour. III:
310; Lond Daer MB.

-ló [-lɔ:] n. flood. See *Gwathló,
Ringló.

*lór [lɒːr] n. (< Silvan) dream. II:
70;III:405n.

Lórien(n) ['lɔːrɩ͵ɛn(n)] nm. place (lór
+ ien(n)) 'Dream-land'. I:239,352;II:
70;III:405n.

-los, see glos(s).

loss [lɒss] n. snow. / Q. losse/ R:
62f. Cf. glos(s).

Lossarnach [͵lɒs'sarnax] nm. place (loss
+ Arnach (place name of unknown origin)) 'Snow-(of)-Arnach'. III:22,407.

lossen ['lɒssɛn] adj. snowy. R:62.

Lossoth ['lɒssɒθ] nm. people (loss +
hoth) 'Snowmen'. III:321f;R:62.

loth-, -loth [lɒθ] n. flower, blossom.
/ Q. †lóte/ I:355;II:70; see Nimloth.

Lothíriel [lɒ'θiːrɩ͵ɛl] nm. pers.
'Flower-noble-woman' ???, 'Flower-
stream-woman'. ??? III:351.

Lothlórien(n) [͵laθ'lɒːrɩ͵ɛn(n)] nm.
place 'Flower-(of)-dream - land', rendered once 'the Dreamflower' (II:70),
and once 'Lórien of the Blossom' (I:
355). I:352,355;II:70;III405n.

Lothron ['lɒθrɒn] n. 'Flowery', the
fifth month, May called Thrimidge in
the Shire. / Q. Lótesse/ III:388.

luin [luˑĩn] adj. blue. / Q. *luine/
Mindolluin II:206; Ered Luin M2.

Lúthien ['luːθɩ͵ɛn] nm. pers. ----.
May be related to S. loth-, Q. †lóte
'flower, blossom'. I:205f.

lyg [lɩg] n. snake. / Q. leuca/ III:
393. α has 'lŷg'. (Eng. lug, a large
marine worm found in sea sand.)

M

Mablung ['mablɒŋ] nm. pers. ----. II:
267-70.

mae [maˑɛ̌] adv. well. I:222. Cf. Q.
Maia.

*magor ['magɒr] n. (len. vagor ['vagɒr])
swordsman. / Q. †macar/ Menelvagor
III:391. Cf. *megil.

mal- [mal-] adj. (len. val [val]))
golden. / Q. †malin/ See Araval, mallorn. (Wel. mâl 'gold'.)

Malbeth ['malbɛθ] nm. pers. 'Golden-
---'. III:54.

†mallen ['mallɛn] adj. golden. / Q.
†malin/ III:235.

Mallor ['mallɒr] nm. pers. 'Golden-
gold' ??? III:318. Cf. glor-, -lor.

mallorn ['mallɒrn] n. (mal + horn) (pl.
mellyrn ['mɛllyrn]) 'golden-tree', a
kind of tree found only in Lothlórien,
characterized by smooth, silver-grey
bark, yellow blossoms, and leaves which
turn gold in autumn, but do not fall
until spring comes. / Q. *malinorne,
ornemalin/ I:349,356ff.

mallos ['mallɒs] n. 'golden-snow' ???,
a yellow flower. III:151.

Malvegil ['malvɛ͵gɩl] nm. pers. (mal +
megil) 'Golden----'. III:318.

-mar [-mar] n. home, dwelling. / Q.
-mar/ I:14,157. Cf. bar(a)-, -bar.

*medui ['mɛduˑɪ̆] adj. (len. vedui
[vɛduˑɪ̆]) last. Cf. mᵊthed, Q. metta.
— na vedui ['na'vɛduˑɪ̆] adv. at last.
I:222;III:330.

†megil ['mɛgɪ̆l] n. (len. vegil [vɛgɪ̆l])
----. / Q. †macil/ See Arvegil, Malvegil.

Melian ['mɛlɪ̆,an] nm. pers. ----. III:
314.

mellon ['mɛl̹lɒn] n. friend. / Q.
†melda ???/ I:3184.,321f. (Skt. mela
'meeting, intercourse'.)

mellyrn, see mallorn.

Melui ['mɛluˑɪ̆] nm. place ----. III:
142.

men- [mɛn-] n. (pl. min- [mɪ̆n-])
region, direction. / Q. †men/ See
menel, Minhiriath.

menel ['mɛnɛl̹] n. (< Q.) (high) heaven,
the sky, the heavens. / Q. menel/ I:
250;R:63f.

Meneldor [mɛ,nɛl̹dɒr] nm. pers. (menel +
tôr) 'Sky-lord'. III:228f.

Menelvagor [mɛ'nɛl̹va,gor] nm. pers.
'Heaven-swordsman', rendered 'Swordsman
of the Sky'. Refers to the constellation Orion. / Q. Menelmacar/ III:91.

†mereth ['mɛrɛθ] n. feasting. III:253.

Merethrond [mɛ'rɛθrɒnd] nm. place
'Feast-hall'. III:253.

methed- [mɛ'θɛd-] adj. last. II:32;
III:433. Cf. *medui, Q. metta.

Methedras [mɛ'θɛdrɑs] nm. place 'Last-
peak'. II:32.

min-¹ [mɪ̆n-] adj. first. See minuial,
Q. Minyatur.

min-² [mɪ̆n-] n. tower. See minas, Mindolluin, Minrimmon.

min-³, see men-.

minas ['mɪ̆nɑs] n. tower. I:257f;II:
249,312;III:243.

Mindolluin [,mɪ̆n'dɒlluˑɪ̆n] nm. place
'Tower-hill-blue'. II:206;III:23.

Minhiriath [,mɪ̆n'hɪ̆rɪ̆,aθ] nm. place
(min-³ + siriath) 'Regions-(of)-the-
streams'. III:321,370.

minno ['mɪ̆nnɒ] v. imper. enter! I:
318f. Cf. men-.

Min-Rimmon ['mɪ̆n'rɪ̆mmɒn] nm. place
(min-² + Rimmon (place name of unknown
origin)) 'Tower-(of)-Rimmon'. III:19,
78,243,407,434;M2. Spelt 'Minrimm⸳⸳'

in III:374;8M2.

minuial [mɪ̆'nuˑɪ̆al] n. (min-¹ + uial)
'first-twilight', that is, morning
twilight, called morrowdim in the
Shire. / Q. tindomÉ/ III:389.

mîr [miːr] n. (len. *vîr, -vir [viːr,
-vir]) 1. jewel. 2. (metaphorically)
star. / Q. *mîre/ I:91;III:393;R:64;
Aravir.

miriel ['miːrɪ̆,ɛl̹] adj. sparkling like
jewels, with light like jewels. I:
250;R:63f.

miruvor ['mɪ̆rɒ,vɒr] n. (< Q. miruvóre)
the cordial of Imladris. I:304.

mith- [mɪ̆θ-] adj. pale grey, hoar.
/ Q. sinda-/ I:212,374;II:278;III:
100,412;G:187.

Mitheithel [,mɪ̆'θeˑɪ̆θɛl̹] nm. river
'Pale-grey - spring', rendered 'Hoarwell' in Common Speech. I:212;G:187.

Mithlond ['mɪ̆θlɒnd] nm. place 'Grey-
haven'. II:203;III:310.

Mithrandir [,mɪ̆θ'randir] nm. pers.
'Grey-wanderer', usually rendered
'Grey Pilgrim' in Common Speech. I:
374;II:278;III:100,365;G:167.

*mithren ['mɪ̆θrɛn] adj. (pl. mithrin
['mɪ̆θrɪ̆n]) grey. / Q. sinda-/ Ered
Mithrin III:346;M1,M2.

mithrin, see *mithren.

mithril ['mɪ̆θrɪ̆l̹] n. (mith + -ril ???)
'grey-flame' ???, called truesilver or
Moria-silver in Common Speech, a metal
found only in Moria. It was ten times
as valuable as gold, and could be
beaten like copper, polished like
glass, and tempered into a state light
yet harder than steel. It resembled
silver, but never tarnished. I:331f.

mor- [mɒr-] adj. black. / Q. *morna/
II:244.

Morannon [mɒ'rannɒn] nm. place 'Black
Gate'. II:244.

Mordor ['mɒrdɒr] nm. place 'Black
Land'. III:430;G:179.

Morgai ['mɒrgaˑɪ̆] nm. place 'Black----',
III:175.

Morgoth ['mɒrgɒθ] nm. pers. 'Black-
---', perhaps 'Black Power', as Morgoth
is called in Common Speech 'the Dark
Power'. III:371,426.

morgul ['mɒrgɒl̹] n. (mor + gul) black
magic, sorcery. I:258.

Morgulduin [‚mɒr'gɔldu·ĩn] nm. river
'Black-magic-river'. II:306;III:85.

Moria ['mɒrɪ‚a] nm. place 'Black-pit',
'Black-chasm'. I:296,309;III:415.

*morn [mɒrn] adj??? (len. vorn [vɒrn])
black ??? / Q. morna ???/ See Aravorn; Eryn Vorn MB.

Morthond ['mɒrθɒnd] nm. place 'Blackroot'. III:43,62,393;G:179.

Morwen ['mɒrwɛn] nm. pers. 'Black----'.
III:350f. Cf. Arwen, Ivorwen.

muil [mu·ɪ̯l] adj. bleak ??? I:390.

N

-n [-n] pers. prn. 1st s. I. / Q. -n,
-nye/ See -chebin, nallon, onen. Cf.
im, nin, anim.

-n(n) [-n(n)] n. (archaic -nd [-nd])
land. / Q. -nde/ III:393.

na [na] prep. to, of, at. / Q. -nna/
I:222,250;III:72;R:63f. Cf. an.

na-chaered [‚na'ǩa·ɛ̃rɛd] adv. to-remote
distance, to lands remote. I:222,250;
III:72;R:63f.

naith [naɪ̯θ] n. 'gore', 'tongue', that
is, anything of roughly triangular
shape. / Q. laMbe ???/ I:361;III:434.

nallon [nallɒn] v. pres. 1st s. I cry.
III:339;R:64. Misspelt 'nallan' in α.

nan [nan] n. vale, dale, valley. / Q.
†nan/ I:296;II:90,157;III:434;G:182.
(Gallic nanto, Wel. nant 'valley'.)

Nanduhirion ['nandɵ'hɪrɪ‚ɒn] nm. place
(nan + du + sirion) 'Valley-(of)-dim
(= overshadowed)-rills', rendered 'Dimrill Dale' in Common Speech. I:296;G:
182.

Nan-tasarion ['nanta'sarɪ‚ɒn] nm. place
'Vale-(of)-willows'. II:72;III:434.

nar-, see naur.

narbeleth ['narbɛ‚lɛθ] n. (naur +
peleth) 1. sun-waning. 2. the fourth
of the six seasons in the Calendar of
Imladris, lasting 54 days. Also called
firith. / Q. lasse-lanta/ III:386.

Narbeleth ['narbɛ‚lɛθ] n. (naur +
peleth) 'Sun-waning', the tenth month
(October), called Winterfilth in the
Shire. / Q. Narquelië/ III:388.

Narchost ['narǩɒst] nm. place 'Fire-
tooth' ??? III:176. Cf. Carchost,
†os(t).

Nardol ['nardɒl] nm. place 'Fire-hill'.
III:19,78,108.

Nargothrond [‚nar'gɵɛrɒnd] nm. place
'Hall of Fiery Power' or 'Hall of Sun
Power' ??? I:330,372;III:322,393,406.
Cf. naur, Morgoth, -hoth, -oth, Agla-
rond, Elrond, merethrond.

Narwain ['narwaɪ̯n] n. (naur + gwain)
'New-sun', the first month (January),
called Afteryule in the Shire. / Q.
Narviny-/ III:388

†naug, nog- [na·ŏg, nɒg-] n. dwarf.
III:415,352. (Skt. naga 'mountain',
ON norg 'dwarf'.)

Naugrim ['na·ŏgrɪm] nm. people 'Dwarf-
folk'. III:415. Cf. nogothrim.

naur, nar-, nŏr- [na·ŏr, nar-, nɒ:r-]
n. 1. fire. 2. sun. / Q. NÁR, fëa-/
I:304,312;III:219,386. Cf. anor,
Anŏrien(n), narbeleth, Narbeleth, Nar-
chost, Nardol, Nargothrond, Narwain,
Nŏrui. (Ar. & Per. nar 'fire'.)

-nd, see -n(n).

-Ndaedelos, form taken by *daedelos
after the article.

nef [nɛv] prep. on this side of,
(here) beyond. I:250,R:63f.

neldor ['nɛḷdɒr] n. ----. II:62.

Neldoreth ['nɛḷdɒ‚rɛθ] nm. place ----.
I:206;II:72;III:338.

nen [nɛn] n. water. I:212,410;III:353.
Cf. nîn, nín-, nin-.

Nenuial [nɛ'nu·ɪal] nm. lake 'Water-
(of)-Twilight', rendered 'Lake Evendim'
in Common Speech. III:331,389;G:188.

ngaurhoth, form taken by *gaurhoth
after the article.

nguruthos, form taken by *guruthos
after *di(n).

nim- [nɪm-] adj. white. See Nimbrethil, Nimloth, Nimrais, Nimrodel.

Nimbrethil ['nɪmbrɛ‚θɪ̯l] nm. place
'White-birch'. I:246.

Nimloth ['nɪmlɒθ] nm. tree 'White-
flower'. III:250,317,388.

Nimrais ['nɪmraɪ̯s] nm. place 'White-
peaks'. I:271;II:293;III:23.

Nimrodel ['nɪmrɒ‚dɛḷ] nm. river 'White-
---'. I:353-7.

nin [nɪn] pers. prn. 1st s. acc. me.
II:339;R:64. Cf. -n, im, anim, Q. -n,
nin.

nîn, nîn-, nin- [niːːn, niːn-, nɪn-]
adj. wet. I:389;G:195. See Nindalf,
Nínui, nen.

Nindalf ['nɪndalv] nm. place (nîn +
talf) 'Wet - flat field', rendered
'Wetwang' in archaic Common Speech.
I:389;III:391;G:195.

Nínui ['niːnuˑɪ̆] n. 'Wet', the second
month (February), called Solmath in the
Shire. / Q. Nénimë/ III:388.

niphredil ['nɪffrɛˌdɪl] n. (nim + pre-
dil ???) a white to pale green flower
which grew on Cerin Amroth in Lothlórien. I:365.

nogothrim [nɒ'gʊΘrɪm] nm. people (naug +
Moth + rim) 'dwarf-men-folk', rendered
'dwarf-folk'. I:320;R:67. Cf. Naugrim.

Nogrod ['nɒgrɒd] nm. place (naug + ørod
???) 'Dwarf-mountain' ??? III:352.
Cf. Damrod, Finrod, Rodyn.

-nor [-nɒr] n. land, country. / Q.
-nóre, -nor, ᵗnórië, -ndóre, -ndor/
See Arnor, Ennor, ennorath. Cf. dor.

noro ['nɒrɒ] v. imper. go! ??? move!
??? hurry! ??? I:225.

Nórui ['nɒːruˑɪ̆] n. 'Sunny', the sixth
month (June), called Forelithe in the
Shire. / Q. Nárië/
LII:388.

Nurn [nurn] nm. place ----. M1,M2.

Núrnen ['nuːrnɛn] nm. lake '----water'.
II:244;III:202,247. Spelt 'Nûrnen' in
αII:244. Spelt 'Nurnen' in M1,M2.

O

o [ɒ] prep. from, of. / Q. -o/ I:250;
R:63f. (Wel. o 'of, from'.)

-on [ɒn] adj. great. / Q. -en/ R:
64f.

ónen ['ɒːnɛn] v. past 1st s. I gave.
III:342. Βγδε read 'Onen' for 'ónen';
apparently the acute accent was missed
from the capital letter. Cf. Q. anna;
also Úrui, Q. Úrimë.

ᵗOnod ['ɒnɒd] n. (pl. Enyd ['ɛnɥd]) Ent.
III:408. (OE ent 'giant'.)

Onodrim [ɒ'nɒdrɪm] nm. people Ent-
folk'. II:45,102;III:408;G:164f.

or-, see aur.

Oraearon [ɒ'raˑɛ̆aˌrɒn] n. 'Great ‘Sea -
day', the sixth day of the Númenorean

week, called Mersday in the Shire.
/ Q. Eärenya/ III:388f.

Oranor ['ɒranɒr] n. 'Sun-day', the
second day of both the Eldarin and
Númenorean weeks, called Sunday in the
Shire. / Q. Anarya/ III:388f.

Orbelain ['ɒrbɛˌlaɪ̆n] n. 'Angelic
Powers - day', the last day of both the
Eldarin and Númenorean weeks, also
called Rodyn; and called Highday in
the Shire. / Q. Valanya/ III:388f.

orch [ɒrx] n. (pl. yrch [ɥrx]) orc,
goblin. H:7,62;I:359,402;III:409;R:66;
G:171. (OE orc 'demon' < Lat. orcus
'underworld, death, Hades'.)

Orcrist ['ɒrkrɪst] nm. obj. (orch +
ris(t)) 'Goblin-cleaver'. H:62,75.

Orgaladh ['ɒrgaˌlað] n. 'Tree-day',
the fourth day of the Númenorean week,
called Trewsday in the Shire. Corresponds to Orgaladhad in the Eldarin
week. / Q. Aldëa/ III:388f.

Orgaladhad [ˌɒr'galaˌðad] n. 'Two
trees - day', the fourth day of the
Eldarin week. Corresponds to Orgaladh
in the Númenorean week. / Q. Aldúya/
III:388f.

Orgilion [ˌɒr'gɪlɪˌɒn] n. 'Stars-day',
the first day of both the Eldarin and
Númenorean weeks, called Sterday in the
Shire. / Q. Elenya/ III:388f.

Orithil ['ɒrɪˌΘɪl] n. 'Moon-day', the
third day of both the Eldarin and Númenorean weeks, called Monday in the
Shire. / Q. Isilya/ III:388f.

Ormenel ['ɒrmɛˌnɛl] n. 'Heavens-day',
the fifth day of both the Eldarin and
Númenorean weeks, called Hevensday or
Hensday in the Shire. / Q. Menelya/
III:388f.

-orn, see -horn.

*or(o)- [ɒr(ɒ)-] n. mountain, mount.
See Orthanc, orod. Cf. Q. Pelóri.

orod ['ɒrɒd] n. (pl. eryd, ered ['ɛrɥd,
'ɛred]) mountain, mount. I:271;II:
293,412;G:178. (Gk. oros 'mountain'.)

Orod-na-Thôn ['ɒrɒdˌnaˈΘɒːːn] nm. place
'Mountain of Pines' ??? II:72;III:431.

Orodreth [ɒ'rɒdrɛΘ] nm. pers. 'Moun-
tain----'. III:319.

Orodruin [ɒ'rɒdruˑɪ̆n] nm. place 'Mountain (of) red flame', rendered 'Fire-
mountain', 'Fiery Mountain', and
'Mountain of Fire' in Common Speech.

I:70f;III:175,412;G:182.

Orophin [ɒ'rɒffʉn] *nm. pers.* 'Mountain-hill' ??? I:357,360.

Orthanc ['ɒrθaŋk] *nm. place* (or(*ǿ*) + thanc *or* orth + anc) 'Mount Fang'. II:160. *Cf.* Durthang, Thangorodrim, Q. anca.

Osgiliath [‚ɒs'gʉlʉ‚aθ] *nm. place* (os(*í*) + giliath) 'Citadel/Fortress-(of)-the-Stars'. I:257;R:65.

Ossir ['ɒssir] *nm. place* 'Fortress-stream' ??? II:72.

Ossiriand [‚ɒs'sʉrʉ‚and] *nm. place* 'Fortress-stream-land' ??? II:72.

†**ost, os(t)-** [ɒst, ɒs(t)-] *n.* (forti-fied) town, fortress, citadel, city. / Q. †osto ???/ I:257;III:435;R:65;G:190. *Cf.* Fornost, Osgiliath, Ossir, Ossiriand.

-oth, *see* -hoth.

P

palan- [palan-] *adv.* (< Q.) abroad, far and wide, afar. / Q. palan-/ R:64f. (Wel. *pell* 'far'.)

palan-díriel ['palan'dʉrʉ‚ɛl] *part. pres.* (palan + tiriel) gazing afar. II:339;R:64f. *Misspelt 'palan-díriel' in* αβγ.

palan-díriel ['palan'di:rʉ‚ɛl] *part. past* (palan + tíriel) (after) having gazed afar. I:250;R:64f.

*pant [pant] *adj.* full, complete. *Cf.* Q. quant-. (Gk. *pan* 'all'.)

parth [parθ] *n.* lawn. I:411.

pedo ['pɛdɒ] *v. imper.* speak!, say! *Both transitive and intransitive.* I:318-22. *Cf.* Q. *Quende.

pel-, -pel [pɛl] *n.* fence. / Q. *pele/ *See* ephel, Pelargir, Pelennor. (OFr. *pel*, Eng. *pale* 'stake, fence, border', < Lat. *pālus* 'stake'.)

Pelargir [pɛ'largir] *nm. place* (pel + ar(*á*) + cîr ???) 'Enclosure-(of)-royal-ships' ??? III:149-52,394.

†**pelen** ['pɛlɛn] *adj.* fenced. *See* Pelennor.

Pelennor [pɛ'lɛnnɒr] *nm. place* (pelen + nor) 'Fenced-land'. III:435.

*peleth ['pɛlɛθ] *n.* (*len.* beleth ['bɛlɛθ]) waning. / Q. †quelië/ *See* narbeleth, Narbeleth.

penna ['pɛnna] *v. pres. s.* slant(s) down, fall(s) slanting *(s.).* I:250;R:63f. *Cf.* *pin(n). (Wel. *pen* 'hill, head'.)

per- [per-, pɛr-] *adj.* (*len.* ber- [ber-, bɛr-]) half. *See* *Peredhel, *Perhael, perian(n).

*Peredhel [pɛ'rɛðɛl] *n.* (*pl.* Peredhil [pɛ'rɛðʉl]) Half-elven. III:314.

*Perhael ['perhaˑɛl] *nm. pers.* (*len.* Berhael ['berhaˑɛl]) 'Half-wise'. *Used to render Westron* Banazîr *'Half-wise' into Sindarin.* Banazîr *is anglicized as* Samwise *(derived from OE* samwîs *'half-wise').* III:231,414.

periain(n), *see* perian(n).

perian(n) ['pɛrʉ‚an(n)] *n.* (*pl.* peri-ain(n) ['pɛrʉ‚aɪn(n)], *g. pl.* perian-nath ['pɛrʉ‚annaθ]) halfling. III:41, 80,135,147,160,231,244,366f,392,394, 408,426;R:67; *Hobbit* III:424; βγδɛI:24. (Per. *peri* 'fairy'.)

periannath, *see* perian(n).

pheriain, *form taken by* periain *after the article.*

pheriannath, *form taken by* periannath *after the article.*

*pin(n) [pʉn(n)] *n.* (*g. pl.* pinnath ['pʉnnaθ]) hill; *g. pl.* (joined) hills, ridge. III:43,435. (Lat. *pinna* 'point', whence Eng. *pinnacle;* Wel. *pen* 'hill, head'.)

pinnath, *see* *pin(n).

Poros ['pɒrɒs] *nm. river* ----. III:329,335,369. *Cf.* Araphor, Celos.

R

†**rais(s),** *see* †ras(s).

rammas ['rammas] *n.* great wall. III:435. (ON *ramr* 'strong'.)

†**randir** ['randir] *n.* wanderer, pilgrim. I:374;II:278;III:100. *Cf.* †rant.

†**rant** [rant] *n.* course, water-channel. III:430;G:191. *Cf.* †randir. (Eng. *rand* 'a strip'; ON *rand* 'border'.)

†**ras(s)** [ras(s)] *n.* (*pl.* †rais(s) [raɪs(s)], *du.* *raw, rau- [raˑŏ] ???) peak. III:391,433; *see* Caradhras, Methedras, Nimrais, Rauros. (Ar. *raas* 'head'.)

rath [raθ] *n.* street. III:40,100. (Scot. *rat* 'scratch, rut, track'.)

Rauros ['raˑörɒs] nm. place (raw + -ros ???) 'Twin-peaks-(of)-foam' ??? I: 389,410.

*raw, see †ras(s).

rem(m) [rɛm(m)] n. mesh. / Q. rembe/ III:393.

*remmen ['rɛmmɛn] adj. (pl. †remmin ['rɛmmɪn]) tangled, woven. I:250; III:393;R:63f.

Remmirath ['rɛmmɪˌraθ] n. g. pl. (rem(m) + mîr + ath) 'The Netted Stars'. Refers to the star cluster of the Pleiades. I:91;III:393.

-ren [-rɛn] adj. suff. (pl. -rin [-rɪn]) -ing, ish, etc. See angren, *mithren, silivren.

rhîw [ʒiːw] n. 1. winter. 2. the fifth of the six seasons in the Calendar of Imladris, lasting 72 days. / Q. hrívë/ III:386. (Wel. rhew 'ice'; Gk. rhigos 'frost, cold'.)

Rhosgobel [ˈʒɒsgɒˌbɛl] nm. place May contain len. -pel or bel as in Bel, Belfalas. Initial Rhos- may be unlenited ros 'foam'. I:269,287.

Rhovanion [ʒɒ'vanɪˌɒn] nm. place ----. III:328f;G:196;M1.

rhu- [ʒɒ-] adj. east, eastern. / Q. rómen/ III:320. Cf. Q. *RÓ.

rhûn [ʒuːn] n. east. / Q. rómen/ III:401.

Rhudaur ['ʒɒdaˑör] nm. place (rhu + taur[2]) 'East-forest'. III:320f,3ö6.

-riel [-rɪˌɛl] n. woman, female ??? / Q. -riel/ See Galadriel.

-ril [-rɪl] n. (<Q. -ril ???) (white) flame ??? / Q. †sil, -ril ???/ See mithril. (Gael. reul 'star'.)

-rim [-rɪm] n. folk, people. I:320, 335ff. See Galadhrim, Naugrim, nogothrim, Onodrim, Rohirrîm, Thangorodrim.

-rin, see -ren.

†ring [rɪŋ] adj. cold ??? / Q. †ringa/ See Ringló, Q. Ringarë.

Ringló ['rɪŋglɒː] nm. river 'Cold-flood' ??? III:43,151,374;TB:8n. Misspelt 'Ringlo' in M1,M2,MB. Cf. Gwath-*Gwathló, Q. LO.

-ris(t) [-rɪs(t)] n. cleaving, cleft, cleaving. See Imladris, Orcrist.

ro- [rɒ-] adj. high. / Q. *TÁR/ See or(o)-, Rodyn, Q. *RÓ.

roch-, roh- [rɒx̌-] n. horse. III:345,

391,393. (Skt. roha 'mounting, riding'; rokha 'rider'.)

Rochand, see Rohan(n).

Rochann, see Rohan(n).

Rodyn ['rɒdɥn] n. 'High----' ???, the last day of both the Eldarin and Númenorian weeks, called Highday in the Shire. Also called Orbelain. / Q. Tárion/ III:388f. Cf. Damrod, Finrod, Nogrod, ro-.

roh-, see roch-.

Rohan(n) ['rɒx̌an(n)] nm. place (roch + an(n); full spelling Rochann, archaic Rochand) 'Horse-land'. III:393.

Roheryn ['rɒx̌ɛˌrɥn] nm. horse (roch + eryn) 'Horse-(of)-the-wood. III:51, 55.

†rohir ['rɒx̌ir] n. (roch + hîr) horse-lord. See Rohirrim.

Rohirrim [rɒ'x̌irrɪm] nm. people (roch + hîr + rim) 'Horse-lord-folk', rendered 'Horse-lords' in Common Speech. I:275;II:111;III:345,407.

-rond [-'rɒnd] n. hall. / Q. *marde/ See Aglarond, Elrond, Merethrond, Nargothrond.

-ros [-rɒs] n. foam. See Andros, Rauros. Cf. Rhosgobel.

Rúmil ['ruːmɪl] nm. pers. ----. I:257, 260f. Cf. Q. Rúmil.

S

†sam(m) [sam(m)] n. (g. pl. sammath ['sammaθ]) chamber. III:219. (Fr. chambre, Ger. Zimmer 'room'.)

sammath, see †sam(m).

sarn [sarn] n. (len. harn [harn]) stone. / Q. †sar/ I:384,401f;G:190; see Celepharn. (Finn. saari 'island'.)

Sarn-athrad ['sarn'aθrad] nm. place 'Stoney-ford', half translated as 'Sarn Ford' in Common Speech'. G:190.

Sauron ['saˑörɒn] nm. pers. ----. I: 24;II:18,80. (Gk. sauros 'lizard'; OE sār 'pain', whence Eng. sore.)

Serni or Sernui ['sɛrnɪ or 'sɛrnuˑi] nm. river (sarn + i or ui ???) 'Stoney' ??? Serni M1,M2,MB; Sernui TB:8n.

sí [siː] adv. here. / Q. sinome/ I: 250;II:339;R:63f.

silivren [sɪ'lɪvrɛn] adj. (siliv- (<Q.

Silima) + ren) (white) glittering,
with crystalline glitter. *This word
would recall the glory of the Silmarils
to Elvish minds.* I:250;R:63f,65.

*sîr, sir- [siːːr, sir- or sɪr-] n. (g.
pl. *siriath ['sɪrɪ,aθ], pl. gen.
*sirion ['sɪrɪ,ɒn]; len. *hîr, hir-,
hiriath, hirion) stream, rill. See
Duhirion, ethir, Linhir, Minhiriath,
Nanduhirion, Sirannon, Sirith. (Scot.
sire 'sewer'; Skt. sri 'to flow', sara
'brook'.)

Sirannon [sɪ'rannɒn] nm. river (sîr +
annon) 'Stream-(of)-gate', rendered
'Gatestream' in Common Speech. I:314.

Sirith ['sɪrɪθ] nm. river 'Streaming'
??? M2.

†suil [su·ɪ̯l] n??? adj??? ----. See
Arassuil.

sûl [suːːl] n. wind. / Q. *súri,
*súle/ I:197;G:195. (Hung. szel
'wind'; OHG seula 'soul, spirit'; Eng.
soul.)

T

*taith [ta·i̯θ] n. (len. daith [da·i̯θ])
mark. / Q. tehta/ See andaith. Cf.
teithant.

talan ['talan] n. wooden platform, rendered 'flet' (OE flet 'floor, ground,
hall'; whence Eng. flat in the sense of
'apartment') in Common Speech. I:357.
(West Country Eng. tallet 'loft' < Wel.
taflod, Ir. tafled 'storey'.)

talf [talv] n. (len. dalf [dalv]) flat
field. G:195.

Targon ['targɒn] n. May be related to
Q. *tarcil 'high-man, king-man' or may
contain -gon 'stone'. III:35.

Tarlang ['tarlaŋ] nm. place ----. In
Common Speech taken as a personal name
so that the ridge of Tarlang was rendered 'Tarlang's Neck'. III:62;G:193.

†tasar ['tasar] n. (gen. pl. tasarion
[ta'sarɪ,ɒn]) willow. II:72;III:434.

Tasarinan [ta'sarɪ,nan] nm. place
'Willow-vale'. II:72;III:259

taur¹ [ta·ɒr] n. (len. daur² [da·ɒr])
forest. / Q. taure/ II:72;III:412;
Rhudaur III:320. (Skt. daru 'tree';
Avestan dauru 'wood'; OIr. daur 'oak'.

*taur², *tor- [ta·ɒr, tɒr-] n. (len.
*daur³, *dor-, -dor [da·ɒr, dɒr])
lord. / Q. tar-/ See Galdor, Gildor,
Meneldor, fhorondor. Cf. *tûr, tur-.

Taur-na-neldor ['ta·ɒr,na'neḷdɒr] nm.
place 'Forest-of----'. II:72.

teithant ['tei̯θant] v. past s. drew
(s.). I:318f. Cf. *taith, echant.

Telchar ['teḷxar] nm. pers. ----. II:
115. (Gk. Telkhines, a supernatural
race of craftsmen.)

*têw [teːːw] n. (pl. tîw [tiːːw]) let-
ter, character. / Q. *tengwa/ I:
395f. (Another possible singular
reconstruction is *taiw.) (Goth.
tiuha 'I draw'; Eng. tee [originally
'mark'] < Ice. tja 'mark', note'.)

Thangorodrim ['θaŋgɒ'rɒdrɪm] nm. place
(thanc or thang + orod + rim) 'Fang
???-(of)-mountain-folk'. I:256;III:
321;III:352,363; ßγδεIII:314. Cf. Durthang, Orthanc.

Tharbad ['θarbad] nm. place ----. I:
13,287,390;III:319,370.

Thingol ['θɪŋgɒl] nm. pers. Thingol is
given the epithet 'Grey-cloak' which
may be a translation of his name.
III:314,406. Cf. Bladorthin, Fingolfin, Golasgil, Legolas.

thiw [θɪw] form taken by tîw after the
article in the Moria West-gate inscription. I:319.

thôn [θoːːn] n. (pl. gen. †thonion
['θɒnɪ,ɒn]) pine ??? II:72.

thond [θɒnd] n. root. III:43,62,393.

-thoniel [-'θɒnɪ,ɛl] n. kindler. / Q.
tintallë/ I:250;II:339;R:63f; Elbereth III:421.

†thonion,   see thôn.

†thoron ['θɒrɒn] n. eagle. III:335.

Thorondir [θɒ'rɒndir] nm. pers. (thoron
+ TIR) 'Eagle-sight'. III:319.

Thorondor [θɒ'rɒndɒr] nm. pers. (thoron
+ taur²) 'Eagle-lord'. III:226.

Thorongil ['θɒrɒŋgɪl] nm. pers. (thoron
+ gil) 'Eagle-(of)-star', rendered
'Eagle of the Star' in Common Speech.
III:335f.

*tîl [tiːːl] n. (len. *dîl, -dil [diːːl,
-dɪl] tine. / Q. †til/ See Celebdil.

*tîn [tiːːn] n. (len. *dîn, -din [diːːn,
-dɪn] star. / Q. tinwe/ See ithildin.

tinúviel [tɪ'nuːvɪ,ɛl] n. nightingale.
I:206;III:428.

TIR [tir] root looking, watching. / Q.
TIR/ R:65.

*tiriel ['tɪrɪ,ɛḷ] *part. pres.* **gazing.**
R:64f.

*tiriel ['tiːrɪ,ɛḷ] *part. past* (after)
having gazed. R:64f.

tirith ['tɪrɪθ] *n.* **guard, ward.** I:258;
TB:8;G:186.

tiro ['tɪrɒ] *v. imper.* **look towards:,
watch over!, guard!** II:339;R:64. *Misspelt 'tiro' in* αβγ.

tîw, *see* ***têw.**

tol [tɒl] *n.* **rock ???, island ???** I:
389, 410ff;II:19;G:194.

Tolbrandir, *error in* αII:237,275 *for*
'Tol Brandir'.

Tolfalas ['tɒlfɑ,las] *nm. place*
'Island-strand' ???, 'Rock-strand' ???
M1.

torech ['tɒrɛx] *n.* **lair.** II:326.

*torn [tɒrn] *n.* (pl. **tyrn** [tyrn]) **down,
in the sense of low grassy hill.** III:
321,367. *Cf.* ***taur²**, tor-, Q. tarma.
(Wel. *tor*, Gael. *torr* 'hill'.)

torog ['tɒrɒg] *n.* **troll.** III:410. *Cf.*
Balrog.

*tum(m) [tɑm(m)] *n.* **valley.** / Q ᵗ**tum-
bale/** *See* **Tumladen**, Q. **tumbale.**

Tumladen ['tɑmlɑ,dɛn] *nm. place* (**tum(m)**
+ **lad** + **en** ???) **'Valley-plainlike' ???**
III:36.

Tuor ['tɒɒr] *nm. pers.* **----.** III:314.

*tûr, tur- [tuːr, tur- *or* tɒr-] *n.* (len.
*dûr, -dur [duːr, -dur]) **lord.** / Q.
-tur/ *See* **Guldur, Turgon.** *Cf.* ***taur².**

Turgon ['turgɒn] *nm. pers.* **'Lord-(of)-
stone' ???** III:314,319,335,350.

Túrin ['tuːrɪn] *nm. pers.* **----.** I:284;
II:337;III:319,335,350;TB:8.

tyrn, *see* ***torn.**

u

ú- ['uː:-] *adv.* **not.** / Q. **ú-/** III:342.
(Eng. *un-*.)

ú-chebin, *see* **-chebin.**

Udûn ['ɒduːn] *nm. place* (**ú** + **dûn** ???)
Hell. III:436.

ui- ['u·ī-] *adv.* **ever, everlastingly.**

/ Q. **oi(o)-/** I:250;II:339;R:62-66.
(Du. *ooit* 'ever'.)

-ui [-u·ī] *adj. suff. s. & pl.* **-y,
-able,** etc. /Q. **-imë/** *See* **Erui,
fanui, ᵗgonui, Hithui, lithui, *medui,
Nínui, Nórui, Sernui, Úrui:** G:178.

uial ['u·ial] *n.* **twilight.** / Q. **tindómë, undómë/** III:389;G:188. *Cf.*
aduial, minuial, Nenuial.

Uilos ['u·īlɒs] *nm. place* **'Ever-snow-
white', rendered 'Everwhite' in Common Speech.** / Q. **Oiolosse/** R:62.

ungol ['ɒŋgɒl] *n.* **spider.** II:326;III:
13;G:181; *Cirith* **Ungol** III:430. *Cf.* Q.
ungwe.

Ungoliant [,ɒŋ'gɒlɪ,ant] *nm. pers.*
'Spider----'. II:332.

ᵗûr [uːr] *n.* **spirit ???** / Q. **óre ???/**
See **gwanûr.**

Úrui ['uːru·ī] *n.* **'Hot', the eighth
month (August), called** *Wedmath* **in the
Shire.** / Q. **Úrimë/** III:388f. *Spelt*
'Urui' in γδε.

V

-vagor, *see* ***magor.**

-val, *see* **mal-.**

vedui, -vedui, *see* ***medui.**

-vegil, *see* ***megil.**

-veleg, *see* ***beleg.**

-vir, *see* **mîr.**

vorn, -vorn, *see* ***morn.**

W

-wain¹ [-waɪn] *adv. indicating super-
lative degree* **most, -est.** *See* **lar-
wain.**

-wain², *see* ***gwain.**

-waith [-waɪθ] *n.* **land, people.** *See*
Enedhwaith, Forodwaith, Haradwaith.

Y

yrch, *see* **orch.**

-yrn, *see* **-horn, -orn.**

ENGLISH~QUENYA/SINDARIN ENTRY INDEX

BASED ON LISTS COMPILED BY NINA CARSON (QUENYA) AND ALEXANDRA TARASOVNA KICENIUK (SINDARIN).

This is mainly an index to the entries in the Quenya and Sindarin dictionaries by alphabetical listing of definitions. It has been expanded and made more useful by giving for an individual definition not only the head under which that definition is found, but also any other headings followed by a definition that means approximately or exactly the same. For example, following Tolkien the Quenya dictionary gives to *linta the definition 'swift', and the Sindarin dictionary gives to bre- the definition 'quick'. In this Index both '*linta' and 'bre-' are listed under both *swift* and *quick*.

For fine shades of meaning, plural forms, other special forms, and other detailed information on Eldarin forms the user must consult the Quenya and Sindarin dictionaries, to which this is the index, or the discussions on grammar and structure.

abide, to: Q. mar-.

abide, I will: Q. maruvan.

-able: Q. -imë; S. -ui.

abroad: Q. palan-; S. palan-.

absent friend: Q. vanimelda ???

afar: Q. palan-; S. palan-.

again: Q. en-.

ah!:   Q. ai; S. ai.

air: Q. vilya.

'Air-one':   Q. Vilya.

alas!:   Q. ai; S. ai.

Aldebaran: S. Borgil.

all: Q. ilye.

all of: Q *ilya ???

alphabet, runic: S. certhas.

alphabet, long runic: S. angerthas.

am: Q. ná.

and: Q. ar; S. a.

Angelic Power: Q. Valar; S. *Balan.

'Angelic Powers-day':   S. Orbelain.

angle: S. egladil.

April: Q. Víresse; S. Gwirith.

are (s.):   Q. ná.

as: Q. ve.

ash: S. *lith.

ashen; ashey; of ash-grey hue: S. lithui.

'Ash-plain':   S. Lithlad.

associated with: Q. -ya.

at: S. na.

at last: S. na vedui.

at once: S. lim ???

August: Q. Úrimë; S. Úrui.

autumn: Q. yávië; S. iavas.

'autumn-day':   Q. yáviérë.

'Bark-(of)-Skin':   S. Fladrif.

battle: S. †dagor.

'Battle Plain':   S. Dagorlad.

be, to: Q. *na-.

be it that: Q. nai.

beard: S. †fang.

'Beard-(of)-Tree':   S. Fangorn.

bearer: Q. *colindo.

beginning: Q. †yesta ???

'beginning-day':   Q. yestarë ???

belonging to: Q. -ië.

beneath: Q. nu; S. *di(n).

between: Q. imbe.

beyond, here: S. nef.

beyond (the borders of):   Q. pella.

birch: S. †brethil.

black: Q. †morna; S. mor-, *morn.

'Black-chasm':   S. Moria.

black deep valley: Q. tumbalemorna.

'Black-forest':   Q. Tauremorna.

'Black Gate':   S. Morannon.

black-handed: Q. morimaite ???

'Black-king':   S. Aravorn.

'Black Land':   S. Mordor.

black magic: S. morgul.

'Black-magic-river':   S. Morgulduin.

'Black-pit':   S. Moria.

'Black Power':   S. Morgoth ???

'Blackroot':   S. Morthond.

black sorcery: S. morgul.

bleak: S. muil.

'Blessed':   Q. Aman ???

blossom: Q. *lóte; S. loth-, -loth.

blue: Q. *luinë; S. luin.

'Blue Mountains':'   S. Eredluin, Ered Luin.

book: Q. parma.

both: Q. -t, te.

bow: Q. lúva.

bread: S. †bas.

bridge: Q. yanta.

bright: S. †calen ???

'Bright-(angelic)-figure - ever - white; 'Bright-(angelic)-figure - (of) - (Mount) - Everwhite':   S. Fanuilos.

bright light: S. *calad.

'bright-region, Great-':   S. Calenardhon.

bright spark: Q. tinwe; S. gil.

brown: S. baran.

by means of: Q. -nen.

century, last year of a: Q. haranyë.

chamber: S. *sam(m).

chant, I will: S. linnathon.

character (written):   Q. *tengwa; S. *têw.

'chasm, Black-':   S. Moria.

children: Q. -sén.

'Children of God':   Q. Erusén.

circle: Q. cor-.

citadel: Q. †osto ???; S. os(t)-.

-ost.

'Citadel-(of)-the-Stars':   S. Osgiliath.

city: S. caras, os(t)-, -ost.

cleaving: S. -ris(t).

cleft: Q. cirya; S. cirith, -ris(t).

'Cleft, Deep Valley (of the)':   S. Imladris.

closed: S. hollen.

cloud (white):   Q. fanya; S. fân.

cloudy: S. fanui.

'Cloudy-head':   S. Fanuidhol.

coast: Q. falas-; S. †falas.

'Coast-lord':   Q. Falastur.

cold: Q. †ringa; S. †ring ???

'Cold-flood':   S. Ringló ???

'Cold-time':   Q. Ringarë.

come, I am: Q. utúlien.

come, to: Q. túl-.

complete: S. *pant.

composed of: Q. -va.

cordial of Imladris: S. miruvor.

countable: Q. †nótimë.

counting: Q. †nót-.

course (of a river):   S. †rant.

cover(s) v. s.:   Q. untúpa.

cover, to: Q. túp-.

crow, a variety of: S. *craban.

cry, I: S. nallon.

crystal substance: Q. Silima.

crystaline glitter, with: S. silivren.

cup: Q. yulma.

'Cutting':   Q. Cermië; S. Cerveth.

dale: Q. †nan; S. nan.

dale, deep: S. imlad.

dark: S. dîr, dur-.

darkness: Q. lumbulë, mornië.

'Dark Power':   S. Morgoth ???

'Dark-sorcery':   S. Guldur ???

day (from sunset to sunset):   Q. ré; S. aur, or-.

day(light):   Q. aurë;   S. calan.

dazzling-white: S. glos(s).

death, dread of: S. *guruthos.

death, overwhelmed by dread of: S. di'nguruthos, di-nguruthos.

death-horror: S. *guruthos.

death-horror, beneath: S. di'nguruthos, di-nguruthos.

December: Q. Ringarë;   S. Girithron.

deep dale: Q. tumbale;   S. imlad.

Deep-elf: Q. Noldo ???

deep valley: Q. tumbale;   S. imlad.

deep valley, black: Q. tumbalemorna.

deep valley, forested: Q. tumbaletaurë.

'Deep Valley (of the) Cleft':   S. Imladris.

demon, fiery: S. Balrog.

demon-folk: S. *gaurhoth ???

'Demon-folk':   S. Gorgoroth ???

departed: Q. vani- ???

departed spirits: S. gwanûr ???

departing friend: Q. vanimelda ???

descend: Q. *NDÚ.

descending: Q. und(u)-.

dim: S. dim.

'Dimrill Dale':   S. Nanduhirion.

'dim (overshadowed) rills: S. Duhirion.

'dim (= overshadowed)-rills, Valley-(of)-':   S. Nanduhirion.

direction: Q. ᵗmen;   S. men-.

doer: Q. -tar.

dome: Q. *telluma.

doom: S. amarth.

double: Q. at-

'double-middle':   Q. atendëa.

down (grassy hill):   S. *torn.

down adv.:   Q. *NDÚ, und(u)-.

down-roof(s):   Q. untúpa.

draught (of beverage):   Q. *yulda.

dread of death: S. *guruthos.

dread of death, overwhelmed by: S. di'nguruthos, di-nguruthos.

dream: S. lôr.

'Dreamflower':   S. Lothlórien(n).

'Dreaming-land':   Q. Lóriende;   S. Lórien(n).

drew v. s.:   S. teithant.

dwarf: S. ᵗnaug, nog-.

dwarf-folk: S. Naugrim, nogothrim.

dwarf-man-folk: S. nogothrim.

'Dwarf-mountain':   S. Nogrod ???

dwelling: Q. -mar, *MBAR;   S. bar(a)-, -bar, -mar.

'Dwelling-of-the-Valar':   Q. Valimar. Valmar.

each: Q. *ilya ???

eagle: S. ᵗthoron.

'Eagle-lord':   S. Thorondor ???

'Eagle of the Star':   S. Thorongil.

'Eagle-sight':   S. Thorondir.

'Eagle-(of)-star':   S. Thorongil.

ears (du.):   S. lhaw.

earth: Q. -ndóre, -ndor, -nóre, -nor;   S. dor, -nor.

east: Q. rómen;   S. amrûn, rhu-, rhûn.

'East, one from':   Q. Rómello.

eastern: S. rhu-

'East-forest':   S. Rhudaur.

East-victor: Q. Rómendacil.

Elf: Q. Elda, *elen-, *Quende;   S. edhel.

elf, Deep-:   Q. Noldo ???

elf, Grey-:   Q. *Sinda.

elf, West-:   Q. Elda;   S. edhel.

'Elf-friend':   Q. Elendil.

'Elf-haven':   S. Edhellond.

'Elf-home':   Q. Eldamar.

'Elfstone':   Q. Elessar.

elven: S. edhellen.

'Elvenhome':   Q. Eldamar.

elvish: S. edhellen.

-en: Q. -in;   S. -en.

'Enclosure-(of)-royal ships':   S. Pelargir.

ending: Q. metta.

'ending-day':   Q. mettarë.

ending of the world: Q. ambar-metta.

Ent: S. †Onod.

Ent-folk: S. Onodrim.

'Ents-land':   S. Enedhwaith, Enedwaith.

-est (degree)*:*   S. -wain.

even thou: Q. elyë.

evendim: Q. undómë; S. aduial.

'Evendim, Lake':   S. Nenuial.

'Evenstar'; 'Evening-star':   Q. Undómiel.

evening twilight: Q. undómë; S. aduial.

ever: Q. oi(o)-, oialë; S. ui-.

ever, for: Q. oialë.

everlastingly: Q. oi(o)-, oialë; S. ui-.

'Ever-snow-white'; 'Everwhite':   Q. Oiolosse; S. Uilos.

exalted: Q. varda.

'Exalted, The':   Q. Varda.

'Exalted-jewel':   Q. Vardamir.

eye; eyesight: S. hen(n).

fading (season)*:*   Q. quellë; S. firith.

fall n.*:*   Q. lanta.

fall v. pl.*:*   Q. lantar.

fall, to: Q. lant-.

fall(s) slanting v. s.*:*   S. penna.

'Fang-(of)-mountain-folk':   S. Thangorodrim ???

far and wide: Q. palan-; S. palan-

far-seer: Q. palantír.

farsighted: Q. palant'ir.

farewell: Q. namárië.

faster: S. lim ???

fate: Q. umbar; S. amarth.

fatherless: S. Ben-adar.

fear, great: S. *daedelos.

'Feast-Hall':   S. Merethrond.

feasting: S. †mereth.

feather: Q. quesse.

February: Q. Nénimë; S. Nínui.

female: Q. -riel; S. -riel.

fence: Q. *pele ???; S. pel, -pel.

fence, outer: S. ephel.

fenced: S. †pelen.

'Fenced-land':   S. Pelennor.

'Fence-mountains':   Q. Pelóri ???

field, flat: S. talf.

fiery demon: S. Balrog.

'Fiery Mountain':   S. Orodruin.

fill, to: Q. quant-

find, thou wilt: Q. hiruvalyë.

find, to: Q. hir-, túv-.

find, will: v. s.*:*   Q. hiruva.

fire: Q. NÁR; S. naur, nar- nór-.

'Fire-hill':   S. Nardol.

'Fire-mountain':   S. Orodruin.

'Fire-tooth':   S. Narchost ???

firmament: Q. menel; S. menel.

first: S. min-[1].

'First-lord':   Q. Minyatur ???

'first-twilight':   S. minuial.

flame, red: Q. NÁR; S. naur, nar- nór-.

'Flame, Red and White':   Q. Narsil.

flame, white: Q. †sil; S. -ril ???

'Flame of the West':   Q. Andúril.

flet: S. talan.

flood: S. -ló.

flower: Q. *lóte; S. loth-, -loth.

'Flower-(of)-dream-land':   S. Lothlórien(n).

'Flowery':   Q. Lótesse; S. Lothron.

flowing: S. dui-.

foam: Q. fal- ???; S. -ros.

foaming wave: Q. fal- ???, falma.

'Foe-hammer':   S. Glamdring.

folk: S. -rim.

for prep.*:*   S. an.

for conj.*:*   Q. an.

for ever: Q. oialë.

for me; for myself: Q. nin;   S. anim.

ford: S. athrad.

'Ford-cold':   S. Ethring ???

'ford, Stoney-':   S. Sarn-athrad.

forest: Q. ᵗtaure;   S. taur¹.

'forest, Black':   Q. Tauremorna.

forested: Q. ᵗtaurëa.

forested deep valley: Q. tumbaletaurëa.

forestmanyshadowed: Q. taurelilómëa.

form assumed by a Vala: Q. fanya;   S. fân.

fortress: Q. osto ???;   S. ᵗost, os(t)-.

'Fortress-lord':   Q. Ostohir ???

'Fortress-stream':   S. Ossir ???

'Fortress-stream-land':   S. Ossiriand ???

'Fortress-(of)-the-Stars':   S. Osgiliath.

forward: S. lim ???

found, I have: Q. *utúvien.

found it, I have: Q. utúvienyes.

Friday: Q. Tárion, Valanya;   S. Orbelain, Rodyn.

friend: Q. ᵗmelda ???, -ndil, -nil;   S. mellon.

friend, absent; friend, departing: Q. vanimelda ???

'Friend of Aman':   Q. Amandil.

from: Q. -llo, -o;   S. o.

'Fruit-gift':   Q. Yavanna ???

'Fruit-giving':   Q. Yavannië ???;   S. Ivanneth ???

full: S. *pant.

'Full-king':   S. Araphant.

gate: Q. ando;   S. annon.

'Gatestream':   S. Sirannon.

gateway: S. fennas.

gave, I: S. ónen.

gazed, (after) having: S. *tíriel.

gazed afar, (after) having: S. palandíriel.

gazing: S. *tiriel.

gazing afar: S. palan-diriel.

gift: Q. anna.

give light!:   Q. ancalima ???

give praise!:   S. eglerio.

glen: Q. tumbale;   S. imlad.

glitter v. pl.:   Q. tintilar.

glitter, to: Q. tintil-.

glitter, with crystaline; glittering (white):   S. silivren.

'Glittering Caves':   S. Aglarond.

gloom: Q. lóme.

gloomy: Q. ᵗlómëa.

'Gloomyland':   Q. Lomëanor.

glorify!:   S. elgerio.

glorious: Q. alcarin.

glory: Q. alcar;   S. aglar.

glory to the: Q. aglar'ni.

go!:   S. noro ???

goblin: S. orch.

'Goblin-cleaver':   S. Orcrist.

God: Q. Eru.

God, Children of: Q. Erusén.

gold n.:   Q. malta.

gold adj.:   Q. ᵗmalin;   S. mal-, ᵗmallen.

gold, like: Q. laurëa;   S. glor-, -lor.

'gold-brown river, long':   S. Baranduin.

golden: Q. ᵗmalin;   S. mal-. ᵗmallen.

golden (coloured):   Q. laurëa;   S. glor-, -lor.

golden brown: S. baran.

'Golden-brown river':   S. Baranduin.

golden colour: Q. laure;   S. glor-, -lor.

golden field flower: S. alfirin.

'Golden-gold':   S. Mallor ???

'Golden-king':   S. Araval.

'Golden-ring.:   S. Cormallen.

'Golden-singing-land-valley':   Q. Laurelindórenan.

'Golden-snow':   S. Mallos ???

'Golden-song':   Q. Laurelin.

golden-tree: Q. *malinorne, ornemalin; S. mallorn.

gore: S. naith.

grade: Q. *tyelle.

great: Q. -en, -le;   S. -on.

great fear: S. *daedelos.

great light: Q. ancalima ???

greatly: Q. andave.

'Great River':   S. Anduin.

Great Sea: Q. ᵗEären;   S. aearon.

'Great Sea-day':   S. Oraearon.

'Great Sea-one':   Q. Eärenya.

great wall: S. rammas.

'Great-watchtower':   Q. Tirion

green: S. gal-, galen.

green leaf: S. lasgalen.

'Greenleaf':   S. Legolas ???

green leafage; green leaved, of green leaves: S. lasgalen.

'Green-lord':   S. Galdor ???

grey: Q. mista ???, ᵗsinda;   S. ᵗgwath, mith-, *mithren.

grey, pale: Q. mista ???;   S. mith-, *mithren.

'Grey (-one)':   Q. *Sinda.

'Greycloak':   S. Thingol ???

grey-country: Q. *sindanórië.

Grey-elf: Q. *Sinda.

Grey-elven: Q. sindarinwa.

Grey-elven language: Q. Sindarin.

'grey-flame':   S. mithril ???

'Grey, wood':   S. Gwathló.

'Grey-haven':   S. Mithlond.

'Grey-leaved':   Q. Lassemista ???

'Grey Pilgrim': 'Grey-wanderer':   S. Mithrandir.

growing: Q. LO.

growth: Q. loa.

guard; guarding: Q. tirith.

guard!:   S. tiro.

hail!:   S. ai.

hair: S. fin-, -fin.

half: S. per-.

half-elven: S. *Peredhel.

halfling: S. perian(n).

'Half-wise':   S. *Perhael.

hall: Q. *marde;   S. -rond.

'Hall of Fiery Power'; 'Hall of Sun Power':   S. Nargothrond ???

halt!:   S. daro.

hand: Q. má-.

-handed: Q. -maitë ???

harbour: S. lond.

harvest: Q. yávië;   S. iavas.

haunted: S. gorgor.

haven: S. lond.

head (= hill, mount):   S. dol.

hearing: S. lhaw.

heart (inner mind):   Q. óre.

heat: Q. úre.

heaven: Q. menel;   S. menel.

'Heaven-day':   S. Orbelain.

'Heaven-friend':   Q. Meneldil.

'Heaven-hill':   Q. Meneltarma ???

'Heaven-lover':   Q. Meneldil.

'Heaven-one':   Q. Menelya.

'Heaven-swordsman':   Q. Menelmacar;   S. Menelvagor.

heavy shadow: Q. lumbule.

heights, to the: Q. tarienna ???

heir: Q. *hilde.

Hell: S. Udûn.

Hensday: Q. Menelya;   S. Ormenel.

her: Q. -rya.

here: Q. sinome;   S. sí.

here beyond: S. nef.

heroes: S. conin ???

Hevensday: Q. Menelya;   S. Ormenel.

high: Q. or(o)-, *TÁR;   S. ro-.

Highday: Q. Tárion, Valanya;   S. Orbelain, Rodyn.

High-elven speech: Q. Quenya.

'High-heaven':   Q. Tarmenel.

'high-man':   Q. *tarcil.

high-white: Q. *tánique.

'High-white-peak':   Q. Tániquetil.

hill: Q. †tarma ???; S. amon, dol, *torn.

'Hill, King-(of the)-':   .Q. Arathorn.

hoar: Q, †mista ???; Q. mith-, *mithren.

'Hoarwell':   S. Mitheithel.

'Hollin (-land)':   S. Eregion.

hollow, a: Q. unque.

'Holly-region':   S. Eregion.

holy: Q. †aire; S. †aer.

holy and queenly: Q. airetári.

holy one: Q. aiya ???

home: Q. -mar; S. bar(a)-, -bar, -mar.

'Home-friend'; 'Home-lover':   Q. Mardil.

hook: Q. ampa.

hope: S. estel.

horse: S. roch-, roh-.

'Horse-land':   S. Rochand, Rochann, Rohan(n).

horse-lord: S. †rohir.

'Horse-lord-folk'; 'Horse-lords':   S. Rohirrim.

'Horse-(of)-the-wood':   S. Roheryn.

'Hot':   Q. Úrimë; S. Úrui.

hour: Q. lúme.

hurry!:   S. noro ???

hymn: S. aerlinn.

I: Q. -n, -nye; S. im, -n.

I am come: Q. utúlien.

I cry: S. nallon.

I gave: S. ónen.

I have found: Q. *utúvien.

I have found it: Q. utúvienyes.

I have kept: S. -chebin.

I have not kept: S. ú-chebin.

I will abide: Q. maruvan.

I will chant, sing: S. linnathon.

icicle: S. aiglos.

impending fate: S. amarth.

in: Q. -nen, -sse.

in song: Q. lírinen.

in the: Q. mí.

in the wind: Q. súrinen.

in this place: Q. sinome; S. sí.

in which: Q. *yasse.

-ing: S. -ren.

inner mind: Q. óre.

innumerable: Q. únótimë.

-ious: Q. -in; S. -en.

iron n.:   Q. anga; S. †ang.

iron adj.:   S. angren.

'Iron-fortress':   S. Angrenost.

'Iron-handed':   Q. Angamaitë ???

'Iron-home':   S. Angmar.

is: Q. ná.

Isengard: S. Angrenost.

-ish: S. -iel, -ren.

island: S. tol ???

'Island-strand':   S. Tolfalas ???

'Isle, Lonely':   Eressëa.

it (acc.):   Q. -s.

January: Q. Narvinyë; S. Narwain.

jaws: Q. anca; S. carach.

jewel: Q. *mír; S. *mîr.

'jewel, Elendil-':   Q. Elendilmir.

'jewel, King-':   S. Aravir.

jewel made of Silima: Q. silmaril.

'Jewel-of-Men':   Q. Atanamir ???

'Jewel-of-Varda':   Q. Vardamir.

jewels, sparkling like, with light like: S. míriel.

'Jewel-woman':   Q. Míriel.

July: Q. Cermië; S. Cerveth.

June: Q. Nárië; S. Nórui.

kept, I have: S. -chebin.

kept, I have not: S. ú-chebin.

kindler: S. -thoniel.

'Kindler, (Star-)':   Q. Tintallë.

'kindler, Star-':   S. Gilthoniel.

king: Q. tar-;   S. ar(a)-, aran.

'King-black':   S. Aravorn.

'King-full':   S. Araphant.

'King-golden':   S. Araval.

'King-jewel':   S. Aravir.

'King-last':   S. Arvedui.

'King-leaf':   S. Araglas ???

'king-man':   Q. *tarcil.

'King-of-Men':   Q. Atanatar ???

'King-of-the-Hill':   S. Arathorn.

'King-of-the-Land':   S. Arador.

'King-of-the-Realm':   S. Aranarth.

'Kings, Pillars of the':   S. Argonath.

kingsfoil: Q. asëa aranion;   S. athelas.

'King-silver':   S. Argeleb.

'King-stoney: S. Argonui.

'King-tree':   S. Aragorn ???

'King-wise':   S. Arahael.

'k-series':   Q. calmatéma.

'kw-series':   Q. quessetéma.

lair: S. torech.

'Lake Evendim':   S. Nenuial.

'Lake-town':   S. Esgaroth ???

lament: Q. nainië.

lamp: Q. calma;   S. *calar.

'Lamp-man':   Q. Calmacil ???

lampwright: S. *celairdan.

land: Q. -nde, -ndóre, -ndor, -nóre, -nor;   S. -an(n), bar(a)-, -bar, dor, -n(n), -nor, -waith.

'Land, Lord-of-the-':   S. Barahir ???

land connected with: S. -ien(n).

'Land-(of)-Pines':   S. Dorthonion.

land of: S. -ien(n).

'Land-of-the-Moon':   S. Ithilien(n).

'Land-of-the-Sun':   S. Anórien(n).

'Land of the Star':   Q. Elenna.

'Land-of-the-Valar':   Q. Valinóre, Valinor.

'Land of the Valley of Singing Gold':   Q. Laurelindórenan.

'Lands, The':   S. Doriath.

lands remote: S. -chaered.

lands remote, to: S. na-chaered.

'Land-(of)-the-Prince':   S. Dor-en-Ernil.

'Langstrand':   S. Anfalas.

last: S. *medui, ᵗmethed.

last, at: S. na vedui.

last day of a year: Q. mettarë.

'Last-king':   S. Arvedui.

'Last-peak':   S. Methedras.

last year of a century: Q. haranyë.

lawn: S. parth.

leaf: Q. lasse;   S. las(s).

'leaf':   S. galenas.

leaf, green; leafage, green: S. lasgalen.

leaf-fall (season):   Q. lasse-lanta, lasselanta.

'Leaflock':   S. Finglas.

leap year: Q. atendëa.

leaved, green; leaves, of green: S. lasgalen.

left, left-hand direction: Q. hyar-.

letter: Q. *tengwa;   S. *têw.

lick, to: Q. láv-.

licked down v. s.:   Q. unduláve.

lie v. s.:   Q. caita.

lie, to: Q. cait-.

lifted up v. s.:   Q. ortane.

lift up, to: Q. ortan-.

light: Q. cal(a).

light, bright: S. *calad.

light, give!; light, great: Q. ancalima ???.

light, of: S. calen ???

'Light-cleft':   Q. Calacirya.

'Light-cleft-land':   Q. *Calaciryan(de).

like gold: Q. laurëa;   S. glor-, -lor.

live!:   S. cuio.

lively: S. bre-.

lo!:   Q. yé.

lock of hair: S. fing.

'Lock of hair - (of) - leaf':   S. Finglas.

lofty: Q. *or(o)-.

lofty-hall: Q. *oromarde.

lone: S. er(e)-.

'Lone':   S. Erui.

'Lone-leaf':   S. Erelas ???

lonely: S. er(e)-.

'Lonely Isle':   Q. Eressëa.

'Lonely Mountain':   S. Erebor.

'Lone-man':   S. Eradan ???

long: S. an(n), anann.

'Long-coast':   S. Anfalas.

'Long-foam':   S. Andros.

long mark: S. andaith.

'Long-river':   S. Anduin.

long rune rows; long runic alphabet: S. angerthas.

long year (= 144 normal years):   Q. yén.

looking: Q. TIR;   S. TIR.

look towards!:   S. tiro.

lord: Q. -her, *tur;   S. ar(a), aran, *hîr, hir-, -hir, *taur², *tûr.

'Lord-blue':   S. Hirluin.

'Lord-of-the-Land':   S. Barahir ???.

'Lord-stone':   S. Hirgon.

'Lord-(of)-stone':   S. Turgon ???

'Lord-(of the)-world':   Q. Turambar.

lost: Q. vanwa.

loud: S. *brui- or *bruin-.

'Loudwater':   S. Bruinen.

lover: Q. -ndil, -nil.

'Lover of Aman':   Q. Amandil.

made v. s.:   S. echant.

magic, black: S. morgul.

maker: S. -dan.

Man: Q. *Atan;   S. adan.

'Man-of-Skill':   S. Curunir.

'Man of the West':   S. Dúnadan.

many: Q. li, -li.

March: Q. Súlimë;   S. Gwaeron.

mark: Q. tehta.   S. *taith.

May: Q. Lótesse;   S. Lothron.

may it be that; maybe: Q. nai.

me: S. nin.

me-for: Q. nin;   S. anim.

mead, a kind of: Q. miruvóre;   S. miruvor.

means of, by: Q. -nen.

meeting: Q. *omentië.

men: Q. Atani;   S. edain, -hoth, -oth.

'Men, Jewel-of-':   Q. Atanamir ???

'Men, King-of-':   Q. Atanatar ???

Mersday: Q. Eärenya;   S. Oraearon.

mesh: Q. rembe;   S. rem(m).

met: S. govannen.

metal: Q. tinco.

middle: Q. end(e)-, †endëa.

middle day: Q. *enderë.

Middle-earth: Q. Endóre;   S. Ennor.

middle-lands: S. ennorath.

Mid-year's Day: Q. loëndë.

mind, inner: Q. óre.

mist: Q. hísië;   S. hith-.

'Mist-peaks':   S. Hithaiglin.

mist-thread: S. hithlain.

'Misty':   Q. Hísimë;   S. Hithui.

'Misty Mountains':   S. Hithaiglin.

Monday: Q. Isilya;   S. Orithil.

month: Q. *asta.

monument: S. haudh ???

Moon: Q. Isil;   S. Ithil.

'Moon, Land-of-the-':   S. Ithilien(n).

'Moon-day':   S. Orithil.

'Moon-one':   Q. Isilya.

morning twilight; morrowdim: Q. tindóme;   S. minuial.

'Mortal-woman':   Q. Fíriel.

most: S. -wain¹.

mound: S. cerin ???, haudh ???

mount: Q. †tarma ???; S. amon, dol, orod.

mountain: S. orod.

'mountain-folk, Fang-(of)-':   S. Thangorodrim ???

'Mountain-hill':   S. Orophin ???

'Mountain of Fire':   S. Orodruin.

'Mountain of Pines':   S. Orod-na-Thôn ???

'Mountain of red flame':   S. Orodruin.

'Mountain Wall':   Q. Pelóri.

'Mount Fang':   S. Orthanc.

mouth: Q. anto.

move!:   S. noro ???

my: Q. *-nya.

myself, for: Q. nin; S. anim

name: Q. esse.

'Necromancer':   S. Guldur ???

nectar: Q. miruvóre.

nectar, sweet: Q. *lisse-miruvóre.

'Netted Stars':   S. Remmirath.

new, newness: Q. †vinyë; S. *gwain.

'New-sun':   Q. Narvinyë; S. Narwain.

night: Q. lóme; S. fuin.

nightingale: S. tinúviel.

'Norbury':   S. Fornost.

north: Q. formen; S. for(o)-, forod, *foron-.

'North-city':   S. Fornost.

northern: S. for(o)-, *foron-.

'North-haven':   S. Forlond.

'North-land':   S. Forodwaith.

not: Q. ú-; S. ú-.

November: Q. Hísimë; S. Hithui.

now: Q. sí. ·

numbering: Q. †nót-.

numberless: Q. únótimë.

Númenorean: Q. *tarcil; S. Dúnadan.

O!:   Q. a; S. a.

Ocean: Q. †Eären; S. aearon.

'Ocean-friend'; 'Ocean-lover':   Q. Eärendil.

October: Q. Narquelië; S. Narbeleth.

of: Q. -o; S. na, o.

of (composed of):   Q. -va.

oh!:   S. a.

old: S. iar-, iaur, ior-.

'Oldest':   S. Iarwain.

'Old-leaf':   S. Iorlas ???

on: Q. -nna.

on this side of: S. nef.

-one: Q. -ya; S. -ian(n) ???

'One, the':   Q. Eru.

'One of Great Light':   Q. Ancalimon ???

one who: Q. -tar.

onward: S. lim ???

open!:   S. edro, lasto ???

-or: Q. -cil ???

orc: S. orch.

Orion: Q. Menelmacar, Telumehtar; S. Menelvagor.

our (of me & him/her/it/them):   Q. *-lma.

our (of me & you):   Q. *-lva.

out: Q. et.

outer fence: S. ephel.

outer ring: S. echor.

outflow: S. ethir.

out of: Q. et.

'Over-heaven':   Q. Tarmenel.

overshadowed: Q. †lómëa; S. du-.

overwhelmed by: S. *di(n).

overwhelmed by dread of death: S. di'nguruthos, di-nguruthos.

pale grey: Q. †mista ???; S. mith-.

'Pale-grey-spring':   S. Mitheithel.

pass n.:   S. cirith.

pass (away), to: Q. váni-.

passage: S. cirith.

passed (away) (pl.):   Q. vánier.

passed (away), having (pl.):　　Q. avá-nier.

passing away:　　Q. vani-.

path:　　Q. *tië.

peak:　　Q. †til; S. *tîl, †ras(s).

'peak, High-white-':　　Q. Tániquetil.

'peak, Red-':　　S. Caradhras.

peaks:　　S. †aiglin, †rais(s).

people:　　S. -hoth, -oth, -rim, -waith.

People of the Stars, one of the:　　Q. *Elda.

People of the Valar, one of the:　　Q. Maia.

person:　　Q. -cil ???; S. -ian(n) ???

pilgrim:　　S. †randir.

'Pillars of the King':　　S. Argonath.

pine:　　S. thôn.

pipeweed:　　S. galenas.

plain:　　S. -lad, talf.

Pleiades:　　S. Remmirath.

Power, Angelic:　　Q. Vala; S. *Balan.

praise!:　　Q. laita; S. eglerio.

praise, to:　　Q. lait-.

praise (them???) both, we will:　　Q. laituvalmet.

prince:　　S. ernil.

'Prince, Land-(of)-the-':　　S. Dor-en-Ernil.

'p-series':　　Q. parmatéma.

queen:　　Q. Tar-, †tári; S. bereth.

quick:　　Q. *linta; S. bre-.

'Quickbeam':　　S. Bregalad.

'quick (lively) moon':　　S. †brethil.

'Quick (lively) Tree':　　S. Bregalad.

radiant form:　　Q. fanya; S. fân.

rage:　　Q. aha.

ravine:　　Q. cirya.

re-:　　Q. en-.

realm:　　Q. arda; S. †ardhon ???, †arth.

'Realm, King-of-the-':　　S. Aranarth.

'Realm-of-the-Edain':　　S. Arthedain.

red:　　Q. *carne; S. car-, caran.

'Red and White Flame':　　Q. Narsil.

red flame:　　Q. NÁR.

'red flame - white flame':　　Q. Narsil.

'Red-hill-country':　　S. Cardolan(n).

'Redhorn':　　S. Caradhras.

'Red-jewelled':　　Q. Carnimírië.

'Red-peak':　　S. Caradhras.

'Red-tooth':　　S. Carchost ???

'Redwater':　　S. Carnen.

refill, will (s.):　　Q. enquantuva.

region:　　Q. arda, †men, -nde; S. †arth, men-, -n(n).

region of the stars:　　Q. menel; S. menel.

'Regions-(of)-the-streams':　　S. Minhiriath.

remote distance:　　S. -chaered.

remote distance, to:　　S. na-chaered.

renewer:　　Q. envinyatar.

reversed:　　Q. nuquerna.

ridge:　　S. pinnath.

right, right-hand direction:　　Q. for-.

rill:　　S. *sîr.

ring:　　Q. corma; S. *côr, cor-.

ring, outer:　　S. echor.

ring-bearer:　　Q. *cormacolindo.

'Ring-day':　　Q. Cormarë.

'Rivendell':　　S. Imladris.

river (large):　　S. duin.

'River-lord':　　S. Duinhir.

'River Running':　　S. Celduin.

road:　　Q. *tië.

rock:　　S. tol ???

'Rock-strand':　　S. Tolfalas ???

roof, to:　　Q. túp-.

root:　　S. thond.

round n.:　　Q. cor-.

royal:　　Q. *TÁR; S. ar(a)-.

'Royal-land':　　S. Arnor.

'Royal One':　　Q. Arantar ???

'Royal Stones, The':　　S. Argonath.

'Royal-water': S. Arnen.

rune: Q. *certa; S. certh.

rune rows: S. certhas.

rune rows, long: S. angerthas.

runic alphabet: S. certhas.

runic alphabet, long: S. angerthas.

running: S. cel-.

'Running River': S. Celduin.

'Running-snow': S. Celos ???

'Samrise': S. *Perhael.

'Saruman': S. Curunír.

Saturday: Q. Elenya; S. Orgilion.

saviours: S. conin ???

say!: S. pedo.

sea: Q. ëar; S. aear.

Sea, Great: Q. †Eären; S. aearon.

'Sea-friend'; 'Sea-lover': Q. Eärnil ???.

'second twilight': S. aduial.

September: Q. Yavannië; S. Ivanneth.

series: Q. téma.

shadow: Q. lóme; S. *dû, du-.

shadow (heavy): Q. lumbulë.

shadowed: Q. †lómëa; S. du-.

'She-that-causes-sparkling'; 'She-that-kindles-lights': Q. Tintallë; S. Gilthoniel.

shine, to: Q. síl-.

shine(s) (s.): Q. síla.

ship: Q. cirya; S. cair.

'Ship friend': Q. Ciryandil.

'Ship-lord': Q. Ciryaher.

'Ship-lover': Q. Ciryandil.

'Ship-man': Q. Ciryatan.

'Shipwright': S. Círdan.

shore: Q. falas-; S. †falas.

sight: S. hen(n).

silence: S. dîn.

silent: S. dínen.

silver: Q. telpe-, †tyelpe; S. celeb.

'Silver-course': S. Celebrant.

'Silver-king': S. Argeleb.

'Silverlode': S. Celebrant.

'Silver-stone': S. Celepharn.

'Silvertine': S. Celebdil.

'Silver-tree': S. Celeborn.

sing, I will: S. linnathon.

'Singing-gold': Q. Laurelin.

'singing-golden-land': Q. lindelorendor.

'Skill, Man-of-': S. Curunír.

'Skinbark': S. Fladrif.

sky: Q. menel, vilya; S. menel.

'Sky, Swordsman of the': Q. Menelmacar; S. Menelmagor.

'Sky-lord': S. Meneldor.

'Sky-one': Q. Vilya.

slant(s) down (s.): S. penna.

slender: S. fim-.

'Slender-flowing-leafage': S. Finduilas.

slim: S. fim-.

'Slim-birch': S. Fimbrethil.

snake: Q. leuca; S. lyg.

snow: Q. losse; S. loss.

'Snow-(of)-Arnach': S. Lossarnach ???

'Snowmen': S. Lossoth.

snow-white: Q. losse; S. glos(s).

'Snow-white': S. Fanuilos.

snowy: S. lossen.

solar year: Q. coranar.

song: Q. †lin(de), *líri; S. lin(n)-.

song, in: Q. lírinen.

song, a mode of: S. ann-thennath.

sorcery: S. gul-, -gul, morgul.

sorcery, black: S. morgul.

'Sorcery-lord': S. Guldur ???

source: S. †eithel.

south: Q. hyarmen; S. har(a)-, harad.

southern: S. har(a)-.

'South-haven': S. Harlond.

'South-land': S. Haradwaith.

'South-people'; 'Southrons': S. Haradrim.

'South-Stoneland': S. Harondor.

'South-victor': Q. Hyarmendacil.

'South-water': S. Harnen.

spark: Q. TIN, tinwe; S. gil.

sparkle: Q. TIN.

sparkle v. pl.: Q. tintilar.

sparkle, to: Q. tintil-.

sparkling like jewels: S. míriel.

speak!: S. pedo.

'Speaker': Q. *Quende.

speaking: S. hu-.

'Speech': Q. Quenya.

spider: S. ungol.

spider's web: Q. ungwe.

spirit: Q. óre, súle; S. †Ûr ???

'Spirit of Fire': Q. Fëanor.

spirits, departed: S. gwanÛr.

spoken: S. lammen ???

spouse: S. bereth.

spring (season): Q. tuilë; S. ethuil.

spring (of water): S. †eithel.

'spring-day': Q. tuilerë.

springing up: Q. LO.

star: Q. EL, elen, tinwe; S. gil, êl, el-, mîr, *tîn.

'Star, Land of the': Q. Elenna.

'Star - (of) - Bright Light': S. Gilgalad.

'Star-foam': S. Elros.

'Star-hall': S. Elrond.

'Star-horselord': S. Elrohir.

'Star-kindler': Q. Tintallë; S. Gilthoniel.

starlight: Q. silme.

'Starlight': S. Gil-galad.

'Star-lord': S. Gildor.

'Star-lover': Q. Elendil.

'Star-man': S. Elladan ???

'starmoon': S. ithildin.

'Star of Elendil': Q. Elendilmir.

'Star-one': Q. Elenya.

'Star-queen': Q. Elentári; S. Elbereth.

Stars, People of the, one of: Q. *Elda.

'stars, region of the': Q. menel; S. menel.

'Stars-day': S. Orgilion.

'star-shadow': Q. tindómë.

steadfast: Q. voron- ???, voronwë; S. bor(o)- ???, -bor ???, -born ???

'Steadfast-friend': Q. Vorondil ???

'Steadfast-jewel': S. Boromir ???

steadfastness: Q. voron- ???; S. bor(o)- ???, -bor ???, -born ???

'Steadfastness, Lover-of-': Q. Vorondil ???

'Steadfast-star': S. Borgil ???

stem: Q. telco.

Sterday: Q. Elenya; S. Orgilion.

stirring (season): Q. coirë; S. echuir.

stone: Q. †sar, †ondo; S. gon-, -gon, †gond ???, gond(o)- ???, sarn.

'Stone-land': S. Gondobar ???, Gondor.

'Stoneland, South': S. Harondor.

'Stone-paths'; 'Stone-singing': S. Gondolin ???

'Stones, The Royal': S. Argonath.

stoney: S. †gonui.

'Stoney': S. Serni ???, Sernui ???

'Stoney-ford': S. Sarn-athrad.

'Stoney-king': S. Argonui.

'Stoning-land': S. Gondor.

strand: Q. falas-; S. †falas.

stream: S. *sîr, sir-.

'Stream-(of)-gate': S. Sirannon.

'Streaming': S. Sirith ???

street: S. rath.

strider: Q. telcontar.

summer: Q. lairë; S. laer.

Sun: Q. †Anar, Anár-, NÁR; S. Anor, Anór-.

'Sun, Land-of-the-': S. Anórien(n).

'Sun-day': S. Oranor.

Sunday: Q. Anarya; S. Oranor.

'Sun-friend': Q. Anardil.

'Sunlending': S. Anórien(n).

sunlight: Q. áre.

'Sun-lover': Q. Anardil.

'Sunny': Q. Nárië; S. Nŏrui.

'Sun-one': Q. Anarya.

sunrise: S. amrûn.

'sun-round': Q. coranar.

sunset: Q. andúnë; S. annûn.

sunset, of the: Q. andú-; S. annú-.

'sun-star': S. elanor.

'sun-waning' (season): S. narbeleth.

'Sun-waning' (month): Q. Narquelië; S. Narbeleth.

'Sutherland': S. Haradwaith.

swan: S. alph.

'Swanfleet': S. Glanduin.

sweet: Q. lisse.

sweet mead; sweet nectar: Q. *lisse-miruvóre.

swift: Q. *linta; S. bre-.

swordsman: Q. †macar; S. *magor.

'Swordsman of the Sky': Q. Menelmacar; S. Menelvagor.

tall: Q. halla; S. †hal ???

'Tall-leaf': S. Hallas ???

'Tall-sight': S. Haldir ???

'Tall-tower': S. Halbarad ???

tangled: S. *remmen.

the: Q. i; S. e(n).

thee, to: S. le.

them: S. hain.

them both: Q. -t, te ???

'thing' of..., beloning to..., connected with...: Q. -ië.

this: S. *hen.

this side of, on: S. nef.

thou: Q. -lyë.

thou, even: Q. elyë.

thou wilt find: Q. hiruvalyë.

thread: S. -lain.

Thursday: Q. Eärenya; S. Oraearon.

tine: Q. †til; S. *tîl.

to: Q. -nna; S. an, na.

to lands remote; to-remote distance: S. na-chaered.

to thee: S. le.

tongue: Q. lambe; S. *lam(m) ???, naith.

tooth: S. -chost ???

torment: Q. nwalme.

tower: S. barad, min-², minas.

'Tower-blue-hill': S. Mindolluin.

'Tower-(of)-Rimmon': S. Min-Rimmon.

'Tower-watching': Q. Minastir ???

town: Q. †osto ???; S. †ost, os(t)-.

treasure: Q. harma.

tree: Q. alda, †alta, †orne; S. †galad, galadh, -horn, -orn.

'tree, golden-': Q. *malinorne, orne-malin; S. mallorn.

'Treebeard': S. Fangorn.

tree beloved of the woodwrights of Gondor: S. lebethron.

'Tree-day': S. Orgaladh.

'Tree-friend': Q. Ornendil.

'Tree-jewel': Q. Aldamir.

'Tree-lover': Q. Ornendil.

'Tree-(of)-Moons': S. Galathilion ???

'Tree-one': Q. Aldëa.

'Tree-people': S. Galadhrim.

trees, two: Q. aldú-; S. †galadhad.

'Tree-shadow': Q. Aldalómë.

tree-tangled: S. *galadhremmen.

'Tree-woman': Q. *Altáriel; S. Galadriel.

tree-woven: S. *galadhremmen.

tremble (pl.): Q. tintilar.

tremble, to: Q. tintil-.

Trewsday: Q. Aldëa; S. Orgaladh.

troll: S. torog.

truesilver: S. mithril.

't-series': Q. tincotéma.

Tuesday: Q. Aldëa; S. Orgaladh.

turned: Q. *querna ???

twilight: Q. tindómë, undómë; S. uial.

twilight, evening: Q. undómë; S.

aduial.

twilight, morning: Q. tindómë; S. minuial.

'Twilight, Water-(of)-':   S. Nenuial.

twinkle v. pl.:   Q. tintilar.

twinkle, to: Q. tintil-.

'Twin-peaks-(of)-foam':   S. Rauros ???

two: Q. at-, -t; S. ad-, -ad.

two trees: Q. aldú-; S. †galadhad.

'Two trees - day':   S. Orgaladhad.

'Two-trees one':   Q. Aldúya.

'ty-series':   Q. tyelpetéma.

'Umbar-victor':   Q. Umbardacil.

uncountable: Q únótimë.

under: Q. nu; S. *di(n).

until, unto: Q. *tenna.

up: Q. *RÓ.

uplift, to: Q. ortan-.

uplifted v. s.:   Q. ortane.

upon: Q. *-nna.

us two (myself & him/her/it):   Q. met.

'Vala-friend':   Q. Valandil.

'Vala-home':   Q. Valimar, Valmar.

'Vala-land':   Q. Valinóre, Valinor.

'Vala-lover':   Q. Valandil.

Valar, People of the, one of: Q. Maia.

vale: Q. †nan; S. nan, *tum(m).

'Vale-(of)-Willows':   S. Nan-tasarion.

valley: Q. †nan; S. nan, *tum(m).

valley, black deep: Q. tumbalemorna.

valley, deep: Q. tumbale; S. imlad.

valley, forested deep: Q. tumbaletaurëa.

'Valley-(of)-dim (= overshadowed)-rills':   S. Nanduhirion.

'Valley-plainlike':   S. Tumladen ???

vault: Q. *telluma.

veil: Q. FANA.

Venus (planet):   Q. Eärendil.

verse: S. linnod ???

victor: Q. -dacil; S. †degil.

voice: Q. †óma.

voiced: S. hu-.

'Voiced-tree':   S. Huorn.

wall, great: S. rammas.

wanderer: S. †randir.

waning: Q. †quelië; S. *peleth.

ward: S. tirith.

watching: Q. TIR; S. TIR.

watch over!:   S. tiro.

'watchtower, Great-':   Q. Tirion.

water: Q. NÉN; S. nen.

water-channel: S. †rant.

'Water-one':   Q. Nenya.

'Water-(of)-Twilight':   S. Nenuial.

'Watery':   Q. Nénimë.

wave, foaming: Q. falma.

way: S. len-.

waybread: S. lembas.

we (I & he/she/it/they):   Q. †-'lme.

we will praise (them???) both: Q. laituvalmet.

web, spider's: Q. ungwe.

Wednesday: Q. Menelya; S. Ormenel.

week: Q. enquië.

well adv.:   S. mae.

west: Q. andú-, andúnë, númen; S. annú-, annûn, dûn, dún-.

'West, Flame of the':   Q. Andúril.

West-elf: Q. *Elda; S. edhel.

'Westering':   Q. Andúnië.

western: Q. andú-; S. annú-, dún-.

'Westernesse':   Q. Númenóre, Númenor.

'Western-tower':   S. Annúminas.

'West-land':   Q. Númenóre, Númenor.

'West-man':   S. Dúnadan.

westmansweed: S. galenas.

wet: S. nîn, nín-, nin-.

'Wet':   Q. Nénimë; S. Nínui.

'Wet-flat field'; 'Wetwang':   S. Nindalf.

wherein: Q. *yasse.

which: Q. *ya.

which, in: Q. *yasse.

white: S. nim-.

white (as snow); white, dazzling; white, snow-:   Q. losse; S. glos(s).

'White-birch':   S. Nimbrethil.

white cloud: Q. fanya; S. fân.

white flame: Q. †sil; S. -riḷ ???

'White-flower':   S. Nimloth.

white glittering: S. silivren.

!White-peaks':   S. Nimrais.

who?:   Q. man.

wild: S. drú- ???, dru- ???.

'Wild Man':   S. Druadan ???, Drúadan ???

'Wild Men, Land-(of)-':   S. Drúwaith ???

will (fut. indicator):   Q. -uva.

will find (s.):   Q. hiruva.

will refill (s.):   Q. enquantuva.

willow: S. †tasar.

'Willows, Vale-(of)-':   S. Nan-tasarion.

'Willow-vale':   S. Tasarinan.

wilt (fut. indicator):   Q. -uva.

wind: Q. súle, *súri; S. †gwae, sûl.

wind, in the: Q. súrinen.

'Windlord':   S. Gwaihir.

window: S. henneth.

'Winds-lord':   S. Gwaihir.

'Windy':   Q. Súlimë; S. Gwaeron.

wing: Q. *ráma.

winter: Q. hríve; S. rhîw.

wise: S. †hael.

'Wise-king':   S. Arahael.

with light like jewels: S. míriel.

Wizard: Q. *Istar; S. Curunír.

woe!:   Q. ai; S. ai.

woman: Q. -riel; S. -riel.

'Woman, Mortal':   Q. Fíriel.

'woman, Tree-':   Q. *Altáriel; S. Galadriel.

'Woman of Great Light':   Q. Ancalimë ???

wood (forest):   S. eryn.

wooden platform: S. talan.

world: Q. ambar.

world-ending: Q. ambar-metta.

woven: S. *remmen.

-wright: S. -dan.

-y: Q. -imë, -in; S. -en, -ui.

year (as a cycle of growth):   Q. loa.

year, long (= 144 normal years):   Q. yén.

year, solar: Q. coranar.

'year-middle':   Q. loëndë.

yellow-brown: S. baran.

PROTO-ELDARIN VOWELS:
A COMPARATIVE SURVEY

Chris Gilson & Bill Welden

'Rare Temples thou hast seen, I know,
And rich for in and outward show:
Survey this Chapell, built, alone,
Without or Lime, or Wood, or Stone:
Then say, if one th'ast seene more fine
Than this, the Fairies once, now Thine.'

Introduction

IN THIS ARTICLE we offer a preliminary assessment of the
developments of the vowels in the Eldarin dialects from the
First Age up to the end of the Third Age. It is at this
later time, namely the century immediately before and after
the War of the Ring, that the majority of the received forms
were recorded in the prototypes of the manuscripts from which
our corpus was edited, translated, and transcribed; and also
at this time that most of the utterances recorded in these
manuscripts were actually spoken. Two languages so recorded
are our present concern—Quenya and Sindarin. These two languages allow comparison of enough regular correspondence
between the phonemes of forms of similar meaning, that their
genetic relation is undoubtable. This necessarily implies an
ancestor language which has been dubbed PROTO-ELDARIN. We
use the comparative method to attempt to recover the structure of Proto-Eldarin.

The primary tool is COMPARATIVE RECONSTRUCTION, a comparison of the structure of several descendent languages to
ascertain the structure of the parent tongue. Every language
has structural units which correspond approximately to the

everyday concept of a 'sound'. These are called PHONEMES.
Each phoneme is actually a set of sounds, and the particular
realization of the phoneme in a word is determined by its
environment. Thus the phoneme /t/ in English is realized as
a voiceless aspirated alveolar stop [tʰ] when it precedes a
stressed syllable; unless it follows /s/, in which case there
is no aspiration [t]; and is realized as an alveolar flap [ɾ]
if it follows a stressed syllable. Cf. taken ['tʰeɪkn],
stale [steɪl], later ['leɪɾəʲ]. The various realizations of
a phoneme are called its ALLOPHONES. The allophones of a
single phoneme are always in COMPLIMENTARY DISTRIBUTION, that
is, two of them cannot both occur in identical environments.
So, for instance, the initial sounds of taught and thought
must be allophones of different phonemes since they occur in
exactly the same environment. Such oppositions as taught/
thought which demarcate phonemes are called MINIMAL PAIRS.
One can determine the phonemes of a language by searching for
minimal pairs, and forming sets of phonetically similar allophones that do NOT occur in such pairs, i.e. are in complimentary distribution.

Now for comparative reconstruction one starts with the
phonemes of the descendent languages and tabulates the correspondences between phonemes in sets of cognate words. For
example, we take the pair Q rembe/S rem and observe the correspondences r/r, e/e, mb/m, e/∅ (zero). Moving on to the
pair Q eleni/S elin we confirm e/e and get the additional
correspondences l/l, e/i, n/n, i/∅. We continue through the
vocabulary attempting to confirm as many correspondences as
possible. Here confirmation is most important in order to
avoid confusion from the results of analogy and inter-
language borrowing. For example, from the pair Q valar/S
-belain the correspondences v/b, a/e, l/l, a/ai are all
valid, and can be confirmed by other pairs; but r/n cannot be
confirmed. And, in fact, from other evidence it appears the
r in the Quenya form is not a regular development, but an
innovation modeled after other plural nouns of Quenya ending
-ar.

Having tabulated the correspondences, we treat each one
as a unit and call it an 'allophone'. We search for phonemes
as if these were the allophones of a presented language; that
is, we formulate sets of phonetically similar correspondences
that are in complimentary distribution. For example, the e/e
and e/i of Q eleni/S elin end up being considered allophones
of the same phoneme which we call *e. The phoneme *e is
realized as the allophone e/i when the following syllable
contains word-final *ī (which in turn is realized as i/∅ when
it occurs word-finally). Once we have established the phonemes and the conditioning environments for the allophones of
each, we can use the phonemes as a shorthand for the cognate

pairs. Thus *elenī, five phonemes in a certain order, implies five allophones, that is, the five correspondences which entail the pair Q elenī/S elin.

The axiom upon which the comparative reconstruction is founded is that given enough data to establish a proper set of correspondences and to allow a rigorous determination of phonemes from them, the reconstruction yields the actual phonemes of the parent language. (Or, to put it another way, we can reinterpret the asterisk at the head of *elenī to mean: 'Assuming there are no bugs in the system, this is a world of Proto-Eldarin, it just isn't attested.' In fact, we use * throughout the article as shorthand for 'unattested', whether the word in question is Proto-Eldarin, Quenya, Sindarin or something in between.) Of course, minimal pairs are rare in a corpus as small as ours, and we must use similar environments rather than identical ones for arbitrating between phonemes. What can amount to a lack of rigor must be overcome using one's imagination and linguistic intuitions.

It should be emphasized that we are dealing only with the structure of historical forms. The theory can guarantee no information about the actual pronunciation of reconstructions (though we can make some guesses). All forms cited in the body of the article are intended as phonemic spellings. Received forms are cited as they occur in the corpus, however, according to the usual practice, with the exception that the macrons marking length in some forms in *The Road Goes Ever On* are regularized as acute accents (´), and the dieresis (¨), employed inconsistently in the corpus for purely pedagogical reasons, has been eliminated throughout. Tolkien's transliteration of Elvish is phonemic for the most part, with notable exceptions such as the circumflexed vowels which are probably allophones of the long vowels. Tolkien sometimes uses 2 letters in combination to represent a phoneme, e.g. *ch, dh*. This system can have its disadvantages—for instance it has been questioned whether *Ethir* contains 4 phonemes or 5—and we have preferred to use diacritics, superscripted letters, and symbols from the International Phonetic Alphabet where the possibilities of the Roman alphabet are inadequate, e.g. θ, n^d. In reconstructed forms long vowels are indicated by the macron.

Another tool of the comparative method is INTERNAL RECONSTRUCTION, that is, comparison of the different phonemic shapes of the same semantic unit within one language to ascertain information about the proto-structure. Every language has minimal semantic units which may correspond to words, but may be shorter. These are called MORPHEMES. For examples, *halves*, phonemically /hævz/, contains two morphemes, the first being /hæv/, the second /z/ the semantic content of which is 'plurality'. /z/ is also said to be one

of the ALLOMORPHS of a single morpheme which includes the
three allomorphs /z/, /əz/ as in *changes*, and /s/ as in
lakes. Allomorphs of one morpheme are in complimentary distribution. Now /hæv/ too is an allomorph along with *half*
/hæf/, and here it is rather straightforward to suggest that
/f/ and /v/ were once allophonic variants of the same phoneme
—other allomorphic pairs that suggest this will occur to the
reader. And, in fact, the Old English progenitors of the *f*
and *v* of modern spelling were written with the same letter,
f, and it is assumed that a single Old English phoneme, written *f*, was realized as [v] between voiced sounds and as [f]
elsewhere.

This type of analysis is often an invaluable suplement
to comparative reconstruction. For example, from the comparative evidence of Q *elda*/S *edhel*, Q *ando*/S *annon*, Q *alda*/S
galadh we can posit a provisional phoneme **d* with various
medial allophones; but we don't know its realization in word-
initial position. Using internal reconstruction, however, we
observe S *Fanuidhol* beside D*ol Amroth*, and Q *tindóme* 'twilight' beside *lóme* 'night', and conclude that **d* is realized
as *l/d* in word-initial position.

Most of the evidence for what we term VOWEL AFFECTION in
this article comes from internal reconstruction. For example, we assume from a few pairs like Q *eleni*/S *elin* that many
plural nouns ended in final **ī*. And, consequently we consider Sindarin singular/plural pairs like *adan*, pl. *edain* or
orch, pl. *yrch* to represent sets of allomorphs which have
split into separate morphemes once the conditioning environment of the final *ī* was lost. It is through this sort of
internal reconstruction that we determine that **a* became *ai*,
*o became *y*, etc., 'by final *ī*-affection.'

Internal reconstruction can also be applied to the
reconstructed proto-language, often extending our purview to
before the point of common origin of the descendent dialects.
For example, from the approximate correspondences: Q *Narquelie*/S *Narbeleth*, Q *Narvinye*/S *Narwain*, Q *Nárie*/S *Nórui* we
reconstruct the following partial Proto-Eldarin forms: **nar-
*narkwel-, **narwiny-*, **nār-*. Now the first syllable of each
of these forms refers to the fires of the Sun, and their common origin seems very plausible. The simplest hypothesis is
that Early Proto-Eldarin long vowels were changed to short
vowels when followed by two consonants, that is to say in
closed syllables, if we divide syllables in a certain way
(see p. 117n). This hypothesis is supported by the rest of
our rather meagre evidence on the point.

It should be noted that while a complex but regular cognate pair like Q *elda*/S *edhel* can be handled quite consistently by our method—the proto-form is **eldā*, **l* is realized
as *l/dh* when medial before **d*, and **d* is realized as *d/el*

when preceded by *eɭ and followed by the last vowel of the
form, and this is not *ɩ—but this complicated conditioning
environment is practically unmanageable. The reason is that
4 or 5 shifts in the phonemic structure of the language bear
on the history of this one form, and the complex environment
is the intersection of the 4 or 5 environments that conditioned these changes. So we attempt to isolate the different
changes in the history of a form. A direct application of
the comparative method provides a starting point, but we find
it desirable to fill in the gap between the start point and
the extant dialects as fully as possible, not least of all
for the improvement in the elegance of our theory that this
can yield.

This article is essentially a tabulation of the reconstructed vowel phonemes of Proto-Eldarin along with cognate
pairs and approximately cognate forms from which they are
abstracted, and an explanation of the environments which con-
dition the various correspondence 'allophones'. We have
tried to include as many cognate sets as was feasible. When
a correspondence is well attested we have not bothered to
cite questionable examples of it. But the mere fact that a
correspondence is not corroborated several times over was
never considered reason enough to exclude it from discussion.
The reader is not to think that this article is a definitive
grammar; rather, we think of it as the first draft of part of
a grammar. The organization of the text and the declarative
aspect of the statements made are intended only to suggest
the latter. It was felt that to qualify every doubtful
statement—there are few unimpeachable in the whole thing—
would be too tedious for the reader, especially since the
credibility of a correspondence is fairly well proportional
to the number of its examples, so the reader can always judge
for himself. This is not to say that every conceivable
theory has been aired; since many are mutually exclusive,
choices have constantly been made using our own intuitions
and personal tastes where the evidence was not decisive.

Finally we would like to note that the authors have had
access to unpublished portions of materials from Tolkien's
'pen', material which unfortunately cannot here be presented
in full by us, nor quoted extensively. However, we have not
refrained from letting such materials bias our interpretation
of the published forms. (The reader is warned, however,
against assuming that the authors know what they are talking
about when this is not clear from the evidence of the article.) In a few places we have taken the liberty of citing
unpublished forms which provide key evidence for our theories, marked of course with an asterisk since they are not in
the official published corpus, and followed by the abbrevia-
tion M (for Manuscript, Materials, or Misleading, take your

pick).

Any reader interested in any portion of this article is welcome to write me personally care of the publisher.

Chris Gilson
March 1976

Short Vowels

THERE WERE FIVE PURE VOWELS in Proto-Eldarin: *i, e, a, o, u*. Each could be either long or short. The short vowels generally remained unchanged in Quenya.

In Sindarin the short vowels could be partially assimilated to a vowel or semi-vowel in an adjacent syllable. This is referred to by Celtic linguists as VOWEL-AFFECTION, by German linguists as UMLAUT. (The English alternations *mouse/ mice, tooth/teeth* show the results of *i*-umlaut: Old English *mȳs* < Germanic **mūsi* plural of **mūs*; OE *tēþ* < **tōþi* plural of **tōþ*.) The changes in Sindarin run along very similar lines to those in Welsh, so we will adopt the Celticists' terminology. There are two kinds of vowel-affection (in Welsh and Sindarin): that due to a sound which is ultimately lost— FINAL AFFECTION; and that due to a sound which remains in some form—INTERNAL AFFECTION.

The varieties of final affection in Sindarin for which we have evidence are:

i...a > e...

u...a > o...

e...ī > i...

e...y > ei... (> ai...)

o...ī > ü (*the Sindarin vocalic* y)

a...ī > ei... (> ai...)

ai...ī > ei... (> ai...)

Note that the ellipsis marks are used here to indicate the syllable boundary. The change *ei > ai* in final syllables was a late phenomenon occuring after older *ai* had become *ae*.[1] By internal affection *a* and *o* were changed to *e* if the following syllable contained an *ī* which was not completely lost (though

---

[1] Compare Middle Welsh (MWel.) *seith* 'seven' = Modern Wel. *saith*; MWel. *mynach* 'monk' pl. *myneich* = Mod. Wel. *mynach* pl. *mynaich*; MWel. *penceirdieid* 'chief bards' = Mod. Wel. *penceirddiaid*.

possibly shortened) or if the following syllable contained an
i, *ei*, *e*, or *ü* (= the Sindarin vocalic *y*) resulting from
final *ī*-affection. The latter we refer to as SECONDARY
AFFECTION. The examples of Sindarin vowel mutations are
included below, listed under the original form of the vowel.

i

PE *i* > Q, S *i*. PE **iθil-* 'moon' > Q *Isil*, S *Ithil*; PE
*lind- 'sing' > Q †*lin(de)*, S *linnathon* 'I will chant'; PE
*minas 'tower' > Q *Minastir*, *Minardil*, S *Minas*; Q *Tániquetil*
'high white peak', S *Nimrais* 'white horns',[2] *Celebdil* 'Silvertine' (*celeb* + **tîl*); Q *tinwe* 'spark, star', S *ithildin*
'starmoon' (*ithil* **tîn*); PE **tir-* 'look toward, watch over'
> Q *Tirion* 'great watch tower', S *Tirith* 'guard, ward'; pos-
sibly PE **gil-* 'star' > Q *Ilmarin* 'star dwelling' (?), S *gil*.

PE *i* > S *e* by final *ā*-affection. PE **sindā* 'grey' > Q
†*sinda*, S **send* (M). The only evidence for this change from
the published corpus is indirect: S *Cair* 'ship' < **ceir* <
**keir*ʸ < PE **kiryā* (= Q *cirya* 'cleft', cf. also *Ciryaher*, one
of the four 'Ship-kings' of Gondor) pl. PE **kirya-i* > **kiryē*
> **kir*ʸ > S **cîr* 'ships' as in *Círdan*; S *-wain* 'new' (as in
Narwain 'new sun, January') < **wein* < **wen*ʸ < PE **winyā*, cf.
Q *Envinyatar* 'Renewer', *Narvinye* 'January'.

We see a third Q *i*...*ya*/S *ai* cognate set in the pair Q
vilya 'air', S †*gwai* 'wind(s)' in *Gwaihir*. We posit the
proto-form **wigyā*, where the voiced palatalized velar **gy*
becomes dental + *y*, that is **dy* (compare this development
with the corresponding voiceless stop *t* + *y* III:392), and *d*
bcomes *l* following a vowel (compare its becoming *l* word-
initially G:179) in Quenya: PE **wigyā* > **widya* > Q *wilya* >
vilya. In Sindarin *i* is affected to *e* and the *g* is spirant-
ized intervocalically (cf. *b* > *v*, *d* > *dh*) and ultimately lost
altogether leaving the palatal glide; initial *w* becomes *gw* as
expected (cf. Q. *Víresse*, S *Gwirith*): PE **wigyā* > **wiγ*ʸ >
*wei > **gwei*. This last becomes S †*gwai* when *ei* > *ai* in
final syllables (cf. *teithant* beside *andaith*). The formation
of the name *Gwaihir* must postdate this change.[3]

---

[2] This is the only example we know of Q *qu* corresponding to S *m*. One
possible proto-form for Q †*nique-*, S *nim-* (*Nimbrethil, Nimloth, Nimrodel*)
would be PE **nipkwe* with loss of *ŋ* by dissimilation in Quenya. In Sindarin we expect the labio-velar *kw* to become a bilabial *p* and then to be
voiced medially as *b* (cf. Q. *Narquelie*, S *Narbeleth*). So with assimilation of the nasal we have *ŋkw* > *mp* > *mb* > *mm* > *m*.

[3] The exact relation between S †*gwae*, †*gwai* can only be guessed at.
Above we assumed the meanings 'wind', 'winds' respectively, and intimated
an analogical source for the alternation, though we have no other example. At least the semantic development of 'air' > 'winds' is possible.

e

PE *e* > Q, S *e*. PE **eldā* 'elf' > Q *Elda*, S *edhel*; PE **elenī* 'stars' > Q *eleni*, S *elin*; Q *Endóre*, S *Ennor* 'Middle-earth'; PE **eresse-* 'lonely' > Q *Eressea* 'the lonely isle', S *Erestor*, *Erebor* 'lonely mountain' (**eres* + **bor*); PE **kwel-* 'wane' > Q *Narquelie*, S *Narbeleth* 'Sun-waning'; PE **pel-* 'fence, boundary' > Q *Pelóri* 'Mountain Wall' (?); *pella* 'beyond (the borders of)', S *Pelennor* 'fenced land'; Q *Quendi* 'speakers', S *pedo* 'speak!, say!'; Q *rembe* 'mesh', S *rem*; PE **kyelpe* 'silver' > Q *tyelpetéma*, S *celeb*.

PE *e* > S *i* by final *ī*-affection. PE **elenī* > S *elin*; *certh* 'rune' pl. *cirth*;[4] *edhel* 'elf' pl. ⵝⵀⵓⵜ (*Edhil*).

On the possibility of **wei* < **wigyā* compare MWel. *carrei* < Lat. *corrigia* 'shoe-string' (Kenneth H. Jackson, *Language and History in Early Britain*, Edinburgh: 1953, pp. 449-50). Prof. Jackson, it should be noted, treats *carrei* as coming from (British) Vulgar Latin **corregia*, finding other examples of Brit. VLat. *e* < *i* + *g* + consonant (462), and does not see *ā*-affection here. But, as he states this is 'the only example' of original *igi* known to me' (449), his particular choice of an etymology seems to be based primarily on the opinion 'that *ā*-affection can be caused by *iā* is unproven and unlikely' (450). Jackson demonstrates the 'unproven' part (575); the upshot being that the combination of final *ā*-affection and *y*-affection in Welsh, *i* > *e* > (vocalic) *y*, is identical to the normal development of unaffected *i* > (vocalic) *y* in stressed syllables, so that in general one cannot demonstrate whether the intermediate *e* stage occurred.

What has all this to do with Sindarin? Well, the similarity of Sindarin phonological history to that of Welsh is well known. But the phonics of Sindarin are to a certain degree simpler. For example, Welsh has 4 high vowels, [i] written *i*, [ɥ] written *u*, [u] written *w*, and a sound somewhere between [ɯ] and [ɨ] in the IPA written *y*; Sindarin has only the first three of these [i, ɥ, u], written respectively *i*, *y*, *u*. Correspondingly, the various vocalic developments which converged to the vowel written *y* in Welsh remained divergent in Sindarin: short *i* normally remains unchanged; *e* is changed to *i* by final *ī*-affection; *o* is changed to *ü* [ɥ] (written *y*) by final *ī*-affection (probably fronted to *ö* [ø] before being raised); *e* seems to become *ei* by final *y*-affection, paralleling the internal *y*-affection of *e* in Welsh. (Refer to examples in the main text.) Consequently, unlike the Welsh situation, the combined effect in Sindarin of *ā*-affection and *y*-affection upon original *i* is different from unaffected *i*, namely *i* > *e* > *ei* as opposed to *i* > *i*. Thus we can tell if the whole process occurred.

Note that if we start with the forms *cair*, *-wain*, and regress through the change *ei* > *ai* and through the alleged final *y*-affection, we arrive at the Pre-Sindarin forms **kerʸ*, **wenʸ*. A priori the question remains: was original *e* raised to *i* in Quenya due to the following *y*, or was original *i* lowered to *e* in Sindarin due to a following *ā*? Clearly Q *Nenya*, *Quenya* contradict the former of these hypotheses, showing as they do that the regular development of **-enyā* in Quenya is *-enya*, not ***-inya*. Hence our avowal of *ā*-affection in Sindarin in these instances.

[4] Although we propose an etymology for *cirth* involving *ī*-affection in the section on *Final Syllables*, it may be that *certh* derives not from PE

Pre-S *e* > S *ei* by final *y*-affection. S *Cair* < **ceir* <
*ker^y (= Q *cirya*); S *-wain* < **wein* < **wen^y* 'new'.

a

PE *a* > Q, S *a*. PE **aklar-* 'glory' > Q *alcar*, S *aglar*
R:65; PE **galdar* 'tree' > Q *alda* gen. pl. *aldaron* (< **galdar*
-on-i), S *galadh*; PE **andon* 'gate' > Q *ando*, S *Annon*; PE
*aŋg 'iron' > Q *anga*, S *Angren*; PE **aθea* > Q *asea*, S *athe-*
las (†*athe* + *las(s)* 'leaf'); PE **karne* 'red' > Q *Carnimírie*
'red-jewelled', S †*caran*; PE **aiare* 'sea' > Q *ear*, S *aear*;
PE **falas* > Q *Falastur* 'Lord of the Coasts', S *Anfalas* 'Langstrand'; Q *fana, fanya*, S *fan-*; Q *hyarmen*, S *harad*; Q
lasse 'leaf', S *las(s)* 'leaf', *Lasgalen* 'greenleaves', *athe-*
las; Q *malta* 'gold', S *mallorn* 'golden tree'; PE **m^bar-*
'dwelling' > Q *oromardi* 'high halls', S *Barad-* 'tower'.

PE *a* > early S *ei* by final *ī*-affection. S *adan* pl.
Edain < **edein* < PE **atanī* = Q *Atani* 'Fathers of Men'; S
Aran 'king' pl. *Erain* > **erein* < **aranī*, cf. Q *aranion* gen.
pl.;[5] S *Barad-* pl. *Beraid*; *perian* 'halfling' pl. *periain*;
-rass 'peak' pl. **raiss* > **rais* as in *Nimrais*.

PE *a* > S *e* by secondary affection. S *adan* pl. *Edain*;
amon 'hill' pl. *emyn*; *Annon* pl. *Ennyn*; *Aran* pl. *Erain*;
Barad-, pl. *Beraid*.

PE *a* > S *e* by internal *ī*-affection. PE **dakīl-* 'victor' (*Hyarmendacil, Rómendacil, Umbardacil*), S †*degil* in

---

*kirtā by *ā*-affection. The Sindarin plural *cirth* could then be the regular result of PE plural **kirtā-i* > **kirtai*. (On the **kir-* we are propos-
ing in these reconstructions cf Q. *cirya* 'cleft', S *cirith* 'cleft, cutting'.) Or *cirth* may be the result of analogy. Once vowel alternation
had been established in various words as a morphological marker it could
be generalized to other forms. Of course, these analogical forms are
themselves indirect evidence of the regular changes, so, as with *cirth*,
we will continue to list all causes of s./pl. vowel alternation as evidence of the results of *ī*-affection.

According to the above proposal of PE **kirtā*, Q *certar* would not be
the regular development of the plural—we would expect ***cirtar*; rather,
it must be a borrowing from Sindarin, probably of an early form something
like **kerθa* or **kerta*. Such as borrowing is not improbable since the
Certhas was a Sindarin invention.

[5] We assume that the name *asea aranion* is Quenya for 'kingsfoil,
i.e. *asea* of the kings'. Just before Aragorn uses the term (III:141) the
herb-master has mentioned 'those who know somewhat of the Valinorean...'
and Aragorn's retort is: 'I do so, and I care not whether you say now
asëa aranion or *kingsfoil....*' Whether or not the herb-master knew the
difference between Quenya and Valinorean, Aragorn certainly does not say
that the phrase he uses is Valinorean, only that he knows some Valinorean, for what it's worth, and that he knows as many words for 'kingsfoil'
as he cares to discuss at the moment.

Findegil; PE **makīl-* > Q †*macil* in *Calimmacil, Narmacil*, S
*megil in *Arvegil, Malvegil*. Also S E*glerio*, the imperative
'praise!', beside a*glar* 'glory'.

o

PE *o* > Q, S *o*. Q *ando* 'gate', S *Annon*; PE **kor-*
'ring, circle' > Q *coranar* 'sun-round',[6] S *Echor* 'outer ring'
(**et* + **kor*); Q *formen*, S *forod*; Q *losse*, S *loss*; PE **mor-*
'black' > Q *morimaite-* 'black-handed' (?), *mornie* 'darkness',
S *Mordor* 'black land', *Morthond* 'blackroot'; PE **gondō*
'stone' > Q *Ondoher*, S *Gondor* 'Stoningland' (**gond* + *dor*);
PE **gornē* 'tree' > Q †*orne* in the Ent phrase *malinornélion
ornemalin*, S *Aragorn, Fangorn*; Q *oro-* 'high', S *orod* 'mountain'; Q *Ostoher*, S *Os(t)giliath* 'Fortress of the Stars'; Q
Voronwe 'steadfast', S *Boromir*.

PE *o* > S *ü* (written *y*) by final *ī*-affection. S *amon*
pl. *emyn*; *Annon* pl. *Ennyn*; *mallorn* pl. *Mellyrn*; *orch* pl.
yrch; *Onodrim* 'Ent-folk', *Enyd* 'Ents'; *orod* pl. *eryd*.[7]

PE *o* > S *e* by secondary affection. S *Enyd, eryd* as
in the above paragraph; also possibly *Enedwaith* < **Ened-
weith* < **onodweiθ* < **onod-waθyā* 'ent-land' (where the second
element contains a color term **waθ-* 'grey', i.e. earth-color'
cf. *Gwathlo* 'Greyflood'), compare also *Drúwaith, Forodwaith,
Haradwaith*.

PE *o* > S *e* by internal *ī*-affection. S **erin* < **orīṇa*
'on the day', see below under 'e'; *Cerin*, which is probably
the plural of †*cor* as in *Echor*, though the exact etymology is
not certain.

---

[6] Note that Q *coranar* 'solar year'—'when considered more or less
astronomically' (App. D, III:385)—in no way depends on assuming a spher-
ical earth, nor contradicts the implication of Tom Bombadil's words,
'When the Elves passed westward, Tom was here already, before the seas
were bent' (I:142) that Middle-earth was flat up to the time that 'Ar-
Pharazōn set foot upon the shores of Aman the Blessed, the Valar laid
down their guardianship and called upon the One, and the world was
changed...and the Undying Lands were removed from the circles of the
world (III:317), after which tumult, undoubtedly including the bending of
the seas, it seems Middle-earth was shaped more or less as it is now.
For *coranar* refers to the seasonal movement of the Sun around the 'circle' or 'ring' of the Zodiac, which is independent of the daily spinning
of the earth (or heavens, depending on which it is conceptually as well
as physically). The Zodiac as a circular band of stars is neatly analogous to both the circular wall of Rammas Echor and to the rings of trees
at Cerin Amroth.

[7] Tolkien gives us both *eryd, ered* as the plurals of *orod*. While
eryd corresponds to other *o/y* pairs, *ered* is the form that occurs in all
the place names: *Eredluin, Ered Lithui, Ered Mithrin, Ered Nimrais*.

PE *o* > Q *u* before *mb*. Q *lumbule* '(heavy) shadow' < PE *dombule* < *dom* + *bule* (?), cf. Q *tindóme* 'morning twilight', *lóme* 'night'; PE *ombar-* 'fate' > Q *umbar*, S *Amarth*[8] 'doom, i.e. impending fate'.

u

PE *u* > Q, S *u*. Q †*tumbale* 'deep valley'. S *Tumladen*; Q *ungwe* 'spider's web', S *Ungol* 'spider'; PE *tur-* 'lord' > Q *Turambar*, *Falastur* 'Lord of the Coasts', S *Turgon*.

PE *u* > S *o* by final *ā*-affection. PE *-uā* > *-uwa* > Q *-uva* the future marker, as in *enquantuva* 'will refill', *hir hiruva* 'will find', *hiruvalye* 'thou wilt find', *maruvan* 'I will abide'. In Sindarin we get PE *-ua* > *-oə* > S *-o* the imperative marker, as in *Cuio* 'live!', *Daro*, *edro* 'open', *minno* 'enter!', *noro*, *pedo* 'speak!, say!', *tiro* 'look towards!'. On the semantic connection between the future and the imperative cf Q *laituvalmet* which clearly has a jussive force and could be translated either 'we will praise them both' or 'let us praise them both'.

Long Vowels

The Proto-Eldarin long vowels in closed syllables[9] were shortened and developed like the short vowels in both Quenya and Sindarin. The long vowels in non-final open syllables remained unchanged in Quenya. In Sindarin the lower ones, *ē*, *ā*, *ō*, were 'raised' and ultimately equated qualitatively with with *i*, *o*, *u* respectively. Original *ī* and *ū* did not change in quality in Sindarin.

Vowel quantity in Sindarin is less straightforward. It does not seem to be related directly to vowel quantity in Proto-Eldarin, but rather to be determined by the stress patterns and syllable shapes in words at certain stages of the language. This is an unfortunately vague observation, but we do not have enough clear etymologies to determine which

---

[8] We would perhaps expect **Omarth* rather than *Amarth*. But there may be a parallel example of assimilation of *o* to *a* in the pair Q *Orome*, S *Araw*, though the etymology of these forms is by no means transparent. Perhaps PE *Oromē* > *Orauʋ* > *Orauw* > *Araw*.

[9] We divide syllables in front of single medial consonants, and between medial pairs of consonants. A CLOSED SYLLABLE is one that ends in a consonant. E.g. *e-le-ni*, *Nú-me-nó-re*, *Hi-thui* contain only OPEN SYLLABLES; *Hil-din-yar*, *An-ger-thas* contain only closed syllables; *lo-en-de*, *ae-a-ron* each contain both.

developments are regular and which analogical
    We will let it suffice to point out one obvious pattern,
the occurrence of long vowels in monosyllables or words
closely related to them: *Dîn, Dûm, dûn, êl, fân, Lhûn, lŷg,
nîn, rhîw, rhûn, Sûl, Tîw, amrûn, annûn, Gwanûr, Orod-na-
Thôn, Udûn.* When final vowels were lost in Sindarin there
was compensatory lengthening of the vowels in singly closed
monosyllables, but not in doubly closed ones, e.g. *alph,
cirth, loss, thond, Tyrn.* This would suggest that in monosyllables with short vowels a single final consonant represents an older gemminate, viz. *Bel, Dol, Fen* (cf. *Fennas*),
gil, glos(s), Hen (cf. *Henneth*), *Nan, Nen* (S *e* < PE *ē* indicates closed syllable), *rem* (cf. ᵗ*remmin*), *Tol.*
    Note that at the time of the lengthening we refer to
above, *o* from original *ā* was still a distinct sound (lower)
than original *o* and was diphthongized to *au* instead of being
lengthened. Thus we get *-Thôn* but *naur, Iaur.*

I

    PE *ī* > Q *í*, S *i, í.*   PE *hīθ- 'mist' > Q *hísie*, S
Hithaiglin 'Misty Mountains';   PE *srīwē 'winter' > Q *hríve*,
S *rhîw*;   PE *mīr- > Q *míri* pl., S *mîr, míriel* 'sparkling like
jewels';   PE *wīr- > Q *Víresse* 'April', S *Gwirith.*

    PE *i* < *ī* in closed syllables.   Q *silme* 'starlight'
beside *síla* 'shines'.

    PE *ī* > Q *i* in final syllables of polysyllabic words: Q
Elendilmir, Vardamir, both containing *mīr; enderi,* containing PE *rī* < *rē-i* pl. of *rē* 'day';   PE *lassī* (< *lasse-i* pl.
of *lasse* 'leaf') > Q *lassi.*   On *ēi* > *ī* see below under
Vowel Contraction.

    Final *ī* causes *ī*-affection in Sindarin.   For details
see above.

ē

    PE *ē* > Q *é*, S *i, í.*   PE *nēn- 'wet' > Q *Nénime* 'Febru-
ary', S *Nínui, nîn* 'wet';   S *erin* 'on (the)...day' (M) <
*orīna < PE *aurēnar = *aurē 'day' (> Q *aure*) + *nar allative
particle (cf. Q *falmalinnar*);   possibly S ᵗ*remmin* 'tangled' <
PE *rembēnar = all. of *rembē 'mesh' (> Q *rembe*).

    PE *e* < *ē* in closed syllables.   Q *Nényo* < PE *nēn-yā;   S
Nen 'water' (? < *nenn < PE *nēn-na).

    PE *ē* > Q *e* in final syllables of polysyllabic words.   Q
tuile, yávie beside *tuilére, yáviére*;   *yáviére* beside *ré*
'day';   ᵗ*orne* beside *ornélion.*

118

Note that in the development of Sindarin final *ē* must have been shortened (on the way to being completely lost) before the change of *ē* to *i*, because original final *ē* does not cause final *ī*-affection, cf. S *rem* < PE **rembē*, S *Fangorn, mallorn* beside Q *ornélion*.

ā

PE *ā* > Q *á*, S *o*, *ó*. PE **yār-* 'age, old' > S *Ioreth* 'aging' (?), *Iorlas* 'old leaf' (**iaur* + **lass*), that these are PE *ā* not *ō* cf. *Iarwain* below; PE **nār-* '(red) fire' > Q *Nárie* 'June', S *Nórui*; PE **anār* 'sun' > Q *Anárion*, S *Anor, Anórien* 'Sunlending'; PE **tār-* 'high' > Q *Tárion* 'Highday', *tárienna* 'on high' (?), **tári* 'queen' as in *airetári-lirinen, Elentári*, S **torn* 'hill'[10] as in *Arathorn, Tyrn* 'downs', *Gildor (gil + *tor), Thorondor (*thoron + *tor), Erestor (*eres + *tor)*.

PE *ā* > S *au* in monosyllables. S *Iaur* 'old'; *naur* 'fire'.

PE *a* < *ā* in closed syllables. S *Iarwain* < PE **yarwinyā* = **yār-winyā* 'old-new, i.e. ageless'; PE **nār-* > Q *Narquelie*, S *Narbeleth* 'sun-waning, October', Q *Narvinye* 'new-sun, January', S *Narwain*, Q *Narmacil, Narsil* 'red and white flame', *Narya*, S *Narchost, Nardol, Nargothrond*; PE **anār* > Q *Anarya* 'Sunday', *Anardil*; PE **tār-* > Q *Tarmenel* 'high-heaven'; Q *anna* 'gift', compare S *Ónen* 'I gave' (*Onen* in βγδε).

PE *ā* > Q *a* in final syllables of polysyllabic words. Q *Telemnar* 'silver sun' (?); *coronar* 'sun-round'; *Atanatar* (< PE **atana* 'man' + **tār* 'high').

Final *ā* causes *ā*-affection in Sindarin. For details see above.

ō

PE *ō* > Q *ó*, S *u*, *ú*. PE **dō-* > Q *lóme* 'night', **lómea* 'gloomy, shadowed', *Undómiel* 'Evenstar', S *Dúath* 'shadow (collective sense)', *Barad-dûr* 'tower-dark'; PE **rō-* 'rising, east' > Q *Rómello* 'from the east', *rómen*, S *rhûn* 'east', *amrûn* 'sunrise', *Rhudaur* 'east forest' (**rhu + taur*); PE **gōr-* 'spirit' > Q *óre* 'heart', S **guruth* 'death, i.e. becoming a spirit' (as in *di'nguruthos* 'beneath-death-horror', cf.

---

[10] We might expect *a* rather than *o* in a closed syllable, but this may be a late noun formation based on the Sindarin adjective **taur, *tor-* 'high'.

also *Gorgor* 'haunted', *Gorthad* 'barrow').[11]
Several Sindarin place-names, all containing the root PE
**n^d̄ōre* 'land, country' (cf. Q. *Númenor, sindanóriello*) show *o*
rather than *u*: *Arnor, Gondor, Mordor, Ennor* 'Middle-earth'.
These perhaps represent a borrowing from Quenya.

PE *ō* > Q *o* in final syllables of polysyllabic words.   Q
miruvor (borrowed into Sindarin) from older *miruvóre*; Q
Númenor < *Númenóre* (III:406); Q *Feanor* 'spirit of fire'[12]
beside *óre* 'heart (inner mind), i.e. spirit' (III:401).

PE *ō* > Q *o* in syllables without primary or secondary
stress. Q *Endóre*, but *Endorenna* which is stressed
ₗ*Endo*'*renna*.

ū

PE *ū* > Q, S *ú*. PE **n^dū-* 'down, west' > Q *númen*, S *dûn*;
PE *andūnē (? < *am-n^dūnē*, cf. S *amrûn*) > Q *andúne* 'sunset,

---

[11] We seem to have another example of PE *ō* > S *ú* in the name *Lúthien*
where the *ú* in an open syllable paralleling the *o* in closed syllables in
Lothron 'May' and *Lothlórien* 'Lórien of the Blossom' (I:355) suggests an
original *ō*. The *t* in Q *Lótesse* 'in flower' (?) i.e. 'May' is difficult
to explain if we have an original PE *lōθē 'flower', but perhaps when Q
th > *s* occurred dissimilation from the following *ss* prevented the change
here and *th* was de-spirantized to *t* instead. In *Lothíriel* the short *o*
suggests that this *th* is derived from a geminate, perhaps *loθ-sīriel
'flowing blossom' (compare *Ethir* < *et + *sir 'outflow', *míriel* 'sparkling'). Note that assuming a root **lōt-* with an extension **lott-* > S
loth- does not help with the name *Lúthien*, which requires a long *ō*. And
the etymology *lúthi (< *lōθē) 'flower' + *-en* (adj. suff., cf. ᵗ*mallen*,
galen) with the meaning 'flowery' is very inviting when we consider that
Lat. *flōrentia* 'flowery' yielded the name *Florence*; thus *Lúthien Tinúviel*
= 'Florence Nightingale'. A very intriguing equation if one recalls that
when Beren 'escaping through great peril' from the Enemy first saw
Lúthien in Neldoreth with '*flowers* of gold / Upon her mantle and her
sleeves', then 'Enchantment *healed* his weary feet'; and later, just
before he called her name, 'He saw the elven-*flowers* spring / About her
feet, and *healed* again' (emphasis ours) he came to her at last; and that
Tolkien probably first recorded the tale of Tinúviel while in the hospi-
tal in England healing from his war wounds, just returned to his wife
whom he had newly wed before going off to the Great War. 'What dreames
may come...Must giue vs pawse.'

[12] This gloss of the name *Feanor* is provided by Clyde S. Kilby in his
essay 'Mythic and Christian Elements in Tolkien' in *Myth, Allegory, and
Gospel*, p. 127. (This essay contains a few statements which are inconsistent with what Tolkien says in *The Lord of the Rings*, but we have no
specific reason to doubt the validity of this particular bit of information.) That the second element of this compound is Q *-or* 'spirit' rather
than S *-nor* 'fire' (< PE *năr-*) is confirmed by the fact that in discussing stress in App. E I (III:394) Tolkien gives 2 lists of examples separated by a semicolon, with *Feanor* included in the sublist of Quenya
forms (the other sublist is composed of Sindarin examples). The implication that *Feanor* is Quenya determines the etymology we have adopted.

west' = S *annûn*; PE *θūlē* > Q *thúle* > *súle* 'spirit', S *Sûl*
'wind';[13] PE *ūr-* 'heat' > Q *úre* (*úr* in αβ) 'heat', *Úrime*
'hot, August' = S *Úrui*.

PE *u* < *ū* in closed syllables. PE *n^dū-n* > *n^dun* > Q *nu*
'under'; compare S *di-* 'beneath' which causes eclipses
(nasal mutation)—thus *di-nguruthos* with *guruthos* 'death
horror' probably related to *gor-* in *Tyrn Gorthad* 'Barrow-
downs'—indicating the presence of a final nasal at an earlier period. The change PE *u* > S *i* was probably restricted
to monosyllables which were never stressed, such as prepositions. But with no other examples the exact conditions are
unrecoverable.

Diphthongs'

For the diphthongs (as for the pure vowels) we assume a
system in Proto-Eldarin like that in Quenya, i.e. six falling
diphthongs: *ui, oi, ai, iu, eu, au*. These were unchanged for
the most part in Quenya, however *ai* and *au* become *e* and *o*
respectively in unstressed syllables and in prevocalic position. In Third Age Quenya *iu* had become a rising diphthong
(*iu* [yu] instead of *iu* [iŭ], cf. App. E [III:394n]).

In Sindarin *oi* merged with *ui*; *ai* became *ae*; *iu* and *eu*
probably both became *ü* (written *y*). The diphthong *au*
remained in stressed monosyllables and certain compounds,
otherwise it was changed to *o*. Sindarin had three other
diphthongs: *ei, ai,* and *oe*. *Ei* arose from original *a* and *ai*
by final *i*-affection, from *e* (and possibly *a*, cf. *Enedwaith*)
by final *y*-affection, and from *eχ* (cf. Q *tehtar* 'signs' S
teithant 'drew'); *ei* was later changed to *ai* in final syllables (including monosyllables).

Oe possibly derives from *oi* in hiatus (like the *oi* in
coincidence as opposed to *coin*) resulting from original *ogi*
and *osi* when *g* and *s* were lost intervocalicly. We have only
one example of this diphthong: in *Nen Hithoel*, which may contain *hiθo-gil* and mean 'water of mist sparks' or *hiθo-sil*
and mean 'water of mist flame'.

---

[13] We do not expect S *s* to correspond with Q *s* from *th*. We might
suggest a PE *sū-* 'wind' with a suffix beginning *r* or *s* in Q *súrinen*
and suffix beginning *l* in Q *Súlime* 'March' and S *Sûl* 'wind' with only
accidental homophony with Q *súle* 'spirit'. On the other hand, it is possible that S *Sûl* is a borrowing from Q *súle* or *Súlime*. (Note, for what
it's worth, that the Sindarin name for March, *Gwaeron*, contains a different morpheme †*gwae* 'wind'. The Quenya name *Súlime* might mean 'spirited'
or 'lively' and have been misinterpreted by the Sindarin borrowers as
meaning 'windy' like their own name.)

Note that S *au* (written *aw* word-finally) also derives
from *au* in hiatus, which is not changed to *o*. Thus *Rauros* =
PE **ras-ū* 'two peaks' (cf. *Methedras* 'last peak', Q *Aldúya*
'two trees day') + **ros* 'foam' (cf. *Cair Andros*); *Lhaw* '(two)
ears' < PE **slasū*.

PE *ui* > Q, S *ui*. PE **luinë* 'blue' > Q *luini* pl., S
luin s. (*Mindolluin*) and pl. (*Eredluin*); PE **tuilë* 'spring'
> Q *tuile*, S *ethuil* (**et* + **tuil*).

PE *oi* > Q *oi*, S *ui*. PE **koi-* 'live, stir' > Q *coire*
'stirring' = S *echuir* (< **eccuir* < **et* + **kuir*), S *Cuio*
'live! (imperative)'; Q *Oiolosse* 'ever snow-white' = S
Uilos.

PE *ai* > Q *ai, e*, S *ae*. PE **airë* 'holy' > Q †*aire*, S
ᴄᴀʏʒɪɴ (*aerlinn* = †*aer* + †*linn* 'song'); PE **lairë* 'summer'
> Q *lairë*, S *laer*; PE **aiare* 'sea' > Q *ear*, S *aear*; Q *Aldea*
'Tree-day' < **aldaia* = **aldā* + **yā* (cf. *Anaryä, Isilya*, etc.
App. D., III:388); S *mae* 'well' in *Mae govannen!* 'well met'
(cf. what Glorfindel says to Aragorn with what he says to
Frodo, I:222) is probably related to Q *Maia* 'Blessed' or
'Good'—we offer the interpretation Melian the Maia = Melian
the Blessed, the Maiar being a race of 'Blessed Ones'.

PE *ai* > S *ei* (> *ai*) by final *ī*-affection. S †*gwae*
'wind' (*Gwaeron* 'March'—on the second element cf. *Lothron*
'May', *Girithron* 'December') pl. †*gwai* (*Gwaihir* = **gwai* +
-hir 'lord of the winds') (see p. 113n).

PE *iu* came to be pronounced as *yu* in Third Age Quenya
(III:294n). If this pronunciation was reflected in the
writing then Q *yuldar* 'draughts', *yulma* 'cup' may derive
from a PE form **iul-*. These are the only Quenya forms in
the corpus that might contain this diphthong. We have no
examples of the Sindarin reflex of PE *iu*; but we are told
(III:393) that S *y* was 'partly derived from older diphthongs
eu, iu.'

PE *eu* > Q *eu*, S *ū* (written *ȳ* in the sole certain example). PE **leukā* 'snake' > Q *leuca*, S *lȳg* (*lyg* in βγδε).

PE *au* > Q *au*, S *o*. PE **aurë* 'day' > Q *aure* 'day-
(light)', S *Or-* in *Oranor* 'Sunday', *Orithil* 'Monday' etc.;
PE **laurë* 'golden light' > Q *laure*, S *Glorfindel* (containing
*glaur 'dazzling-gold', cf. *glos* 'dazzling-white' R:62); PE
*nauk- 'dwarf' > Arch. S. *Naugrim* 'dwarf-folk (of the Elder
Days)', S *Nogrod* 'dwarf-height (?)' 'dwarf-mountain (?)',
nogothrim 'dwarf-folk'.

PE *au* > Q *o* in syllables without primary or secondary
stress. Q *Lindelorendor* 'land of singing gold' containing
laure 'gold', stressed *'Lindelo'rendor*.

PE *au* > S *au* in monosyllables. PE **aurë* > S *aur* 'day';

PE *taurẽ 'forest' > Q (Entish) Taurelilómea 'forestmanyshadowed', S Taur (in Taur e-Ndaedelos, Taur-na-Neldor, Rhudaur
'east-forest').

Vowel Contraction

The evidence we possess for vowel contraction in late
Proto-Eldarin is wholly tied up with the problem of reconstructing the noun declension of Proto-Eldarin. We are particularly hampered in our investigation by the affects of
analogy, which we expect to be widespread in the area of morphological categories. Without a large number of examples we
can rarely be sure that the forms we have to work with are
the result of regular phonetic changes rather than generaliz-
ations based on other forms which existed in the language but
are not extant in the corpus we possess.

The reader will have observed above that we suggest a
Proto-Eldarin plural marker *-i and genitive marker *-on.
Juxtaposed they yield a plural genitive marker *-on-i. With
the loss of final consonants and final short vowels in Quenya
(see below) we would expect the genitive singular marker *-on
to become Q -o and the genitive plural marker *-oni to become
Q -on. Thus airetário 'holy queen's', Oiolosseo gen. of Oiolosse, aldaron 'of trees', malinornélion 'of many gold
trees'.

The combinations ão and ao were contracted to õ
which became o in final syllables in Quenya. Thus Calacirya
gen. Calaciryo (*kiryã-on > †ciryo), ómaryo 'of her voice'
beside má-rya-t 'hands-her-two' (R:59), Varda gen. Vardo.

The plural marker *-i would normally be lost when
affixed to a Proto-Eldarin stem ending in a single consonant. But the stem consonant would be preserved (in some
form) while being lost in the singular. Thus plural and
singular remained distinct. For example, PE s. *balar pl.
*balar-i yield Q s. vala pl. Valar. Also the adverbial case
markers: PE loc. s. *-sen pl. *-sen-i > Q s. -sse (Lóriendesse 'in Lórien') pl. -ssen (yassen 'in which [pl.]'); PE
all. s. *-nar pl. *-nar-i > Q s. -nna (tárienna 'on high')
pl. -nnar (falmalinnar). Note also the plural genitive -on
< *-on-i mentioned above.

Now the combinations ẽi and ei were contracted to ĩ.
Thus Q mí 'in the' < *mei < PE *m^{b}e 'in' + i 'the' (cf. Q
imbe 'between', S *ben 'in the' [M] Iarwain Ben-adar 'Old-
new in the Beginning' [?]). And the Proto-Eldarin forms
ending in ẽ or e would have plurals in -ĩ (which causes final
ĩ-affection in Sindarin). This was shortened to -i in Quenya

in polysyllabic words. Thus *lasse* pl. *lassi*, *ré* 'day',
enderi 'middle days'. Pairs like *yén* pl. *yéni* probably arose
from something like PE **yēne* pl. **yēne-i*. These patterns
were undoubtedly generalized as well to other Quenya forms
ending in -*e* or a consonant.

We have just scratched the surface of possible speculation in the area of Eldarin morphology. But these comments
will suffice we think to illuminate the two clear cases of
vowel contraction in Proto-Eldarin.

Final Syllables

In reconstructing Proto-Eldarin form from Quenya and
Sindarin cognates we have assumed certain regular changes in
final syllables in the separate development of each language.

In Quenya there are three basic changes. To begin with,
and in effect simultaneously, (1) final consonants were lost
and (2) certain consonant groups were not tolerated word-
finally. Thirdly, and more recently, long vowels in various
syllables were shortened, except in monosyllables.

On the loss of final consonants cf. Q *ando*, S *annon*,
where Sindarin may preserve an original final *n* (though what
the conditions of such a preservation could be is not clear,
and these words may not in fact be exact cognates). The best
evidence for this loss is indirect: If in the Quenya singu-
lar/plural oppositions *vala/Valar*, -*o*/-*on*, -*nna*/-*nnar*, -*sse*/
-*ssen* we attempt to isolate a unified 'sign' of the plural,
we can at best say that it is a consonantal suffix. Within
the context of Quenya alone we cannot explain the variation
as to specific suffix, except to classify the cases that have
an -*r* and those that have an -*n*. However, to attack the
problem historically, if we suppose that word final consonants were lost at an earlier stage of the language, we can
reconstruct proto-forms such that the consonants occur in
both the singular and plural. Thus their variety is due to
their being originally part of distinct case suffixes—-*r*
(nom.), -*on* (gen.), -*nar* (all.), -*sen* (loc.)—rather than
integral signs of the plural. The plural was originally
marked by a final short vowel, identical for all cases, which
was lost (see next paragraph) leaving the originally internal consonant to mark the plural in Quenya, e.g. PE **bala-r-i*
nom. pl. > Q *Valar*.

The one example we have of a polysyllabic Quenya word
with a long vowel in its final syllable is *palantír* 'far-
seer',[14] which may preserve its *í* by analogy with the plural

---

[14] Two if *Erusén* is Quenya. Cf. R:66.

form *palantíri* and the example of other Quenya nouns that
follow the pattern PLURAL = SINGULAR + *i*: *yén* pl. *yéni*, *elen*
pl. *eleni*. Note that in the personal name *Tar-Palantir*,
where it would be separate mentally from the rest of the
declension, we may have the same form with a regularly shortened final syllable.

In the development of Sindarin (1) words ending in a
consonant lost that consonant, then (2) all words ultimately
lost their final vowel (whether long or short). Thus with an
original final consonant: PE **fala-sen* 'at the wave(s)' >
*falase > S †*falas* 'strand' (*Anfalas*, *Belfalas*); PE **galdar*
'tree' > **galða* > **galð* > S *galadh*. PE **dō-siri-on-i* 'shadowed rill' gen. pl. > S *Duhirion* 'Dimrill'; PE **gornē* 'tree'
(Q *ornélion*) appearing in S *Fangorn*, *Aragorn*.

Because of the decay in final syllables of Eldarin forms
we are often unable to determine the precise final sounds of
the proto-stage. So, for example, S *fân*, *fan-* 'cloud' = Q
fana 'veil'[15] could be descended from either PE **fanar* or
*fanā. The Quenya pl. *fanar*, presumably from PE **fanari*,
would point to PE **fanar*, but this plural form could be a
Quenya innovation. In some instances we seem to have
reflexes of both these endings, e.g. we assume PE **winyā* to
account for the diphthong in S *-wain*, while on the other hand
Q *Vinyarion* seems to contain a PE **winyar*. Perhaps the *-ar*
and *-ā* marked two different cases in Proto-Eldarin which,
falling together in the singular in both Quenya and Sindarin,
were also syncretized in the plural, with one or the other of
the cases being generalized in specific instances. This
would neatly account for the fact that Quenya makes no apparent distinction between the nominative and accusative, but
has an otherwise quite elaborate case system. Thus S *certh*
(and presumably Q **certa*) represents both PE **kertar* and
*kertā, but PE **kertar-i* is generalized in Q *Certar* while PE
*kerta-i may account for S *cirth* (< **kerθī* < **kertai*; but see
p. 114n).

Svarabhakti

Certain consonant clusters in Sindarin monosyllables
developed an epenthetic vowel. This probably started as a
weak central vowel [ə], and was then assimilated to the vowel
in the now preceding syllable. This phenomenon is called

---

[15] Although Q *fanya* (a 'derivative' of *fana*) means 'cloud', according to R:66, S *fân* 'cloud' was 'originally identical' to Q *fana*; and carried the same connotations.

SVARABHAKTI. It occurred in Welsh and Cornish (though the specific consonants involved are different). The combinations *ld* *lð*, *ðl*, *lb*, *rd* are involved in svarabhakti in Sindarin.
Thus *galð 'tree' > *galəð.> S galað (written galadh); *cald 'light' (< PE *caltā) > *caləd > S *calad in Gil-galad; PE *eldā (Q elda) > *eðl > *eðəl > S edhel; PE *kyelpe 'silver' (Q tyelpe-) > *kelb > *keləb > S celeb. Some of Barad, harad, forod, orod pl. ered undoubtedly involve svarabhakti with the cluster *rd*, though possibly not all of them.

Acknowledgments

This article is lengthy, and we hope ponderous, enough to justify the grateful acknowledgment by its authors of those who engendered and helped bring it to fruition. First and foremost we thank Paula Marmor; whose 'Notes toward as System of Sindarin Vowel Shifts' inspired our own effort, and in fact provided the conceptual kernal of which it is to a large extent an expansion (and we hope a revivication); whose chaperoning of various heated arguments between the authors transformed a sometimes sterile interaction into a collaboration; and whose incessant pleas for something to publish, and other sorts of cajolement, ultimately inveigled a response. Next we thank Jim Allan, the numerous products of whose tireless typewriter have continued to instruct us from the moment we first opened *A Glossary of the Eldarin Tongues*. His efforts include the final typing of our article, during which drudgery he patiently endured our idiosyncracies and corrected our more blatent blunders. We should mention: Charles Kester, who was the first (as far as we know) to use the term 'Proto-Eldarin' in the sense we have adopted and to attempt the reconstruction of Proto-Eldarin forms, all in a brief but very thought-provoking letter in *Parma* 1; Björn Fromén, who offered the stop-gap and stimulus of a fresh point of view; Bob Foster, the value of whose *Guide to Middle-Earth* as a tool for onomastic research is proverbial. Last we would thank Raimo Antilla, linguist and teacher, who is largely responsible for what understanding of the comparative method we here display. His *Introduction to Historical and Comparitive Linguistics* (New York: Macmillan, 1972) we highly recommend. It is from this abundantly instructive book that the attempts at explanation in our Introduction are gleaned, though of course we must claim responsibility for any vagaries or misconceptions.

PROTO-ELDARIN VOWELS

Vowel Summary Chart: by Jim Allan

The transformations of the preceding article are generalized here. All but the most complex changes appear. / / = unstressed and/or in a final syllable. | | *= stressed, originally singly-closed, monosyllable.* ∿ *= in alternation with.* ... *= syllable boundary.* V *= any vowel.* V[i] *= vowel shifted towards i or i-diphthong. Note that long vowels in Proto-Eldarin normally become the corresponding short vowel in a closed syllable in Proto-Eldarin, so that transformations ascribed to the short vowels may also occur with originally long vowels.*

QUENYA		PROTO-ELDARIN		SINDARIN
i	⟵	i	⟶	i |î|
i...a	⟵	i...ā	⟶	e... |ê...|
i...ya	⟵	i...yā	⟶	ei... ∿ ai... |ai...|
í /i/	⟵	ī	⟶	i ∿ í |î|
yu(?) iu(?)	⟵	iu	⟶	ü = ⟨y⟩
iht	⟵	iχt	⟶	íth |îth|
e	⟵	e	⟶	e |ê|
e...i	⟵	e...ī	⟶	i... |î...|
é /e/	⟵	ĕ	⟶	i ∿ í |î|
eu	⟵	eu	⟶	ü = ⟨y⟩
eht	⟵	eχt	⟶	eith ∿ aith |aith|
a	⟵	a	⟶	a |ā|
a...i	⟵	a...ī	⟶	ei... ∿ ai... |ai...|
a...V...i	⟵	a ..V...ī	⟶	a...V[i]...
á /a/	⟵	ā	⟶	o ∿ ó |au|
ea	⟵	āyā	⟶	ei ∿ ai |ai|
ai	⟵	ai	⟶	ae
ai...i	⟵	ai...ī	⟶	ei... ∿ ai... |ai...|
au /o/	⟵	au	⟶	o |au/aw|
aht	⟵	aχt	⟶	aeth
o	⟵	o	⟶	o |ō|
o...i	⟵	o...ī	⟶	ü... = ⟨y...⟩
o...V...i	⟵	o...V...ī	⟶	e...V[i]...
ó /o/	⟵	ō	⟶	u ∿ ú |û|
oi	⟵	oi	⟶	ui
oht	⟵	oχt	⟶	oeth
umb	⟵	omb	⟶	om(m) (?)
u	⟵	u	⟶	u |û|
u...a	⟵	u...ā	⟶	o... |ō...|
ú /u/	⟵	ū	⟶	u ∿ ú |û|
ui	⟵	ui	⟶	ui
uht	⟵	uχt	⟶	uith

No long variant of ũ written y in Sindarin is given here. However, if the form lŷg found in α is correct, rather than the lyg of βγδε, then the occurrence of long ũ/y can be predicted on the pattern of other alternations of long and short vowels in Sindarin.

The complete vowel + χt series has been given here from Welsh parallels.

PROTO-ELDARIN CONSONANTS

Jim Allan

compiled & expanded from notes by
Chris Gilson & Bill Welden

A SUGGESTED DEVELOPMENT OF THE CONSONANTS OF Quenya and Sindarin is given in the table beginning on page 135. A simplified listing follows here, in which consonant clusters and the more complicated changes are not included. This simplified listing gives the symbol for the phoneme in Proto-Eldarin, and its realization in Tolkien's spelling in word-initial position in the Third Age in Quenya and Sindarin (Q/S). In a few instances a more archaic value is given in parentheses. The consonants are arranged so as to make clear what seems to us the most systematic way of ordering them in Proto-Eldarin.

Voiceless:

*p	> p/p		*f	> f/f
*t	> t/t		*θ	> θ (th)/th
			*s	> s/s
*ky	> ty/c		*χy	> hy/h
*k	> c/c		*χ	> h/h
*kw	> qu/p		*χw	> hw/f

Voiced:

*b	> v/b		*w	> v (w)/gw
*d	> l/d		*r	> r/r
			*l	> l/l
*gy	> ly/i		*y	> y/i
*g	> Ø/g			
*gw	> v (w)/b			

128

Nasal:

*m^b > m/b		*m > m/m
*n^d > n/d		*n > n/n
*$ŋ^g$ > n *(ng)* $/g$		*ŋ > n *(ng)* $/ng$

The nasals are a much more complex problem than the chart suggests. Further nasal combinations are included in the more complete chart. It is doubtful that *ŋ occurred initially save in the combinations *ŋg, *ŋk and their palatal and labialized extensions.

For the velars we have indicated regular velars (*k, *χ, *g), palatal velars (*ky, *χy, *gy), and labialized velars (*kw, *χw, *gw). It appears that these functioned as units in Proto-Eldarin rather than as clusters, as, for example, paralleling forms beginning *kye- and *kwe- we have forms beginning *pe-, *te- and *ke-, but no forms beginning *pye-, *pwe-, or *twe-. (See below for examples.) This rudimentary pattern may be an accident of the paucity of data, but it would seem to indicate that it is best to consider these as single consonants. They might well be written *k^y, k^w, g^y, etc. to emphasize this; or diacritics might be used for palatalization and velarization. However, there is, as yet, no evidence that we need to distinguish between these and corresponding combinations (between *g^w and *gw from *g + *w for example), and so the simpler form of notation without superscripts or diacritics has been used here.

With the nasals it is a different matter. We get, for one example, two sorts of Quenya/Sindarin correspondences that we must trace back to some sort of *nd. One is exemplified by Q *ando*/S *annon*, Q *Endóre*/S *Ennor*, and is distinctly traced back by Tolkien to an original *nd, one of three nasal 'combinations' (*mb, nd, ŋg*) 'which were specially favoured in the Eldarin languages at an earlier stage' (III:393). Tolkien makes is quite clear that this 'combination' became *nn* usually (sometimes shortened to *n*), but remained *nd* in certain circumstances. But in contrast to this Q *nd*/S *nn* correspondence we also find a Q *nd*/S *d* correspondence exemplified by Q *Quendi* 'Speakers' compared to S *pedo* 'speak!', and possibly by Q *undu-* 'down' compared to S *Udûn* 'Hell'. It fits the evidence to postulate a series of what we might call NASAL STOPS (*m^b, *n^d, *$ŋ^g$) in opposition to both the simple nasal continuants (*m, *n, *ŋ) and the nasal + voiced stop combinations (*mb, *nd, *ŋg). Of course, it is possible that further evidence would prove that our nasal stops are only allophones of the nasal + voiced stop combinations, perhaps conditioned by the original length of the preceding vowel, or by stress, or that the picture is confused by nasal combinations being changed in certain environments at one period in the languages, and the unchanged nasal combinations being

subject to further different changes at a later period.
Whatever are the actual facts, the use a series of nasal
stops in our reconstructions does at least allow us to conveniently symbolize the two different sets of Quenya/Sinda-
rin correspondences in a clear manner.

Tolkien mentions that Q *ty* 'was derived mainly from *c* or
t + y' (III:392). That is, PE **ky* and PE **ty* fell together
in Quenya as *ty*. Tolkien also indicates that Q *hy* 'was
usually derived from *sy-* and *khy-*' (III:393). That is, PE
*χy and PE **sy* fell together in Quenya as *hy*. From these
two examples a full dental + *y* series has been given in the
large chart with their probable Quenya reflexes based on the
two samples given by Tolkien. The pairs are, in each case,
enclosed in braces {} to indicate that they have fallen
together, though in fact it is not certain that they have
also fallen together in Sindarin as the chart indicates.

Voiceless Stops:

For PE **p* there is Q *pella* 'beyond'/S **pel* 'fence' in
ephel.

For PE **t* there is Q *tehta* 'mark'/S *teithant* 'drew'
with the lenition to *d* appearing in S *andaith* 'long mark';
also, Q *tinwe* 'star' compared with S *ithildin* 'starmoon'.
The combinations **tp*, **ts*, **tk* are realized in S *ephel* 'outer
fence' (> **et + *pel*), S *ethir* 'outflow' (> **et + *sir*), and
S *echor* 'outer ring' (> **et + *kor*). Tolkien indicates that
ph in *ephel* 'represents a long *ff* (from *pp*)' (III:392), and
so presumably *echor* comes from earlier **ekkor*. That the
these doublings contain an assimilated *t* is suggested by
the Quenya word *et* 'out' which supplies the required meaning,
as well as from parallels in Welsh of *d* + consonant producing
a double consonant. So PE **tt* should normally produce S *th*,
which process is verified by Q *metta* 'ending' compared with S
methed- 'last'.

We have Q ⁺*tyelpe* corresponding to S *celeb*, and from
Tolkien's indication that Q *ty* derives mainly from PE **ty* or
*ky must postulate PE **tyelpē* or **kyelpē*. Sindarin lenition
is found in *Argeleb*. The Quenya variant *telpe* in *Telperion*
might respresent loss of *y* from dissimilation from the *i* in
the ending.

For PE **k* we have Q *corma*/S ⁺*cor* 'ring', and with lenition in Sindarin, Q *cal(a)-* 'light'/S *Gil-galad* 'Star-(of)-
Bright-Light'. Also with lenition is Q *alcar*/S *aglar* 'glory'
with metathesis of the original **kl* to **lk* = *lc* in Quenya.
For original PE **lk* see below.

For PE **kw* we have Q *Quendi* 'Speakers' compared to S
pedo 'speak!'. Lenition of S *p* to *b* is found in Q *Narquelie*/S *Narbeleth* 'Sun-waning'.

Voiced Stops:

The voiced stops have different reflexes when preceded
by their corresponding nasals, and these nasal + voiced stop
reflexes have been given a separate section at the end of the
Consonant Summay Chart. Also, for *rd and *ld see the section on Voiced Continuants.

For PE *b we have only Q vala/S *balan, the plural of
*balan—ᵗbelain—being found in Orbelain 'Day-(of the)-Valar'.

For PE *d we have Q lóme 'shadow, night' with the original d still preserved following n in the Quenya compounds
tindóme 'star-shadow' and undóme 'down-shadow'. In Sindarin
we find dúath 'the shadows' and Duhirion 'Shadowed-rills'.
Also, Tolkien points out that original duinē (> S duin
'river') 'would have been luine (in Quenya initial d became
l), but the word was not used' (G:179).

For PE *dy/gy we have followed the pattern of the corresponding voiceless PE *ty/ky, and assumed a possible connection between Q vilya 'air' and S ᵗgwai 'winds'. An original *gwidyā or *gwigyā is postulated, producing Early Quenya
wilya > vilya. In archaic Sindarin we would get *gwigʸ >
*gweig lenited to *gweiɣ (written *gweigh) > ᵗgwai in Third
Age Sindarin. The singular ᵗgwae may have developed analog-
ically with other ae/ai singular and plural pairs. But
it is not impossible that the change of ɣ (gh) to ∅ may have
caused a lengthening of the preceding diphthong ei so that
it became ae.

For PE *g we have Q ᵗondo (in Ondoher) and S gond(o)-
(in Gondobar, Gondolin).

PE *gw largely fell together with PE *b in Third Age
Quenya and in Sindarin, as both became Q v and S b~v. We
can suggest that Q voron- is cognate with S bor(o)-, but cannot tell whether they derive from PE *bor- or *gwor-. Q
varda 'exalted' may be related to S barad 'tower' (if barad
does not, in fact, contain original *mᵇar-), but the proto-
form of the stem may be either *bar- or *gwar-. We know that
we must construct the proto-form for Q *vala/S *balan as
something like *balan-, not **gwalan-, only because vala is
the Quenya letter name for ♫ which stood for v also in early
Quenya, as opposed to ♫ which stood for w in early Quenya.
If vilya (earlier wilya) is not a cognate of S ᵗgwai (as
suggested in the discussion of PE *w below), its initial v
might descend from PE *gw. It is likely that early Q w from
PE *gw would remain w in late Quenya internally in certain
enivronments, as it does in the nasal combinations. Hence
this has been indicated on the chart. It also seems likely
that PE *igw, *egw, *agw, *ugw would become, respectively,
*iw > iu, *ew > eu, *aw > au, *uw > ú in at least some
environments, hence the u in the chart. PE *ogw should,
likewise, become ou, but as this diphthong does not occur in

Quenya it would seem that it fell together with *au*, *ó*, or *ú*.

Voiceless Continuants:

PE **f* remaining *f* in Quenya and Sindarin is exemplified by Q *fana*, S *fân*. In Sindarin final written *f* in Tolkien's transcription indicates the sound [v], not [f]. There are no pairs which indicate whether this final *f* normally derives from PE **f* or from PE **b* > S *b* lenited to *v* written *f*. But Tolkien does tell us that *ph* is used in his writing of Sindarin for the sound [f] '(*a*) where the *f*-sound occurs at the end of a word, as in *alph* "swan"; (*b*) where the *f*-sound is related to or derived from *p*...; (*c*) in the middle of a few words where it represents a long *ff* (from *pp*)...' (III:392). One implication of this is that final *ph* is NOT 'related to or derived from *p*' or Tolkien would not have listed it separately from *ph* from *p*. The only other consonant it might derive from is *f*. So it is indicated on the chart that final *ph* derives from PE **f*. As to final *f* representing [v], the Sindarin pair *alph* and *talf* indicate that it is not, at least in every case, just a voiced allophone of original **f*, but probably derives from original PE **b*. But why then does Tolkien use the transliteration *f* if it is misleading not only in respect to pronunciation, but in respect to etymology? A possible solution is that Sindarin final *f* from PE **f* did become voiced to [v] in most cases, and thus fell together with Sindarin final *v* from PE **b* and **m*, and that *f* was used finally to indicate final [v] from whatever source. However following *l*, and possibly in some other circumstances, *f* retained its original pronuncation [f], and then Tolkien has used the writing *ph*. That is, *alph* would come from earlier **alf*, but **talf* would come from earlier **talb* or **talm* (< PE **talmā* [?]), or even **talw*. This hypothesis does account for the small number of examples and few facts available.

PE **θ* appears in Q *isil* (earlier *ithil*)/S *ithil*, and in Q *Hísime*/S *Hithui*. Quenya internal *s* would normally be derived from PE **θ* rather than from PE **s* which internally becomes *r* in Third Age Quenya.

PE **s* remains in Quenya and Sindarin initially. In Sindarin it lenits to *h* in lenition position, as indicated by S *sir-* 'stream' in *Sirannon* 'Gatestream' and *Duhirion* 'Shadowed-streams', with *h* in some cases entirely disappearing. In Quenya PE **s* became *z* between vowels and probably in some other internal environments, and *z* later became *r*. Where possible the Quenya letter names begin with the sound which they represent and the use of the the letter name *áze* for ʒ indicates that *z* was not found initially in early Quenya. The change of *s* > *z* > *r* may also be demonstrated in English in the pair *was* and *were*. In Germanic, PIE **s*

became *z* in most places internally, but remained *s* when the
main stress of the word fell on the vowel directly preceding.
Thus in Germanic we would have found **ik 'wasð* but **wē
wē'zun.* In Old English, after Gmc. **z* had become *r*, we find
ic 'wæs / wē 'wǣron > ME *ɩ 'was / wē 'weren* > *I was / we were.*
In Quenya we find *Minastan* and *Minardil* in which the *s/z*
correspondence may arise from an original **s* > *z* > *r* in
Minardil. That Q *r* may represent PE **s* opens another possibility in respect to plurals. Let us assume PE **kertas,* pl.
*kertasi > **kertas,* pl. **kertazi* > Early Q **certā,* pl.
*certaz > Third Age Q **certa,* pl. **certar.* A possible Sindarin sequence would be PE **kertas,* pl. **kertasi* > **kerta,*
pl. **kertas* > **kert,* pl. **kertas* > S *certh,* pl. *certhas.*
That is, *certhas* would be an archaic plural along side the
regular plural *cirth* formed by analogy, and would have developed the specialized meaning 'set of runes, i.e., runic
alphabet', while *cirth* would simply mean 'runes'. Similarly,
rammas 'great wall' might originally mean 'fortifications'
and *fennas* 'gateway' might mean 'set of gates'. One of the
difficulties with this theory is that the final *s* on *certhas,*
fennas, and *rammas* would seem to have to derive from PE **ss*
as we would expect simple PE **s* to lenit to *h* or to vanish.
We would be forced to assume either that final *s* generally
does not undergo lenition in Sindarin, or that the necessity
of retaining a plural marker prevented *s* from lenition when
it filled that function. Further evidence is required.

   PE **ss* generally remains in both Quenya and Sindarin,
thus Q *losse*/S *loss* 'snow'. It, of course, often simplified
to *s* when final as in Q *Oiolosse* than S *Uilos,* and in some
cases may have become simple *s* elsewhere in Quenya or Sindarin or both. Tolkien indicates that PE **sl* and **sr* become
voiceless *l* and voiceless *r* respectively, written *hl* and *hr*
in Quenya and transliterated by Tolkien as *lh* and *rh* for
Sindarin (III:392). The only pair of words for either is
Q *hríve*/S *rhîw* 'winter'. PE **sw,* giving Q, S *hw* appears on
the chart by analogy with **sr,* **sl,* and **sy.*

   PE **sy* and **χy* both produce Q *hy* and S *h* according to
Tolkien (III:393). Compare Q *hyarmen* and S *harad,* both meaning 'south'.

   PE **χ* was still pronounced as [x] in most positions in
Early Quenya, but in Third Age Quenya it had come to be pro-
as [h] save in the combination *ht* (< PE **χt*) and is written
h. In Sindarin *ch* in *carach, torech,* and *Rochann* can best
be explained as representing PE **χ.* This *ch* is not found
initially in the corpus, and it would seem to follow that
intial PE **χ* became *h* in Sindarin, which is found corresponding to Q initial *h*: Q *Hísime*/S *Hithui,* Q *halla*/S *hal-.* On
this interpretation, when compounds were formed in which the
the second element began with *h* < PE **χ* the *h* would still

remain as *h*, even though it was now medial. For example:
†*rooh* + *ann* → *Roohann* with medial * oh*, but *bar(a)* + *hir* (as in
Hirgon) → *Barahir*. It is assumed in this argument that S
-*hir*—cognate with Q -*her* (see *Ciryaher*)—derives from PE
*χ*ir-. But, our information on medial *h* and *oh* in Sindarin
is somewhat confused by the fact that *oh* came to be pronounced [h] in the speech of Gondor—save finally and immediately preceding *t*—and this change in pronunciation has
been followed by a change from *oh* to *h* in the spelling of
some names (III:391). Accordingly, we cannot be certain that
a medial *h* in a name does not, in fact, stand for *oh* as it
would be spelt by the Elves themselves. PE *χ*t probably derives mostly from earlier *kt. It is written *ht* in Quenya,
and retains its original pronunciation of [xt] following *a*,
o, or *u*. Following *i* or *e* it is pronounced [çt]. The Sindarin change of PE *χ*t to *eth* or *ith* has been covered on the
Vowel Summary Chart on page 127. The only pair for this
change is Q *tehta*/S *taith*.

It is assumed that PE *χ*w parallels the developments of
PE *kw and *gw, and so produces Q *hw* and S *f*.

Tolkien talks of the use of a simple raised stem to
represent breath *h* in Early Quenya (III:401n.). This may
indicate that Early Quenya had a breath *h* [h] phonemically
distinct from spirant *h* [x], derived from a PE *h distinct
from PE *χ. This PE *h would presumably also appear in Sindarin as *h*. It would be represented by Q *halla*/S *hal*- since
halla is the name given the raised stem used to represent it
in Quenya, and it is possible that *h* in either or both of the
pairs Q *Hísime*/S *Hithui*, Q -*her*/S -*hir* derives from original
*h rather than *χ as suggested in the discussion of *χ. PE
*h has accordingly been included in the Consonant Summary
Chart, but the reader should note the scanty evidence for its
existence. It might be that the raised stem was only adopted
into the writing of Quenya after spirant *h* had become breath
h initially.

Voiced Continuants:

For PE *w we have Q *Víresse*/S *Gwirith*, and apparently
Q *van*-/S *gwan*- in *gwanûr*. We may also have Q *vilya*/S †*gwai*
if the correspondence suggested in the discussion on PE *dy/
gy* is correct. It is thought that though *w* became *v* initially in Quenya it would have remained *w* internally in some
environments. See, for example, *Elwe*. The combinations *iw,
*ew, *aw, *uw would probably have become in at least some
environments, respectively, *iu, eu, au, ú*, and *ow would have
become *au* or *ó* or *ú*. The change of PE *w to S initial *gw* is
paralleled by the change of primitive Celtic *w to Welsh
initial *gw. The consonant *w* was more strongly pronounced

Consonant Summary Chart

This chart is fully discussed and explained in the text. ∿ = *in alternation with, being used in Sindarin with the lenited form of the consonant, and in Quenya for correspondences of a similar sort; / is used when the alternation of sounds is not simple lenition or, in Quenya, similar to lenition. Final forms are indicated by a preceding hyphen, that is, -rth means final rth.*

QUENYA		PROTO-ELDARIN				SINDARIN
Voiceless Stops:						
p	←	p			→	p ∿ b
t	←	t			→	t ∿ʼd
(?)	←	tp	→	pp	→	ph
tt	←	tt	→	tt	→	th
ts	←	ts	→	tth	→	th
(?)	←	tk	→	kk	→	ch
ty/t	←	{ ty / ky }			→	c ∿ g
c	←	k			→	c ∿ g
qu	←	kw			→	p ∿ b
Voiced Stops:						
v	←	b			→	b ∿ v
l	←	d			→	d ∿ dh
ly	←	{ dy / gy }	→	g ∿ gh	→	g ∿ ∅
∅	←	g	→	g ∿ gh	→	g ∿ ∅
v/w/u ←	w ←	gw			→	b ∿ v
Voiceless Continuants:						
f	←		f		→	f/-ph
s	← th ←		θ		→	th
s ∿ r ←	s ∿ z ←	s			→	s ∿ h/∅
ss	←	ss			→	ss
hr	←	sr			→	rh ∿ r
hl	←	sl			→	lh ∿ l
hw	←	sw			→	hw ∿ w
hy	←	{ sy / χy }			→	h/∅
h	←	χ			→	h/∅/ch
ht	←	χt			→	eth/itn
hw	←	χw			→	f
h	←	h			→	h/∅

continued on p. 139

initially than medially, so eventually initial [w] became
[ɣw] which became [gw]. The same process occured in Romance
languages, and has even gone a stage further in pronunciation, with [gw] becoming simple [g]. For example, Gmc.
*werra produced Eng. war but Fr. guerre [geːʀ]; OE wigle
produced Eng. wile directly but Eng. guile through Old
French.
    For PE *r we have Q rembe/S rem(m), Q ring-/S ⁺ring.
For the Quenya reflexes of *r + the voiced and voiceless
stops it has been assumed that the stops behaved normally,
save that *d remained d following *r rather than becoming l.
The Sindarin reflexes for PE *rp, *rt, *rk are based on
the pair Q *certa/S certh (see also S certhas) and on the
parallel development in Welsh (Lat. corpus 'body', portus
'port', arca 'box' adopted into British became, respectively, Welsh corff, porth, arch). S orch might come from a
PE *ork-. The Sindarin reflexes for PE *rb, *rd, *rg are all
taken from the parallel of Q arda with S ⁺arth, but also S
Calenardhon. It would appear that PE *rd became S rdh
medially, but rth finally. The final rth generally remained
in compounds formed after the change in which it was now in
a medial position, as Arthedain (not **Ardhedain) indicates.
S orch might come from a PE *org- (cf. gorgûn, the word for
'orc' in the speech of the Wild Men of Drúadan Forest [III:
106]). The correspondence Q rómen/S rhûn is inexplicable
from data now available.
    Early Quenya had both a trilled r and an untrilled r.
The letter name of the latter is óre, indicating that it was
not found initially. This might have been an allophone of
trilled r, but might also have a different origin. However,
by the Third Age the two r's have fallen together in Quenya,
and if S -ûr in gwanûr is indeed cognate with Q óre, then
the untrilled r of Early Quenya appears as trilled r in Third
Age Sindarin also. This is as much as one can say from current data.
    PE *l appears in the pair Q losse/S loss and elsewhere.
We have pairs for three of the PE *l + stop combinations: *lp
in Q ⁺tyelpe/S celeb, *lt in Q ⁺alta/S ⁺galad, *ld in Q alda/
S galadh. The other combinations are given parallel Quenya
and Sindarin reflexes in the chart, incorporating the normal
change of PE *b and *g to Q v and Ø respectively. But the
pronunciation of Q lv was often, in fact, [lb]; for, Tolkien
says that for 'lv, not for lw, many speakers, especially
Elves, used lb' (III:399). In the chart the symbol ⟨ᵛ⟩ is
used to indicate a duplication of whatever vowel precedes the
l. The Sindarin reflexes for PE *lk and *lg are uncertain
because we do not know how strongly the vowel ᵛ had developed
at the period when Early S ɣ (gh) disappeared. They might
have become lv. The evolution PE *ld > Q lvdh does not fit

the pair Q *Elda/S edhel* at all. For both the PE *r and *l combinations more data is badly needed. It is possible that stress or original vowel length or both are needed to establish a complete set of accurate reflexes. The chart may be considered only to give some of the reflexes that occur with these combinations. PE *y generally remains in Quenya (but cf. Q *Aldea* < *alda* + *ya*) and is written *i* in Sindarin. It might in some cases be represented by *e* in Sindarin, as PE *ay would likely become *ai which produces S *ae*, hence the *e* on the chart.

Nasal Stops:

For PE **m^b* we postulate a Proto-Eldarin stem **m^bar*- 'dwell' which appears in Quenya in mar- 'dwell', *marde 'hall', *Eldamar* 'Elvenhome', *ambar* 'world'; and appears in Sindarin in *Gondobar*, *Barahir* 'Lord-(of the)-Land', and possibly in *barad* 'tower'. The Sindarin form -*mar* found in *Angmar* is taken as a borrowing from Quenya, or as a development from **m^bar* after it has become *mbar in some medial environment in Proto-Eldarin.

For PE **n^d* we have the pair Q *Quendi* 'Speakers'/S *pedo* 'speak!'. Also, we postulate a Proto-Eldarin stem **n^dū*- 'down, descend', which appears in Quenya in *númen* 'west', *nuquerna* 'reversed', *undu*- 'down', and *andúne* 'sunset'; and appears in Sindarin in *dûn* 'west', *di(n)* 'beneath', *annûn* 'sunset'. Here S *annûn* is either a borrowing from Quenya, or descends from **n^dū*- after it became *ndū- in a medial environment, or represents, as would Q *andúne*, some such Proto-Eldarin combination as *am + **n^dūnē* → *andūnē as is suggested by S *amrûn* 'sunrise'. PE **n^dū*- may also appear in S *Udûn* 'Hell'. Finally, we postulate PE **n^dōrē* whence Q -*nóre*, -*nor* 'land' (in *Númenóre*, *Númenor*, *Valinóre*, *Valinor*), -*nórie* 'country' (in *sindanóriello*); and whence S *dor*.(found also in the compound names *Eriador*, *Gondor*, *Mordor*, *Neldor*). The Sindarin form -*nor* found only in *Arnor* would be either a borrowing from Quenya or descend from PE **n^dōrē* only after it had become *ndōrē in some medial environment in Proto-Eldarin.

For PE **ŋ^g* we have no apparent correspondences unless Q *nol*- in *noldo* (earlier *ngoldo*) and S *gul*- in *Guldur*, *morgul* both represent a PE **ŋ^gŏl*-. Its reflexes on the chart follow the pattern of PE **m^b* and **n^d*, taking into account initial [ŋ] in Quenya had become [n] in the Third Age, and is so written by Tolkien (III:392).

In S *Gondobar*, *pedo*, and *Udûn* we note that *b* and *d* derived from Proto-Eldarin nasal stops do not undergo lenition. The easiest way to explain this is that they became doubled consonants, and thus withstood lenition, only

becoming single consonants after medial lenition had ceased
to be a living process. When intial they would have simplified phonetically to single consonants much earlier, but may
still have been treated as though double and so have escaped
lenition. That we find *Eriador* rather than **Eriadhor* might
suggest this, but we do not really have sufficient examples
to make a decision.

PE $*n^dy$, η^gy, η^g, η^gw appear on the chart with reflexes
on analogy with m^b, n^d, and the simple voiced stops. No pairs
are found in the extant corpus.

Nasal Continuants:

PE *m* is represented by Q min-/S min-, Q metta/S
methed-, Q morna/S mor-. With lenition in Sindarin we find
Q Silima/S silivren, Q Menelmacar/S Menelvagor.

PE *n* is represented by Q Narquelie/S Narbeleth, Q N n
Nénime/S Nínui. For *nb* we have S lembas from len + bas.
As S Anborn indicates, new combinations of nb may remain nb,
unless we here have a rule in in which n + b → mb but n(n) +
b → nb. For *nr* we have Caradhras from caran + ras(s).
There seems no reason why it would not remain nr in Quenya.
The double nn occurs in Q anna, probably from PE *nn, and
there seems no reason why it should change in Sindarin.

PE *ny/ɲy* appears on the chart with reflexes on analogy
with the other nasal continuants and the other Proto-Eldarin
palatals.

PE *ŋ* may have existed only as an allophone of *n* in the
combinations *ŋk*, *ŋg* and in their extensions in -y and -w.
If it did appear in other environments it has in its reflexes fallen together with *ŋg* and cannot now be distinguished from it by the available data.

Nasal & Voiceless Stop Combinations:

In Quenya the combinations mp, nt, nc, and nqu are all
found in the extant corpus, and were common enough to have
special letters in the tengwar to represent them. It seems
most reasonable to derive them from PE *mp, *nt, *ŋk, and
*ŋkw respectively. PE *nty/ɲky would become Q nty just as PE
*ty/ky become Q ty.

In Sindarin we find find -nt and -nc in the extent corpus (Celebrant, Orthanc) in final position, and presumably
-mp would also occur finally. Medially we have a single
Quenya/Sindarin pair: Q †nique (found in Tániquetil 'High-
white-peak') and S nim- (found in Nimrais 'White-peaks', Nimloth 'White-flower'). A posited PE *niŋkwē would become Q
†nique by dissimilation of the second nasal. In Pre-Sindarin
we would have the change of PE *kw to p, as indicated by Q
Quendi 'Speakers' but S pedo 'speak!'. The preceding *ŋ

QUENYA			PROTO-ELDARIN			SINDARIN

continued from p. 135

Voiced Continuants:

v/w/u	←	w/u	←	w	⇒	gw ᴠ w/u
r	←			r	⇒	r
rp	←			rp	⇒	rph
rt	←			rt	⇒	rth
rc	←			rk	⇒	rch
rv	←			rb	⇒	rv/-rph
rd	←			rd	⇒	rdh/-rth
r	←			rg	⇒	r/-rch
l	←			l	⇒	l
lp	←			lp	⇒	lʋb
lt	←			lt	⇒	lʋd
lc	←			lk	⇒	l (???)
lv	←			lb	⇒	lʋf
ld	←			ld	⇒	lʋdh
l	←			lg	⇒	l (???)
y	←			y	⇒	i/e

Nasal Stops:

m/mb	←	m^b	⇒	bb	⇒	b
n/nd	←	n^d	⇒	dd	⇒	d
ny/ndy	←	$\left\{ \begin{array}{c} n^dy \\ ŋ^gy \end{array} \right\}$	⇒	gi	⇒	gi ᴠ e/i
n/ng	← ng/ng ←	$ŋ^g$	⇒	gg	⇒	g
nw/ngw	← ngw/ngw ←	$ŋ^gw$	⇒	bb	⇒	b

Nasal Continuants:

m	←	m	⇒	m ᴠ mh	⇒	m ᴠ v
n	←	n	⇒			n
(?)	←	nb	⇒			mb
nr	←	nr	⇒			ndh
nn	←	nn	⇒			nn
ny	←	$\left\{ \begin{array}{c} ny \\ ŋy \end{array} \right\}$	⇒			ng
n/ng	← ng/ng ←	ŋ	⇒			ng

Nasal & Voiceless Stop Combinations:

mp	←	mp	⇒	⇒	m/mm/-mp
nt	←	nt	⇒	⇒	nn/-nt
nty	←	$\left\{ \begin{array}{c} nty \\ ŋky \end{array} \right\}$		⇒	ng/-nc
nc	←	ŋk		⇒	ng/-nc
nqu	←	ŋkw	⇒	mp ⇒	m/mm/-mp

continued on p. 141

would become *m* by assimilation to *p*, producing the form
nimpe. If *p*, *t*, *k*, were subject to lenition medially when
preceded by a nasal, then *mp* will become *mb* medially, and
nimpe will become *nimbe*, which with loss of the final vowel
will become *nimb*. So *mp* will have fallen together with
original *mb*, and will simplify to *m* (III:393), producing the
required S *nim-*. Another possibility is that Pre-Sindarin
mp, *nt*, *ŋk*, following the pattern of Welsh, became *mm̥*,
nn̥, *ŋŋ̊*, the voiceless stop becoming a voicless nasal by
assimilation to the preceding voiced nasal. In Modern Welsh
these have been simplified to *m*, *n* or *nn*, and *ŋ* (written *ng*)
save immediately preceding the stress, where they appear as
mh, *nh*, and *ŋh* (written *ngh*). In Third Age Sindarin voiceless nasals did not normally occur, and so if they ever did
occur, we must assume that they had fallen together with the
voiced nasals. But, whichever of the two processes we posit,
we arrive at the same results: medial *mp* > S *m* or *mm*, medial
nt > S *nn*, and medial *ŋk* > S *ng*.
S *niphredil*, the name of a white flower, probably comes
from an earlier *nimp* + *pretil*.

Nasal & Voiced Stop Combinations:

The Proto-Eldarin nasal + voiced stop combinations
remain unchanged in Quenya. In Sindarin their reflexes are
given by Tolkien in Appendix E I, following the list of particular consonants (III:393), and the chart is taken from
the information given there.
Sindarin medial *m* will almost always derive from PE *mb*,
mp, *ŋgw*, or *ŋkw*, not from *m* which will have lenited to *v*.
Tolkien says double *mm* was used 'in cases where otherwise the
stress might be in doubt' (III:393), but *lammen*, *rammas*, and
sammath would be stressed identically if spelt **lamen*,
**ramas*, and **samath*. It seems we need an additional rule:
that final *m* from earlier *mb* is written *mm* when a suffix
beginning with a vowel is added.
In Sindarin *n* immediately preceding a consonant and
final *n* in dissylabic and polysyllabic words often represents
an earlier *nn*.

Before Proto-Eldarin

From a comparison of forms in reconstructed Proto-
Eldarin and from a look at relationships within Quenya and
Sindarin or between the two languages not accounted for by
Proto-Eldarin, it is possible to delve back even farther,
though not with any great assurance.
Q *súle* and *súri* both mean 'wind', indicating perhaps

QUENYA	PROTO-ELDARIN			SINDARIN
continued from p. 139				
Nasal & Voiced Stop Combinations:				
mb	← mb	→		m/mm
nd	← nd	→		nn/nd
ndr	← ndr	→		ndr
ndy	← $\left\{ \begin{array}{l} \text{ndy} \\ \text{ŋgy} \end{array} \right\}$	→		ng
ng	← ŋg	→		ng
ngw	← ŋgw	→ mb	→	m/mm

an original connection between *r* and *l* in some cases. There
might also be an earlier relationship between *s* and *θ*. If
PE *nār- indicating 'red, hot, fire' came to mean 'sun' by
prefixing of its vowel to produce *anār-, should not PE *sil-
meaning 'white, cold, light' also mean 'moon' by prefixing of
its vowel to produce *isil-. But the PE form is, in fact,
*iθil-. Do we have here a variant form of *SIL, perhaps from
another dialect, realized in Proto-Eldarin as *θIL? Q
sinda- 'grey' begins with *s* derived from PE *s, not *θ (M),
but S *Thingol* does look like it might mean 'Grey-cloak'.
Also, what of S *hith-* 'mist', *mith-* 'grey', *lith-* 'ash', and
ithil 'moon', all of which seem to revolve around a meaning
something like 'grey' or 'grey stuff'?
 There are some indications of early metathesis of consonants. PE *tal- would appear in S *talan* 'platform', *talf*
'flat field', while PE *lat would appear in S -*lad* 'plain'.
PE *miθ- appears in Sindarin as *mith-* 'grey'; when metathe-
sized we would get PE *θim- which might appear in S *Thingol*
with *m* assimilated to the following *g*. With change of *θ to
*s in one language or dialect before the Proto-Eldarin
period we would get PE *sim- which would appear in Quenya in
sinda- 'grey', again with assimilation of *m*. PE *dui- 'flow'
(as in S *duin* 'river') would metathesize to *iud- which might
become in Quenya—with the normal change of PE *d to *l—*yul*-
as in Q *yulma* 'cup', *yuldar* 'draughts'. The same result
would be achieved from metathesis of PE *lui- 'blue', perhaps
originally meaning 'water-colour'? Legolas is once called
'Greenleaf' which looks like it might be a gloss of his name.
But, while -*las* means 'leaf', the word for 'green' is *galen*
as in *Lasgalen*, not *lego-*. But might not both *gal-* and *leg-*
mean 'green', deriving from a Pre-Proto-Eldarin metathesis
pair that we might construct as *gæl- and *læg? Of course,
we then have to account for why PE *g does not lenit in *Legolas*.

One definite linkage can be made between Q *tengwa* and *tehta*. Assuming a stem meaning 'mark' in the form *teg-* the developments would run:

teg + *mā* → *tegmā* > *teŋ^{g}wā* > Q *tengwa*

teg + *tā* → *tegtā* > *tektā* > *teχtā* > Q *tehta*

The plural Sindarin form *tîw* is harder to account for. One way is to assume a derivation from *tegmā* as follows:

tegma > *teγβ̃* > S *têw*, pl. *tîw*

If the γ remained as an *i*, the singular might be *teiw*, which would also pluralize as *tîw*. The difficulty with this is that we have no parallel examples of a Sindarin word that must be derived from an archaic Proto-Eldarin form before the resolution of velar stop + nasal to nasal stop + velar.

ELVISH LOANWORDS

IN INDO-EUROPEAN:

CULTURAL IMPLICATIONS

Lise Menn

Paper read at the 1st International Conference of the Society for Elvish Studies, Oswego, N.Y., July 1976.

WE CANNOT DOUBT THAT SPEAKERS OF QUENYA, Sindarin, or both, had contact with the speakers of Proto-Indo-European, for as I will show, the descendants of some Elvish loanwords are found well-distributed in the Indo-European languages. Let us begin by considering two clear cases which should erase all lingering doubt.

A Sindarin word which should be familiar to all my listeners is *craban, a large crow-like bird; the word is actually attested in the plural, crebain. It was certainly borrowed during the time when there was an actual community of PIE speakers, because we can construct a good proto-form *krew underlying Latin corvus, Sanskrit karawa, and allowing for augments and other derivational processes, also underlying Lithuanian krauklỹs, Old Norse hrafn, Old English hræfn, and Greek koraks, all of which, of course, mean either 'crow', or 'raven'.

Less well-known, perhaps, but more reliable (being free from the possibility of onomatopoeic creation) is the appearance of the Sindarin word for 'swan', alph, which is found in Indo-European generally meaning either 'swan' or 'white': Latin albus 'white', Greek alphos '(white) skin rash', Old High German albiz, Old Norse elptr, and Russian lebed, all preserving the original meaning 'swan'. The PIE reconstructed form would be $*ə_2 elbh-$, but since it corresponds to a

vowel-initial Sindarin form, we have grounds for surmising
that the borrowing took place at a time in the history of
Indo-European when the laryngeal had been phonetically much
reduced in prevocalic position, and had perhaps already disappeared after giving rise to the vowel coloring.

Such loanwords denoting specific animal or plant names
help to establish the chronology of language contact, but
they raise more questions than they answer. We cannot tell
from such commonplace sorts of borrowings whether these Sindarin speakers were Elves or Humans, whether the contact was
friendly or hostile, of long or short duration, whether or
not our linguistic ancestors understood anything that the
Sindarin speakers may have tried to teach them of Elvish culture, or whether any material objects that we might expect to
excavate someday were involved in any cultural heritage.

However, a search of the available materials on Elvish
can give us the answers to all these questions, and the conclusions to which we are inevitably led are of the greatest
importance. While some details remain obscure, we can be
certain of the main point: Speakers of Sindarin, undoubtedly
Grey-elves, lived in close and amicable contact with the
speakers of Proto-Indo-European for a considerable length of
time, perhaps several hundred years.

During this time, they attempted to communicate some of
their enlightened philosophy and religion, but the followers
of the warrior sky god, the Thunderer, reached only a limited
understanding, and what they had understood quickly became
garbled and then submerged after contact with the Elves was
lost. Material objects of Elvish manufacture were known to
the Proto-Indo-European community, at least objects of silver
and wrought iron. It is in fact from the treatment of S †ang
'iron', in the Indo-European languages that we deduce the
conclusion that Grey-elves themselves had contact with our
linguistic ancestors.

Let me develop this reasoning at once. What we can see
from the meanings of the PIE root, which we shall refer to as
*angʷ- for convenience, is that †ang was known to the PIE
community only as denoting elaborate wrought-iron decorative
objects, and not either massive cast-iron or forged-iron
weaponry. The most prominent meaning of *angʷ- is in fact
'eel' (Russian úgorʹ) or 'snake' (Latin anguis, Lithuanian
angìs); in the Greek and Germanic sensibility, the root
retained its wider meaning, and can denote almost anything
curved: from ankles and angles to fishhooks (Gk. ánkōn '
'elbow, angle, curved horns of a lyre', ankístron 'fishhook';
OE ancléow 'ankle'; OE anga, OHG ango 'hook'; OE angel, OHG
angul 'fishhook'—whence Eng. angling); in Gothic it occurs
concerned with bending the neck.

Now we know that the Elves were masters of all metalwork,

including weapons manufacture; the fact that †*ang* is not used
for weapons is therefore of great significance. Clearly the
Sindar, finding the Thunderer's followers a bloodthirstier
crew than the Edain and their kin, did their best to keep the
very existence of iron and steel weapons a secret from their
Bronze Age neighbors. While tales of certain objects necessarily leaked into legend, such as the source tale for the
divinely-wrought armor of Achilles, the Elves were essentially successful, and the Bronze Age did not come to a pre-
mature end.

This tells us that the Sindarin speakers who had contact
with our linguistic ancestors were indeed Elves and not
Humans. For when have Humans restrained themselves from
trade in armaments? Humans have kept secrets of manufacture
for varying periods of time in order to maintain military and
economic superiority, but to have hidden, for several hundred
years, the very existence of superior weapons from a war-
loving community shows a superhuman restraint and morality
which could only have been maintained by Elves.

Two points remain to be established in the argument: How
do we know that the contact period did extend over such an
extended period of time? And, how do we know that it was
amicable enough for weapons trade to have taken place?

We have ample evidence to warrent the necessary conclusions, for we have a group of loanwords which show that the
contact between peoples was of sufficient intimacy to permit
the teaching of philosophy and religion, and another (over-
lapping) group of words which show that the contact was of
sufficient strength to permit the borrowing of words of the
most basic vocabulary, including at least one derivational
morpheme. Let us consider these groups now.

Again, there is one word which will have been obvious to
all of you, the Elvish root *mor-* 'black' (*Moria, Morannon,
Morthond*). This probably entered PIE as the root **mer-* 'to
die', and was originally a euphemism that we may translate as
'to go into darkness'. However, the literal meaning is preserved in the Greek word *morphnos* 'of dark color'. In the
adoption of Sindarin *car-* 'red' as **krew-*, the Indo-European
root for thick blood or flesh (Gk. *kre(w)as*, 'meat', Lat.
cruor 'clotting blood', Skt. *kravis-* 'raw flesh', ON *hrar*
'raw', Eng. *raw*, Lat. *carn-* 'flesh') we see the use of a
euphemism by the Elves: Our carnivorous PIE community must
have had eating habits revolting indeed to the vegetarian
Elves. Probably there is no Sindarin word for flesh used as
food, and they may have had trouble bringing themselves to
speak directly of the haunches of boar and venison being
eaten directly by their human hosts. They probably referred
to it as 'that which is red', and this must have become
upper-class human usage, and eventually general.

α

The likelihood of there having been such occasional
shared feasts is increased by the existence of another loan-
word that might well be associated with ceremonial feasting.
This is the word for 'silver', *celeb*, mentioned earlier.
(Cf. *Celebdil* 'Silvertine'.) *Celeb* appears in an obscure
Greek word, *kelébē*, a bowl of some sort, which suggests that
silver vessels made by the Elves were known to Humans. We
may speculate that these *kelébai* were gifts of Elves to
Humans, since it is unlikely that true commercial transactions took place between the peoples, and presumably Humans
raiding Elvenhalls for treasure would meet with less success
than did Bilbo Baggins and the Dwarves when they were merely
grabbing for dinner in Mirkwood. The correspondence with the
Slavic words of 'silver', such as Russian *serebró*, Old Church
Slavonic *sirebro* is plausible, but connection with the Germanic words such as English *silver* would have to involve borrowing of a Slavic form by Proto-Germanic speakers. This
might have taken place, of course, but there is no evidence
except for the resemblance of the words; that is, no independent evidence for such a borrowing from Slavic into Germanic,
and so we cannot rely on etymology.

Leaving these later internal IE affairs and returning to
the Elvish words, I would like to draw your attention to an
etymology that has certain phonological problems but suggests
something more of the incompatibilities between the Elves and
our linguistic ancestors. There is a fascinating connection
between Quenya *áre* and PIE *awe-* 'air, wind', which is found
in Greek *aer* 'lower atmosphere', Sanskrit *vati* 'blows', Latin
ventus 'wind', and of course English *wind*. If the 'starlight
on the Western Seas' (III:308) figures strongly in Elvish
rhyme, surely the sunlight on the sea is of no less spiritual
importance. I think we may see here the results of Sindarin
attempts to convey the glory of Elvenhome, which they themselves had never seen, to mortals of non-Númenorean descent;
light on the ocean that conveyed no material advantage was of
no interest to such Humans; all they could make out of it was
wind, wind to fill ships' sails.

A similar psychic distance between Elves and Humans can
be read from the appearance of the Sindarin *gor-* 'death'
(*Cirith Gorgor*, *Tyrn Gorthad*) in the IE root **gʷor-* 'devour'
(Lat. *vor-* as in 'voracious', Skt. *girati* 'devours', Old
Church Slavonic *žrěti* 'to devour', Russ. *górlo* 'throat', OHG
querdar 'bait', Gk. *boros* 'greedy'). The Elvish notion of
death, a long sleep and an awakening 'beyond the Sundering
Seas' (I:206) for Elves, separate from a similar long-sleep-
and-awakening for Humans, was beyond the comprehension of
those who needed to believe in an immediate awakening in the
afterlife.

Our linguistic ancestors were willing to believe, however, that death for the Elves might be quite a different
matter from death for themselves. They were, after all,
humanly jealous of the Elves' near-immortality. And so they

had their own theory: they whispered that it was all lies
about the Elves' far future awakening in a separate sphere
from Humans. After all, if Men in the afterlife never met
dead Elves, there could be another explanation. Perhaps, in
payment for their long lives in this world, Elves died
entirely and had no afterlife at all, were consumed utterly.
So S *gor-* became IE *g^wor-*.

Other borrowings from Sindarin are less revealing of the
relations between Elves and the PIE community, but they are
further evidence for the rich contact that I claim existed.
We have S *br-* 'noise' (*Bruinen* = 'Loudwater'), clearly the
same as IE *$bhre$-m* (Gk. *brontē* 'thunder', Skt. *bhṛmi-h*
'active', movable; whirlwind', Lat. *fremitus* 'muttering, mur-
muring, roar'); we have a correspondence between Elvish *van-*
'gone, lost' and the IE root *wa (Lat. *vādo* 'go', also OHG
watan; Lat. *vastus* 'waste, deserted', OIr. *fáss* 'empty');
Sindarin *aglar* 'glory' appears in Greek *aglaia* 'splendor,
brightness', to which Walde suggests we compare *glaks* 'owl',
that is, 'the one with sparkling eyes'. Other reflexes of
this loanword appear in derivatives from the form *$g'el$*
'bright, sparkling', including German *klein* 'little' and Old
English *clæne* 'clean'.

We should give special attention to the borrowing of the
nominalizing or concretizing suffix *-ma* which we see operat-
ing in Quenya: cf. *cor-* 'round', *corma* 'ring'; or *cal-*
'light', *calma* 'lamp'; and also in such words as *parma*
'book', *ancalima* 'great light bearer'. This is found in
Indo-European as *-mo*, and English speakers will recognize it
in borrowings from Greek—*stigma*, *schema*, *syntagma*, *enigma*,
and the like.

This borrowing is further confirmation of the type of
relation between Elves and Humans that we have reconstructed,
because the borrowing of affixes is less common than the borrowing of stems. One of the situations in which affix-
borrowing can take place is when there has been a wholesale
importation of a great number of words, some containing the
affix in question and some containing only the stems which
appeared combined with that affix—such was the case when the
suffix *-able* came into English from French. But borrowing
from Sindarin, as far as we can tell, never took place on
that kind of scale in PIE. The other common situation for
affix-borrowing, however, fits what we know of the cultural
levels of the Sindar and our Bronze Age linguistic borebears:
the language of a less technically advanced society picks up
on an affix of a language of a more advanced society as a
learned term—e.g. the adoption of *-ize* in English (directly
from French *-iser*, ultimately from Greek *-izein* via Late
Latin *-izāre*).

We should mention in passing the absence of a good

argument to connect S *lith* 'ash' with PIE **lidh-* 'cut, hurt', the ancestor of Greek *lithos* 'stone'. A connection presumably would have to be through volcanic products, and its plausibility would have to rest on evidence of volcanoes in the area where the Sindar and the PIE-speaking community had contact.

Elvish royal authority must have made considerable impression in PIE-speakers, because we find the stem *tar-* 'royal' in the form **terg^w-*, whose reflexex include Sanskrit *tarjati*, 'threaten, frighten', Greek *tárbos* 'fear', and Latin *torvus* 'wild, dark'. We might gather from the Latin meanings, especially, that the Elves maintained a forest territory as their sole domain, more like Mirkwood than like Lórien.

Naturally, in this study, we must mount a special search for IE borrowings of the favorite Elvish morpheme *el-* 'star'. It quickly becomes apparent that that meaning has been lost, and even its derived force as designating the Elves themselves, 'the People of the Stars' (III:416) is often hard to discern. It might seem obvious that the word *elf* itself preserves the name, but there is a very serious difficulty with this etymology, for the Germanic word from which *elf* comes is reconstructed as **albiz*, and is generally considered to be derived from the root for 'white' that we derived earlier from S *alph* 'swan'. Unless we can account for the vowel change, we must regard the connection between *elf* and *el-* as spurious.

On the other hand, true descendants of *el-* can be found. Two IE sets of tree names, 'elm' and 'alder', show it, e.g. Old High German *elira*, Russian *ól'kha* 'alder'; Latin *ulmus* 'elm'. Certain birds and animals may also contain the *el-*, especially 'elk'; probably these trees and creatures were characteristic inhabitants of the Elves' woodland kingdom. In Greek, however, we find traces of the Elves' influence in much weightier matters. Our attention is drawn to an unexplained and isolated epithet of the shining sun, *ēléktōr*—the word from which the better known *ḗlektron* 'amber'; also 'an alloy of gold and silver' is derived. The details are lost, but an Elvish origin for this word is clearly plausible. We also find *eléō* '(I) take pity on', which might once have meant 'I behave in accordance with Elvish teachings'.

Finally, Greek shows us hitherto totally unsuspected links between the Elves' faith and the evolution of the Indo-European pantheon. Notice the name of the city of Eleusis, home of the Eleusinian mysteries, the secret worship of Demeter and Persephone. Might these rites have been a debased derivative of the devotion paid to Elbereth? We shall now answer this question in the affirmative. One further word is all that we need: *elaia* 'olive'. The olive, staple crop of

the Mediterranean, gift of Athene to mankind—so the Greeks
knew it. But consider Athene, warrior, goddess of wisdom,
teacher of crafts. Is she indeed the virgin daughter of the
brain of Zeus? I think not. I claim that she is none other ·
than Elbereth as remodeled by a patriarchal society, even
though her name is borne only by her legendary gift, the
olive tree. Consider Elbereth—Varda 'the Exalted', Queen of
the Valar—whose true name is never mentioned in *The Lord of
the Rings*. Fully equal in authority and wisdom to her more
aloof husband, the Elder King, Elbereth is now and must
always have been a compelling divine figure, especially to
women. I think it is clear that she was adopted for a time
into the Indo-European pantheon. And she could not survive
as a member of the Thunderer's coterie; there was no way in
which a patriarchal society could sustain her worship. Even
as the story of the Ring comes down to us somewhat remodeled
by Men, so that Elven women are only shown to us as greater
than their husbands if they were of a higher kindred, so was
Elbereth remodeled—in fact, divided, polarized. On the one
hand, as a nurturing, directly powerful, richly female divinity, she is reduced to a mysterious and irrational earth-
mother similar to the one of the Mediterranean cults. On the
other hand, as the figure of divine wisdom she could not be
anyone's wife, for then she would have been her husband's
equal in the crafts of war and in rational thought. So she
became the virgin daughter of Zeus-father to the Greeks, and
was lost entirely to the harsher peoples of Northern Europe.
Again, Humans were unable to receive or maintain the enlightened teachings of the Elves.

   To end this paper on a less somber note, I return to a
favorite word and a favorite speaking-people, the Ents. The
name of the Ents has come down to us, as far as I know, only
in Old English. There it was already obscure; in Old English
sources, such as those that underlie the great poem 'The Wanderer', Ents were conceived of as the vanished builders of
the great ruined stone buildings which had actually been constructed by the Romans. So we read:

   oþ-þæt burgwara breahtma lease,
   eald enta ge-weorc idlu stondon.

'until, without the revelry of inhabitants, the old works of
the Ents stood empty' ('The Wanderer', lines 86-87).

   Now, at the time of the composition of 'The Wanderer',
the ruined buildings of the Romans were actually no longer
thought to be the works of super-humans. But the phrase
ealda enta ge-weorc had become fixed, and it takes us back
several hundred years before the probable date of the composition of 'The Wanderer', to a time when the Romans' art of
moving stone with levers and winches was forgotten, when the

Romans themselves were forgotten (the last legions were with-
drawn about 410 A.D.; the invasions of the Angles, Saxons,
and Jutes came during the period 450-55; 'The Wanderer' post-
dates the Christianization of England, which took place during the seventh century A.D.). The Old English word *ent* is
usually translated 'giant', and the association with trees is
nowhere indicated. But we can see the Treeherds, called *Enyd*
in Sindarin, were dimly remembered in English legend when the
name of the Romans was forgotten: a vanished people of great
size and strength who had moved tremendous stones. The destruction of stone-walled Isengard by the Ents had an echo
preserved to this day in the poety of the English language.

‡   ‡   ‡   ‡   ‡   ‡   ‡   ‡   ‡

ADDITIONAL NOTES

Internal evidence alone would rule out an explanation of
shared morphemes as being due to common ancestry of the
Elvish tongues and Indo-European, and the nature of the
shared morphemes considered together with the relative cultural backwardness of our linguistic ancestors as compared
with the Elves rules out the possiblity of Elvish having borrowed most of the words under discussion from Humans. (The
words for crow/raven and for swan could have been borrowed
by Sindarin from PIE; we cannot resolve this question without
knowing the names of those birds in Quenya; obviously, if
related words are found in the language of those who left
Middle-earth so long ago, the chances that those words were
learned from Humans becomes vanishingly small.)

It should be noted that Tolkien does not at any point
deal with a possible historical connection between the Elvish
tongues and extant languages. He does make it clear that
Elvish languages are unrelated to the Common Speech, Weston,
which he rendered into English, but Westron is not related to
any living tongue that I know of, and certainly not IE.

I am assuming that the Elf-Human contact discussed here
was contact between the Sindar, that is, the Grey-elves, and
Humans. There is no direct linguistic evidence for this
assumption; Quenya could be the source of the Elvish words,
for none of the words under discussion happen to reconstruct
in such a way that they could only have come from Sindarin.
It is also not impossible that Wood-elves, whose language
must have been rich with loanwords from Quenya and Sindarin,
were those who made the contact reconstructed in this paper,
but since we know only a fragment or two of the Wood-elves'
language, placing them in this intermediary role is entirely
conjectural. In any case, my arguments for the most part

would require only superficial changes in order to accomo-
date such a hypothesis if it should be proven true.

The Calendar of Imladris

A NOTE BY JIM ALLAN

Λ SURPRISING SIMILARITY between the Elvish Calendar of Imladris and the French Revolutionary Calendar is revealed by
the following listing of month names.

	QUENYA	SINDARIN		REVOLUTIONARY	
1.	Narvinyë	Narwain	*'New-sun'*	Nivôse	*'Snowy'*
2.	Nénimë	Nínui	*'Wet'*	Pluviôse	*'Rainy'*
3.	Súlimë	Gwaeron	*'Windy'*	Ventôse	*'Windy'*
4.	Víressë	Gwirith	*?*	Germinal	*'Seed-time'*
5.	Lótessë	Lothron	*'Flowery'*	Floréal	*'Blossoming'*
6.	Nárië	Nórui	*'Sunny'*	Prairial	*'Meadowy'*
7.	Cermië	Cerveth	*'Cutting'*	Messidor	*'Harvest'*
8.	Úrimë	Úrui	*'Hot'*	Thermidor	*'Hot'*
9.	Yavannië	Ivanneth	*'Fruit-giving'*	Fructidor	*'In-fruit'*
10.	Narquelië	Narbeleth	*'Sun-waning'*	Vendémiaire	*'Vintage'*
11.	Hísimë	Hithui	*'Misty'*	Brumaire	*'Misty'*
12.	Ringarë	Girithron	*'Cold-tide?'*	Frimaire	*'Frosty'*

The month names of the French Revolutionary Calendar
were partly modeled on old Germanic month names, but no surviving list of the old German months corresponds so closely
to the Calendar of Imladris. The only real differences
are that the Calendar of Imladris contains some month names
referring to the sun.

Víressë/Gwirith may also refer to planting, or might
have reference to the increasing brightness of the sun.

TOLKIEN'S PRONUNCIATION: SOME OBSERVATIONS

Laurence J. Krieg

THE RECENT RELEASE OF RECORDINGS made in 1952 of J. R. R. Tolkien reading selections from his then-unpublished *Lord of the Rings*[1] has made it possible for devoted students of his Elvish languages to get a new insight into their intended pronunciation.

I was asked by Jim Allan to use the facilities of the Phonetics Laboratory at the University of Michigan to make a detailed examination of these recordings with particular attention to certain sounds in Quenya and Sindarin whose pronunciation is not made clear by the descriptions in Tolkien's published work. This I have done (with considerable interest, I might add); from the examination I have made several observations in addition to those specifically requested by Jim, and I'd like to pass them along.

The first matter one must consider is this: to what extent does Tolkien's reading or reciting represent Quenya and Sindarin? A ticklish matter, that! In terms of the 'real' (that is, non-fictional) world, Tolkien invented two languages, so what he intended is the sum-total of what the languages are. One might then ask whether his pronunciation actually represents what he intended the pronunciation to be; I know one person who invented a language and had considerable difficulty in pronouncing it, though the language in question (David Strecker's Kungapuker) was designed specifically to be fiendishly difficult to pronounce! In Tolkien's

---

[1] *J. R. R. TOLKIEN reads and sings his THE HOBBIT and The Fellowship of the Ring* and *J. R. R. TOLKIEN reads and sings his THE LORD OF THE RINGS: The Two Towers: The Return of the King* (New York: Caedmon Records, No. TC 1477 and No. 1478, 1975).

case, of course, the languages were not intended to be difficult: Tolkien used sounds which he considered to be beautiful; esthetic concerns were very important to him, and he was
skilled at pronunciation and recitation. Still, he is not
really a 'native speaker': his parents didn't teach him
Quenya and Sindarin when he was an infant.

Within the fictional framework, Tolkien never claimed to
have special competence in speaking Quenya or Sindarin: he
was simply the translator of certain documents which inexpli-
cably came into his possession, and the last native speakers
of the languages went beyond the circles of this world many
hundreds of centuries ago. As with any 'dead' language, the
scholar who deciphers the written records will certainly have
the best available understanding of their former pronunciation in antiquity, but would lay no claim to be able to pronounce them 'natively' himself.

If there were to arise some discrepancy between Tolkien's pronunciation and his written description of the pronunciation, what should we make of it? There are two possible causes for such a difference: first, because Tolkien was
unable to achieve the pronunciation he specified (or at
least, not consistently); and second, because at the the time
he pronounced the word or text he intended it to be pronounced one way, but later he revised this invented phonology and published a description of the results of the revision. Both these possibilities bear some consideration in
general, apart from any actual differences between what Tolkien 'practised' and what he 'preached'.

As to the possibility that Tolkien did not (consistently) achieve the pronunciation he specified: again, there
are two possible causes. First, his native (English) phonological system interfered with his Quenya or Sindarin pronunciation; and second, that the stylistic differences by which
Tolkien conveyed differences in mood and textual type were
expressed to some extent in departures from Quenya or Sindarin phonology. This latter might be the case in his rendering of some Sindarin or Quenya names in English sentences.

Everyone who learns a language after about the age of
eleven or twelve will have some difficulty speaking that language without some interference from the phonological system
(or systems) he learned earlier. This is what accounts for
'foreign' accents of all kinds. The interference is generally systematic: sounds in the native language will tend to
substitute for sounds in the foreign language, and contrasts
made between sound-types in the foreign language but not in
the native language will tend to be lost. In order to be
able to detect such interference, it is helpful to know what
the patterns and sounds of the native language are, so I will
go into some detail on Tolkien's English sound system.

As for stylistic differences: there are several interesting changes that Tolkien makes in his reading when he wishes to express the differences between kinds of people speaking and kinds of text being read. First, of course, there is his 'ordinary' way of speaking, which he uses for reading text which (generally) serves to convey information about the plot. This contrasts with 'elevated' and 'character' styles: the elevated style being used to recite epic poetry and portions of text which are poetic, or epic deeds (such as the ride of the Rohirrim). Characters who have their own peculiar style include Samwise and Gollum.

Let us turn now to the possibility that Tolkien revised his phonology between the time he made the recording and the publication of *The Lord of the Rings*. There were revisions, of course; perhaps most noticeable is the change in Galadriel's Farewell, lines 2 and 3:

Inyar únóti nar ve rámar aldaron > Yéni únótimë ve rámar aldaron!
inyar ve linte yulmar vánier > Yéni ve lintë yuldar avánier

Clyde Kilby tells us (in *Tolkien & The Silmarillion*) that Tolkien had such a delight in his lack of consistency that it could best be described as *contrasistency*, so we should always be prepared to find differences in Tolkien's work of different periods. None the less, his pronunciation (as recorded) is close enough to his descriptions (as published) that we can say with certainty that there were no major revisions in the Elvish phonology between recording and publication.

My transcriptions use the symbols of the International Phonetic Alphabet, with the value of the vowels following the system used in *Handbook of the Linguistic Geography of New England* (Hans Kirath, Providence, Rhode Island: Brown University, 1939) and in subsequent American dialect surveys.

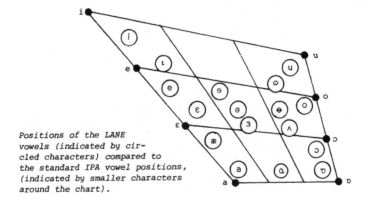

Positions of the LANE vowels (indicated by circled characters) compared to the standard IPA vowel positions, (indicated by smaller characters around the chart).

The transcription of any speech as recorded is based on a comparison between the acoustic signals and a set of 'archetypal' sounds which are somehow stored in the brain of the person doing the transcription. They depend on the quality of the recording and on the ability of the transcriber to make consistent judgements. These judgements can be aided by machines which translate the acoustic patterns into visual or digital patterns, but when the signal lies close to the boundary line between two archetypal sounds the person doing the transcription must make a choice. The person reading the transcription must bear in mind that any symbol represents not A SOUND but any one of A NUMBER OF POSSIBLE SOUNDS in a limited acoustic space.

The distinction which Jim had difficulty with, for which he asked me to listen, was that between [ʊ] and [ɔ]. Most English dialects have either one or the other, or neither (except in certain environments): it is what is generally referred to as the 'short *o*', which in many dialects is farther back when followed by /r ɪ g/ than in other environments. The Quenya 'short *o*' should, from published descriptions, be [ɔ], while the Sindarin *o*, long and short, would be normal and lengthened versions of [ʊ]. Now the difference between these two is that [ɔ] has the lips slightly more rounded (but not much), and the back of the tongue is slightly higher (but not much) than [ʊ]. Acoustically, the first and second formants, which are very close together in both these sounds, are slightly lower in [ɔ].[2] It is this lowering that the transcriber must listen for in the recording, since the lip rounding of the speaker can't be used as a clue.

Note on Tolkien's Reading Styles

The 'elevated' style differs from the ordinary primarily in rhythm and intonation (including the ways in which sounds blend in to one another during fast speech), and the pronunciation of the letter *r*. I didn't notice any other variation in the individual sounds, either consonants or vowels.

'Elevated' rhythm is characterized by greater regularity in the duration ratio between stressed and unstressed syllables (an effect which is characteristic of poetry in English). 'Elevated' intonation appears to use certain patterns

---

[2] *[Different vowels are distinguishable from one another because they have different sound intensities at different frequencies. On an ACOUSTIC SPECTROGRAPH the frequencies of the most intensity for any vowel appear as dark bands, forming a sound spectrum of light and dark. The dark bands are called FORMANTS; the band of lowest frequency is the first format, the next highest band the second formant, and so forth. The first three formants alone are necessary for vowel identification. —J.A.]*

in preference to others, though I haven't studied this aspect
in detail.
It is in the pronunciation of *r* that the difference is
most noticeable. There appears to be a set of /r/ pronunciations ordered according to degree of elevation of style:

trilled *r*	[r]	most elevated
tapped *r*	[ɾ]	
approximant *r*	[ɹ]	
lengthen preceding vowel	[:]	least elevated

In his ordinary pronunciation, syllable-initial /r/ is an
alveolar approximant [ɹ], while syllable-final /r/ simply
makes the preceding vowel longer, as in most speech of England at the present time. But the more elevated the style,
the more likely the /r/ is to be tapped or trilled.
I'll leave the description of the 'character' styles to
others, since an impressionistic description is of little use
here. I have not used the character styles for vowel analysis anyway.

Tolkien's English

Now for some observations about Tolkien's manner of
speaking English in general.
Tolkien's vowels seem normal enough, though I have not
had the leisure to do a detailed analysis. Such a full description would be best done in chart form, using the center
frequency of the first and second formants to plot the loca-
tion of the vowel in a two dimensional space which corresponds rather closely with the physical space in which the
vowels are produced in the mouth. (This correspondence
between format pattern and articulation exists because the
frequency of the first formant depends largely on the size of
the cavity beneath the narrowest place in the mouth, while
that of the second format is related to the size of the cavity in front of the constriction.)
The only noteworthy consonants are /r/ and /ŋg/. In
addition to what was mentioned under 'elevated style' about
/r/, it often happens that when two vowels occur together in
speech they are separated by an epenthetic /r/. As in many
Midland dialects of English, Tolkien sometimes pronounces the
combination ⟨ng⟩ between vowels as [ŋg] when standard English
has [ŋ]; for example, in reciting 'The Song of Beren and
Lúthien', *in the forest singing sorrowless* has *singing* come
out as ['sɪŋgɪŋ] where we would say ['sɪŋɪŋ]. Tolkien's pronunciation of other consonants does not differ notably from
that of standard British or American speech.
There are a number of individual words which Tolkien

pronounces in 'nonstandard' ways:

iron [ˈɑ�·yɾən]

again [əˈgeɪn] (This is standard British, but not American)

herbs [hɜ·bz], rather than [ɜ·bz]

Tolkien's Elvish

Was there any evidence that Tolkien's English interfered with his pronunciation of Elvish? Probably the most outstanding example is in the first line of the Sindarin poem 'A Elbereth Gilthoniel' sung by Arwen in Elrond's Hall of Fire (I:250;R:63f.). Tolkien starts out [ɑ·ˈɾɛlbɛɾɛθ] with the epenthetic /r/ separating what would otherwise be two continuous vowels. In the fifth line, the *o* of *o galadhremmin* is very centralized [ə]; centralizing of unstressed vowels is characteristic of English, but not (according to Tolkien's descriptions) of Sindarin.

In the Quenya poem 'Galadriel's Lament in Lórien' English influences are not so easy to notice. In *laurië*, pronounced [ˈlaŏɾiɛ] in the spoken version, the second element of the diphthong is a short [o] rather than a short [ɔ] or [u]. This is characteristic of English, but Tolkien does not mention that Quenya diphthongs are not pronounced as spelled. In the sung version, the second element is even lower [ʊ]. Another feature of English which I noticed in the sung version (but not in the spoken) was that the lengthened /e/ at the end of some words tended to drift toward a higher position. This was true of *lumbulë* and of the first *namárië*.

There is one phenomenon whose status I'm not sure of: the pronunciation of *fanyar* in both spoken and sung versions of 'Galadriel's Lament' lacks the final (pluralizing) /r/. This could either be an error conditioned by his usual dropping of syllable-final /r/ in English, or conditioned by the relative difficulty of pronouncing /r + m/ in rapid succession (since the next word is *máryat* and since neither preceding nor following vowel is lengthened in either version).

There are a number of cases in which the pronunciation differs from the text due to 'processing' errors not connected with language phonology. These are slips of the tongue which happen to people even when they speak their own language, and are apparently due to the way in which the brain processes spoken languages. In the 8th line of the sung version of 'Galadriel's Lament', we hear...[ˌnɛn ɪnˈkwɑ·ˈntuˌvɑ···] when the spelling and the spoken version lead us to expect [ˌnin ɛnˈkwɑ··ntuˌvɑ···]. This metathesis of similar vowels is quite frequent in ordinary speech and reading, and I would have been surprised to find no instances of it in

TOLKIEN'S PRONUNCIATION

SOME EXAMPLES OF TOLKIEN'S PRONUNCIATION:

'A Elbereth Gilthoniel'

From the 'Song of the Mounds of Mundburg'

1 aˑ ˈrɛlbɛrɛθ gɪlˈθᴐniɛl
2 siˈlɛvrɛn ˈpɛna miˑriɛl
3 oˠː ˈmɛnɛl ˈaggla ˈrɛlɛnaθ
4 na ˈxaɛərɛd ˈpalan ˈdiˑriəl
5 ə ˌgalaˈðrɛmmɪn ˈɛnᴐraθ
6 faˈnutlᴐs lɛ ˈlɪnəðᴐn
7 nɛv ˈa�...

5 ðɛɛ̯ ˈθeodn ˌfɛl, ˈθɛŋglɪŋ ˈmaytɪˆ
8 ... ˈhaˑdɪŋ əṅ ˈguˑðˌlaˑv
9 ˈduˑnhɛrə n ˈdɛʊrˌwɪnə, ˈdaᴐtiˠ ˈgrɪmˌbɛᴐld
10 ˈhɛrɪˌfarə ɛnd ˈhɛruˌbrænd, ˈhᴐrn ɛn
    ˈfæˠstrɛd 12 ...ˈmᴐndˌboˑrg...
    13 ... ˈlᴐˑdz əv ˈgandᴐr
14 naγðə ˈhɪrˌlutn ðə fɛˑə...
15 mᴐr fᴐrlʊŋ ði eᴐld... 16 ...ˈarˌnax...
18 ˈdɛrᴐˌfɪn ɛn ˈdᴐtlɪn... 19 ... mᴐrθʊnd...
22 ...ˈgᴐ‹nˌdᴐr
27 ˈrrrɛd fɛl ðə ˈdʃu ɪn ˈrrammᴐs ˈɛxᴐrr

'Namárië: Galadriel's Lament in Lórien'

Spoken version:

1 ˈaˑy ˈlaᴐ̆riɛ ˈlantaꞎ ˈlassi
   suˑ(ˑ)rinɛn
2 ˈɪppar uˑˈnoˠˑtʰi naˑr vɛ
   ˈraˑma ˈraldarᴐn
3 ˈinˌyar vɛ ˈlɪntĕ ˈyuˑlmar ˈvaˑɲɛr
4 mi ˌᴐrᴐˈmardi ˈlɪssɪˆ
   ˌmɪruˠˈvᴐˑriˠva
5 ˌanˈduˑnɛ pɛlla ˈvardᴐ ˈtɛllomaꞎ
6 nu lutni ˈyassɛn ˈtɪnˌtɪlar i
   ˈɛlɛˌni
7 ˌoˑˈmaˑˈiᴐ ˌaɛrɪˈtaˑri
   ˈliriɛn
8 ˈsiˑ ˈman i ˈyulma niˠnᵈ
   ɛnˈkwantuˌva
9 ˌaˑn ˈsiˑ tɪnˈtallɛ ˈvarda
   ˌᴐyᴐˈlᴐssiᴐ
10 vɛ ˈfanya ˈmarʃat ˌɛlɛnˈtari ˈᴐrtənɛ
11 a ˈriʎyə ˈtiˑɛ ˌrunduˈlaˑvɛ
    ˈlumbᴐlɛ
12 az ˈsɪndaˌnᴐriɛllᴐ ˈkʰayta
    mᴐːrniə
13 ˈfalmaˌlɪnna ˈrɪmbɛ mɛt
    ar ˈhiˑsie
14 ˌᴐnˈtuppa ˌkalaˈkɪlyoˆm ˈmiˑri
    ˈᴐyalɛ
15 ˌsiˑ ˈvanwa ˌna... ˈrᴐˑmɛllᴐ
    ˈvanwa... ˈvaliˌnar
16 ˌnaˈmaˑriˌeˑ ˌnay
    ˈhɪruˠˌvalyɛ ˈvaltˆˌmaˑr
17 ˌnaˠy ˈɛllyɛ ˌhɪˌruˌva
    ˌnaˈmaˑriɛ

Sung version:

aˑˑiˑˑˑ ˈlaᴐ̆rie ˈlantar ˈlasi
suˑrinɛˑˑˑn
ˈiˑɲyar uˑˈnoˆˑtɪ ˌnaˑr vɛ
ˈraˑmarᵃˈralˑdᴐn
ˈiˑɲya vɪˠ ˈlɪntɪˠ ˈyolˑmar ˈvaˑˑniɛr
mi ˈᴐrᴐˈmaˑrdi ˈlɪˑˑssɪˠ
mɪrᴐˈvᴐˑˑrɛˈvaˑˑˑ
ˈaˑˑnˈduˑnɛ pɛlla ˈvaˑrdᴐ ˈtɛˑlomah
ˈnuˑ loˈɪnɪˆ ˈyassɛnṅ ˈtɪntɪˌlar i
ˈɛlɛnɪˠ
ˈoˠˑˈmaˑrʃᴐ ˈaᴐ̆ɛrɪˠˈtaˑˑri
ˈlɪˑꞎriˌnɛˑˑˑˑn
ˈsiˑˑ ˈman i ˈyolma ˌnɛn
ɪnˈkwaˑˑntuˌvaˑˑˑˑ
ˈaˑˑ ˈsiˑ tɪnˈtallɛˆ ˈvarda
ˈᴐyᴐˈlᴐssɛˌᴐ
ˈveˑ ˈfaˑɲya ˈmaˑˑrɛt ˈɛlɛnˈtari ˈᴐrtaˌne
aˑ ˈrɪlya ˈtyɛr uˠnduˈlaˑˑˑvɛ
ˈluˑˑmbuˑˌlɛˑˑˑe
ˈaˑˑˑ ˈsɪndaˑˈnoˠrɪˈɛˆttᴐ ˈkayta
ˈmᴐˑrniˌe
i ˈvalmaˈlɪnnaˑ ˈrɪˑmbɛ ˈmɛt
ˈaˑˑꞎh ˈyiˑsiˌe
ŋˈtuˑpʰa ˈkaˑlaˈkɪlyʊ miˑərɪ
ᴐˑyalɛ
ˈsiˑˑ ˈvaˑnwa ˈnaˑˑ ˈrᴐˑˑˌmɛˑlˌlᴐ
ˈvaˑnwa ˈvalimˑaˑˑˑˑˑꞎ
ˈnaˑˑˈmaˑˑˌriˑˈɛˑˑˑˑeˑˑ ˈnaˑˑ
yirᴐˈvaˑlˌyaˆˑ ˈvaˑliˌmaˑˑˑˑꞎ
ˈnaˑɪ ˈyɛˑlyɪ ˈçyɪˌruˈvaˑˑˑˑˑ
ˈnaˑˑ ˈmᴐˑˑˑˌriˑˈeˑˑˑˑ

158

Tolkien's reading. Two lines further down, we hear *máryat* 'her hands (*dual*)' as ['mɑ·rɛt], with the palatalized /ry/ coming out as a raised following vowel, rather than ['mɑ·ɾ- yɑt]. In the second line of the sung version *rámar aldaron* comes out as ['rɑ·mɑrᵃr'ɑl·dɒn] rather than ['rɑ·mɑr 'ɑldɑ- rɒn]: one syllable from the second word is transferred to the first word in anticipation.

Another phenomenon which seems to be linked to general speech processing problems (but may be due to interference with some aspect of Tolkien's speech which I didn't notice in English) is this: when the vowel /ɛ/ is pronounced rap- idly, it sometimes comes out as if it had been /ɪ/. In Quenya this happens in both versions with the last vowel of *lisse-*, and in the sung version the final *e*'s of *ve lintë* in in the preceding line as well. *Airetári-* has the sound [ɪ] in the second syllable of both versions as well. In the Sin- darin poem 'A Elbereth Gilthoniel', we hear the opposite mis- take in line 2: *silivren* comes out as [si'lɛvrɛn].

Another set of inconsistencies connected with the *r* sounds in 'Galadriel's Lament' are these: in the phrase *ar sindanóriello* we hear [az 'sɪn...] in the spoken version, and ['ɑ·· 'sɪn...] in the sung version. According to the des- cription, it should be [(')ar 'sin...].

There are a number of other minor slips which would be too exhausting to catalog thoroughly. The majority of sounds are enough like the descriptions that we can confirm each by the other, and the discrepancies that do occur can (except as noted above) be explained either as interference from English or as processing errors common to everyone's speech.

OTHER
TONGUES

Jim Allan

KHUZDUL

ΚHUZDUL WAS THE SECRET SPEECH of the Dwarves which they did
not willingly teach to those of other races, even to
friends. After the destructions of their ancient dwellings
the Dwarves used more and more the languages of those Men
among whom they dwelt, and Khuzdul ceased to be a tongue for
everyday use, but rather a tongue of lore and learning,
learned after infancy.

There are not sufficient examples of Khuzdul published
to allow a listing of the sounds which might be considered
complete. But the following incomplete list has been compiled, using Tolkien's orthography:

a, ai, b, d, e, g, i, k, kh, l, m, n, r, sh, th, u, z.

In Khuzdul *kh* and *th* 'are aspirates, that is *t* or *k* followed
by an *h*, more or less as in *backhand, outhouse'* (III:395),
represented by [tʰ] and [kʰ] in the International Phonetic
Alphabet, not by [θ] and [x]. *Sh* would represent a sound
similar to the [ʃ] represented by English *sh*. 'Some Dwarves
are said to have used a back or uvular r' (III:392), that is,
[ʀ], heard in French and many German dialects. The exact
pronunciation of the vowels is not given. They would not
have differed too widely from their counterparts in the Eldarin languages.

Khuzdul, like the Semitic languages of our own time, is
based on a system of triliteral roots. That is, the roots
are not themselves pronounceable words, but consist of three
consonants without vowels. In English—and other Indo-
European languages—forms are created mainly be the addition
of prefixes and suffixes to the root. In the Semitic languages prefixes and suffixes are used, but only along with

insertion and changing of vowels between the three root consonants. For example, from the Hebrew root *MLK* 'royal' derives *melek* 'king', *malk* 'king of', *malak* 'he reigned', *mal-
kāh* 'queen', *mōlek* 'reigning, ruler', *timlōk* 'she will
reign', *mᵉlūkāh* 'kingship', *mamlīk* 'making reign', *malkūt*
'royalty', *mamlakah* 'kingdom', and numerous other forms.
In Khuzdul we can isolate the root *KʰZD*, whence *Khazâd*,
'Dwarves', *Khazad-* 'Dwarvish', and *Khuzdul*, the name of the
Dwarvish language. The three basic consonants of a root can
be isolated in many of the other forms: *BRZ* in *Baraz*, *KʰLD*
in *kheled*, probably *ZRB* in *mazarbul*.

The only example of any sentences in Khuzdul are *Baruk
Khazâd! Khazâd aimênu!* 'Axes of the Dwarves! The Dwarves are
upon you!' (III:411). From this it can be seen that the
genitive can be indicated by placing the genitive noun following the main noun, that the definite article is lacking,
and that the present tense of the verb 'to be' is omitted.
The rest of the corpus is mainly names, and even when we
possess a corresponding Common Speech or Sindarin name we
cannot be sure the meanings correspond, save where Tolkien
tells us they do.

The following is a complete listing of published Khuzdul
forms:

aimênu, *prep. + prn. 2nd pl.* upon you.
III:411.

Azanulbizar, *nm. place* 'Valley of the
dim (overshadowed) rills', *rendered*
'Dimrill Dale' *in Common Speech.* / S.
Nanduhirion/ I:296;G:182. *See* -ul.

Baraz, *nm. mountain* see **Barazinbar**.
I:296.

Barazinbar, *nm. mountain* rendered 'Red-
horn' *in Common Speech.* / S. Caradhras/
The shortened form **Baraz** *is also used.*
I:296.

baruk, *n. pl.* axes. III:411.

Bundushathūr, *nm. mountain* 'Cloudy-
head'. / S. Fanuidhol/ *The shortened
form* **Shathūr** *is also used.* I:296;G:182.

dūm, *n. (gen. dūmu)* mansion. / Q.
*marde, S. -rond/ I:296,333ℓ;III:415.

Khazad-, *adj.* of Dwarves. III:415.

Khazâd, *n. pl.* Dwarves. III:411.

Khazad-dūm. *nm. place (gen. Khazad-dūmu)*
'Dwarf-mansion', *rendered* Phurunargian
'Dwarf-delving' *in archaic Westron'.*
Named Moria 'Black Chasm' *in Sindarin.*

I:296,333ℓ;III:415;G:183.

kheled, *n.* glass. G:190.

Kheled-zâram, *nm. lake* 'Glass-lake',
rendered 'Mirrormere' *in Common Speech.*
I:296;G:190.

Khuzdul, *n.* 'Dwarvish', the language
of the Dwarves. III:392,404. *See* -ul.

Kibil-nâla, *nm. river* The Common
Speech name is 'Silverlode' *translated
from S.* Celebrant. *Cf. S.* celeb. I:
296;G:191.

mazarbul, *n. pl.* records. I:335f.

Shathūr, *nm. mountain* see **Bundushathūr**.
I:296.

Tharkūn, *nm. pers.* name used by Gandalf among the Dwarves. *May be related
to Q.* *tarcil. II:279.

-u, *gen. indicator* of. / Q. -o/ *See*
Khazad-dūmu.

-ul, *adj. suff.???* See Azanulbizar,
Khuzdul, 'Fundinul' I:333ℓ.

zâram, *n.* lake. G:190.

Zirak, *nm. mountain* see **Zirak-zigil**.

I:296.

Zirak-zigil, *nm. mountain* *The Common Speech name is 'Silvertine' translated*

from S. Celebdil. *The shortened form* Zirak *is also used.* I:296;G:191.

Balin's tomb inscription (I:333) is the sole example of Khuzdul written in *certar*. It transliterates as follows:

B A L I N

F U ND I N U L

U Z B A D KH A Z A D D Ū M U

· B A L I N S Λ N O V F U ND I N L O R D O V M O R I A ·

Balin and *Fundin* are, of course, not the true secret Khuzdul names of Balin and his father, but their outer names, in the Northern Speech. See p. 220f.

THE BLACK SPEECH

THE BLACK SPEECH was made by Sauron in the Dark Years of the
Second Age to be the common language for all those under
his power. This he failed to accomplish, and after his downfall at the end of the Second Age the tongue, in its classic
form, died out. The language would have been used chiefly by
Orcs; but Orcs had little love for language and used it care-
lessly, so that it would have become greatly distorted in
their mouths after Sauron's first downfall, where it survived
at all.

When, at the end of the Third Age, Sauron rose to power
again, he revived the Black Speech, and it became again a
tongue for his servants, including the Orcs of Mordor.

There are not sufficient published examples of words
in the Black Speech to allow a listing of its sounds that can
with any confidence be called complete. But the following
are the sounds found in our corpus, in Tolkien's orthography:

*a, ai, b, d, g, gh, h, i, k, l, m, n, nk, o, p, r, s, sh, t,
th, u, z.*

From Orc names, possibly not in the Black Speech, can be
added:

au, f, kh.

Th, kh, and *gh* represent spirants, that is [θ], [x], and
[ɣ]. *Sh* would represent a sound similar to [ʃ] represented
by English *sh.* 'The Orcs...are said to have used a back or
uvular *r*' (III:392), that is, [ʀ], heard in French and in
many German dialects. This may have been the proper value
for *r* in Classic Black Speech.

Tolkien uses both the acute accent and the circumflex
to mark long vowels in words and names from the Black Speech.

This is probably to be taken as an inconsistency on Tolkien's part, not as an indication that Black Speech has two sorts of long vowels.

The following list gives all words in the Black Speech found with meanings in the published corpus. Other words and names from the Black Speech and Orkish will be treated later.

agh, *conj.* and. / Q. ar, S. a/ I: 267.

ash, *adj.* one. I:267.

†bûrz, *adj.* dark. / S. dûr/ II:49 169.

burzum, *n.* darkness. / Q. mornië/ I:267.

durb-, *v. stem* to rule. — durbatulûk, *v. infinitive + prn. 3rd pl. + 'ûk'* to rule them all. I:267.

ghâsh, *n.* fire. / Q. NÁR, S. naur/ I:341;III:409.

gimb-, *v. stem* to find. / Q. hirtûv-/ — gimbatul, *v. infinitive + prn. 3rd pl.* to find them. I:267.

gûl, *n.* wraith(s). G:172. (Eng. *ghoul* < Ar. *ghûl* 'evil demon that robs graves and feeds on the dead'.)

-hai, *n.* people, folk. / S. -hoth, -oth, -rim/ II:149;III:410.

-ishi, *post.* in. / Q. -sse/ I:267.

krimp-, *v. stem* to bind. — krimpatul, *v. infinitive + prn. 3rd pl.* to bind them. I:267.

†lug, *n.* tower. / S. barad, min-[2], minas/ II:49,169.

Lugburz, *nm. place* 'Tower-dark', rendered 'Dark Tower' in Common

Speech. / S. Barad-dûr/ *II:49,169.

nazg, *n.* ring. / Q. corma, S. *côr, cor-/ I:267. (Ir. *nasc* 'ring'.)

Nazgûl, *n.* (nazg + gûl) Ringwraith(s). I:263;II:49;G:172.

olog, *n.* an especially large, strong, and intelligent kind of troll developed by Sauron toward the end of the Third Age. It could endure the sun as long as Sauron maintained his power over it. III:410.

Olog-hai, *nm. people* 'Olog-folk'. See olog. III:410.

sharkû, *n.* (< a debased form of Black Speech used by the Orc soldiers of Lugburz) old man. III:298,410.

snaga, *n.* slave. *Used by the Uruk-hai and other great Orcs as the name for the lesser Orcs.* III:409.

thrak-, *v. stem* to bring. — thrakatulûk, *v. infinitive + prn. 3rd pl. + 'ûk'* to bring them all. I: 267.

-ûk, *adj.* all. I:267.

uruk, *n.* great soldier orc. III:409. *Cf.* S. orch.

Uruk-hai, *nm. people.* 'Uruk-folk'. See uruk. III:409.

Mark Mandel, in his analysis of the Black Speech ('The Ring Inscription', *Tolkien Journal* 1:2, Oct., 1965) identifies -*at* as a suffix indicating purpose, and -*ul* as the third personal plural pronoun in the forms *durbatulûk*, *gimbatul*, *krimpatul*, and *durbatulûk*. But Judy Winn Bell ('The Language of J.R.R. Tolkien in *The Lord of the Rings*', *Mythcon I Proceedings*, ed. Glen GoodKnight, 1971, pp.38-39) suggests that -*a* marks the purpose infinitive and that -*tul* is the pronoun 'them'. Both analyses are equally possible.

BLACK SPEECH

   Not translated by Tolkien in the published text is the
curse uttered by one of the Orcs of the Dark Tower against
Uglúk and the Orcs of Isengard: *Uglúk u bagronk sha pushdug
Saruman-glob búbhosh skai* (II:48). Tolkien identifies this
as a debased form of the Black Speech used by Orcs of the
Tower (III:410).
   Probably from the Black Speech are the names *Gothmog*,
and *Grishnákh*, belonging respectively to the lieutenant of
Minas Morgul and to an Orc captain of soldiers from the Dark
Tower. Other Orc names that may contain, at least, elements
from the Black Speech, if they are not pure Black Speech,
are: *Azog, Bolg, Gorbag, Lagduf, Lugdush, Mauhúr, Muzgash,
Radbug, Shagrat, Ufthak,* and *Uglúk*. But the Orc name *Golfimbul* is of Northern origin (see p. 226).

THE ADÛNAIC LANGUAGES

IN HIS WRITINGS ON THE THIRD AGE of Middle-earth Tolkien has
   generally represented Weston, the predominant tongue for the
whole region west of the Sea of Rhûn and north of Harad, by
English. Other tongues related to Westron, and names in
these tongues, he has represented by other languages from the
Germanic family related to English. Thus, the Northmen of
east Rhovanion are given Gothic names (III:326), the Rohirrim speak Old English and have names in the same tongue, the
outer Mannish names of the Dwarves are of Old Norse formation, and the long personal names of certain upper class Hobbit families are early medieval names of Germanic origin.

   This process of translation of languages of the Third
Age to those of our own age or of the comparatively recent
past means that the published corpus contains little data on
these original tongues. What knowledge is available is sum-
marized below.

   The ancestor of Westron is called by Tolkien *Adûnaic*.
It was the ancestral language of those men whom the Elves
called the Edain, and was also the tongue of their descendants, the Númenoreans, whom the Elves called the Dúnedain.
Like Khuzdul and the Semitic languages of our own age, the
Adûnaic generally derived its forms form roots of three
consonants by the addition of various vowels, suffixes, prefixes, and infixes. Only a few forms have been published:
kalab 'fall down' (TS:23), *pharas* 'gold' (III:392); the names
of five Númenorean kings: *Ar-Adûnakhôr* 'Lord of the West',
Ar-Zimrathôn, *Ar-Sakalthôr*, *Ar-Gimilzôr*, *Ar-Insiladûn*, *Ar-
Pharazôn* entitled 'the Golden' (III:315-17); *Akallabêth*
'Great Fall' (TS:23), the name of a work recounting the downfall of Númenor; and *Adrahil* and *Imrahil*, the names of two
princes of Dol Amroth at the close of the Third Age (Tolkien

tells us that '*Jmrahil* is a Númenorean name' [III:391 *CH*]).
The doubling of the middle root consonant indicates
intensity, as in Hebrew; hence *Akallabêth* means 'GREAT Fall'
(TS:23).

The name of the language, *Adûnaic*, is partly Englished
through the suffix -*ic* commonly used in denoting languages
and language families (e.g. *Germanic*, *Celtic*, *Italic*, *Slavic*,
Hebraic, *Altaic*, *Aramaic*). But the element *adûn*- occurs in
the royal names *Ar-Inziladûn* and *Ar-Adûnakhôr*; the latter
is glossed as 'Lord of the West', and accordingly †*adûn* may
be taken as word meaning 'west' (borrowed from S *dûn* 'west'),
so that *Adûnaic* may be translated 'West-speech' or something
of the kind. Tolkien, as mentioned above, calls its principal
descendant *Westron* which supports the hypothesis. Another
possibility is that †*adûn* is related to S *adan*, in which case
we would have to take -*khôr* or -*akhôr* as the element meaning
'west', and assign to †*adûn* the meaning 'lord'. It is not
impossible that the race of the Edain called themselves 'The
Lords', and that S *adan* is, in fact, borrowed from Adûnaic.
The Quenya form *Atan* would show a substitution of *t* for *d*
because in Quenya *d* can only occur following *n*, *r*, *l*, and so
the closest sound that could occur in other environments was
substituted.

Westron began as a kind of trade lingo used along the
coasts of Middle-earth where the Númenoreans had forts and
harbours. Basically, it was Adûnaic mixed with words from
other Mannish tongues. After the fall of Númenor the few
survivors who founded the kingdoms of Arnor and Gondor from
the Númenorean possessions in Middle-earth naturally used
Westron rather than Adûnaic as the common speech for their
realms, though they enriched it with many words drawn from
Sindarin and Quenya.

The only words we have which are definitely identifiable
as standard Westron are *banakil* 'halfling' (III:416), *kali*
'jolly, gay' (III:414), *Karningul* 'Rivendell' (III:412),
Phurunargian 'Dwarf-delving' a word of antique form (III:
415), and *tarkil* 'one of Númenorean descent' derived from
Q *tarcil* (III:409). Possibly *mûmak*, pl. *mûmakil* 'elephant'
(II:269;III:101) should also be included, but it may rather
be a word derived from a tongue of the Haradrim.

The speech of various other Men of those days was often
related to Westron, for not all the Edain journeyed to Númenor at the beginning of the Second Age, and there were other
men, kindred to the Edain, who spoke tongues very similar to
Adûnaic, if not Adûnaic itself. Such a language, or group of
similar languages, was spoken in the upper Vales of Anduin in
the middle of the Third Age, and was ancestral to the speech
of the Men of the Vales of Anduin and to the speech of the

ADÛNAIC

Rohirrim at the end of the Third Age, tongues still very
closely related, perhaps even to be described as differing
dialects of the same tongue. Compared to Westron these
tongues were archaic, that is, they resembled more closely
the original Adûnaic than did Westron. Names and words from
these tongues Tolkien has rendered in Old English so that
some of the feeling of the relationships comes through,
though of course Rohirric is not ancestral to the Common
Speech in any sense. (If an more exact parallel between
Westron and Rohirric were desired it might be found in
Modern English compared to Modern Frisian.)

Tolkien does provide a few of true words of these related languages: Rohirric *kûd-dûkan* 'hole-dweller' (III:416),
glossed by the invented OE form *holbytla* ['hɔlˌbʉtla] 'hole-
builder' (III:408); *kastu*, glossed by OE *māðm* [mɑːðm]
'treasure, jewel, ornament, gift' (III:414f); *trahan*, glossed
by OE *smygel* ['smʉɣɛl] 'burrow' (III:414); the related name
Trahald 'burrowing, worming in', glossed by the invented OE
form *Sméagol* ['smeˑɑɣɔl] of the same meaning; and the name
Nahald 'secret', glossed by the invented OE form *Déagol*
['deˑɑɣɔl] of the same meaning (III:415). (In the record
*J. R. R. TOLKIEN reads and sings his THE LORD OF THE RINGS:
The Two Towers: The Return of the King* Tolkien represents
Gollum as pronouncing his original name as ['smiːˌɡʊɫ].
We may suppose that the Stoors of the Angle—like the Hobbits
of the Shire—had by 2463 long ago adopted Westron and forgotten their earlier tongue, and that such old names in this
tongue that were still preserved among them had become
changed in pronunciation.)

The Hobbits of the Shire are said to have spoken a
rustic version of Westron, with the addition of some words
still retained from their former language, that of the Vales
of Anduin, closely related to Rohirric. It is difficult to
decide which words are peculiar to the Shire dialect and
which are belong to normal Westron. The only words definitely identified as peculiar to Hobbit Westron are *kuduk*
'hobbit' derived from *kûd-dûkan*; *kast* 'mathom' from *kastu*;
and *trân* 'smial' from *trahan*. Tolkien, as indicated by the
meanings here given, represents these words in English by
corresponding forms not part of standard English. They are,
of course, to be pronounced as in Modern English, not
like the Old English forms on which they are based, that is,
as ['hʊbɪt], ['mæðəm], and ['smaɪəl] (rhyming with *dial*
rather than with *smile* [smaɫl] for those who make a distinction).

Slightly archaic elements are said to appear in certain
of the Hobbit family names and traditional given names: *banazîr* 'halfwise' (cf. *banakil* 'halfling'), glossed as OE *samwîs*
['sʊmwiːs] modernized to *Samwise* ['sæmwaɪz] (III:414); *-bas*

ADÛNAIC

'-wich, -wick' (III:416); *galab-* 'game' (III:416); *gamba* 'buck' (III:416); *hloth* 'a two roomed dwelling or hole, cottage' (III:416); *hlothram(a)* 'cottager, cotman' (III:416); *hlothran* (*hloth* + *ran(u)*) 'cottage town, cotton' (III:416); *ran(u)* 'a group of *hloths* on a hill-side (= town, -ton)' (III:416); *ranugad* 'stay-at-home', glossed as OE *hāmfæst* ['hɑ:mvæst], modernized as *Hamfast* ['hæmfæst] (III:414); †*zara* 'old' (III:416). Tolkien represents the change from the village name *Galabas* to the surname *Galbasi* reduced to *Galpsi* by the translated name *Gamwich* (pronounced as though it were *Gammidge*) from whence comes the surname *Gammidgy* reduced to *Gamgee* (III:383,416).

The following elements appear in Hobbit geographical names: *bralda* 'ale'; *branda* 'border, march'; *hîm* 'heady'; *nîn* 'water' (III:416); and, of course, *Sûza* 'the Shire' (I: 270;III:412).

We have no information on any of the genuine words or names from the Northern Speech of Dale.

The strong influence of the Elvish tongues can be seen even in the few forms we have for the Adûnaic languages. The possible relationship between Adûnaic †*adûn* and S *dûn* has already been covered. *Ar-* in the Adûnaic royal names appears to be cognate with S *ara(n)-* 'king, lord'. S *nen* 'water' is probably connected with Westron *nîn* 'water'. The form *banakil* 'halfling' ends in what appears to be the Quenya ending *-cil*. Compare also †*narg* in *Phurunargian* 'Dwarf-delving' with S †*naug* 'dwarf'.

172

MORE OBSCURE LANGUAGES

Alien to Westron, or very distantly related, was the speech of the Men of Dunland. They were descendants of people who had once dwelt in the vales of the White Mountains. The only word of Dunlendish to appear in the published corpus is the name *Forgoil*, said to mean 'Strawheads', which they applied to tne Rohirrim. Indeed, the name which the Dunlendings called themselves and that which they called their land are lost to us. *Dunland* and *Dunlending* are Old English, standing for Rohirric names. They contain *dunn* 'dark, swarthy' (III:408).

The Men of Bree were descended from the ancestors of the Dunlendings, and formerly spoke a related speech, though by the end of the Third Age they had long used Westron and had forgotten their earlier tongue. Of the Hobbits, many of the Stoors had formerly dwelt in what was later known as northern Dunland, and 'appear to have adopted a language related to Dunlendish before they came north to the Shire. Thus both the Bree-men and the Hobbits of the Marish and Buckland (mostly descended from these Stoors) retained personal and place names from their former languages. Tol-has changed these into names of Celtic derivation. E.g., from a British form meaning 'hill', which appears in Welsh as *bre*, comes *Bree*. The element is found in English place names as *Bray* in Devonshire, with the addition of *-don* 'down' in *Bredon* in Worcestershire and in *Breedon* in Leistershire, and with the addition of *-hill* as *Brill* in Buckinghamshire. *Chet* in *Chetwood* and *Archet* derives from a British form meaning 'forest, wood', whence Welsh *coed* 'wood'. It appears in many English place names, including *Cheetwood* in Lancashire and *Chetwode* in Buckinghamshire. *Ar-* in *Archet* means 'high' from British *ard*; thus, 'High-wood'. *Combe* derives from OE *cumb* 'hollow, valley', a loan-word from British, cognate with Welsh *cwm* of the same meaning. It appears in many English place names in the forms *comb*, *combe*, *coomb*, and *coombe*. In Rohan is found the *Deeping Coomb*, that is, the 'Valley belonging to the Deep', in reference to *Helm's Deep* (G:181).

The personal names peculiar to the Hobbits of Buckland were, according to Tolkien, no doubt inherited from the former language of the Stoors of Dunland (III:413). Tolkien claims not to have altered them, perhaps because they already 'had a style that we should perhaps fell vaguely to be "Celtic"' (III:413). They are discussed fully beginning on page 198.

The only other Celtic geographical name in the corpus is *Carrock* from a Celtic form meaning 'rock', cognate with Welsh *careg* 'rock, stone' and Gaelic *carraig* 'headland, cliff, crag, rock'. English *crag* is also related. *Carrock Fell* is a mountain peak in the Skiddaw group in Cumberland.

In Gondor were old names of unknown origin descending from languages long extinct. The place names are *Arnach*, *Eilenach*, *Erech*, and *Rimmon*. These are not unlike Sindarin forms in their appearance, and it may be that some of the names listed in the Sindarin dictionary belong here instead. Both *Erech* and *Rimmon* may be familiar to some as Biblical names. *Erech* occurs in Genesis 10:10 as the Hebrew name for the ancient city of *Uruk* in Mesopotamia, the modern *Warka*. *Rimmon* appears in the place name *'Ēn-Rimmōn* 'Spring of Rimmon' in Joshua 19:7 (as two names, *'Ayin, Rimmōn* 'Spring, Rimmon' in I Chronicles 4:32) and in Nehemiah 11:29. In II Kings 5:18 *Rimmōn* is used as a name for the Canaanite god Ba'al Hadad. It is, in fact, a common name for Hadad the thunder god, and means something like 'Roarer'. There is no connection with the homonymous Hebrew word *rimmōn* 'pomegranite'. The names *Erech* and *Rimmon* and the Sindarin name *Lebennin* (reminiscent of Mount *Lebanon*) give a slightly eastern flavour to Gondor to the modern reader, and help suggest its antiquity.

Umbar also was a geographical name of forgotten origin, not be be connected with Q *umbar* 'fate'.

One personal name, *Forlong*, is said to be of the same kind. (III:407)

Another language or language group probably gives the name *Khand*, applied to a land to the south-east of Mordor. Tolkien refers to 'Variags of Khand' who fight in the Battle of the Pelennor (III:121,123). *Variag* may be the true name for the inhabitants of Khand, but *Variag* also occurs as a Russian name 〈Варяг〉 for the Varangian Guard, the Norse bodyguard of the Emperors of Constantinople. The Norse form of their name, *Væringi*, means 'Sworn-ones' and refers to their status as mercenaries sworn to the service of the emperor. The **Variags** founded Kiev. In modern Russian *Variág* is sometimes used as a name for a travelling pedlar.

It may be that in the Third Age a similar group of northern mercenaries served the Lord of Khand, and that Tolkien has adopted the Slavic term for the Varangian Guard as a reasonable equivalent.

Another name of the same kind, for which a Slavic substitution would have been made, is the original behind *Radagast*. Early chroniclers speak of a Slavic god named *Radegást* ⟨*Padeɜdcm*⟩. His temple was at Rethra (earlier *Radogoszsz*), made of wood, and rested on animal horns. Its outside was covered with figures of the gods. Within were kept special insignia and a stabled horse. Some believe that the reference is to a different god altogether, and that the name of the town has been erroneously applied to the god. Certainly two of the wizards are known to us primarily by names given them by Men in their own languages—then translated by Tolkien as *Gandalf* and *Saruman*—and Radagast's name might be expected to be in a Mannish tongue of the east, for he appears to dwell there more than do Gandalf or Saruman.

A southern speech is rendered by Latin when Gandalf says he was known as *Incánus* in the South (II:279); for *incānus* is Latin for 'grey'. This same speech may be behind the Latin term *Flammifer* given to Eärendil's Star (the planet Venus) by Bilbo in his song in the House of Elrond (I:249). *Flammifer* derives from *flamma* 'flame' and *ferre* 'to carry', and so means 'Flame-bearing' or 'Flame-bearer'. It occurs in Latin as an adjective with the general meaning 'fiery'. Its use in Bilbo's poem recalls the normal Latin word for the planet Venus as a morning star, *Lucifer* 'Light-bearer'. But, of course, the adoption of *Lucifer* as a byname for the devil spoiled it for Tolkien's purpose.

The language indicated is probably one of the tongues of the Haradrim. It must be remembered that Gondor at one time extended far into the South.

For the Wild Men of Drúadan Forest we have only one word, *gorgûn* 'orcs'.

We have no words in the tongue of the Snowmen of the Ice Bay of Forochel.

OTHER TONGUES OF ELVES

Tolkien states 'Of the Eldarin tongues two are found in this book: the High-elven or *Quenya*, and the Grey-elven or *Sindarin*' (III:405). This clearly indicates that more than

these two Eldarin tongues existed, but of the other(s) we
know nothing.

As to the East-elves, their languages do not appear at
all in the corpus, save that Tolkien does say that *'Lórien,
Caras Galadon* [sic], *Amroth, Nimrodel* are probably of Silvan
origin, adapted to Sindarin' (III:405n).

ENTISH

Tolkien describes Entish as follows:

> The language that they had made was unlike all others:
> slow, sonorous, agglomerated, repetitive, indeed long-
> winded; formed of a multiplicity of vowel-shades and dis-
> tinctions of tone and quantity which even the loremasters
> of the Eldar had not attempted to represent in writing.
> They used it only among themselves; but had no need to
> keep it secret, for no others could learn it.   (III:409)

A great increase in distinctions of vowel-colour, tone,
and quantity ought to have made possible the transmission of
a greater amount of data in less time than in any human language. That Entish was still an unbelievably slow means of
transmitting information by human terms indicates how unin-
terested in haste the Ents were. But it would have been
an exceedingly precise tongue.

A speech in Entish, if it could be understood by human
ears, would perhaps be like a very verbose and involved kind
of poetry. There would be repetitions upon repetitions upon
repetitions, with slight variations. If there was anything
that we might call a sentence, it might proceed in a sort of
spiral fashion, winding in to the main point, and then winding out again, touching all along the way on what has already
been said and what will be said.

Entish may have lacked anything that might be called a
common noun, for Ents would be able to take the time and use
the complexities of their tongue to describe every object and
person in a way that would, in effect, give it a distinct
proper name of its own. Treebeard gives part of the name for
the hill on which he stands as *a-lalla-lalla-rumba-kamanda-
lindor-burúmë* (II:68). Tolkien notes this single representation of a fragment of true Entish is 'probably very inac-
curate' (III:409n).

The slowness of Entish is in part because the Ents can
and do use other tongues—those of Elves and Men—when they
have need of hasty speech, and so preserve the purity of
their own tongue. Treebeard says of Entish, 'It is a lovely
language, but it takes a very long time to say anything in

it, because we do not say anything in it, unless it is worth
taking a long time to say, and to listen to' (II:68).

VALINOREAN

The Valar, it seems, had their own tongue. Q *miruvóre*
was said by the Eldar to come from the language of the Valar
and to be the name of the drink poured out at their festi-
vals. The meaning of the name is not known. The Eldar
believed, though they were not certain, that it was made from
honey of the undying flowers in the gardens of Yavanna.
Tolkien compares this with νέκταρ (*nectar*), the drink of the
Olympian gods. (R:61)

When Aragorn seeks the herb called *athelas* in Sindarin
and *kingsfoil* in Common Speech a conversation occurs between
himself and the herb-master in which it is implied that *aséa
aranion* is the Valinorean name for this plant (III:141).
The name appears, however, very much Quenya in its form.
It may be that the herb-master is using *Valinorean* here to
mean 'Quenya', for Quenya is the speech of the Elves who
returned from Valinor. Or the relationship may be that the
Elvish tongues in part descend from Valinorean. It is my
opinion that the name is genuine Valinorean. But see page
115, note 5, for an opposing view.

PERSONAL NAMES

AN ETYMOLOGICAL EXCURSION
AMONG THE SHIRE FOLK

Paula Marmor

Note: Abbreviations such as ED and AS indicate references. See conclusion of article.

THE NAMES OF THE HOBBITS may first be divided into two types: those represented by Celtic words or in a style resembling Celtic and those of Germanic origin. The Celtic represents a former language of the Stoors, probably related to Dunlendish and to the former language of the Men of the Bree-land (III:408,413). The Germanic terms represent tongues of Men of the Vales of Anduin, originally akin to the language of Rohan, and more distantly to Westron (represented in *The Lord of the Rings* by modern English).

The names of the two brothers who led the first group of Hobbits west into the land beyond the Brandywine, *Marcho* and *Blanco* are either both Germanic, or one Celtic and one Germanic, indicating there was already some mixture of both language groups. You see, *Marcho* is from an old element *marka* 'horse' found both in the Germanic and Celtic languages: OHG *marh*, OE *mearh*, Wel. *march*, Gael. *marc*. (Modern Eng. *mare* derives from OE *mere* the feminine from of *mearh*.) *Blanco* is OE *blanca* 'horse', cognate with ON *blakkr* 'horse, steed' (ED). (The element *blank-* originally meant 'shining white', and was probably once applied to white horses only.) These two brothers present an interesting parallel with Hengest (or Hengist) and Horsa, the two Saxon brothers who traditionally led the first Germanic people into Britain, especially when one considers that *hengest* and *horsa* are both Old English words for 'horse'. Hengest was the founder of the kingdom of Kent, and quick perusal of an encyclopedia

will show that the geography of that portion of England is
similar to that of the Shire: the North Downs above, more
hill country to the west, a body of water to the east (the
Brandywine in one case and the Straits of Dover in the
other), and marshy fen country to the southeast.

Of course there are those scholars (the kind that don't
believe in Elves) who insist that Hengest and Horsa are mythical figures. The White Horse carved on the Berkshire Downs
is supposed to be their symbol (ED), and considering their
names it IS possible that they were created to fit their
trademark. The White Horse was later used as the banner of
several Anglo-Saxon kings (DC) (sound familiar?).

But that isn't all! If one goes back to the premise
that the Shire represents southeast and south-central England, with the Straits of Dover and the Channel as the
Brandywine, one is led to conclude that the Buckland represents Brittany. This is further supported by the fact that
Brittany (according to the standard tradition) was settled
from a band of Britons led by one CONAN MERIADOC! (AB:33,93).
(Curiouser and curiouser.) Buckland, in turn, is the Anglo-
Saxon *bocland* or 'bookland', duty-free estates granted by
deed by the old Kings of England (see 'Anglo-Saxon laws', EA,
Vol. 1, p. 845). (Now you know why I called this an excur-
sion.)

The Germanic Hobbit names are actually different stages
of development, words preserved in various states of evolution. The older names are the Frankish and Gothic names
still in use among the Tooks and Bolgers (*Peregrin*, *Fredegar*,
Isembold III:411). These names (as well as the names used in
Rohan) are usually two unconnected words: *Fredegar* 'peace·
spear' (ED;W); *Isembold* 'iron·bold' (ED). Some of the names
used in Europe at this time (the early Middle Ages) were
Latin, as *Peregrin* 'foreign', used of a stranger or a wanderer (W;AS). Some of the names in use among the Shire folk
were worn-down forms of these names, as *Tobald*, for *Theobald*,
OE *Þēodbeald* 'people·bold' (W) (*þēod* is also found in *Éothēod*
'Horse-people' or 'Horse-nation' [OEH]); *Harding* for *Hardwine*
'strong·friend' (ED).

Most of the other Hobbit names are either descriptive
(*Hamfast* 'stay-at-home', *Hending* 'friendly' from old *hende*
'amiable' [ES]), geographical (*Holman* 'one from the Holm
[a flat land between the twistings of a river or small island
in the stream]' [ES] [Geographical names are often passed
down and soon have no significance.]), or are apparently
meaningless (*Frodo*, *Drogo*, *Odo*)—leaving out the jewel- and
flower-type girls' names.

But lo! These names are not meaningless. In Anglo-
Saxon times (and among the Saxons after the conquest) it was

common to give nicknames for the older names, as *Sicca* for
Sigmund, *Betta* for *Beorhtnoth* (AS). The name *Frodo* (ON
Fróði, OHG *Fruoti*) means 'wise', specifically 'wise in
ancient lore'. *Otho* and *Odo* are variants of a Germanic root
meaning 'prosperity' (AS:78); compare the Bolger name *Odova-
car*. *Drogo* is an old word meaning 'carrier', replaced in the
Middle Ages by *Drew* (ES;AS). *Falco* is a name with origins
beyond recorded Germanic history. Weekley (ED) considers it
the origin of *Falcon*; Smith (AS) rather connects it with
Fulc, *Folc* 'people, fólk' (compare the Rohan name *Folcwine*).
Many of these short names are descriptive, as *Longo* and
Largo. A recorded Old English nickname which would prove
interesting is *Baga* or *Bacga*, meaning 'Fat-one' (apropos).
This would gave a clue to the formation of last names in the
major families of the Shire.

The Oldbucks (later Brandybucks) reckoned their descent
from Bucca of the Marish (*Bucca* is an Old English name from
either OE *bucc* 'male deer' or OE *bucca* 'he-goat' [G:161]).
This Bucca was a famous character round-abouts, and references to 'Old Bucca's grandson' or 'Miss Peony over at Old
Bucca's place' would devolve into the name *Oldbuck* in no
time. In like manner, a rather influential Hobbit, one Baga,
would leave his mark on his family. The Old English word for
Baga's people would be *Bagingas* (cf. *Eorlingas*, *Helmingas*),
which would probably become *Baggins* with a few centuries.
(*Boffin* may have been formed the same way from the lost
Middle-English name *Bofa*, of uncertain etymology, although it
may be cognate with *boy* [ED].) *Baggins* may also have contained a jesting reference to *bag* for *badger*: *Bagshot* is a
name occuring in England, meaning *Bag's Holt* 'badger's wood
or thicket' (ES). (The *brock* of *Brockhouse* and *Brockenbores*
also means 'badger'—this. is similar to the naming of Hobbits
as *Grubbs* and *Maggots*, not to mention *Hornblower*, a dialectical English name for the hornworm [W]. [Tolkien, however,
claims that *Grubb* 'is meant to recall the English verb *grub*
'dig, root, in the ground' (G:167); that *Maggot* is 'intended
to be a "meaningless" name, hobbit-like in sound' and that
'it is an accident that *maggot* is an English word meaning
"grub", "larva"' (G:169); and that *Hornblower* is an occupational surname (G:168).])

The Tooks may have taken their name from an old word
tuck, from French *estoc* 'a short sword' (ED). This would be
a logical name for a particularly adventurous Hobbit. The
name may also be a short form for something like *Theogar* or
Theogund. (Compare *Tobold* from *Theobald*; *Togo* is a name that
occurs in the Shire.) The name *Took* might also have come
from either of two Old English uncompounded names: *Toki*,
whence modern *Tooke*; and *Tucca*, whence *Tuck* (but this looks

more like *Tûk*). The meanings of the names are lost to us.
See C. M. Mathews, *English Surnames*.

A *bilbo* is a Spanish sword, from Bilbao, not a likely
Hobbit name. But *bil* 'sword' is found in those old Germanic
names, as *Bilihar* and *Biligarda* (AS:79). *Bilbo* may then be
shortened from *Bilberht* or *Bilibald*. (*Bilibald Baggins*? I
don't believe it. Not a word....) Thomas of Otterbourne, in
a 15th(?) century manuscript, records a king of Mercia named
Bilba as the father of the famous Penda, but this seems an
error for the name *Wibba* (TM:1715).

References:

AB   E. K. Chambers, *Arthur of Britain*. New York: Oçtober House, 1967.
AS   Elsdon C. Smith. *American Surnames*. Philadephia: Chilton Book Co.,
        1969.
DC   Grant Udon. *A Dictionary of Chivalry*. New York (printed in Great
        Britain): Thomas Y. Crowell Co., 1968.
EA   *Encyclopedia Americana*. New York: Americana Corp., 1970.
ED   Earnest Weekley. *An Etymological Dictionary of Modern English*. 2
        volumes. New York: Dover Publications, 1967.
ES   Charles Wareing Beardsley. *English Surnames: Their Sources and Sig-
        nifications*. 1889; rpt. Rutland Vermont: Charles E. Tuttle Co.,
        1968.
OEH Marjorie Anderson and Blanche Cotton Williams. *Old English Hand-
        book*. Cambridge, Mass.: Houghton-Mifflin Co., 1935.
TM   Jacob Grimm. *Teutonic Mythology*. Trans. James Steven Stallybrass.
        4 volumes. 1883, 1888; rpt. New York: Dover Publications, 1966.
W   *Webster's New International Dictionary* (unabridged). 2nd edition.
        Springfield, Mass.: G. & C. Merriam Co.

THE GIVING OF NAMES

Jim Allan

Note: Full bibliographical references for citations from works other than Tolkien's will be found following this article.

THE GERMANIC SYSTEM OF NOMENCLATURE

ONE CAN EASILY conceive of a society in which personal names
are totally meaningless and chosen entirely at random. But
none such exists on Earth, or has existed so far as we know.
Even in our own culture, where most personal names used convey no meaning to the ordinary person, picking a random   collection of normal English sounds is not how names are generally arrived at. Usually a child's parents will not invent
a name, but will pick one from the hoard of traditional names
that have come down to us—from the names that are in use at
the present time. A name too far removed from the norm would
be thought FUNNY, and most parents aren't eager to burden
their child with a name that may invite ridicule. When an
odd name is given, it is usually because the name has some
particular value to the parents that outweighs its oddness.
(Perhaps it is traditional within the family, or is the name
of some person the parents admire. Or, it might be a statement of the parents' desire to be unconventional.) A personal name may be very revealing.

The traditional stock of names does slowly change. A
name here and there falls into disuse. And old, seldom used
name regains popularity. Names from other cultures are
adopted and their foreignness forgotten. Occasionally new
names are simply created, and become popular, e.g. *Wendy*,
first used by James M. Barrie in his play *Peter Pan*.

GIVING OF NAMES

The normal name pattern on our Society is for a person to possess three names: first that which the parents usually intend to be the name of common use (sometimes in what is an accepted normal familar form, as *Bob* for *Robert*, *Pat* for *Patricia*); second, a name often less common which will not normally be used and may be represented only the its initial letter even in a full writing of the name; and last, the final name of the parents, called the SURNAME. A woman changes her surname for that of a man she marries.

Of course there are variations on this pattern. Some of these are usual enough to be called normal: the use of the second name rather than the first for common use; the lack of a second name; a greater number of names than three; the use of a name for common use that is not one of the names given to the person. Some are less normal: the retaining of her original surname by a married woman (though this is becoming more frequent). Rarer still is the omission of the surname entirely, or of the other names. I am aware of no instance in our society of anyone insisting on his or her surname being listed first or centrally rather than last, though in the Chinese system the surname always comes first.

In short, our culture, like others, has a system of traditional rules and a stock of traditional names that members of the society seldom ignore.

The Germanic speaking peoples from their first appearance in history show a unique system of name-giving which is only gradually lost in the Middle Ages, This system and many of the same names are found in all branches of the Germanic family, and is also that found more-or-less intact in *The Lord of the Rings*. (Perhaps we are to suppose that it was preserved in Europe until the coming of the Germanic speaking peoples who took it as their own.)

Germanic names normally consist of two parts, called THEMES; that is, two short words. For example: *Alfred* is OE *ælf* 'elf' + *ræd* 'counsel, rede'; *Gertrude* is OHG *ger* 'spear' + *trut* 'dear'. A limited stock of themes is used. A few are sometimes found as the first element in a name, and sometimes as the second (OE *beorht* 'bright' in *Beorhtwulf* 'Bright·wolf' and in *Æðelbeorht* 'Noble·bright'); but most are found only in one position or in the other. It is not clear to what extent the Germanic peoples of the fourth of tenth centuries actually thought about the meanings of these names, and to what extent they were compiled on other grounds (as will follow). It can be said that the meaning of a name was not the primary consideration, and was probably largely ignored.

More important in the choosing of names was the principle of VARIATION, in which a continuity between names was established by retaining one of the elements in a name and

varying the other. For example, in the royal family of the
Anglican kingdom of Bernicia, King *Æðelfrið* (fl. 593-614)
named his sons: *Eanfrið, Offa, Oswudu, Oslaf, Oslac, Osweald*,
and *Oswiu*. He has named his eldest son, *Eanfrið*, by taking
his own name and changing the first theme, *æðel-*, to *ean-*.
This is known as FRONT VARIATION. Save for *Offa*, the other
names of the king's sons all begin with the theme *os-*,
apparently to recall their uncle, *Æðelfrið*'s brother, whose
name was *Osmær*. These names differ from *Osmær* and from each
other by variation of the second element, that is, by END
VARIATION.

Oswiu's sons were named: *Eahlfrið, Ealhflæd, Osþryð,
Ecgfrið, Ealdfrið, Ælfflæd*, and *Ælfwine*. The themes *os-* and
-frið both reoccur; *ealh-* is used for the first two brothers
born one after the other, and *ælf-* is used for the last pair
of brothers. Ealdfrið's sons were named *Offa, Osred*, and
Oslac. Ælfwine's son was also named *Oslac*.

The shuffling of themes is typical in Germanic geneol-
ogies. The themes used were most often chosen from themes
found in the names of close relatives, joined in new combinations. More information on maternal relatives and other
children would probably show this even more clearly.

Note also that all these names begin with a vowel.
Early Germanic verse was predominantly—if not exclusively—
alliterative, and was the means by which the speakers of the
Germanic languages preserved their history and traditions,
recited euologies, and otherwise gave outlet to their literary powers. So families tended to choose names all beginning
with the same consonant, or with a vowel, to allow the names
to be used together easily in this kind of verse. (In alliterative verse any initial vowel may alliterate with any other
initial vowel.) For example, the royaly family of Essex concentrated on initial *s*; examples of the names are: *Sledda,
Sæbeorht, Seaxa, Seaxred, Sigebeorht, Sæwearld, Sigefrið,
Sigehere, Sebbi, Sigeheard, Selefrið, Sigebeald, Sigemund,
Swiðred, Swiðhelm, Swæfred, Selered, Sigered*. In the royal
family of Wessex *c* was most used: *Cerdic, Creoda, Cynric,
Ceawlin, Cuðwine, Cynebeald, Ceadda, Cuðwulf, Cwichelm, Ceol-
ric, Ceolwulf, Cynegils, Coenfus, Coenwealh, Cyneburg, Cent-
wine, Coenbeorht, Ceolwald, Coenred, Cwenburg, Cuðburg, Ceadwalla*.

These same principles applied on the continent. The
genealogy of the Merovingian monarchs of the Franks shows
reoccurence of the same themes and concentration on the initial consonant *ch*. *Chlodio* is the father of *Merovech*, father
of *Childeric*. His children are *Chlodovech* (combining *chlod-*
from *Chlodio* with *-vech* from *Merovech*, alliterating with
Childeric), *Albofled, Audelfled* (repeating *-fled* from *Albofled*), and *Lanthechild* (with *-child* from *child-* in *Childeric*).

Chlodovech was father of *Theuderic* (*-ric* for *Childeric*),
who was father of *Theudebert*, who was father of *Theudebald*
(three names showing end-variation on the theme *theude-*).
Backtracking, a son of *Chlodovech* whose name is unknown begot
Chlodomer (*chlodo-* from *Chlodovech*), *Childebert* (*childe-*
from *Childeric*, *-bert* also in the name of his cousin *Theudo-
bert*), *Chlothar*, and *Clotild* (representing *chlodo-* as in
Chlodovech and *Chlodomer* + *-child* as in *Lanthechild* and
initially in *Childeric*). *Chlodomer* was the father of *Theudovald* (cf. his second cousin *Theudobald*), *Gunthar* (his mother
was named *Guntheuc*), and *Chlodovald* (*chlodo-* as in his father
Chlodomer and great-grandfather *Chlodovech* + *vald* as in the
name of his brother *Theudovald*).

T. H. White comments on this kind of system in his *The
Once and Future King*:

> In those days you generally named your children in the
> same way as we name foxhounds and foals today. If you
> happened to be Queen Morgause and had four children,
> you put a G in all their names (Gawaine, Agravaine,
> Gaheris, and Gareth)—, and naturally if your brothers
> happened to be called Ban and Bors, you were doomed to
> be called Gwenbors yourself. It made it easier to
> remember who you were.

ELVISH NAMES

We have no extensive genealogical material for the
Elves, save for the lineage of the Half-elven. This is given
in part below:

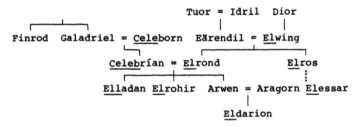

Some variation of themes occurs. All *Elwing*'s descendants
save for *Arwen* and the mortal descendants of *Elros* have names
beginning in *El(l)-*. *Celeb-* appears both in *Celeborn*'s name
and in that of his daughter *Celebrían*. *Tuor*'s father is
named *Huor*, perhaps here a case of front variation.

In the names of the royal houses of Númenor, Arnor, and
Gondor, there is a repetition of themes, and some repetition

of names. But only a few examples occur of systematic variation. In the northern line there is *Celebrindor* son of
Celepharn. In the southern line there is much use of the
theme -*(n)dil* 'friend, lover', so that the pair *Anardil* son
of *Eärendil* cannot be taken as significant. Of more
importance is that the brother of *Tarannon*, the first childless king, was named *Tarciryan*, the two brothers' names
having the same initial theme. *Ciryan-* occurs again as an
initial theme in the name of *Tarciryan*'s grandson *Ciryandil*.
Also, the brother of *Narmacil*, the second childless king,
was named *Calmacil*, so that both brothers' names end in the
theme -*macil*. Other father-and-son pairs in this genealogy
are *Eldacar* son of *Valacar*, *Minastan* son of *Minardil*, and
Eärnur son of *Eärnil*.

The House of the Stewards shows no theme variation
save for the front variation in the names *Boromir* and *Faramir*.

The name of the Prince of Dol Amroth at the end of the
Third Age was *Imrahil* (said to be a Númenorean (= Adûnaic)
name (III:391). The name of his predecessor, probably his
father, was *Adrahil* (III:336), showing what appears to be
front variation.

To summarize, it would seem that the Elvish names used
by the Dúnedain resembled those of Germanic nomenclature in
being composed of two themes, and these themes could be
combined into different names. But the Germanic practise of
a regular variation on the same themes within a family was
only occasionally followed by the royal lines of the north
and of Gondor, and by the House of Stewards. Alliteration
of names within a family was not followed either.

Names were sometimes picked for meaning, as *Hyarmendacil*
'South-victor', *Rómendacil* 'East-victor', *Elessar Telcontar*
'Elf-stone Strider'; but these are all names taken by kings
after they have ascended the throne. *Arvedui* 'Last-king' is
a name bestowed because of the prophecy that he shall be
the last king of Arnor. The names of the Stewards and, we
are told, of other men and women of the Dúnedain were 'often
the names of Elves or Men remembered in the songs and histories of the First Age (as *Beren*, *Húrin*)' (III:406n).

OLD RHOVANION NAMES

Tolkien uses Gothic names for the people of Rhovanion
in the eleventh century of the Third Age. *Vidugavia*, the
name of their most powerful king, is *vidu* 'wood, forest' +
gavia 'one of a district', for *gavi* means 'district'. *Gavia*
might have meant either 'lord' (as lord of a district) or
simply 'man' (as a countryman), so the name might be translated 'Wood-lord' or 'Wood-man'. The name appears in

GIVING OF NAMES

Germanic literature as *Witugouwo*, *Witicho*, *Witege*, and *Wittich*, and is applied to a son (in one source two sons) of the famous Weland Smith (Grimm:376,1392).

Vidumavi, the name of Vidugavia's daugther, means 'Woodmaiden.

Her son, by Valacar prince of Gondor, was called in his youth *Vinitharya*, to be broken as *vinid + harya*. *Harya* derives from *hari* 'army' and can be rendered 'army-man'. *Vinid* is usually taken as referring to the *Vinidi* 'Wends', the name of a Slavic tribe in eastern Germany, though Sändig (173) suggests instead a lost word meaning 'pasture-land'. If these names are meant to be translations of the originals, rather than just substitutions, and if the first meaning of *vinid-* is taken, we may suppose that the original name contained the name of some eastern people of Rhovanion. But meaning is probably not important here, any more than it was to most bearers of the Gothic name, who would have had as much connexion with the Wends as most bearers of the modern name *Frank* have with France. The name appear in Jordanes, Latinized as *Vinitharius*, applied to an early king of the Ostrogoths. Gaulish forms are *Winedharius*, *Winettharius*, *Viniterius*, and *Guineterius*. The standard German from is *Winidhere*.

The end variation of *Vidugavia* and *Vidumavi* and the initial *v* on all three shows full use of the Germanic system.

HOBBIT NAMES

Five different sorts of personal names can be distinguished among the Hobbits:

1) High-sounding names taken mostly from legends of the past concerning both Hobbits and Men, e.g. *Bandobras*, *Peregrin*, *Fredegar*, *Menegilda*. Their use is peculiar to a few old artistocratic families, such as the Tooks and the Bolgers. Most of the names of this kind can be found in the Took genealogy of Appendix C.

2) Short meaningless names, the male names ending in *-a* (usually changed to *-o* by Tolkien) and the female names ending in *-o* or *-e* (changed to *-a* by Tolkien), e.g. *Bilbo*, *Frodo*, *Odo*, *Dora*. They were the most normal kind of Hobbit name, and especially used by the middle class. Most of them can be found in the Baggins genealogy of Appendix C.

3) Short names of Old English or similar origin, e.g.

Samwise, Hamfast, Halfast, Carl. These are used
mainly by peasants and small tradesmen. Most of
them can be found in the Longfather Tree of Master
Samwise in Appendix C. No female names of this
kind occur in the corpus.

4) Names of flowers or jewels, e.g. *Belladonna, Rose,
Berylla, Ruby*. These kinds are used only for
females.

5) Names of a vaguely Celtic style, e.g. *Rorimac, Saradoc, Bombadil, Berilac*. These are peculiar to the
Bucklanders, apparently derived from the former
language of the southern Stoors. Save for *Bombadil*
and *Kalimac*, they can all be found in the Brandybuck genealogy in Appendix C. No female names of
this kind occur in the corpus.

High-Sounding Names:

MASCULINE NAMES

Adalgrim, *adal* 'noble' + *grim*
'fierce'.

Adelard, *adel* 'noble' + *hard* 'strong'.

Bandobras, *bando* < *band* 'band,
stripe, banner' + *bras* 'arm'.

Doderic, < *Theuderic, theud* 'people'
+ *ric* 'rule, reign'. Takes such
forms as *Theodoric, Dietrich*.

Everard, *ever, eber* 'boar' + *hard*
'strong'.

Fastolph, *fast* 'firm' + *wulf* 'wolf'.

Ferdibrand, *ferdi, frede* 'peace' +
brand 'torch, brand, sword'.

Ferdinand, *ferdi, frede* 'peace' +
nand 'bold'.

Ferumbras, perhaps French *feron* 'iron-
worker, blacksmith' (< Lat. *ferrum*
'iron') + *bras* 'arm'.

Filibert, *fili* 'very' + *berht* 'bright'.
The modern English form is *Fullbright*.

Flambard, *flam* 'flame' + *bard* 'battle-
axe'.

Fortinbras, *fortin* perhaps derives
originally from *fard-* 'journey' (cf.
Eng. *to fare, forth*) and the name
would derive from an earlier *Forti-
bras*. But it would probably be
understood as from French *fortin*

'strong' (a diminutive of normal
fort 'strong') + *bras* 'arm',

Fredegar, *ferdi, frede* 'peace' + *gar*
'spear' (cf. Eng. *gore*).

Gerontius, Lat. *Gerontius* < Gk. *Gerón-
tios* < *géron* 'old', thus meaning
'Old-man'. A popular name in the
Late Roman Empire, it entered into
British and became Welsh *Gereint*.
Cf. Eng. *gerontology*.

Gundabald, *gund* 'battle' + *bald*
'bold'.

Hildibrand, *hild* 'battle' + *brand*
'torch, brand, sword'.

Hildifons, *hild* 'battle' + *fons*
'ready'.

Hildigrim, *hild* 'battle' + *grim*
'fierce'.

Ilberic. < *Alberic, alb* 'elf' + *ric*
'reign, rule'. *Alberic* is a dwarf-
king in medieval German heroic literature, and is used by Wagner in
his operatic Ring cycle.

Isembard, *isen* 'iron' + *bard* 'battle-
axe'.

Isembold, *isen* 'iron' + *bald, bold*
'bold'.

Isengar, *isen* 'iron' + *gar* 'spear' (cf.
Eng. *gore*).

Isumbras, *isen* 'iron' + *bras* 'arm'.

Odovacar, *aud* 'wealth' + *vacar* 'watchful'.

Paladin, Italian *paladino* < Lat. *palatīnus* 'palace officer'. Used of the twelve peers of Charlemagne.

Peregrin, Lat. *peregrīnus* 'foreign' < *peregrē* 'abroad' < *per agrī* 'out of the field'. It was used as a term for someone who wandered abroad. It produced the Late Latin form *pelegrīnus* by dissimilation, whence Old French *peligrin*, whence Middle Eng. *pelegrim*, whence Mod. Eng. *pilgrim*.

Reginard, *ragin* 'counsel' + *hard* 'strong'. Further reduced, this becomes *Reynard*, the name given the fox in medieval French beast fable.

Rudigar, *hrod* 'fame' + *gar* 'spear' (cf. Eng. *gore*).

Rufus, Lat. *rūfus* 'red, reddish, red-haired'.

Sigismond, *sigis* 'victory' + *mund* 'hand, protection'.

Tobald (Toby), < *Theudebald*, *theud* 'people' + *bald* 'bold'.

Willibald, *wilja* 'wish, desire' + *bald* 'bold'.

FEMININE NAMES

Aldarida, *ald* 'old' + *rid* 'travel, ride'.

Hildigard, *hild* 'battle' + *gard* 'protection'.

Menegilda, *manag* 'much' (related to Eng. *many*) + *hild* 'battle'.

Rosamunda, *hros* 'horse' (related to Eng. *horse*) + *mund* 'hand, protection'. But in medieval times this etymology was forgotten and it was understood as Lat. *rosa* 'rose' + *munda* 'pure'.

The reader may recognize above in the elements *adal-*, *adel-*, 'noble' and *alb-* 'elf' the German cognates to the themes *æðel-* and *ælf-* found in the Old English names already discussed, and in *-hild* 'battle' may be discerned the *child-*, *-child* of the Merovingian genealogy.

Short Meaningless Names

A complete listing of the short meaningless Hobbit names follows:

> *Masculine:* Balbo, Bilbo, Bingo, Blanco, Bodo, Bungo, Drogo, Dudo, Falco, Folco, Fosco, Frodo, Griffo, Hugo, Largo, Longo, Lotho, Marcho, Matta (Mat), Milo, Minto, Mosco, Moto, Mungo, Odo, Olo, Otho, Polo, Ponto, Porto, Posco, Sancho, Togo, Talma (Tim), Tomba (Tom).
> *Feminine:* Belba, Chica, Cora, Dora, Hanna, Hilda, Linda, Nina, Prisca, Tanta.

As Paul Marmor has indicated in her 'Etymological Excursion Among the Shire Folk' many of these names are similar to shortened forms of the high sounding names. It is possible that some of them are intended by Tolkien as short forms of such names, and should not be in this list. But a comparison of these with similar Old English and Germanic names, though of interest in showing how few of the names cannot be easily matched up, tells us nothing about Hobbit nomenclature. So it will be set aside. All the names above may be found in III:380-383 (the Hobbit genealogies), 413.

GIVING OF NAMES

Old English and Similar Names

The following list includes a few names from Bree, Mannish as well as Hobbit, as they are of the same kind. Page references are given to all names to found in the genealogy of Samwise in Appendix C. The English etymologies of the names *Bill*, *Bob*, *Harry*, *Hob*, *Jack*, *Jolly*, *Matt*, *Nibs*, *Nick*, *Nob*, *Perry-the-Winkle*, *Robin*, *Rowlie*, *Ted*, *Will*, and *Willie* may have nothing to do with their use by Tolkien in *The Lord of the Rings*.

Andwise (Andy), OE *andwīs* 'expert', skilful'.

Anson, to be understood as *Andson* 'Son of Andy'.

Barliman, *barley* + *man*, a name 'suitable to an innkeeper and ale-brewer' (G:162). A Man in Bree. I:164ff.

Bill, in English a variant for Will, but see the short meaningless name Biːbo. A Hobbit TB:42. A Man in Bree I:177.

Bob, in English a diminutive of *Robert* (*hrod* 'fame' + *berht* 'bright'). A Hobbit in Bree. I:165.

Bowman, *bowman*.

Bucca, Either from 'Old English *bucc* 'male deer' (fallow or roe), or *bucca* 'he-goat' (G:161). Becomes Modern Eng. *buck*, as in the Hobbit surnames *Oldbuck*, *Brandybuck*. III:368.

Carl, OE *carl* 'man' < ON *karl* 'old man, man, servant'; introduced into England by the Danes; cognate with OE *ceorl* 'freeman of low degree', whence Mod. Eng. *churl*.

Cotman, ME, OE *cot* 'cottage, hut' + *mann* 'person'.

Cottar, ME *cottar* 'cotter, cottager' < OFr. *cotier* < *cote* < OE *cot* 'cottage, hut'.

Elfstan, *elf* + *stan* 'stone'. Translation of Q Elessar. III:378.

Erling, OE *Eorling* 'descendant of a worthy man'.

Fastred, OE *fæstrǣd* 'steadfast, constant' < *fæst* 'firm' *rǣd* 'counsel'.

Halfast (Hal), OE *hālfæst* 'pious ???, healthy ???' < *hāl* 'whole, healthy, hale' + *fæst* 'firm'.

Halfred, OE *healfrēad* 'reddish', but perhaps understood as from *healf* 'half' + *rǣd* 'counsel'.

Hamfast (Ham), OE *hāmfæst* 'resident, stay-at-home' < *hām* 'home' + *fæst* 'firm, fixed'.

Hamson, 'Son of Ham'.

Harding, 'Strong-one', < OE *heard* 'strong' + *-ing* 'one of'.

Harry, in English a variant (through *Herry*) of *Henry* (*hagin* 'enclosure' + *ric* 'rule, reign'). A Man in Bree. I:163.

Hending, 'Skilful-one, Courteous-one', < ME 'skilful, courteous' + *-ing* 'one of'.

Hob, in English a pet form of *Robin* , (see Robin), used to mean 'rustic person', but also 'fairy'. May here be intended as a shortening of *Hobbit* (*hol* 'hole' + *bytla* 'builder'.)

Hobson, 'Son of Hob'.

Holfast, 'Hole-dweller', < OE *hol* 'hole' + *fæst* 'firm, fixed'.

Holman (Hom), taken to be from OE *hol* 'hole' + *mann* 'person' (G:168). The English surname Holman is from OE *holm* 'river-island' + *mann* 'person'.

Jack, in English taken as a familiar form of *John*, though in fact derived from French *Jacques* from *Jacob*, Used to mean 'fellow', and to indicate the male of certain animals'. TB:43.

Jolly, ME *jolif* < OFr. *jolif* 'merry, happy' < ON *jól* 'Yule'.

Mat, in English a familiar form for *Matthew* (< Heb. *Mattíyāh* < *Mattityāh* 'Gift-(of)-Yah(weh)'). But see the short meaningless name Matta. A Man in Bree. (III:271).

Nibs, a term of mock respect. May be from *Nob* (see **Nob**).

Nick, in English a short form of *Nicholas* < Gk. *Nīkólāos* (*nīkē* 'victory' + *lāós* 'people'). Used of the devil in *Old Nick*.

Nob, in English a slang term of disrespect for a person of high position. Probably from *nob* as a slang term for 'head', a mispelling of *knob*. A Hobbit in Bree. I:165.

Perry-the-Winkle, a nonsense name from *periwinckle*, the name of both a marine mollusc (< OE *pīnewincle* < Lat. *pīna* 'mussel' + OE *wincel* 'that which turns, pulley') and of a creeping evergreen plant (< Lat. *pervinca*). TB:42ff.

Robin, *diminutive of Rob*, a familiar form of *Robert* (*hrod* 'fame' + *berht* 'bright'). ˌRobin Goodfellow is the name of a mischievous fairy, also called *Puck*.

Rowlie, in English a diminutive of *Rowland* (*hrod* 'fame' + *land* 'land'). A Man in Bree. III:271.

Samwise (Sam), OE *samwīs* 'half-wise, simple'.

Ted, in English a familiar form of *Thaddeus* (Aram. *tᵉdaiyā* 'breasts') and *Theodore* (Gk. *theós* 'god' + *dōron* 'gift'). I:53.

Tolman (Tom), OE *tōl* 'tool' + *mann* 'person'.

Tom, in English a familiar form of *Thomas* (Syr. *tōmā* 'twin'), but here to be taken from **Tolman** or from the short meaningless name *Tomba*, or from other such forms. A dweller in the Old Forest, prob. from *Tomba*, a partial rhyme with his surname *Bombadil*. I:130ff. A Man in Bree. III:271.

Wilcome (Will), OE *wilcuma* 'welcome guest' < *willa* 'will, pleasure' + *cuma* 'guest, one who comes'.

Will, in English a familiar form of *William* (*wilja* 'wish, desire' + *helm* 'protection'), but see **Wilcome** and the high sounding name **Willbald**. I: 168.

Willie, a diminutive of **Will**. A Hobbit in Bree. III:271.

Wiseman, OE *wīse* 'wise' + *mann* 'person'.

Of the same kind are the names of the trolls in *The Hobbit*, *Bert*, *Tom*, and *William* (*Bill*).

Flower and Jewel Names

The flower and jewel names were given to female Hobbits to signify beauty and preciousness. The star name *Estella* is of the same sort, and is included here. So also is the name of Tom Bombadil's wife, *Goldberry*.

FLOWER NAMES

Amaranth, Gk. *amárantos* 'unfading' < *a-* 'not' + *marainein* 'quench, waste away'. Originally used for a mythical undying flower. Applied to a family of plants (*Amaranthaceae*) and a genus within the family (*Amaranthus*). Members of the *Amaranthus* family usually have colourful leaves and, in some species, showy tassellike heads if flowers, as *love-lies-bleeding*, *pigweed*, *tumbleweed*.

Angelica, MLat. *(herba) angelica* 'angelic (plant)', so named for its medicinal properties. Used of any of a number of related plants (genus *Angelica*) of the parsley family, with tall stalks, large divided leaves, clusters of white or greenish flowers, and roots and fruit used in flavouring, perfumes, and medicine.

Asphodel, Gk. *asphódelos* of uncertain origin. Seems to have originally referred to flowers of the daffodil type (*daffodil* < Du. *de affodil* 'the asphodel), but used today for any of a genus (*Asphodeline*) of plants of the lily family having fleshy roots, narrow leaves, and white or yellow flowers like lilies; or any of a genus (*Asphodelus*) of similar plants, but with leafless flower stems.

Bell, used of flowers so shaped, as *Bluebell* and *Harbell*, both with blue bell-shaped flowers; especially used of the genera *Campanula* and *Mertensia*. The name *bellflower* is used for any of the *Campanulae*, a genus marked by showy bell-shaped flowers of white, pink, or blue, and also is used to designate the family of the Campanulacae which includes the *Campanulae*.

Belladonna, understood as from It. *bella* 'beautiful' + *donna* 'lady', but actually developed from MLat. *bladone* 'nightshade', probably of Gaulish origin. A poisonous plant of the nightshade family, with purplish or reddish bell-shaped flowers and shiny black berries. A cosmetic was formerly made from it.

Camellia, named from the Jesuit traveller George Joseph Kamel who brought specimans from Japan to London in 1738. A genus (*Camellia*) of Asiatic evergreen trees and shrubs of the tea family, with glossy evergreen leaves and waxy, roselike flowers.

Celandine, Gk. *khelīdónion* < *khelīdŏn* 'swallow'; also called *Swallowwort*. It is a weedy plant of the poppy family, with deeply divided leaves and yellow flowers and juice, its Latin name being *Chelidonium majus*. The name *Lesser Celandine* is given to *Raniculus ficaria*, a perennial plant of the buttercup family, with yellow flowers.

Daisy, OE *dæges eage* 'day's eye', so called in reference to it's opening its flower each morning. See Gollum's riddle beginning '*An eye in a blue face...*'. A plant (*Chrysanthemum leucathemum*) of the composite family, bearing flowers with white radiating petals around a yellow disk.

Eglantine, Fr. *églentine* 'dog rose (the flower)' < *églantier* 'dog rose (the bush)' < MFr. *aiglent* < Late Lat. **aquilentus*, **aculentus* < Lat. *aculeus* 'spine, prickle', diminutive of *acus* 'needle'. Used in English as a name for the *sweetbriar* (*Rosa eglantaria*), a European rose with hooked spines, sweet-scented leaves, and usually pink

flowers.

Elanor, S *él* 'star' + *anor* 'sun': 'sun-star'. A small star-shaped golden flower that grew on Cerin Amroth in Lothlórien.

Gilly, *Gillyflower* < OFr. *gilotre*, *girofre* 'clove' < Gk. *karyóphyllon* 'clove tree' < *káryon* 'nut' + *phýllon* 'leaf'. Refers to any of several plants in the genus *Dianthus* with clove-scented flowers, as the *clove pink*. It is also used as a name for those members of the mustard family also called *stocks*, and those known as *wallflowers*.

Goldberry, *gold* + *berry*. No plant of this name in fact exists. I:130ff;G:167.

Goldilocks, *gold* + *locks (of hair)*. Name 'sometimes given to flowers of the buttercup kind' (G:169), as the *Wood Goldilocks* (*Ranunculus auricomus*), a plant with kidney shaped lobed basal leaves, dissected stem leaves, and yellow petalled flowers with dark centres. Another plant called *Goldilocks* is *Crinitaria linosyris* in the Daisy family, marked by dissected leaves and small clumped yellow flowers.

Laura, familiar form of Lat. *Laurentia* 'Woman of Laurentum', *Laurentum* meaning 'Town of Bay Trees' < *laurus* 'bay tree, laurel tree'.

Lily, OE *lilie* < Lat. *līlium* < Coptic *hrēri*, *hlēli* < Egyp. *ḥrr-t* 'lily'. Name given to all plants of the genus *Lilium* characterized by white or coloured trumpet shaped flowers. It is also applied to plants whose flowers resemble those of true lilies, such as the *water lily*.

Lobelia, named from the Flemish botonost Matthias de L'Obel (1538-1616). A genus of the bellflower (Campanulacae) family, having white, blue, or red flowers of very irregular shape.

Malva, Lat. *malva* 'mallow'. Eng. *mallow* > OE *mealuwe* < Lat. *malva* < Heb. *malūᵃḥ* 'mallow' < *mélaḥ* 'salt'. Used of a genus (*Malva*) of plants with dissected or lobed leaves and pink or white loosely petalled flowers. Includes the *musk mallow*, *dwarf mallow*, *long-hairy mallow*, *marsh mallow*, *rose mallow*.

Marigold, *Mary* + *gold*. Any of a genus
(*Tagetes*) of annual plants of the
daisy family with red, yellow, or,
orange flowers of petals radiating
from a darker centre.

May, Lat. *Maia*, a month named after
Maia, a goddess of increase and
growth from Pre-Lat. *magja* 'she who
brings increase' related to *magnus*
'great'. Used as a name for the
English hawthorn (*Crataegus oxyacan-
tha*), a thorny shrub or small tree
with small lobed leaves and white,
pink, or red blossoms. Also found
is *mayweed* (for **maythe-weed* < OE
mageðe 'stinking camomile', probably
related to *mægeð* 'maid'.) Used for
stinking camomile or *dog fennel*,
an annual weed (*Anthemis cotula*) of
the daisy family with flowers with
white radiating petals and yellow
centres, and an offensive smell.
The name is also used for the
distantly related *scented mayweed*
(*Matricaria recutita*) with droopy
white petals radiating from yellow
conical centres, and a pleasant arom-
atic smell; and *scentless mayweed*
(*Tripleurospermum maritimum*) with no
smell.

Melilot, ME *melilot* < MFr. *mélilot* <
Gk. *melilōtos* < *méli* 'honey' + *lōtós*
'lotus'. Used of the genus *Melilotus*
covering the various kinds of *sweet
clover*, annual or biennial plants of
the legume family, with small white
or yellow flowers, leaflets in groups
of three, and single-seeded pods.

Mentha, Lat. *mentha* 'mint'. A genus
of plants marked by purple flowers
clustered in heads and leaves used
for flavouring and medicine.

Mimosa, Mod. Lat. *mimosa* derived from
Lat. *mimus* 'actor, mime', in reference to the ability of some of the
members of the *Mimosa* family to mimic
animal life in moving leaves and
stalks when touched. The *Mimosae*
include trees, shrubs, and herbs of
the legume family, growing in warm
regions, usually with bipinnate
leaves and heads or spikes of small
white, yellow, or pink flowers.

Mirabella, Fr. *mirabelle* < Lat. *myro-
balanum* 'palm tree fruit' < Gk.

myrobalanan < *myron* 'perfume, unguent'
+ *balanos* 'acorn, date'. Applied
to a European variety of the plum
tree.

Myrtle, MLat. *murtillus*, a diminutive
of Lat. *murtus*, *myrtus* < Gk. *mýrtos*
< Phoen. **murra* 'bitter gum' > Sem.
MRR 'bitter'. Applied to plants of
the genus *Myrtus* marked by evergreen
leaves, white or pinkish flowers, and
dark, fragrant berries.

Pansy, Fr. *pensée* 'thought' (fem. past
participle) < Lat. *pēnsāre* 'to weigh
carefully, ponder'. Applied to a
small garden plant (*Viola tricolor*)
of the violet family, with broad,
flat, velvety petals in many colours.

Peony, ME *piony* < OFr. *peonie* < Lat.
paeonia < Gk. *paiōniā* 'beloning to
Paion'; *Paiōn* was the name of the god
of healing' < *paíō*, *paíein* 'to touch'.
Used for any of a genus (*Paeonia*) of
the buttercup family of perennial,
often double-flowered, plants with
large double-flowered, plants with
showy flowers.

Pervinca, Lat. *pervinca* 'periwinkle'
< *pervincire* 'to entwine, bind' <
per- 'thoroughly' + *wincire* 'to bind,
fetter'. Applied to any of the genus
Vinca of trailing or erect, evergreen
plants of the dogbane family, especially a European creeper (*Vinca
minor*) with blue, white, or pink flowers, grown as ground cover.

Pimpernel, ME *pympernele* < OFr. *pimpre-
nelle* 'burnet' < MLat. *pimpernella*, a
changed diminutive of Lat. *piper* 'pep-
per', so called because its fruits
resembled peppercorns. Used of a
genus (*Anagallis*) of the primrose family, with red, white, or blue, star-
like flowers which close in bad
weather.

Poppy, OE *popig* < *popæg* < Late Lat.
*papāvum < Lat. *papāver* 'poppy'. Used
for any of a genus (*Papaver*) of
annual and perennial plants of the
poppy family, having a milky juice,
showy pink, white, red, orange, or
yellow flowers, and capsules containing many small seeds.

Primrose, ME *primerole* < OFr. *primerole*
< MLat. *primula* 'primrose'. The word
has been confused with *rose*. Used for

plants of the the genus *Primula* of the primrose family, having variously coloured tubelike corollas with five spreading lobes, most often thought of as that shade of yellow called *primrose*. See **Primula**.

Primula, Lat. *primula* 'primrose', diminutive of *primus* 'first'; so named because it flowers in early spring. See **Primrose**.

Rosa, Lat. *rosa* 'rose' < Gk. *rhódon* < *wródon* < OIran. *wrda-* 'rose < IE *wrdho-* 'thorn, bramble'. Used of a genus (*Rosa*) of shrubs of the rose family, usually with prickly stems, alternate compound leaves, and five-parted, usually fragrant flowers of red, pink, white, yellow, having many stamens. See **Rosamunda**, **Rose (Rosie)**.

Rosamunda, in medieval times generally taken to be Lat. *rosa* 'rose' + *munda* 'pure'; but in fact from Gmc. *hros* 'horse' (related to Eng. *horse*) + *mund* 'hand, protection'.

Rose (Rosie), Lat. *rosa* 'rose'. See **Rosa**.

Rowan, of Scandinavina origin, cf. ON *reynir*, *ron*, Swed. *ronn* 'rowan'; akin to ON *rauð* 'red' from the colour of its berries. Used of the European mountain ash (*Sorbus aucuparia*), a tree with pinnately compound leaves, white flowers, and red berries.

Salvia, Lat. *salvia* 'sage' < *salvus* 'safe, whole' from its reputed healing powers. Used for any of a genus (*Salvia*) of plants of the mint family, having two-lipped corolla and two stamens, known as *sages* in English. Some varieties are cultivated for ornament and others for flavouring.

JEWEL NAMES

Adamanta, ME *adamant* < OFr. *adamant* (oblique case) < Lat. *adamantem* (acc. of *adamās*) < Gk. *adámās* < *a-* 'not' + *daman* 'subdue, tame'. Used of a mythical hard stone or metal too hard to be broken, sometimes identified with iron, but more often with diamond. Also identified with the lodestone or magnet in medieval times from confusion with Lat. *adamāre* 'to love passionately'.

Berylla, feminine form of Lat. *beryllus* 'beryl' < Gk. *bếryllos* < Prakrit *vēruliya* < *vēluriya* < *Vēlūr*, the name of a city, now called *Bēlūr*. *Beryl* is a hard, lustrous mineral (*beryllium aluminum silicate*, $Be_3Al_2Si_6O_{18}$) occuring in hexagonal crystals, usually blue, green, pink, or yellow in colour. A blue or green colour is usually associated with beryl. Emerald and Aquamarine are varieties of beryl.

Diamond, ME *diamant*, *diamaunt* < OFr. *diamant* < Late Lat. *diamantem* (acc. of *diamās*) < Gk. *adamās* 'not conquerable' (see **Adamanta**) combined with *diaphanēs* 'transparent'. Used of the hardest natural substance, almost pure carbon in transparent crystalline form.

Esmeralda, Sp. *esmaralda* 'emerald' < Lat. *smaragdus* < Gk. *smáragdos*, *máragdos* < a Semitic language; cf. Heb. *bāréqet*, Akkadian *barraqtu* 'emerald' < BRQ 'flash'. Used of a bright-green, transparent, precious stone, a variety of *beryl*. See **Berylla**. Eng. *emerald* < OFr. *esmeralde*, *esmeraude*.

Pearl, ME *perle* < MFr. *perle* < It. *perla* < Vulgar Lat. *perla* < Lat. *perna* 'ham, sea mussel, pearl' combined with *sphaerula* 'little ball', a diminutive of *sphaera* 'ball, sphere'. Used of a rounded, iridescent, usually white or bluish-grey, hard growth formed within the shell of some oysters and certain other mollusks.

Ruby, ME *ruby* < OFr. *rubi* < MLat. *rubīnus* < Lat. *rubeus* 'red' < *rubēre* 'to be red'. Used of a clear, deep-red, precious stone, a variety of corundum (Al_2O_3), the natural substance second only to diamond in hardness.

STAR NAMES

Estella, Sp. *estella* 'star' < Lat. *stēlla* 'star' < *stērla*. *Estella* occurs only in the β text of the genealogies of the Tooks and the Brandybucks, where it is the name of the sister of Fredegar Bolger, born S.R. 1385, and wife of Meriadoc Brandybuck.

Note that in the flower names also the style varies according to social class. The Tooks and Brandybucks use high-sounding and exotic names like *Belladonna*, *Pimpernel*, *Eglantine*, *Amaranth*, *Asphodel*, and *Celandine*. The Bagginses use more ordinary names, such as *Lily*, *Angelica*, *Peony*, *Poppy*, and *Daisy*. Some of the same names appear in Samwise's genealogy, such as *Lily* and *Daisy*, but the slightly more exotic *Angelica* and *Peony* do not appear. Instead are some other short names: *Rowan*, *May*, *Bell*, *Marigold*. The difference can be most clearly seen where different names for the same flower are used: high-sounding *Rosamunda Took*, simpler *Rosa Baggins*, and the entirely unpretentious *Rose Greenhand* and *Rose Cotton*; the high-sounding *Primula Brandybuck* compared with the simple *Primrose Gamgee*.

The jewel names seem mostly used by the nobility. Of the six names found, *Esmeralda* and *Pearl* were given to born Tooks, *Adamanta* and *Diamond* belong to women who marry into the Took line and who probably belong to the same social class, and *Berylla* and *Ruby* belong, respectively, to a Boffin and a Bolger who marry into the somewhat *nouveau riche* Baggins family. Samwise names one of his daughters *Ruby*, but at a date when he has been Mayor of the Shire for 11 years.

The Celtic-sounding Names

Tolkien remarks on the Brandybuck names and his treatment of them as follows:

> The names of the Bucklanders were different from those
> of the rest of the Shire. The folk of the Marish and
> their offshoot across the Brandywine were in many ways
> peculiar, as has been told. It was from the former lan-
> guage of the southern Stoors, no doubt, that they inher-
> ited many of their very odd names. These I have actually
> left unaltered, for if queer now, they were queer in their
> own day. They had a style that we should perhaps feel
> vaguely to be 'Celtic'.
>
> Since the survival of traces of the older language of
> the Stoors and the Bree-men resembled the survival of
> Celtic elements in England, I have sometimes imitated the
> latter in my translation. Thus Bree, Combe (Coomb),
> Archet, and Chetwood are modelled on relics of British
> nomenclature, chosen according to sense: *bree* 'hill',
> *chet* 'wood'. But only one personal name has been altered
> in this way. Meriadoc was chosen to fit the fact that
> this character's shortened name, Kali, meant in Westron
> 'jolly, gay', though it was actually an abbreviation of
> the now unmeaning Buckland name Kalimac. (III:413f)

The difference in style of these Buckland names comes out

clearly in an examination of the male names in the Brandybuck genealogy (ignoring, of course, the two Germanic names
Doderic and *Ilberic*). There is a predominance of voiced
consonants: *b, d, g, m, n, l, r*. The only voiceless stop
found is *c/k*, and the only voiceless spirant is *s*; these
occur only initially and finally. All names end in *-as*,
-ac, or *-oc*. It is, of course, impossible to say how many
of these peculiarities are illusions arising from the small
corpus of names.

   There are two names not in the Brandybuck genealogy
that call for attention as well. One is *Bombadil*, for Tolkien says that the Bucklanders 'probably gave him this name
(it is Bucklandish in form) to add to his many older ones'
(TB:9n). This name lacks the ordinary ending of the Brandybuck names, but otherwise agrees with their phonetic style,
and may be accepted as a name of the same sort. Tolkien
also refers to *Gorhendad* Oldbuck in a note at the head of
the genealogy. But *Gorhendad* is perfect Welsh for 'great-
grandfather' from *gor* 'over, sur-' + *hen* 'old' + *tad*
'father'. Since Tolkien has stated he has not changed any
of the original Brandybuck names save for *Kalimac*, and since
it seems unlikely that the person in question would have
been given as a child a name meaning 'great-grandfather',
we must here have to do with a kind of title rather than a
name. Apparently the southern Stoors retained, after sett-
ling in the Shire, certain old words from their former
tongue, including one meaning something like 'great-
grandfather' or 'forefather' or 'ancestor'. This was
applied as a title or nickname to the old founder of Buckland
to the extent that it replaced his true name. Since the
nickname or title was a word understood in Buckland still,
unlike the normal Buckland names whose meanings had been long
lost, Tolkien naturally translated it. The word was not
generally known outside of Buckland and was from the old language of the southern Stoors, and so Tolkien translated it by
a corresponding Welsh form,

   Of the names that Tolkien definitely claims not to have
changed, two of them might actually be Celtic as they stand:
Madoc and *Marmadoc*. Several of the rest are very close to
actual Celtic names, and these and many of those that remain
bear a close resemblance to another group of names from a
literary tradition that also strikes the ear as Celtic.
   From the sixth century onward in Wales, Cornwall, and
Brittany, tales were told of a certain Arthur and his men.
It was mainly through minstrels and story tellers of the
Breton race that these tales were so spread throughout Europe
that by the twelfth century the MATIÈRE DE BRETAGNE had
become the third great source for romance language poetry,
along with the MATIÈRE DE ROME (Classical mythology and

history) and the MATIÈRE DE FRANCE (the tales of Charlemagne
and his twelve peers). The personal names in the stories of
Arthur varied somewhat in Breton mouths from the forms found
in Wales, for over the centuries the speech of the Welsh and
Bretons had fallen apart. When French romancers and poets
began to retell the stories of Arthur's men and to create
new tales of the same kind the name underwent further dis-
tortions and modifications, in part to fit the French language, and in part because the French found it difficult to
correctly remember and reproduce the unfamiliar Celtic names.
Further changes occurred when the stories were taken from
French and put into English.

For example, in Malory's *Le Morte Arthur* Arthur's right-
hand man, called *Kei Hir* by the Welsh, has become three separate individuals with three different names: *Kay the Senes-
chal, Colgrevaunce* (< Fr. *Calogrenant*, probably corrupted
from *Cai lo grenant* 'Kay the grumbler'), and *Kehydyns*. For
Welsh *Bedwyr* Malory has *Bedyvere*; for *Llakheu* he has *Borre/
Bohart* (< Fr. *Lohot*); for *Drystan* he has *Trystram*; for *Esyllt*
he has *Isoude*; for *Ritta* he has *Rience*; for *Avallakh* he has
Avylyon (< Fr. *Avalon*) and *Evelake*; for *Melwas* he has *Mellya-
gaunce*; for *Baedon ap Cuil* he has *Bagdemagus* (< Fr. *Bade-
magu*); for *Edern ap Nud* he has *Idrus son of Ewayne*; for
Gweir ap Llwkh he has *Harry le Fise Lake* (< Fr. *Erec li filz
de Lac*); and for *Gilvaethwy ap Dôn* he has *Gryflet le Fise de
Deu* (< Fr. *Girflet li filz de Do(n)*). A larger number of
names have no exact Welsh counterpart.

The names in Malory and in other treatments of the
Arthurian tales can be divided into four general classes:
1) names of obvious non-Celtic origin, usually either French
or Latin; 2) genuine Celtic names; 3) names that are distor-
tions of genuine Celtic names; and 4) invented names following vaguely the style of the genuine Celtic names and the
distorted Celtic names, as well as the style of similarly
invented names. The entire nomenclature system may be called
PSEUDO-CELTIC, with the understanding that a few genuine
Celtic names still remain in a reasonably pure state. This
pseudo-Celtic Arthurian nomenclature closely resembles the
Brandybuck nomenclature.

Before considering the names in detail, there are some
points on spelling to be dealt with. First, in medieval
spellings *k* and *c* were often interchanged in representation
of the [k] sound. *C* was more common in French, Breton, Welsh
names transcribed in Latin texts, and is used in modern
Welsh.. *K* was more common in medieval Welsh and in later
medieval English. So we can expect to find a name sometimes
with *c*, sometimes with *k*, and sometimes with *ck*.

Second, some medieval English authors, such as Malory,
use *y* where we would use *i*. (Indeed, *i* is often substituted

for *y* even in the names in modernized texts. or in retellings.)

Third, in medieval French words had two cases: the nominative and the oblique. A name was usually placed in the nominative by adding *s* or *z* to its oblique form, sometimes replacing the original final consonant. When this happened, the final consonant tended to be forgotten in the oblique case also, or was replaced by *t*. For example, *Arthur* was originally rendered in French by *Artus* in the nominative case and by *Artur* in the oblique, but the oblique form was soon changed to *Artu*. The genuine Celtic name *Caradoc* appears in medieval French in the nominative with such forms as *Carados*, *Caradus*, *Caradas*, *Caradués*, and in the oblique as *Caradoc*, *Carador*, *Caradot*, *Caradué*, *Caradeu*. We find the closely related names *Meliadoc*, *Meliadas*, and *Meliadus*. *Erec* sometimes appears as *Erés*. The Celtic name *Meriadoc* usually appears as *Meriadués* in both nominative and oblique cases; similarly *Patrick* is always *Patris*. So, it will not seem too unusual if the Brandybuck names ending in *c* had variants ending in *s*.

Berilac, A similar name is given to the Green Knight in the fifteenth century alliterative poem *Sir Gawain and the Green Knight*. In the edition of the poem edited by J. R. R. Tolkien and E. V. Gordon (Oxford: Clarendon Press, 1926), the following note appears:

Bercilak de Hautdesert: the correct reading of the name (*Bernlak* in former eds.) is due to Hulbert (*Manly Anniversary Studies in Lang. and Lit.*, Chicago, 1923, p. 12). The name *Bercilak* is the same as *Bertelak* (in the Middle English prose Merlin romance) and Old French *Bertolais* (nom. case; the acc. was *Bertolai*, earlier *Bertolac*). None of the other knights bearing the name can be certainly identified with the Green Knight. The name *Bertolac* is of Celtic origin, probably from an original *Brettūlakos*, à derivative of *Britto* 'a Briton' (so Max Förster).

It should be noted that it is not clear whether the fourth letter should be read as *c* or *t*. In the revision of the Tolkien and Gordon edition brought out in 1967 by Norman Davis, and using in part notes collected by Tolkien, the form *Bertilak* appears instead of *Bercilak*, and the form with the *t* is also used in Tolkien's own translation in *Sir Gawain and the Green Knight: Pearl: Sir Orfeo* (London: Allen & Unwin, 1975; New York: Houghton Mifflin, 1975).

The *Bertolai* or *Bertelak* mentioned by Tolkien also appears in the French *Vulgate Merlin* and in the prose *Lancelot*, and is the only figure of a similar name to that of the Green Knight to be at all connected with Arthur. The other figures named *Bertolais* all appear in the Charlemagne cycle. The *Bertolais* of the *Lancelot* and *Merlin* resembles the *Bercilak/Bertilak* of the English poem in being part of a plot against Guinivere.

R. S. Loomis, in *Celtic Myth and Arthurian Legend* (New York: Columbia Univ. Press, 1927), derived the name in the English poem from Irish *brachlach* 'churl' on the basis of an eighth century Irish tale, *Briciu's Feast*, in which there occurs a more primitive rendition of the head-cutting episode of *Sir Gawain*, and a churl (*brachlach*) plays the role there assigned to the Green Knight.

The Brandybuck name *Berilak* is then, the name of the Green Knight, less the disputed letter.

Bombadil, Paula Marmor has pointed out that the name resembles *bobadil*, an obsolete word for 'braggart'; cf. the character *Bobadil* in Jonson's *Every man in his humour*. The name derives from *Boabdil*, the name of the last Moorish king of Granada, a Spanish corruption of Arab. *Abū Abd'illāh* 'Father (of the) Servant-(of)-Allah'. (Ernest Weekley, *An etymological dictionary of Modern English*, 1921; reprinted New York: Dover Publications, 1967.)

Dinodas, This appears to be a rearrangement of **Dodinas** below.

Dodinas, *Dodynas le Saveage* is one of the more prominent of the lesser Knights of the Round Table in Malory's *Le Morte Darthur* (IV:26;VII:28,29;VIII:9,15-17;IX:35;X:4,66; XVIII:11;XIX:1,2,11). His name is rendered *Dodinas* in editions with modernized spelling. The same knight appears as *Doddinaual de Sauage* in *Sir Gawain and the Green Knight*, as *Dedyne* in *Ywain and Gawain*, as *Dodynell*, *Dodynax*, *Dodineax*, *Dodynalx*, etc. in the English prose *Merlin*. In French prose and poetic Arthurian romances he is also a common figure as *Dodin(i)el*, *-iau*, *-iaus*, *-ia(u)x*, *-et*, *-és*, etc. He is always a secondary character.

The ONLY other personage of the same name in medieval literature is Dodinaus the son of Corbarant of Oliferne in *La Chanson du Chevalier au Cygne et de Godefroid de Boullon*, which belongs to the Charlemagne cycle.

The name *Dodiniel* (whose nominative form yields Malory's *Dodynas*) appears to be a diminutive of *Dodins*, the spelling found in two of the earliest romances—the name appears once in each. E. Brugger suggests that *Dodins* is, in turn, a diminutive form of a theme *dod-* found in Old French names and in Fr. *dodiner*, *dodelliner* 'to swing', *dorloter* 'to pamper', and in Portuguese *doído* 'foolish'. He thinks *Dodins* would mean 'foolish one, simpleton', and *Dodiniel* would mean 'little fool' ('Bliocadron, the Father of Perceval', *Medieval Studies in Memory of Gertrude Schoepperle Loomis*, Paris, 1927, p. 169).

The form *Dodynas* is peculiar to Malory.

Gorbadoc, This name is a slight alteration of *Gorboduc* or *Gorbodugu*, a pre-Roman king of Britain in the mostly fictional twelfth century *Historia Regum Britanniae* 'History of the Kings of Britain' by Galfridus Monemutensis (Geoffrey of Monmouth). This history was written to provide a coherent and sufficiently glorious past for pre-Saxon Britain, and it devotes more space to the reign of Arthur than to that of any other ruler. It is the earliest extant account of Arthur of a reasonable length, and later chronicles draw extensively from it.

The British name *Gorboduc* becomes *Gwrvoddw* in medieval Welsh (*Gwrfoddw* in modern spelling), and in *The Mabinogion* Gwrvoddw Hen appears as one of the brothers of Arthur's mother. (The identity of *Gorboduc* and *Gwrvoddw* was pointed out in 'The treatment of personal names in the Early Welsh versions of *Historia Regum Britanniae*', a paper read, by the author Bryn F. Roberts, at the 10th International Arthurian Congress, Nantes, Brittany, August 1972.)

Might there be some significance in the earliest preserved tragic play in English being *Gorboduc, the tragedy of Ferrex and Porrex*, by Thomas Sackville (!) and Thomas Norton?

Gorbulas, This seems to combine the first part of **Gorbadoc** with the second part of **Orgulas**.

Gormadoc, The element *gor-*, which in Welsh means 'over, sur-', has been prefixed to **Madoc**.

Kalimac, The closest parallel to this name is *Silimac* in Manassier's continuation to the *Perceval* of Chrétien de Troyes. The name is also spelt *Silemarc* and *Sorlimac*. Not very close.

The ending *-mac* also appears on **Merimac**.

Tolkien has replaced this name by the genuine Celtic name *Meriadoc*. In the form *Meiriadoc* this is the name of an area one mile south of St. Asaph in Denbighshire. According to C. M. Yonge it means 'sea-protection'. As a personal name *Meriadoc* is found only in Brittany. In the *Historia Regum Britaniae* and in Breton tradition a certain CONAN MERIADOC is credited

with the founding of the British settlement in Gaul under the direction
of the Emperor Magnus Maximus—the
settlement which later became Brittany. Welsh tradition agrees with
this, but save when translating from
or citing the *Historia* it never gives
Conan (in Welsh *Cynan*) the surname
Meriadoc.

There are three Meriadocs in
Arthurian romance. The first is a
Breton lord (*Meriadu*) in *Guigemar*, a
lay of Marie de France. The second is
the hero of the *Historia Meriadoci*, a
twelfth century Arthurian romance
written in Latin. The third (*Meriadués*) is the hero of a poem titled *Li
Chevaliers as deus espees* 'The Knight
with the two swords', the first part
of which parallels almost exactly the
early sections of the later story of
Balaain (or Balin) as found in the so-
called *Huth Merlin* and in Book II of
Malory's *Le Morte Darthur*.

A fourth Meriadoc appeared in the
lost portion of the *Tristan* of Thomas
of Britain as revealed by the German,
Norwegian, and English romances based
on it. The English version, *Sir
Tristrem*, gives his name the form
Meriadok. He plays the role of the
betrayer of Tristan and Isold to King
Mark and corresponds to Malory's Sir
Andred.

Madoc, This is a genuine Welsh name in
use since Roman times, if not before.
It is a derivative of *mad* 'fortunate'.
Forms of the name include *Matôc*,
Madauc, *Madawg*, *Madog*, *Maddok*, *Mad-
dock*.

Perhaps the most interesting historical Madoc is the son of Owain
Gwenydd who, according to a tradition
predating Columbus, discovered a new
land out in the Atlantic in or about
A.D. 1170. There is some evidence
that the now extinct Mandan Indian
tribe were descended in part from a
colony founded by this Madoc. (Richard Deacon, *Madoc and the Discovery of
America*, London: Frederick Muller
Ltd., 1967.)

Malory mentions a *Madok de la Mon-
tayne* in *Le Morte Darthur* (IX:27), and
a *Maduc le Noir* appears in two French
Arthurian sources: *La Vengeance
Raguidel* by Raoul de Houdenc and the
so-called *Livre d'Artus*. Welsh

tradition knows of a half-brother to
Arthur named *Madog ap Uther* (Rachel
Bromwich, *Trioedd Ynys Prydein: The
Welsh Triads*, Cardiff: University of
Wales Press, 1961). The name does not
otherwise appear in connection with
Arthur.

Marmadas, An *-as* variation on **Marmadoc**.
Cf. **Merimas**, **Saradas**.

Marmadoc, The name *Marmaduke*, commonly
spelt *Marmaduc* in medieval times, is
peculiar to Yorkshire, but fairly common there from the twelfth century
onwards, particularly around Thirsk.
In the *Doomsday Book*, Wellburg, about
13 miles from Thirsk, is said to be
held by Fredegist and MELMIDOC, the
name of the latter apparently being an
early form of *Marmaduc* and to be derived from Irish *Maelmaedoc* 'Servant-
(of)-Maedoc'. Or might it be interpreted as 'Maedoc the Servant'? The
Brandybuck genealogy gives us Marmadoc son of Madoc son of Gormadoc
which might come out as—taking these
as Welsh—'Madoc the Servant' son of
'Madoc' son of 'High-Madoc'.

Marroc, In Malory's *Le Morte Darthur*,
Marrok is mentioned twice as one of
the Knights of the Round Table (V:8;
XIX:11). The form *Marrok* occurs only
here, though what seems to be the same
person is found in other English
Arthurian romances as *Marrake*, as well
as once as *Marrike*, once as *Merrake*,
once as *Mewreke*, and once as *Marroke*.
Malory refers to a lost story about
him, for he calls him 'sir Marrok the
good knyght that was betrayed with
his wyff, for she made hym seven yere
a warwolff' (XIX:11; the Winchester
ms. reads in error 'he made hym seven
...').

The name may be a variant of *Merrick* < *Merick* < *Almeric* < Gmc. *alm* (<
amal) 'strive, labour' + *ric* 'rule,
reign'; it may be from the Welsh name
Meyric; it may be from *Merrick*, a peak
in southern Scotland; it may be from
Maurice < Late Lat. *Mauritius*, *Mauri-
cius* < Lat. *Maurus* 'Mauritanian,
Moor' < Gk. *maurun* 'to darken'; or it
may be from *Mauruc de la Roche*, the
name of a knight of Arthur in the
Vulgate Merlin and its English translations.

Meriadoc, See **Kalimac**.

Merimac, *Merrimac* or *Merrimack* is the name of a river running through New Hampshire and Massachusetts, probably meaning 'deep place' in Algonquin; but a similar word in Middle-west Algonquin dialects means 'catfish' whence the name of the Meramec River in Missouri, and the name of the town of Merrimac, Illinois, opposite the mouth of the river (George R. Stewart, *American Place-Names,* New York: Oxford Univ. Press, 1970). The Merrimac River gave its name to the U.S. government frigate Merrimac, which was built in 1855 and sunk by the Monitor in 1862.

This alone of the Brandybuck names has a parallel which is neither Celtic part of the pseudo-Celtic Arthurian material. But it strikes the ear as a name in the same style.

Merimas, An *-as* variation on Merimac. Cf. Marmadas, Saradas.

Orgulas, The adjective *orgulous* 'proud, haughty' is used frequently by Malory in his *Le Morte Darthur*; it is an anglicized form of a French word appearing in Modern French as *orgueilleux*. The closest it comes to being a name in Malory is as a title of a minor Knight of the Round Table, Bellyaunce le Orgulus (VIII:41;XIX: 11;XX:8), and in the name Castle *Orgulous* (IX:3f).

In French romances several characters appear called *l'Orgueilleus* 'the Proud One'. Most notable is *L'Oguelleus de la Lande* 'the Proud One of the Glade', who plays a part in Chrétien's *Perceval*, in his *Erec et Enide*, in the so-called *Didot Perceval*, in the *Perlesvaux*, in Renaut de Beaujeu's *Le Bel Inconnu*, and in Jehan's *Les Mervelles de Rigomer*. The German poet Wolfram von Eschenbach makes of *l'Orgueilleus de la Lande* the proper name Orilus de Lalander.

Other characters with this title are Li Orgueilleus de la Gaudine, Li Orguelleus de la Roche, a giant l'Orguillos, and a giant Orguilleus.

Rorimac (Rory), *Rory* is a northern Irish from of the Celtic name *Rhuadri* or *Rhuaidhri* 'red, ruddy'. Rory O'More was an ancient Irish hero. The name is confused with, or per-

haps originally corrupted from the Germanic name *Roderick* (hrod 'fame' + ric 'reign, rule') which appears in Welsh as *Rhydderch*.

C. M. Yonge states (II:104) that *Rory* is the familiar name for the fox in many Highland tales which tell of his shrewdness. (The full name for the fox is *madadh ruadh* 'red dog', often shortened to *ruadh* or *ray*.) So it is fitting to learn of RORY Brandybuck that 'neither age nor an enormous dinner had clouded his wits' (I:39).

Sadoc, Two knight named *Sadok/Saduk/ Sadocke/Sadoke* appear in Malory's *Le Morte Darthur*. The first is a Cornish knight, hostile to King Mark and friendly to Sir Trystram (VII:27,29; IX:33,35,50f) who becomes a Knight of the Round Table (XIX:11) and a supporter of Launcelot in his war with Arthur (XIX:11;XX:5.18). The second is a knight of Orkney (X:68).

Both appear in the French Arthurian romances with at least four other Sadocs, and characters bearing the same name are found in the non-Arthurian *Li Romanz d'Athis et Prophilias ou l'Estoire d'Athenas* and in the Arseual text of *Le Roman d'Alexandre*.

There is also a genuine Welsh name *Cadoc,* later *Cadawg*, from *cad* 'battle', which is of interest when looked at beside Saradoc and Seredic. The name appears twice in French Arthurian poems.

Saradas, An *-as* variation on Saradoc. Cf. Marmadas, Merimas.

Saradoc, Among the names of the Knights of the Round Table listed in 'Les Devises des arms de tous les chevaliers de la Table Ronde' at the beginning of the 1501 edition of the romance of *Giron le Courtois* is *Saradoc des Sept Fontaines*. The name appears as *Surados* in Robinson's *Ancient Order and Societe and Unitie Laudable of Prince Arthure, and his knightly Armory of the Round Table*.

Saradoc is also reminiscent of the genuine Celtic name *Caradoc*, meaning 'kind, amiable'. There have been numerous Caradocs of historical importance, of which the earliest, and probably the most famous, is that *Caratacos*, Latinized as *Caractacus*, the British chieftain who fought so

valiently against the Romans during
the reign of Claudius.

Several Caradocs appear in Arthurian romance, of which only one is
of importance. This is he called
Caradoc Brecbras 'Strong-arm' in
early historical sources. He appears
in medieval Welsh as Caradawg Vrech-
vras and in French as Carados Briebras 'Short-arm'. He was apparently
an historical sixth century British
ruler with lands both in Britain and
Brittany. In the first continuation
of the Perceval of Chrétien de Troyes
a King Carados of Nantes (in Brittany) is introduced as step-father to
Carados Briebras. Upon his death the
younger Carados inherits the throne.
In the prose romances the two are
confounded into one person who
appears in Malory as King Carados of
Scotlonde (!) (I:9,12,15,15;VIII:20,
21;IX:25,30,31,33;X:36;XIX:11).

Two other knights called Carados
appear in Malory, one is the giant
Sir Carados of the Dolerous Tower who
is slain by Launcelot (VI:8;VII:27,
29,30;VIII:28;XX:1,15), the other
is an old knight who invites Sir
Gawayne to pass the night with him
(IV:22).

Other lesser characters named Caradoc appear in various French Romances

Seredic, Seredic resembles the real
Welsh name Ceredic (later Ceredig),
and indeed suggests the pronunciation
that an English reader who knew
nothing of Welsh would be likely to
give the name. (In fact, the initial
c represents [k], not [s].) Ceredic
is a variant of Caradoc. The most
notable bearer of the name in this
form would be Ceredic Guletic—later
his name is spelt Ceredig Wledig—,
the son of the fifth century chief
Cunedag Guletic/Cunedda Wledig who
drove the Goidels/Gaels out of what
is now North Wales and divided the
region among his sons. Ceredic took
the region now called after him: Cere-
digion in Welsh, and Cardiganshire in
English. One of Ceredic's nephews
was Caswallon Llaw Hir, King of

Gwynedd, the original behind Malory's
King Cradelmant of North Wales.

A variation of Ceredic is Cerdic or
Ceardic, a form found not among the
Welsh but among the West Saxons,
borne, surprisingly enough, by the
traditional founder of the royal house
of Wessex. Other anglicized forms of
Celtic names appearing among the descendants of this Cerdic are Cadda/
Ceadda and Ceadwalla. Cerdic may,
despite the official genealogy tracing
him to Woden, have been of Celtic
descent in part. Even the offical
genealogy says nothing of his maternal
lineage or the maternal lineages of
his immediate forebears.

This Cerdic, following the dates
in the Anglo-Saxon Chronicle, would
have flourished during the Arthurian
period. But he is not mentioned in
any of the Arthurian chronicles or
romances, unless he is to be identified with either Cheldric or Chelric,
Saxon chiefs who war on Arthur in the
Historia Regum Britanniae, or unless
he is hidden under one of the Caradocs
of the French Arthurian romances.

Tolkien says of these Wessex names:
The names from which Cerdic and
Ceadwalla were derived may be
assumed to have had some such late
British form as Car[a]díc and Cad-
wallón. In the West-Saxon forms the
accent was shifted back to accord
with normal Germanic initial stress.
In Ceadwalla, and probably in Cerdic, the initial c had been fronted,
and the pronunciation intended was
probably nearer modern English ch
than k. (EW:9)

Seredic might then be taken as a
sort of modern form of Cerdic. (The
modern name Cedric, with initial [s],
comes, in fact, from Cerdic via a
remodelling of the name by Sir Walter
Scott in his novel Ivanhoe.) And,
just as the sons and grandsons of the
founder of the royal line of Wessex
have Old English names, not Celtic
names, so the sons of Seredic Brandybuck bear Germanic names: Doderic and
Ilberic.

From the above it is clear why these names strike the
ear as 'vaguely Celtic'. Almost all are identical or not too
different from British names of the sixth century, or names
from the Arthurian cycle, or both. The only exceptions are

GIVING OF NAMES

Bombadil, *Gorbulas*, *Kalimac*, *Marmadoc* and its *-as* variant
(*Marmadas*), and *Merimac* and its *-as* variant (*Merimas*). But,
of these, *Marmadoc* is genuinely Celtic, *Rorimac* is half-
Celtic, and *Gorbulas* is a combination of *Gorbadoc* and *Orgulas*. Only *Bombadil*, *Kalimac*, and *Merimac* (with *Merimas*) are
completely outside the Celtic and Arthurian pseudo-Celtic
boundaries.

The *-as* ending is very frequent in Malory's *Le Morte
Darthur*, which gives us:

> Ballias, Baudas, Brastias, Caulas, Claudas, Damas, Dar-.
> ras, Dodynas, Dynas, Elyas, Florydas, Gwynas, Hellyas,
> Ladynas, Lucas, Melyas, Melyodas, Pelleas, Placidas,
> Taulas.

Melyodas is, in fact, derived from an earlier *Meliadoc*, perhaps originally a variant of *Meriadoc*. The *-as* ending is
also common on Sindarin names.

The Brandybucks also had the custom of giving a meaning-
ful nickname in the Common Speech to the head of the family:
Broadbelt, *Deep-delver*, *Goldfather*, *Magnificent*, *Masterful*,
Proudneck, and *Scattergold*.

Surnames

In most societies there will be more than one bearer for
most given names. An additional name or epithet therefore
becomes necessary to help in distinguishing between bearers
of the same name. This may be the name of the father—or
more rarely the mother—, as *Anderson*, *Johnson*. They may
describe a particular characteristic of the person, as
Short, *Armstrong*; often an occupation as *Smith*, *Cartwright*,
Fuller, or a place of residence or origin as *London*, *Street-
field*. Towards the end of the medieval period it became more
and more common for such surnames to be inherited in the male
line, and so become family names. A woman, upon marriage,
would normally give up the family surname she had used since
birth—her MAIDEN NAME—and take instead her husband's family
surname.

The same evolution of family surnames passed on in the
male line had occurred among the Hobbits of the Shire by
the end of the Third Age, and was also found among the Men
and Hobbits of Bree. It may have been known elsewhere.
Aragorn intends to make *Telcontar* the name of his house, to
be born by all the heirs of his body, with no indication that
any novelty of nomenclature is being proposed (III:139).
But, Tolkien stresses that the practise of the Hobbits and
the Men of Bree was unusual for those days (III:413). In
Gondor inherited surnames may have been used only in certain
noble families.

GIVING OF NAMES

Some of the older Hobbit surnames were not of known meaning, or at least the meaning was not obvious from a superficial look: *Baggins* (jestingly connected with 'bag' in the place name *Bag End* 'cul-de-sac' and in Bilbo's riddling conversation with Smaug), *Boffin* (representing *Bophîn*), *Bunce*, *Maggot* (Tolkien says 'it is an accident that *maggot* is an English word meaning "grub", "larva" [G:169]), *Rumble* (Tolkien indicates 'it had no meaning (at that time) in the Shire' [G:172]), and *Took* (representing *Tûk*).

Some surnames came from the common practise of living underground in holes: *Banks* (meaning 'slopes'), *Brockhouse* 'Badger-house', *Burrowes* (H, Ch. 19), *Burrows*, *Grubb* (recalling 'the English verb *grub* "dig, root, in the ground"' [G: 167]), *Sandheaver*, *Smallburrow*, and *Underhill*. *Banks*, *Brockhouse*, and *Underhill*, were also Bree names, as were *Longholes*, *Tunelly*. *Hobbit* itself is a name of the same kind, being a worn down form of *Holbytla* 'Hole-builder', and seems originally to have been a name applied by the Fallohides and Stoors to the Harfoots who alone consistently dwelt in burrows by choice (III:408).

Surnames of geographical import are *Brandybuck* (with reference to the Brandywine), *Cotton* (*cot* 'cottage, hut' + -*ton* 'town' < OE *tūn* 'village' [G:162]), *Gamgee* (< *Gammidgy* 'person of *Gamwich* [pronounced *Gammidge*]), *Noakes* 'one of Noake' (*Noake* < OE *atten oke* 'at the oak' [G:170]), and *Sackville.* Bandobras Tooks is said to have been the ancestor of 'the North-tooks of Long Cleeve' and Peregrin Took marries 'Diamond of Long Cleeve' (III:381). It may be that *of Long Cleeve* is a full family surname.

Surnames indicating a particular physical or mental characteristics are: *Brown*, *Brownlock*, *Fairbairn* 'Fairchild' (G:165), *Goodbody*, *Goodchild*, *Greenhand* (meaning skilled in the care of plants), *Headstrong*, *Proudfoot* (in reference to large feet), *Puddifoot* 'Puddle-foot' (a jesting name for Hobbits of the Marish), *Sandyman* (probably possessing red, sand-coloured hair), *Twofoot*, and *Whitfoot* 'Whitefoot'. The characteristic of tubbiness appears in *Bolger* (from the same source as Eng. *bulge* [G:180]), *Bracegirdle* ('with reference to the hobbit tendency to be fat and so to strain their belts' [G:161]), *Chubb* (taken as from *chubby* [G:162]), and *Pott* (TB:42). *Goldworthy* may mean 'very worthy' or contain a reference to golden hair. *Goold* also means 'gold'.

Occupational surnames are: *Butcher* (TB:42), *Gardner*, *Hayward* (*hay* 'fence' [cf. *hedge*] + *ward* 'guard' [G:168]), *Hogg* (TB:42; he or an ancestor probably raised pigs), *Hornblower* (G:168), and *Roper*. The name *Smith* does not occur; that sort of work would be done by travelling Dwarves.

The surname *Oldbuck* carries the memory of Bucca of the
Marish, the founder of the family (G:179).

The names of the three varieties of Hobbits are also
names denoting physical characteristics. *Harfoot* would be
ME *Herfoot* from OE *Hǽrfōt* 'Hair-foot' (G:167), and is probably a name given them by Men when they first entered Eriador,
for all Halflings had hair upon their feet and so *Harfoot*
does not do as a name to distinguish between types of Hobbits. But when the other varieties came into Eriador and
found already there a many of their own race called Harfoots,
the name was kept to denote that particular variety of Hobbit. *Stoor* represents ME *stor*, *stur*, from OE *stōr* 'hard,
strong' (G:174), for 'the Stoors were broader. heavier in
build; their feet and hands were larger' (I:12). *Fallowhide*
would be OE *Fealohӯd* 'Yellow-skin, Pale-skin', the element
fealo surviving in Modern English only as *fallow* in *fallow
deer*, the name of a small European deer (*Dama. dama*) having
a yellowish coat spotted with white in summer (G:165).
'The Fallowhides were fairer of skin and also of hair' (I:
12).

In Bree the family names of Men were usually taken from
plants: *Appledore* ('an old word for "apple-tree" [it survives in English place-names]' [G:160]}, *Butterbur* (a name
given to any of several plants of the genus *Petasites* with
small purplish or whitish flowers and large heart-shaped
leaves; the Common Butterbur [*Petasites hybridus* or *Petasites
vulgaris*] is especially intended [G:162]), *Ferny*, *Goatleaf*
(a name for the honeysuckle or woodbine, the French *chèvre-
feuille* [G:166f]), *Heathertoes*, *Pickthorn*, and *Thistlewool*.
Tolkien tells us that 'some of the hobbits had similar
names' (I:167), but only gives the example of *Mugwort*, a
plant (*Artemisia vulgaris*) with pinnate leaves and very small
orange flowers (G:169). But Tolkien implies that *Heathertoes*
was originally used as a Hobbit surname, for he says that it
was 'presumably a joke of the Big Folk, meaning that the Little Folk, wandering unshold, collected heather, twigs and
leaves between their toes' (G:168).

In Bree, at least, surnames had been inherited through
families for so long that their origin as nicknames were
almost forgotten. The Underhills of Staddle 'could not
imagine sharing a name without being related, they took Frodo
to heart as a long-lost cousin' (I:167). In the Shire the
same is true among the upper classes. The only change of
family name occurs when two such names are conjoined, as
Chubb-Baggins and *Sackville-Baggins*. But in the genealogy
of Samwise the surnames still tend to remain epithets and
are easily modified or changed for others. Hamfast of Gamwich (Galabas) passes on to this son Wiseman the surname
Gamwich (*Galabas*). But when it reaches Wiseman's son Hob,

it becomes *Gammidge* (**Galbas* ?), and then changes further
into a diminutive form *Gammidgy* (**Galbasi* ?). When Hob
passes it on to his son Hobson it assumes the final form
Gamgee (*Galpsi*). Hobson had set himself up as rope maker,
and so came to be called *Roper Gamgee*. His eldest son, Andwise, inherited the business, and as a surname used *Roper*.
not *Gamgee*. The second son, Hamfast, who takes up gardening,
retains the surname *Gamgee*, and it appears as the surname of
his son, Samwise, throughout the main text of *The Lord of the
Rings*. But in the genealogy the word *gardener* appears in
parentheses following his name; at the end of Appendix D
there is reference to 'old Sam Gardner's birthday'; and
Samwise's eldest son is named *Frodo Gardner*, and his son
Holfast Gardner. The surname has changed again. The Took
genealogy records that Peregrin's son Faramir married 'Goldilocks daughter of Master Samwise', not 'Goldilocks Gamgee'
or 'Goldilocks Gardner'.

The Choosing of Names

In the Took family the Germanic system of front and
end variation is found in full flower, along with a tendency
to relate names by alliteration. *Isengrin* is the father of
Isumbras, repeating the initial *Isen-*. *Isumbras* names his
sons *Ferumbras* and *Bandobras*, and the son of Ferumbras is
named *Fortinbras*. All four names are front variations on
-*bras*, and *Fortinbras* alliterates with *Ferumbras*.

But the name of Fortinbras' son, *Gerontius*, does not
fit at all. It means 'Old-one', and he was also known as the
Old Took. So the name might be one taken late in life,
replacing an earlier name, or might have been a name given
in prophecy.

With Gerontius' sons the system returns to normal.
His first, third, fifth, seventh, and last children are
named, respectively, *Isengrim, Isumbras, Isembold, Isembard*,
and *Isengar*, all end variations on *isen-*. His second,
fourth, sixth, and eighth children are named, respectively,
Hildigard, Hildigrim, Hildifons, and *Hildibrand*, all end
variations on *hild-*. The three young daughters reveal a
light jest: *Belladonna* and *Mirabella*, the names of the eldest
and youngest, are both plant names, but the name of the
middle daughter, *Donnamira* is not, nor is it a Germanic name.
The other two names have been treated as Germanic names, been
broken up into supposed themes (*bella, donna, mira*), and
a new name created from two of the themes: *Donnamira*. So
the names make a cycle: *bella·donna·mira·bella·donna·mira·
bella·donna·mira·bella·donna* ...

Isembard is father of *Flambard*, father of *Adelard*,
father of *Reginard* and *Everard*. The theme -*bard* has been

kept for one generation, then replaced by the rhyming theme
-(h)ard. *Isumbras* is father of *Fortinbras*, father of
Ferumbras, front variations on *-bras*. *Hildigrim* is father
of *Adalgrim*, but again the pattern breaks, as Adalgrim's
son is named *Paladin*. Paladin names his children in alliteration with his own name: *Pearl*, *Pimpernel*, *Pervinca*, *Peregrin*.

The Brandybuck names seem to show an awareness of the
Germanic system. *Gormadoc* is father of *Madoc*, *Sadoc*, and
Marroc, all ending in *-oc*, and two ending in *-doc*. *Madoc*
is father of *Marmadok*. But Marmadoc's sons are named *Gorbadoc* and *Orgulas*, which don't fit very well. However, Orgulas' son is named *Gorbulas*, which looks like a sort of
combination of themes made out of *Gorbadoc* and *Orgulas*.
The name of Gorbulas' son *Marmadas* only carries on the *-as*
ending, but he names his children *Merimas*, *Mentha*, and *Melilot*, which alliterate with each other and his own name.
In *Saradas*, father of *Seredic*, father of *Doderic* and *Ilberic*,
an *s* alliteration is carried on for one generation (with
sarad- and *sered-* possibly being thought of as variants on
the same theme), and an *-ic* ending occurs on the name of a
father and his two sons. Note also the apparent recombination of elements in *Dodinas* and *Dinodas*, the names of two
brothers.

The short names in the Baggins genealogy do not permit
the same degree of recombination of themes that we find in
the Took genealogy. But some attempt seems to have been made
to compensate by greater use of alliteration. *Ponto* is
father of *Polo*, father of *Prisca* and *Posco*, father of *Ponto*,
Porto, and *Peony*. *Peony* marries *Milo* Burrows, and his children are named *Mosco*, *Moto*, *Myrtle*, and *Minto*. Another alliterating group of siblings are *Dora*, *Drogo*, and *Dudo*, the last
having a child named *Daisy*. *Bilbo* is son of *Bungo* and nephew
to *Belba* and *Bingo*; all three are sons of *Mungo*, son of
Balbo. Here we have a predominance of names beginning with
b, and recurring similarities in the rest of the names. *Otho*
Sackville-Baggins marries *Lobelia* Bracegirdle, and it is not
too surprising that they name their son *Lotho*.

In Samwise's genealogy the Germanic system of variation
is not clearly visible. We do have *Tolman*, son of *Tolman*,
son of *Holman*, son of *Cotman*; and *Halfast* son of *Halfred*,
nephew to *Hamfast*. And there are signs of alliteration:
Cottar is father to *Cotman* and *Carl*; *Hob* is father to *Hobson*, father to *Halfred* (*Halfast*'s father) and *Hamfast*, father
to *Hamson* and *Halfred*. But Hobson and Hamfast also have
children whose names do not alliterate. Names seem more
often to be chosen because they have already been used in the
family: *Hamfast* son of Samwise is grandson to *Hamfast* Gamgee,
who is great-great-grandson to *Hamfast* of Gamwich; there are

two *Halfreds*, related to each other as nephew and uncle, two
Wilcomes related in the same way, two *Daisys* who are niece
and aunt, two *Mays* who are niece and aunt, and other more
distant repetitions of a name twice within a family.

One custom not found in the other genealogies is that
of naming the eldest son by suffixing *-son* to a short form of
the father's name: *Anson* is the only son of *Andwise* (*Andy*);
Hamson is the eldest son of *Hamfast* (*Ham*); *Hobson* is the only
son of *Hob*.

Names may be descriptive. Tolkien notes that the use
of names of yellow flowers as *Daisy* and *Marigold* in the Gamgee line 'suggests that there was a "Fallowhide" strain' (G:
169), indicating these names were applied because of fair
hair and complexion.

Sam's naming of his children is instructive. The eldest
is named *Elanor* after the golden flower of Lothlórien, for
he believes she will be particularly beautiful (III:306).
A golden flower is especially suitable, as most of 'the
children born or begotten in that year...had a rich golden
hair that had been rare among hobbits' (III:303). Sam had
already announced that he planned to name his eldest son
after Frodo (III:306), and as Frodo prepares to depart for
the West he tells Sam, 'Frodo-lad will come, and Rosie-lass,
and Merry, and Goldilocks, and Pippin; and perhaps more that
I cannot see' (III:309). This is partly prophecy—the children are born and named in the precise order Frodo spells out
—but it indicates that Sam might be expected to name his
children after their mother, Rose, and three of his closest
friends. *Goldilocks* may also have been the name of a person
of some importance to Sam or Rose, though the name appears
nowhere in the genealogies. Note that Sam uses the familiar
forms *Merry* and *Pippin* for his sons' full names, not the
longer *Meriadoc* and *Peregrin*. These high forms would seem
too grandiose for the like of him and his family. Of his
other sons' names, *Hamfast* is that of his father, *Bilbo* is
in memory of the old family friend and Sam's first teacher
of Elvish lore, *Tolman* is the name of Rose's father and
eldest brother. Only *Robin* remains unexplained; it may be
from Robin Smallburrow, Sam's old friend who served as a
Sherriff under the ruffians only because compelled to do so
(III:281), and no doubt took part in their overthrow in the
scouring of the Shire. As to the names of Sam's other
daughters, *Daisy* was also the name of one of Sam's sisters;
but it and *Primrose* both suggest fairness, and—like *Elanor*
and *Goldilocks*—suggest that the Fallowhide strain in Sam's
family, 'increased by the favour of Galadriel, became notable
in his children' (G:169). As to *Ruby*, we can only guess as
to the particular reason why this name was chosen.

GIVING OF NAMES

Pronunciation

The Hobbit names have been mostly translated into modern
English forms, or adapted to modern English, and are to be so
pronounced (III:391). That is, pronounce both personal and
place names as you would expect them to be pronounced according to the normal sounds suggested by English spelling.
For example: *Bilbo* ['bɪlboʊ], *Frodo* ['fɹoʊdoʊ], *Samwise*
['sæmwaɪz], *Fredegar* ['fɹɛdəˌgaɹ], *Lotho* ['loʊθoʊ], *Lobelia*
[loʊ'biːlyə], *Bandobras* ['bændʊˌbɹɑz], *Gerontius* [dʒə'rɒn-
tʃəs], *Isengrim* ['aɪznˌgɹɪm], *Baggins* ['bægɪnz], *Took* [tʰʊk],
Gamgee ['gæmdʒiː], *Bolger* ['bʊldʒəɹ], *Brandybuck* ['bɹændɪ-
ˌbʌk], *Boffin* ['bʊfɪn].
Meriadoc should have a flavour of Welsh: ['mɛrɪ'adʊk].
The place name *Michel Delving* is ['mɪtʃl 'dɛlvɪŋ], as in
Mitchel, not *Michael*. *Michel* is an old word meaning 'great'
related to *much*, perhaps more familiar through its northern
form *mickle*.

NAMES OF THE ROHIRRIM

On Old English

Tolkien represents the true language of the Rohirrim
by Old English. The only samples of speech in this tongue
are Éomer's cry *Westu Théoden hál!* 'Be-thou Théoden well
(*hál* = HALE, WHOLE)!'(II:122); and Éowyn's farewell *Ferthu
Théoden hál!* 'Go-thou Théoden in health!' (II:127), in which
ferthu is to be pronounced ['fɛɹðoʊ] and *hál* [haːl]. *Fer*
is the same as our modern *fare*, as in 'How did he fare?',
and Éowyn's sentence might also be rendered 'Farewell, Théoden!' or 'Fare-thee-well, Théoden!'.
The names of persons and places in Rohan have also been
rendered into Old English, with some change of spelling when
the spelling conventions of Old English and Modern English
differ, and an occasional partial modernization. The pronunciation intended is in question. Tolkien indicates that
they are to be pronounced with the same letter values given
for Elvish, but this results in deviations both from the
pronunciation of Old English as generally reconstructed and
from the pronunciation of Modern English. Tolkien specifically gives the pronunciation of the diphthongs *éa* and *éo* as
representings sounds like 'the *ea* of English *bear*, and the *eo*
of *Theobald*' (III:395). The *éa* value indicated is [ɛə̌] (following the so-called RECEIVED PRONUNCIATION accepted as
'standard' British English), which is close enough to the
normal reconstructed pronunciations of [æə̌] for short *ea* and
[ɛ·ǎ] for long *éa*. But the indicated value for *éo*, [ɪ·ə̌], is
nothing like the normally given [e·ɔ̌].

212

In the Tolkien recordings the *éo* of the Rohirric names
is rendered variously in Laurence Krieg's notes as [eo, eʊ,
eˑʊ, eˑʊ, eɔ, eˑe, eʌ], all reasonable approximations for
[eˑɔ]. Accordingly, it has been taken that the names are to
pronounced following the pronunciation reconstructed for
them by modern scholars, and that pronunciation will be the
one given.

Each name, when introduced, will be respelt in Old
English fashion (unless there would be no change in form),
given its probable pronunciation, and then, in SMALL CAPI-
TALS, the form this would taken in modern English will be
given where modern words descended from the Old English
words exist (though often not in common use). If such a
modern form also expresses adequately the meaning of the
original, then no further translation will be given.

Some notes on Old English spelling may help to show how
the pronunciations given are arrived at:

> *c* is generally [k], but is usually fronted before
> the front vowels *e*, *i*, *y*, to something like that
> of Modern English *ch* [tʃ].
>
> *sc* generally represents Modern English *sh* [ʃ].
>
> *g* is sometimes [g], but is fronted to [y] before the
> front vowels *e*, *i*, *y* (modern forms usually show
> *y* or *i*); and is lenited to [ɣ] when falling between
> the back vowels *a*, *o*, *u* (modern forms usually show
> *w*).
>
> *cg* generally represents Modern English *dg* [dʒ].
>
> *þ* and *ð* are used interchangeably for the sounds [θ] and
> [ð]; the same word or name will be spelt now with
> one and now with the other on the same page of a
> manuscript.
>
> *f*, *s*, and *þ/ð* indicate voicless spirants [f, s, θ] save
> medially between voiced sounds (and probably ini-
> tially and finally in a few unstressed monosyllables)
> where they are lenited to the corresponding voiced
> spirants [v, z, ð].

A certain amount of confusion arises because Tolkien
uses Old English both for Rohirric names and archaic Common
Speech names. For example, as indicated by Tolkien's pronunciation on the recordings and by his notes in G:187f,
Isengard 'Iron-enclosure', represents an archaic name in
Common Speech, to be properly given a modern English pronunciation ['aɪzənˌgaɪd] (and so with other names containing
OE *īsen* 'iron'. Perhaps to make a distinction, Tolkien uses
the variant Old English form *īren* in the Rohirric mountain
name *Irensaga* (Īrensaga ['iːɹɛnˌsɑɣɑ] IRON-SAW).

It should be noted that the forms Tolkien uses indicate
that Rohirric is not represented by the Wessex dialect, the

so-called standard Old English dialect in which most of the
surviving literature is written, but in what appears to be
either Kentish, or a sourthern variety of Mercian. Thus
names are often closer in form to a Modern English equivalent than would be the case if the Wessex dialect were being
used.

The ending -*a* on many names is a simple masculine ending, to be rendered, if at all, by 'man of, one of'.

All names discussed can be found in *The Lord of the
Rings* either through its Index or in the section THE HOUSE OF
EORL in Appendix A.

The Royal Names

The royal names tend to be words with meanings such as
'lord', 'chief', 'ruler'. They will often be found to have
fitting connatations of other sorts.

The earliest name in the lineage is *Frumgar* [ˈfɹomˌgɑr]
'First-spear', a word used to mean 'chieftain, patriarch,
noble'. His son bears the alliterating name *Fram* [fɹom]
'firm, stout, valiant, bold', and lives up to it in slaying
the dragon *Scatha* (Scaða [ˈskaða] SCATHE) 'injurer, enemy,
robber'. This was a name of Norse/Danish origin; the true
Old English cognate was pronounced [ˈʃaða].

A descendant of Fram is *Léod* [leˑɔd], whose name funda-
mentally means 'people, nation', but which was also used
to mean 'prince, chief, king'. His son is *Eorl* ([ɛɔɹl] EARL)
which originally meant only 'brave man, warrior'. But the
cognate Danish word *jarl* was used for a nobleman of very
high rank, and after the Danish invasion *eorl* began to be
used as the English counterpart. After the Norman conquest
eorl, erl was adopted as the English equivalent of MFr. *conte*
'count'.

Eorl's son has the name *Brego* [ˈbɹɛgɔ] 'ruler, chief,
lord'. The Norse cognate is *Bragi*, the name of the god of
poetry and also of an historical poet Bragi the Old. Brego
names his first son *Baldor* [ˈbɑldɔɹ] 'bold-one', alliterating
with *Brego*, and named his second *Aldar* [ˈɑldɔɹ] 'old-one', a
sort of front variation on his brother's name. (The Wessex
forms are *Bealdor* and *Ealdor*.) *Baldor* is used in poetry as
a term for 'lord, master, hero'. This *Baldor* is as bold as
his name, daring the Paths of the Dead; but he does not
return. *Baldr*, the name of the Norse god who died, seems
to be cognate with *Baldor*. *Aldor* was used as a title for a
leader or chief of any age, and still survives today in the
title *alderman* from OE *aldormann*. But this Aldor did live
long and became known as 'Aldor the Old'.

Aldor's son is named *Fréa* [fɹɛˑɑ] 'lord', cognate with
Norse *Freyr*, the name of the god of fertility and prosperity.

214

He ushers in a period of prosperity and calm that continues
under his son *Fréawine* ['fɹɛ·ɑ̆ˌwɪnɛ] 'lord-friend', and under
his grandson *Goldwine* ['gɔld̦ˌwɪnɛ] 'gold-friend'. (Note
the systematic variation in these names.)

Then follow *Déor* [de·ɔ̆ɹ] 'brave, bold' (that is, possessing the qualities of a *déor* 'wild animal') and his son
Gram [gɹʊm] 'fierce, angry', a word related to *grim* 'cruel,
fierce, severe'.

The children of *Gram* were *Helm Hammerhand* (Helm Hamer-
hand ['hɛlm 'hʊmɛɹˌxʊnd]) and a daughter *Hild* [hɪld] 'Battle'. *Helm* means 'protection, portector'; its special use
for protecting headgear—a HELM—is a secondary development.
The names of Helm's sons, alliterating with his own name and
that of his sister, were *Haleth* (Hæleð ['hælɛθ]) 'man, hero,
fighter' and *Háma* (['hɑːmɑ] HOME) 'home-one, he-of-the home'.
Helm left his name on the geography of Rohan with *Helm's
Deep, Helm's Dike,* and *Helm's Gate,* as well as in the names
Hornburg ['hɔɹnˌbɔɹy] 'horn-fort, horn-BOROUGH' and *Hornrock*
where the element *horn* refers to 'Helm's great horn, supposed
still at times to be heard blowing' (G:187), and is not used
with the meaning 'peak' as in *Starkhorn* (Starchorn ['stɑɹk-
ˌhɔɹn]) 'stiff-, rigid-, strong-peak' (meaning 'a horn [peak]
"standing up stiff like a spike"' [G:192]) and in *Thrihyrne*
(Prihyrne ['θɹɪˌçɥɹnɛ] THREE-HORNED).

The next king, lord of the remnant that survived the
invading Dunlendings, was named *Fréaláf* ['fɹɛ·ɑ̆ˌlɑːf] 'lord-
(of a)-remnant'; -*láf* is related to the verb 'to leave' and
means 'that which is LEFT'. Fréaláf may have changed his
name, or expanded it from simple *Fréa*, when he took the
throne.

Fréaláf is succeeded by his son *Brytta* ['bɹɥttɑ]
'bestower, dispenser, distributor, prince', also called by
his people—as we might expect if he did what his name
implies—*Léofa* (['le·ɔ̆vɑ] LIEF) 'beloved'. His son and suc-
cessor was named *Walda* (['wɑldɑ] WIELDER) 'master, ruler'.
(It would be *Wealda* in the Wessex dialect.) *Bretwalda* was
a title given to some of the earliest Anglo-Saxon kings who
could make some show of ruling all of southern Britain.
The element *bret-* is taken to mean 'British', a variant of
bryt- 'Briton, British'. But *bret-* also occurs as a variant
of *bryt-* as in *Brytta* above. Note that the warlike names
of Helm's generation and the preceding ones have disappeared. Perhaps after the decimation by the Dunlendings
battle no longer seemed so very glorious.

Next ruled *Folca* (['fɔlkɑ] FOLK) 'he of the people =
ruler', slain by the great boar of *Everholt* (Eferholt ['ɛvɛɹ-
hɔlt]) 'boar-wood'. He was succeeded by his son *Folcwine*
['fɔlkˌwɪnɛ] 'people-friend'. Folcwine's three sons all have
names beginning with *f* like that of their father and

grandfather: *Folcred* (Folcred ['fɔlk̩ɹɛd] FOLK-REDE) 'people-
counsel' (and he would have succeeded to the throne if he
had lived), *Fastred* (Fæstred ['fæst̩ɹɛd] FAST-REDE) 'firm-
counsel' (a front variation on *Folcred*), and *Fengel* ['fɛŋgɛl]
'grasper, embracer = prince, lord, ʌing'.

Used in Old English verse as a poetic term for 'king,
lord' the original meaning of *Fengel*, 'grasper', was not
remembered. But Fengel deserved the name in the original
sense, being 'greedy of food and gold, and at strife with his
marshals and with his children' (III:350), a FANGED man
indeed.

The name of Fengel's son is a kind of front variation
of his own: *Thengel* (Þengel ['θɛŋgɛl]) 'king, lord', a variation on *þegn* 'thane'. His son and daughter were given names
that alliterated with his own and were end variations of
each other: *Théoden* (Þēoden ['θeˑɔdɛn]) 'lord, ruler, prince'
(< *þēod* 'people') and *Théodwyn* (Þēodwyn ['θeˑɔd̩wɥn])
'people-joy' (probably to be understood as 'she who is the
people's delight; for -*wyn*, see WINsome = *joysome*). Théoden's
son was named *Théodred* (Þēodrēd [θeˑɔd̩ɹɛd]) 'people-counsel',
another end variation. Théoden was given the surname *Ednew*
(Ednīwe ['ɛd̩niːwɛ]) 'renewed' after his death in memory of how
he fell into a decline but, stirred by Gandalf, roused himself and led his people to battle and himself to a glorious
death.

Théodwyn married the Chief Marshal of Rohan, named
Éomund ['eˑɔ̩mɔnd] 'horse-protection', from *eoh* [ɛɔx] 'horse'
+ *mund* 'hand, protection'. (*Eoh* appears also in *éored*
['eˑɔɹɛd] 'mounted troop, band of knights'.) Their children
are *Éomer* ['eˑɔ̩mɛɹ] 'horse-famous' (the form in Wessex dialect is *Eomær*) and a daughter *Éowyn* ['eˑɔ̩wɥn] 'horse-joy'
with a name composed of the first theme in her father's name
and the second theme in her mother's name). Éomer was given
the surname *Éadig* ['æˑɑ̃dɪy] 'wealthy, prosperous'. His son,
in alliteration with his own name, was called *Elfwine* ['ɛlv-
̩wɪnɛ] 'elf-friend', a rendering of Q *Elendil*. (The Wessex
dialect form is *Ælfwine*.)

The royal names meaning 'prince', 'chief', 'warrior'
were, for the most part, not actually used as given names
in Old English. In Searle's *Onomasticon Anglo-Saxonicum*
there are no occurrences listed for *Aldor*, *Baldor*, *Eorl*,
Fengel, *Frumgar*, *Thengel*, or *Théoden*. *Brego* only occurs as
an initial theme in longer names, e.g. *Bregusiwth*, *Breguwine*.
Fréa appears alone only as the name of a god, and as a theme
in the names *Fréaláf*, *Fréawaru*, and *Fréawine*. *Fréaláf*
appears only in genealogies as the grandfather of the god
Woden. In one text *Fréawine* appears instead in error; this
name appears elsewhere only in genealogies as the great-
great-grandson of the god Woden and the great-great-great

GIVING OF NAMES

grandfather of Cerdic, traditionally the first king of Wessex, and once in a later historical context. (*Fréawaru* is
only known from the poem *Beowulf* where she appears as the
daughter of King Hroðgar and the betrothed of Froda.)
Other names in the royal family occur in Searle, but with
only one or two entries each, save for *Éomer* and *Elfwine*
which are quite common in their more normal forms *Éomær* and
Ælfwine.

Meaningful Names

Some others of Rohan besides royalty bear names appro-
priate°to their character, or to the part they play in the
tale. *Ceorl* ([tʃɛɔɹl] CHURL) 'freeman, man; hero' is the
name of the knight of Rohan who tells Éomer that all has been
lost at the Fords of Isen: a faithful follower, who is
delighted that Théoden has now ridden forth to fight in the
battle. The great warrior who commands the forces of Rohan
at the Second Battle of the Isen and arrives with his forces
in time to complete the rout of Saruman's troops at the
second Battle of the Hornburg is named *Erkenbrand* (Ercenbrand
['ɛɹkɛnˌbɹɒnd]) (in Wessex dialect *Eorconbrand*) 'noble-
brand'. The theme *ercen-, eorcon-* appears also in OE *eorcan-
stān, earcnan-stān* 'precious stone', whence the modernized
Arkenstone, the name given to the great gem found by the
Dwarves in Erebor in *The Hobbit*. The Old Norse form is *iark-
nasteinn*. The name of Théoden's doorward and the captain of
his guard, whose charge is the safety of the king and his
house, is *Háma* (['hɑːmɑ] HOME) 'he of the home'.
Certain personal names are probably nicknames
rather than names given at birth. *Gamling* (Gameling ['gɒmɛ-
ˌlɪŋ]) 'old man' is the name of an old man, leader of those
who guard Helm's Dike. *Gléowine* ['gleˑɔˌwɪnɛ] 'music-friend'
is the name of Théoden's minstrel; *gléo* is Mod. Engl. GLEE.
Wídfara (['wiːdˌvɑɹɑ] WIDE-FARER) 'far-traveller' is the name
of a man who lives on the open Wold, and probably travels far
on it as a herdsman. *Wormtunge* (Wyrmtunga ['wʉɹmˌtoŋɑ])
'snake-tongue' is one nickname hardly needed, for we are
given that the true name of the person in question is *Gríma*
['gɹiːmɑ] 'mask, helmet' son of *Gálmód* (['gɑːlˌmoːd] ---MOOD)
'licentious', a good name for a traitor who hides his true
face and his secret lust for Éowyn. To Morwen of Lossarnach,
wife of King Thengel, the Rohirrim gave the name *Steelsheen*
(Stȳlscīene ['stʉːlˌʃiˑɛnɛ]. Meriadoc of the Shire they
named *Holdwine* ['hɔldˌwɪnɛ] 'gracious-friend'.
Gandalf is given the epithet *Grayhame* (Grēghama ['gɹeˑy-
ˌxɒmɑ]) 'grey-coat' by Éomer and the name *Láthspell* (Lāðspel
['lɑːθˌspɛl] 'ill-news' by Gríma. When Éowyn rides in secret
with the Rohirrim to Gondor she uses the name *Dernhelm*
['dɛɹnˌçɛlm] 'hidden-protection'. (In German this would be

217

Tarnhelm, which is the name of the helmet of invisibility and
shape-changing in Wagner's operatic Ring cyċle.)
    The Vala named *Oromë* in Quenya and *Araw* in Sindarin was
named *Béma* ['beːma] 'trumpet-man' (< OE *bēme, bīeme* 'trumpet') in Rohan and the Vales of Anduin. Tom Bombadil's name
among the same folk was *Orald* ['ɔɹɑld] (in Wessex dialect
Oreald) 'very very old', cognate with Modern Germ *uralt* of
the same meaning. *Saruman* (Sarumann ['sɑɹo̩ˌmɒnn]) (Wessex
dialect *Searomann*) 'skill-person, cunning-person' is a translation of the wizard's Sindarin name *Curunír* 'Man-of-Skill'.
    The Rohirrim also named places in their own tongue,
translating the meaning of the Common Speech or Elvish names
with more or less accuracy. *Minas Tirith/the Tower of Guard*
they named *Mundburg* ['mɒndˌboɹɣ] 'protecting-city'. *Gondor*
'Stone-land' they named *Stoning-land* (Stāningland ['staːnɪŋg-
ˌlɒnd]) 'stone-people-land'. The region of *Anórien* they
named *Sunlending* (Sunnlending ['sɒnnˌlɛndɪŋg]) 'sun-land-
people'. The element *-ing* originally meant 'son of', later
was used more generally for 'descendant of' or merely 'people
of', and only later still became a general adjectival ending.
The insistance of the Rohirrim in including a word for
'people' in these names—though no such occurs in the originals—indicates that, to them, psychologically, it was
the race and kindred that was more important in determining
who you were than the place where you dwelt. Their own name
for themselves was *Eorlingas* ['ɛɔɹˌlɪŋgas] 'the people of
Eorl'. The name of their old homeland in the north was actually their own name for themselves *Éothéod* (Ēoþēod ['eˑɔ-
ˌðeˑɔd]) 'horse-people'. Their new land they named 'the Mark
of the Riders' *Riddena-mearc* ['rɪdˌdɛnɑˌmæɞ̆ɹk], later shortened to *Riddermark* (Riddermærc ['rɪddɛɹˌmæɹk]) (see *Riddermark* in the Index). *Mark* means 'border (land)'.
    In the Vales of Anduin dwelt one *Beorn* [beˑɔɹn] 'man;
prince, warrior'; a word cognate with OHG *baro* 'warrior,
man', whence *baron*. In early medieval times it was not an
uncommon name, and came to be considered the equivalent of
the Old Norse name *Bjǫrn*, which means 'bear'. The name is
therefore a suitable one for a were-bear, though actually
the two names are not cognates: *bjǫrn* is related to OE
bera (> *bear*) and OHG *bero*, and originally meant 'brown one'.
His son's name was *Grimbeorn* ['gɹɪmˌbeˑɔrn] 'fierce-warrior,
severe-prince'.

Other Names of Rohan

    Names of Men: *Déorwine* ['deˑɔ̆ɹˌwɪnɛ] 'fierce-friend'
(see *Déor* above), perhaps understood as 'dear-friend'; *Dún-
here* ['duːnˌçɛɹɛ] 'hill-warrior'; *Elfhelm* ['ɛlfˌhɛlm] 'elf-
protection'; *Éothain* (Ēoþegn ['eˑɔ̆ˌðɛyn]) 'horse-servant';
Fastred (Fæstred ['fæstˌɹɛd]) 'firm-counsel, constant'; *Freca*

218

([ˈfɹɛkɑ] FREAK) 'warrior, hero' related to *frek* 'greedy'; *Garúlf* [ˈgɑɹˌuːlf] 'spear-wolf'; *Grimbold* [ˈgɹɪmˌbɔld] 'fierce-bold'; *Guthláf* (Gúðláf [ˈgoðˌlɑːf]) 'war-remnant'; *Harding* [ˈhɑɹdɪŋ] 'strong-one'; *Herefara* [ˈhɛɹɛˌvɑɹɑ] 'host-wanderer'; *Herubrand* [ˈhɛɹoˌbɹɒnd] (in Wessex dialect *Heorubrand*) 'sword-brand'; *Horn* ([hɔɹn] HORN); *Ingold* [ˈɪŋˌgɔld] 'king(?)-gold'; *Wulf* ([wolf] WOLF).

Names of Steeds: *Arod* [ˈɑɹɔd] 'swift'; *Felaróf* [ˈfɛlɑˌɹoːf] 'very-strong, very-vigourous'; *Firefoot* (Fȳrfōt [ˈfyːɹˌvoːt]); *Hasufel* [hɑzoˌvɛl] 'grey-skin'; *Lightfoot* (Līhtfōt [ˈliːçtˌfoːt]); *Shadowfax* (Sceadufæx [ˈʃɑdoˌvæks]) 'shadow-coat', that is, 'having shadow-grey mane (and coat)'; *Snowmane* (Snāwmana [ˈsnɑːwˌmɒnɑ]); *Stybba* ([ˈstɥbbɑ] STUBBY); *Windfola* ([ˈwɪndˌvɔlɑ] WIND-FOAL). The descendants of Felaróf were known as the *mearas* [ˈmæðɹɑs]; this is the plural of OE *mearh* 'horse, steed'. The feminine is *mere*, whence Mod. Eng. *mare*.

Names of Swords: *Gúthwine* (Gúðwine [ˈguːðˌwɪnɛ]) 'war-friend'; *Herugrim* [ˈhɛɹoˌgɹɪm] (in Wessex dialect *Heorugrim* 'sword-fierce'.

Names of Peoples

Most of the race names are of Old English derivation, probably representing in some cases the Common Speech form, but in others Tolkien indicates particularly that the form found is that used in the language of the Vales of Anduin and of Rohan.

Elf, of course, is OE *elf* [ɛlf] (in Wessex dialect *ælf*).

Ent, we are told, was the form of the name of this people in the language of Rohan and in the languages of the Vales of Anduin (III:408;G:164). OE *ent* [ɛnt] means 'giant'. It may either be supposed that Tolkien used the Old English word because of a slight resemblance to S *Onod* (pl. *Enyd*), or that the Old English word is indeed to be taken as a true survival from the Third Age, though with distorted meaning.

Orc, Tolkien indicates, 'is the form of the name that other races had for this foul people as it was in the language of Rohan' (III:409). In Old English *orc* [ɔɹk] is used of some kind of demonic creature. A plural form *orcnéas* is also found. The derivation of these words in Old English is not known, though some have suggested Lat. *Orcus*, a name for the god of the dead; but this too is of uncertain origin. We are probably to suppose that OE *orc*, and possibly Lat. *Orcus*, are true survivals of Third Age tradition.

Púkel-men contains OE *púcel* [ˈpuːkɛl] 'goblin', a diminutive of the stem *puc-* 'goblin'. The traditional English goblin Puck has a name from this stem. It also survives in Mod. Eng. *pug*.

GIVING OF NAMES

Warg, the name given to the kind of wolf found in the
Misty Mountains and in the Vales of Anduin, represents OE
wearg [wæðɹy] 'outlaw, felon', used metaphorically to mean
'wolf'. However, its original base meaning was 'wolf', a
meaning still retained by ON *vargr* 'wolf', used metaphorically to mean 'outlaw, felon'.

Woses is a modernization (= Westronization) of Old
English (= Rohirric) *wāsa* ['wɑːzɑ], pl. *wasan*. It is only
found in Old English in the combination form *wuduwāsa* 'wood-
wose', indicating some kind of wild man, or satyr, or demon
living in the forest. It still survives in heraldry as
woodhouse, the name for the wild hairy man dressed in leaves
often used as a supporter.

Etten- in the place names *Ettendales* and *Ettenmoors* is
an old word for 'giant, from OE *eoten* 'giant', cognate with
ON *jǫtunn* 'giant'. Aragorn explains *Ettenmoors* as being 'the
troll-fells north of Rivendell' (I:212), so we might take
etten as an older word for 'troll', perhaps still used as
the normal word in the speech of the Men of the Vales of
Anduin and in Rohan in the form *eoten*. Or it might refer
to the Stone-giants of the Misty Mountains who appear in *The
Hobbit*, and are probably best taken as a peculiar variety of
troll; larger than the normal variety, tending to be less
hostile. (*Troll* itself is a word of Old Norse origin,
adopted into English from Scandinavian folk takes in the
middle of the nineteenth century. It was originally used
to mean 'giant, monster', but in modern folklore of Sweden
and Denmark is applied rather to creatures of the Dwarf
sort.)

NORTHERN NAMES

Tolkien writes:

> Gimli's own name, however, and the names of all his
> kin, are of Northern (Mannish) origin. Their own secret
> and 'inner names,' their true names, the Dwarves have
> never revealed to any one of alien race. Not even on
> their tombs to they inscribe them. (III:411)

> The still more northerly language of Dale is in this
> book seen only in the names of the Dwarves that came
> from that region and so used the languages of the Men
> there, taking their 'outer' names in that tongue.
> (III:415)

For the original Northern names, in a language related
to Westron, Tolkien substitutes names taken from the Scandinavian tongues, mostly from variant forms of a list of Dwarf
names which is to be found in manuscripts of both the poem

GIVING OF NAMES

Vǫluspá 'Wise-woman's Prophecy' (included in the collection
of Icelandic mythological and heroic poetry known as the
Elder Edda or Poetic Edda) and in the *Gylfaginning* 'Beguiling
of Gylfi' in the Prose Edda, a handbook of poetic lore and
technique by Snorri Sturlason. The names appear somewhat
Anglicized by Tolkien, mainly in his omission of the final
r or *n* from many of the names, and by his change of *v* to
w. (In Old Norse and most Germanic languages original *w*
became *v*, but it remained *w* in English.) This presumably
indicates the names are to be pronounced as seems most natural in English, though use of [ɑ] instead of [æ] for *a*
would be desirable.

The dwarf list, with its introduction, is given here,
following the version found in *Die Lieder der Älterene Edde
(Sæmundar Edda)* (ed. Karl Hildebrand, Schöingh, 1904). The
text followed includes all the names used by Tolkien save
for *Óin*, and is preferable for our purposes to the lists in
the versions of the Prose Edda which are longer, but omit
several of Tolkien's names. I have ventured to change the
text in three places following some of the variant versions:
I have placed *Óinn* in the last line of stanza 11 where the
original has *Ái* (a name repeated in stanza 15), and replaced
Aurvangr 'Gravel-plain' (stanza 13) and *Hlévangr* 'Sheltered-
plain' (stanza 15) by the probably more correct *Aurvargr* and
Hlévargr. Names used by Tolkien are underscored.

9. Geŋgu regin ǫll   á røkstóla
   Went the gods all   *to council*

   ginnheilug goþ,   ok of þat gǽttusk:
   very holy gods,   *and over that took charge:*

   hverr skyldi dverga   drótt of skepja
   who   should dwarves'   *race   create*

   ór Brimis blóþi   ok ór Blaíns leggjum.
   from Briming-one's blood and from Black-one's limbs.

10. Þar vas Mótsognir   mǽztr of orþinn
    There was Rage-roaring   master   made of

    dverga allra,   en <u>Durinn</u> annarr;
    all dwarves   *and Sleeper next;*

    þeir mannlíkun   mǫrg of gørþu
    they manlike forms   many of   did make

    dvergar í jǫrþu,   sem <u>Durinn</u> sagþi.
    dwarves in the earth, as   Sleeper said.

11. Nyi ok Niþi,   Norþri ok Suþri
    New-moon and Old-moon, North-one and South-one

    Austri ok Vestri,   Alþjófr, <u>Dvalinn</u>,
    East-one and West-one, All-thief, Torpid,

Nár ok Naïnn,   Nípingr, Daïnn,
Corpse and Corpselike, Pinch, Deadlike,

Bífurr, Bǫfurr,   Bǫmburr, Nóri,
Trembling, ???,   Bulging, Peewee,

Ánn ok Ónarr,   Óinn, Mjǫþvitnir.
Blade(?) and Starer, Fearful, Mead-wolf.

12. Viggr ok Gandalfr,   Vindalfr, Þraïnn
    Spear and Sorcery-elf,   Wind-elf,   Stubborn

    Þekkr ok Þórinn,   Þrór, Vitr ok Litr,
    Beloved and Bold,   Boar, Wise and Ruddy,

    Nyr ok Nýráþr,   nú hefk dverga
    New and Ingenious,   now have I dwarves

    — Reginn ok Ráþsviþr —   rétt of talþa
    — Powerful and Counsel-wise — rightly told of.

13. Fíli, Kíli,   Fundinn, Náli,
    File, Wedge,   Found-one, Axle,

    Heptifíli,   Hannarr, Sviurr,
    Handle-file,   Skilled,   ???

    Frár, Hornbori,   Frǽgi ok Lóni,
    Swift, Hornborer,   Famous and Lazy,

    Aurvargr, Jari,   Eikinskjaldi.
    Gravel-wolf, Warrior, Of-the-Oakenshield.

14. Mál es dverga   i Dvalins liþi
    The account of the dwarves in Torpid's people

    ljóna kindum   til Lofars telja;
    to the sons of men down to Stooper is to be told;

    þeir es sóttu   frá salar steini
    they who sought   from the stone of the halls

    aurvanga sjǫt   til jǫruvalla.
    to gravel-plain's seat to sand-fields.

15. Þar vas Draupnir   ok Dolgþrasir,
    There was Dripper   and Battle-eager,

    Hǫr, Haugspori,   Hlévargr, Gloïnn,
    High, Barrow-treader, Lee-wolf,   Glowing-one,

    Dóri, Óri,   Dúfr, Andvari,
    Borer, Furious,   Nodder, Gentle-breeze,

    Skirfir, Virfir,   Skáfiþr, Aï.
    Maker of Herring- , Dyer, Slant-board, Great-grandfather.
    bone panelling

16. Alfr ok Yngvi,   Eikinskjaldi,
    Elf and ???,   Of-the-Oakenshield,

    Fjalarr ok Frosti,   Fiþr ok Ginnarr;
    Paneller and Frosty,   Wizard and Deceiver;

    þat mun ǽ uppi,   meþan ǫld lifir,
    that shall be aye remembered, while men live,

langniþja tal, *til* Lofars hafat.
the genealogical reckoning, down to Stooper.

The meanings of all these names are not as clear as
the above translations suggest. *Bífurr* might also be from
Frisian or Low German *bever* 'beaver', often used in the
sense of 'hard worker' as in the English expressions 'busy as
a beaver' and 'eager beaver'. In Modern Icelandic *bifurr*
means not only 'beaver' but 'mood, thought, inclination'.
Durinn is to be understood as 'Sleeper, Sleepy' as a development of the stem *dúrr-* 'slumber, sleep'. This is probably
what Tolkien intends, for 'the Sleeper' is a good outer name
for the Longbeards to give to their first king who, it is
prophesied, will one day awake from his sleep and again
reign in Moria, of which the crown of stars in the Mirrormere is a sign. But *Durin* may rather be from *dyrr* 'door'.
　　Bǫmburr is originally derived from *bumba* 'drum'. In
Modern Norwegian it is used of a pregnant woman with a swol-
len figure, and in Modern Icelandic it is used not only for
'drum', but for the belly of a pot.
　　Gandalfr or *Gandálfr* is found outside the list applied
to men. The precise meaning of *gand-* is not known. It is
used in old Icelandic literature in words and phrases denoting magical activity such as *gamdum renna* 'to run by *gand*', a
term for astral projection. In Chapter 125 of *Njalssaga* a
certain Hildiglum sees a figure riding furiously through the
air, He is later told, 'You have seen the *gandreiðr*, and
that is always a portent of disaster'. In other contexts
gand refers to a magic wand or crystal. *Gand-* is also an
initial theme in other Germanic names, such as *Gandabert*,
Gandalbald, *Ganthare*, and a name found in such forms as
Gandulf, *Gandolpho*, *Gandolf* in which the second element is
-wulf 'wolf'. Its original meaning is not known.
　　Þrór 'boar' is from a stem meaning 'to expand', and
Tolkien's *Thrór* expands the diggings and wealth of the
Lonely Mountain. His son *Thráin* 'Stubborn' lives up to his
name by stubbornly going off to Erebor again.
　　Narvi is one of Tolkien's dwarf names that does not
appear in the list from the Eddas, but it does occur in the
Prose Edda, spelt both *Narvi* and *Narfi*. It is the name of
one of the sons of the god Loki, and its meaning is doubtful.

The Dwarf-names used by Tolkien which are not found in
the Eddas are derived from Old Norse elements on patterns
suggested by the names taken from the list.
　　Balin may be from *bál* 'fire', and mean 'Burning-one'.
(The *-inn* termination in these names indicates a past participle form.) But the name is familiar to English readers
from Malory's *Le Morte Darthur*, Book II of which recounts the
adventures of a certain Syr Balyn le Savage. The name

is usually modernized to *Balin* in editions which do not
retain the original spellings. In Malory's source for this
tale, the so-called *Huth Merlin*, the knight is named *Balaain*.
The tale climaxes in a battle between Balin/Balaain and his
brother Balan/Balaan in which both are slain. A source for
this is sometimes seen in the *Historia Regum Britanniae* of
Geoffrey of Monmouth. Geoffrey tells us of a British king
named *Belinus* who wars against his brother *Brennius*. The
names look suspiciously like Latinizations of the names of
two British gods—*Beli* and *Brân* is they are called in med-.
ieval literature. Indeed, in Welsh translations of the *Historia* these are the forms that appear. So what may be
preserved here are different distorted versions of a conflict between two cults, or perhaps an account of a cult in
in which the strife between two gods was of importance.
In the medieval Welsh collection of tales known as *The Mabinogion*, in the story 'Branwen daughter of Llŷr', the conflict
occurs again in another guise. Here Brân is a king of Britain, but also a giant, whose huge size is made much of. He
is slain while on an expedition to Ireland, whereupon a
certain Caswallawn son of Beli(!) accomplishes the death of
Brân's son Caradoc, who had been left as regent, and takes
the throne. Beli is here regarded as having reigned before
Brân—the sequence actually runs as follows: Beli, Lludd son
of Beli, Brân son of Llŷr, Caradoc son of Brân as regent,
Caswallawn son of Beli—so that here the feud between the
gods is made one between royal houses. Now to the point of
this digression: a passage in the Arthurian romance *Erec et.
Enide* of the twelfth century French poet Chrétien de Troyes
reads as follows:

> The lord of the dwarfs came next, Bilis, the king of
> Antipodes. This king of whom I speak was a dwarf himself
> and own brother of Brien. Bilis, on the one hand, was
> the smallest of all the dwarfs, while his brother Brien
> was a half-foot or full foot taller than any other knight
> in the kingdom.

Like the Brân of *The Mabinogion* Chrétien's Brien is the tall-
est in the kingdom. Just as Brân is brother to Beli in the
tradition recorded in Geoffrey, so Chrétien's Brien has a
brother named Bilis. Accordingly, it is suggested that the
gold Beli—whence Malory's *Balyn*—was a dwarf.

Borin might be intended to derived from ON *bora* 'to bore
holes' and thus mean 'Borer'. Compare *Dóri* and *Hornbori* in
the Dwarf list.

Farin is ON *farinn* and means 'travelled-one'.

Flói might be connected with ON *flóa* 'to boil, to
flood'. *Flói* does occur as a word with the meaning 'marshy
moor' or 'bay, large firth', which may seem inappropriate.

But *Lóni*, as Björn Fromén has pointed out to me, also means
'little bay' as well as 'lazy' as I gave in may translation
of the name in the list, and Tolkien may have used *Flói* as
another name of the same sort.
Frerin may be intended to be related to the Dwarf-name
Frár 'Swift', and mean the same. Or it might represent
frérinn 'frozen' (cf. *Frosti* in the list), the short *e* being
a typographical error.
Frór is a variant spelling of *Frár* 'Swift', found in
the Dwarf list.
Gimli appears once in the *Vǫluspá* of the Poetic Edda
and three times in the Prose Edda. It is a dative form.
The *Vǫluspá* prophecies that at the end of our present world
a new one shall rise in which a gold hall shall stand *á gimli*
where the righteous shall dwell for ever. In the Prose Edda
it is said that this hall *á gimli* stands at the southern
end of heaven, and shall remain when heaven and earth have
passed away. There are three heavens, each above and to the
south of the one below, This hall is the third, and is now
inhabited solely by the Light-elves. The nominative form of
this name is usually given as *Gimlé* from *gim* 'fire' + *hlé*
'shelter, lee', though Grimm (p. 823) prposed **gimill* as an
Icelandic form of OHG and Old Saxon *himil* 'heaven'. As a
personal name, *Gimli* would mean 'One-of-Gimlé/Gimill'. And
it is said that Gimli did finally go to the Undying Lands.
Gróin and *Grór* are from *gróa* 'to grow', both meaning
'Growing-one'. As already indicated *Thrór* can be translated
'Increasing-one', and some versions of the Dwarf list give
the name *Thróin* (*Þróinn*) with the same meaning.
Dís, the name of Thorin's sister, is an element found
in Nordic names (*Herdís, Hjordís, Jodís, Valdís, Vigdís*)
and usually taken to mean 'sister'. Its original meaning
was probably 'goddess'.

It is not certain that *Mim*, the name of a Dwarf of the
First Age (TB:8), is intended to be of Old Norse formation.
If it is, it can be connected with various figures in Norse
myth and legend which probably derive from a single original.
In German heroic literature Mime is a dwarf smith who counts
among his pupils the famous Velent (Weland). In the Norse
Þiðrekssaga this smith appears as *Mimi* and raises the young
hero Sigurð. In Saxo's compilation of Danish saga the
hero Hotherus must obtain an enchanted sword from a *sylvarum
satyrus* named *Mimingus*. Danish ballads tell of the dwarf-
knight *Miemering* who was also versed in smith-craft. In the
Eddas and in Snorri Sturlasson's *Heimskringla* a mysterious
Mimir appears as guardian of the fountain of wisdom, and
later his head, prserved by the god *Óðinn*, gives wise advise.
The name would be based on Gmc. **mim-* 'measure, think,
reckon'.

There aré a few non-Dwarf names of Scandinavian origin also.

Bain represents ON *Beinn* 'Mover'.

Bard and *Brand* are common Germanic elements meaning respectively 'Battle-axe' and 'Brand'.

Forn, one of the names of Tom Bombadil means 'Old, Ancient'. •

Golfimbul means 'Wind-terrible'. *Gol-* means 'wind'. *Fimbul* means 'might' or 'great'; it is used only five times in Old Icelandic poetry. The German cognate *fimmel* means 'iron wedge', and Swedish *fimmel* is the name for the handle of a sledge hammer. As to the derivation of *golf* from this name, in fact it is not certain where the name of the game came from. Danish *kolf* 'club' or Scottish *gowf* 'strike' are the usual suggestions. Of course, we are probably to suppose that Tolkien has substituted *golf* for a Hobbit game using some sort of stick or club to knock a ball into or through some kind of opening, and then modeled the name *Golfimbul* to parallel the relationship between the real name of the goblin and the original game.

The Dwarf names use rhyme to show close family relationship. *Thrór*, *Frór*, and *Grór* are brothers, as are *Thorin* and *Frerin*, and *Fíli* and *Kíli*. Rhyme connecting two brothers with their father is seen with *Balin* and *Dwalin* the sons of *Fundin* (the father rhyme being less full) and with *Óin* and *Glóin* the sons of *Gróin*. Simple father and son rhymes are seen in *Óin* son of *Glóin*, *Dáin* I son of *Náin* II, and *Dáin* II son of *Náin*. Less full rhyme appear in *Fundin* son of *Farin* son of *Borin*. In this last the first two names alliterate. Alliteration linking father and son is to be found in *Thorin* I son of *Thráin* I, in *Thorin* II son of *Thráin* II son of *Thrór*, and in *Gimli* son of *Glóin*. The only example of of alliteration between the names of brothers is the pair *Bofur* and *Bombur* (H:174).

THE NAMES OF THE EARLY EDAIN AND OLD ENGLISH

Some of the names of the Edain of the First Age, presented as Elvish, are close to or indentical with Old English forms. *Beren* is an adjective meaning 'of barley', and is found as an alternative spelling for both *biren* 'she-bear' and *berœrn* 'barn'. *Dior* is a variant of *Dēor* 'brave, fierce; dear'. *Hador* means 'brightness'.

In *Eärendel* is seen OE *earendel*, interpreted in glosses by Lat. *jubar* 'brightness, light'. It may have been reduced to meaning just that, but was earlier the name of a star or planet (probably Venus). It is used in this earlier sense

GIVING OF NAMES

in a fragment of an Old English hymn in the *Codex Exoniensis*:

Eala Earendel, engla beorhtast,   O Earendel, brightest of angels,
ofer middangeard monnum sended,   over Middle-earth sent to men,
and sõõfæsta sunnan leoma   and true light of the sun
torht ofer tunglas, þu tïda   radiant above the stars, which
   gehwane   thou
of sylfum þe symle Inïfhtes!   of thyself ever enlighteneth!

    The Old Norse form of the name is *Ǫrvandill*. In the Prose Edda it is told that the god Thór carried him out of Jǫtunheim (Giant-home) in a basket on his back, but one toe stuck out and became frozen, whereupon Thór broke it off and flung it into the sky to become the star named *Ǫrvandils-tá*. The same personage appears in German literature as *Erentel*, and is hero of a poem in which he suffers shipwreck and wins the hand of Breide, fairest of women.

THE HOBBIT MONTH NAMES

    Tolkien represents the names of the months in the Shire by modernized forms of the Old English month names as follows:

1. Afteryule *OE æfter Gēola 'after Winter-Solstice'.*
2. Solmath *OE Solmõnað 'Mud-month'. Sol means 'mud, soil'.*
3. Rethe *OE Hrēõmõnað 'Glory-month'. Bede in De Temporium Ratione claims Hretha was the name of a goddess.*
4. Astron *OE Ēastron 'Easter'. Bede calls this Eosturmonath and claims Eostre was the name of a goddess.*
5. Thrimidge *OE Þri-milce 'Three milk-givings'. Bede says that at this time of year cows were milked three times a day.*
6. Forelithe *OE ǣrra Līða 'before Līða'. The word Līða probably originally meant 'moon'. It would seem to refer, in this case, to either the first new moon before or after the summer solstice.*
7. Afterlithe *OE æfter Līða 'after Līða'.*
8. Wedmath *OE Wēodmõnað 'Grass-month'. OE wēod becomes Modern English weed.*
9. Halimath *OE Hāligmõnað 'Holy-month'. Bede says this was the month for making sacrifice.*
10. Winterfilth *OE Winterfylleð 'Winter-filling'. This month filled out the end of the year before a New Year reckoned in the autumn.*
11. Blotmath *OE Blõtmõnað 'Sacrifice-month'. In this month surplus stock was slaughtered to prepare for winter.*
12. Foreyule *OE ǣrra Gēola 'before Winter-Solstice'.*

    Of the Bree month names that differed from those in most of the Shire, *Harvestmath* (Hærfestmõnað) and *Yulemath*

227

GIVING OF NAMES

(Gēolmōnaŏ) are genuine Old English month names found as
variants for *Hāligmōnaŏ* and *ǣrra Gēola*. The rest are good
Old English forms. *Frery* (the Bree name for *Afteryule*) is
frēorig 'freezing'. *Chithing* (for *Astron*) is from *cīŏing*
'germinating'. *Mede* (for *Afterlithe*) is *mǣd* 'meadow, mead'.
Wintring (for *Winterfilth*) means 'Wintry'. *Blooting* (for
Blotmath) is from *blōt* 'sacrifice'.

Bibliography

Ackerman, Robert W. *An Index of the Arthurian Names in Middle English.*
Stanford University Publications, Language and Literature X.
Stanford-London, 1952.
Chrétien de Troyes. 'Erec et Enide' in *Arthurian Romances.* Trans. W. W.
Comfort. Everyman's: London, 1955.
Epstein, E. L. 'The Novels of J. R. R. Tolkien and the Ethnology of Med-
ieval Christendom', *Philological Quarterly* 48:4 (Oct. 1969), 517-
525.
Flutre, L.-F. *Table des Noms Propres avec toutes leurs variantes figur-
ant dans les Romans du Moyen Age écrits en français ou en provençal et
actuellement publiés ou analysés.* Centre d'Études Supérieurs de Civi-
lization Médiévale: Poitiers, 1962.
Gould, C. N. 'Dwarf-Names: a study in Old Icelandic religion', *Proceedings of the Modern Language Association,* 44 (Dec. 1929), 939-67.
Grimm, Jacob. *Teutonic Mythology.* Trans. James Steven Stallybrass. 4
volumes. 1883, 1888; rpt. New York: Dover Publications, 1967.
Hall, John R. Clark. *A Concise Anglo-Saxon Dictionary.* 4th ed. Cam-
bridge: University Press, 1969.
Klein, Ernest. *A Comprehensive Etymological Dictionary of the English
Language.* Amsterdam, London, New York: Elsevier Pub. Co., 1971.
Langlois, Ernest. *Table des Noms Propres de toute nature compris dans
les Chansons de Geste impreós.* Paris: 1904.
Malory, Sir Thomas. *Malory: Works.* Ed. Eugène Vinaver. London: Oxford
Univ. Press, 1956.
Morlet, Marie-Thérèse. *Les Noms de personne sur le territoire de l'anci-
enne Gaule du VIe au XIIe siècle.* Paris: Éditions du Centre national
de la Recherche scientifique, 1968.
Ryan, J. S. 'German Mythology Applied—The Extension of the Literary
Folk Memory', *Folklore,* 78:77 (Spring, 1966), pp. 45-59.
Searle, William George. *Onomasticon Anglo-Saxonicum.* Cambridge: Univ.
Press, 1897.
Siebs, Benno Eide. *Die Personennamen der Germanen.* Niederwalluf, Weis-
baden: Dr. Martin Sändig oHG, 1970.
Sommer, H. Oskar. *The Vulgate Version of the Arthurian Romances.* 8 vol.
Washington, 1908-16; see Vol. 8: *Index of Names and Places to Volumes
I-VII.*
Vigfusson, Gudbrand. *An Icelandic-English Dictionary.* Oxford: Clarendon
Press, 1957.
West, G. D. *An Index of Proper Names in French Arthurian Verse Romances
1150-1300.* Toronto: Univ. of Toronto Press, 1969.
Wythycombe, E. S. *The Oxford Dictionary of English Christian Names.* 2nd
ed. Oxford: Clarendon Press, 1950.
Yonge, Charlotte M. *History of Christian Names.* London, 1863.

(Various other sources have been used to verify minor pieces of information, some of which are given in the body of the article.)

WRITING SYSTEMS

THE TENGWAR OF FËANOR

Laurence J. Krieg

[This article was originally intended to appear as a separate pamphlet, and was written accordingly. The version which appears here has been revised by the editor of this book to make it more useful in its present context. —J.A.]

<u>HOW TO LEARN THE TENGWAR</u>

THE BEST WAY TO START OUT is to decipher some Sindarin.
Begin with the Moria Gate inscription (I:318/399). (In
this section page references are made first to the three
volume hardcover editions, and then, following the slash
/, to the Ballantine edition.) Don't look at the transliteration at the bottom of the page until you have done your
own transcription using the Tengwar Fact Sheet Chart on page
237 or the chart of the Mode of Beleriand on page 247. (On
the Tengwar Fact Sheet chart the Sindarin values for the letters are in the lower right-hand corner of each box.) Then
take Tolkien's transliteration at the bottom of the Moria
Gate inscription and see if you can put it back into Sindarin without looking at the inscription itself until you're
done with the whole thing.
    The other Sindarin inscription is of 'A Elbereth Gil-
thoniel' (R:62). Transliterate it into roman letters, check
your efforts, and then work from the poem as Tolkien gives it
in roman script to tengwar. When you are satisfied with your
ability to transliterate these two, try a few other Sindarin
words and phrases, such as:
- Gandalf's fire-lighting spell (I:312/390).
- Gandalf's door-opening spell (I:320/400).
- Gilraen's *linnod* at her parting with Aragorn, her son (III:
    342/426).

231

- the Sindarin parts of the praise to the Hobbits:
  Cuio i Pheriain anann! Aglar'ni Pheriannath!
  Daur a Berhael, Connin en Annûn! Eglerio!
- the Elvish names on the maps, most of which are Sindarin.
- the names of the Heirs of Isildur after Eärendur (III:318/
  394).

After you are familiar with Sindarin, you will need to
learn how to read vowels written as *tehtar*. Read about vowels on page 236 following, then start with some Quenya transliteration. The only sample of Quenya done by Tolkien is *Ai!
laurie lantar lassi súrinen...* 'Galadriel's Farewell' (R:57).
Quenya is quite different from Sindarin, so this is likely to
go slowly at first. Quenya values for the letters are in the
upper right-hand corner of each box of the Tengwar Fact Sheet,
or turn to the chart of late Quenya values on page 245. When
you have transliterated this poem both ways and feel that
you understand the way Quenya writing works, try transliterating some other words and phrases in Quenya, such as:
- Gildor's greeting to Frodo in the Shire (I:90/119); the
  last word is given with a slightly different ending in
  different editions (see page 20).
- Elendil's words when he arrived on the shores of Middle-
  earth (III:245/303).
- the names of the Kings and Queens of Númenor up to *Tar-
  Calmacil* (III:315/390).
- the names of the Kings and Stewards of Gondor, and of the
  Kings of Arnor up to Eärendur (III:318/394).

The only sample of Black Speech is the Ring Inscription
(I:59/94; transliterated I:267/333). Note that the tehta *⌒*
is *u* here. There are no transcriptions of Westron.

Finally, there is the title-page inscription, one of
the two samples of English that we have. It is more difficult than the other inscriptions because it uses many abbreviations, the letters overlap and tangle, and (more basically) the tengwar were not designed for the English language,
and Tolkien did not make a systematic attempt to adapt the
elvish letters to our tongue. Read the paragraph about this
inscription (III:400/499) and set to work with the title
page and either the central values in the Tengwar Fact Sheet
or those in the chart for Westron and Black Speech on page
247. The values of the letters correspond generally to those
of Westron/Black Speech.

After deciphering all the inscriptions and transliterating into tengwar most of the Quenya and Sindarin phrases and
names—assuming you are still interested in the tengwar—you
can devise for yourself a mode for writing English. This is
necessary if you want to keep in practice, since you will

need to read and write more in order to do so, but there isn't enough Quenya or Sindarin to make this possible.

Making up your own mode for English can be a complicated task, but it doesn't HAVE to be if you assign one tengwa to each roman letter and follow the English spelling. The alternatives—phonemic or morphophonemic modes—are more exciting but require more patience.

TENGWAR FACT SHEET NOTES

THE PURPOSE OF THE CHART on page 237 is to help people look up information on all modes of the tengwar quickly and easily. It can be duplicated and carried around with one.

TO START WITH THE BASICS, here are the meanings of some terms:

TENGWAR: 'Letters'. One of them is *tengwa* 'letter'.

TINCOTÉMA: 'Tinco-series'—that is, the series of letters in column I, rows 1-6. These are DENTALS: sounds make—like the letter *tinco*—with the tip of the tongue against (or close to) the teeth. (The name of each letter contains an example of the sound involved in Quenya, usually the first sound in the name.)

PARMATÉMA: 'Parma-series'—letters which, like the letter *parma*, are pronounced with the lips.

CALMATEMA: 'calma-series', in Quenya and Sindarin pronounced with the back of the tongue close to the roof of the mouth.

QUESSETÉMA: 'quesse-series', in Quenya and Sindarin, made with the back of the tongue close to the roof of the mouth while the lips are slightly pursed to make a *w*-sound.

TEHTA: 'mark', a diacritical mark used with the Tengwar consonants to indicate vowels, added length, nasality, and other such things.

QUENYA: 'speech', the language of the High Elves who crossed the Sea during the First Age and dwelt in Eldamar. Some Quenya-speakers were exiles in Middle-earth during the First, Second, and Third Ages.

SINDARIN: 'grey-elven', the language of the Grey Elves who remained in Middle-earth during the First, Second, and Third Ages.

WESTRON: the 'Common Speech' spoken or understood by most men, hobbits, and other creatures during the Third Age of Middle-earth.

BLACK SPEECH: the language used by Sauron for inscribing the One Ring.

EXPLANATION OF THE KEY

The Key is in the lower right-hand corner of the chart. This explanation starts with the upper left of the key and works across.

STD NO.: 'Standard Number'. Nos. 1-36 were given their
numbers by Tolkien in his chart (III:396). The rest are num-
bered here in hopes of providing a standard by which we can
refer to the rest of the letters and signs without writing
them down.

QUENYA NAME: Since speakers of the Quenya language first
used the Tengwar as they are shown here, the names they gave
the letters became standard in Middle-earth no matter what
language the letters were used for (III:400f). Most of the
names are common words that begin with the letter's sound; in
rows 2 and 4 the letter's sound is preceded by a vowel as
those sounds did not occur at the beginnings of words in
Quenya. Tehtar had no names that we know of, except for the
length mark, which was called *andaith*.

The Quenya name is written first in tengwar, then in
roman letters. We don't have Tolkien's spellings of the
names in Tengwar, so they are our best guesses. Probably
most of the *a*'s were not marked, since they were predictable
(III:399). Some of the letters originally had one sound in
Quenya but gradually changed to another. When this happened
the name sometimes changed; for these letters the old name
and the new name are separated by a slash (/).

QUENYA, SINDARIN AND WESTRON/BLACK SPEECH VALUES are
given in the right-hand portion of each box. Center left is
Westron/Black Speech (both languages used mostly the same
letter values), upper right is Quenya, and lower right is
Sindarin. In each case the small roman letter(s) are the
pronunciation, represented by symbols of the International
Phonetic Alphabet; the larger italic letters below are letters used by Tolkien when transliterating the Tengwar into
our writing.

Some of these letters are preceded by an asterisk,
which means that they do not occur in any of the inscriptions but that their pronunciation is guessed from the way
the system works. When the letter and/or pronunciation does
not occur or has not been observed in the words of one of the
languages, a dash (-) has been placed where it would have
been.

CORRESPONDING RUNES: With the earliest runes (cirth)
there was no systematic relationship between the shape of a
rune and its sound. But Daeron revised the cirth so that the
shape of each rune bore a regular relationship to the shape
of the corresponding tengwa. For example, when the bow of
the tengwar is doubled, the branch of the rune is doubled
(as with *tinco* ᴘ:ᚱ and *ando* ᴘᴏ :ᚠ). When the stem of the
tengwa is lowered, the branch of the rune points right; when
the stem of the tengwa is raised, the branch of the rune
points left (as with *tinco* ᴘ:ᚱ and *thúle* ᑋ:ᚵ).

The chart gives the corresponding rune for each tengwa;
but for historical and other reasons a rune is not always
PRONOUNCED the same way as its corresponding tengwa. For the
pronunciation of the runes, see the very clear and easy-to-
use chart in III:402-03, and pages 284 and 286 of this book.

TRANSLATION OF QUENYA NAME: What the name of the letter
means in English. This is given by Tolkien (III:401).

INDIVIDUAL LETTERS:

9. Originally pronounced in Quenya as θ = *th* in *thing*,
it came to be pronounced s in Quenya of the Third Age.

10. The Sindarin f sound was sometimes spelled *ph* by
Tolkien in his transcriptions. A note (III:392) explains:
'It is used (*a*) where the *f*-sound occurs at the end of a
word, as in *alph* "swan"; (*b*) where the *f*-sound is related to
or derived from a *p*, as in *i-Pheriannath* "the Halflings"
(*perian*); (*c*) in the middle of a few words where it represents a long *ff* (from *pp*) as in *Ephel* "outer fence"; and (*d*)
in Adûnaic and Westron, as in *Ar-Pharazôn* (*pharaz* 'gold').'

11. This letter in Quenya was originally like German *ch*,
but eventually softened to a sound like English *h* except
before *t*. In Sindarin it retained the original *ch* [x]
sound in the speech of the Elves. In Quenya x occurred in
the combinations *aht*, *oht*, *uht*; and ç occurred in the combinations *eht* and *iht*.

19. In Quenya the original ŋ sound of the letter was
lost, and it came to be pronounced like 17, n. As a result
19 was apparently not used in late Quenya.

20. Like 19, the original ŋ sound change to *n* in Quenya.
(The name *ngwalme* is misprinted *ywalme* in β.).

22. The β sound is given here as the most likely pronunciation of this sound in relation to others in the chart.
But by the Third Age it was probably usually normal v.

23. This should have represented a velar approximant in
Quenya, which is what most back and central vowels can be
considered varities of. So it would make an excellant vowel
carrier. Jim Allan has speculated that it was used as a
vowel carrier until replaced by ı except for the combination
cı, where it was retained for esthetic reasons.)

24. The ? value in Westron/Black Speech was originally
a speculation on Jim Allan's part, later confirmed from some
unpublished material.

26. On the pattern of human languages, the pronunciation
would normally be closer to ɟ, a voiceless spirant or approximant, than to ɾ, a voiceless trill.

30, 32. These are reversed forms of 29 and 31 respectively, which were sometimes used when the space above was
needed for vowel signs.

31, 32. In Quenya these letters were originally used for the *z* sound, but the sound gradually came to be pronounced like *r*. Since there was no need for three *r* symbols (with 21 and 25), the letters 31 and 32 were used by the Quenya speakers of the Third Age for a double (long) *ss*.

35, 36. These two were used as vowels in Sindarin. In Tolkien's transcription of *Namárië* they are used only for semi-vowels at the ends of diphthongs like *eye* /ai/ and *ow* /au/, spelled ả and ỏ respectively.

37. This archaic Quenya letter was no longer used in the Third Age.

DOUBLE-STEM LETTERS. 'The original Fëanorian system also possessed a grade with extended stems, both above and below the line.' þ þ ƌ ƌ 'These usually represented aspirated consonants (e.g. *t+h*, *p+h*, *k+h*)ₒ, but might represent other consonantal variations required. They were not needed in the languages of the Third Age that used this script; but the extended forms were much used as variants (more clearly distinguished from Grade 1) of Grades 3 and 4' (III:398). An extended version of 11 ƌ may be seen in the ring inscription. Tolkien elsewhere makes use of extended forms as abbreviations: ⱬ *of* ⱨ *the* ⱬ *of the*.

VOWELS

There are two ways of writing the vowels using tengwar. They could be written out like the vowels in the Roman alphabet, in which case the letters were largely derived from shapes in Row 6. This is called a 'full mode'. Letters 23, 24, 30, 35, 36, and 41 were used as vowels as shown in the lower line of the chart. For example: ᴧᴍᴪᴫ *ennyn*, ᴄᴍᴄᴫ *annon* ỉᴫ *im*. A dot is often placed over ᴄ and ꞇ to mark these as separate letters, and not a curl or a stem belonging to an adjacent letter.

The other way of writing vowels was to use smaller symbols placed over the consonants. In Quenya (and languages like French and Spanish) where words often end with vowels, they are placed over the preceding consonant: ᴧᵹᴃᵹ *hiruvalye* Quenya 'thou wilt find', ᵹᴛᴍ *lantar* Quenya 'fall (pl.)'. In Sindarin and Westron (and languages like English) which often have words ending with consonants, vowel signs were written over the following consonant: ᴍᴍ *ennyn*, ᴍᵹ *annon*, ᴃᴉ *im*. When there was no consonant in the right place, the vowel sign was placed on a CARRIER, 38, which had no value by itself in this system: ꞇ ᴉᵹᴍ *i eleni* Quenya 'the stars', ᴃᵹᴉᵼ *Moria* (as in Sindarin). In the chart, vowel signs (*tehtar*) are shown above the corresponding 'full' vowel sign; they are numbers 40, 42, 43, 44, 45, 46 (and 47). In the title page inscription ˝ is used for a vocalic *y* in ᴘᴧᴊ

TENGWAR FACT SHEET

Compiled by Laurence J. Krieg

	I Tincotéma	II Parmatéma	III Calmatéma	IV Quessetéma
1	1 TINCO — metal — t, t, t, t	2 PARMA — book — p, p, p, p	3 CALMA — lamp — tʃ/ch, c, k, c	4 QUESSE — feather — kʷ/qu, k, k, ·kʷ
2	5 ANDO — gate — nd, nd, d, d	6 UMBAR — fate — mb, mb, b, b	7 ANGA — iron — ŋg/ng, ng, dʒ/j, g	8 UNGWE — spider's web — ŋgʷ/ngw, g, g, gw
3	9 THÚLE/SÚLE — spirit — θ/s, th/s, θ, th	10 FORMEN — north — f, f, f/ph, f/ph	11 HARMA/AHA — treasure/rage — ç·x/h, h, ʃ/sh, x/ch	12 HWESTA — breeze — hw, x/kh, ·xʷ
4	13 ANTO — mouth — nt, nt, ð/dh, dh	14 AMPA — hook — mp, mp, v, v	15 ANCA — jaws — ŋk/nk, nc, ʒ/zh, ɣ/gh	16 UNQUE — a hollow — ŋkʷ/nqu, nquʷ, ɣh, ·ɣʷ(=w)
5	17 NÚMEN — west — n, n, n, nn	18 MALTA — gold — m, m, m, mm	19 NGOLDO/NOLDO — of the Noldor — ŋ/n, ng/n, ɲ/ny, ng	20 NGWALME/NWALME — torment — ŋʷ/nʷ, ngw, ng, ·ŋʷ
6	21 ÓRE — heart (inner mind) — ɹ/r, r, n	22 VALA — angelic power — β,v/v, w, m	23 ANNA — gift — –, y, y, o	24 WILYA/VILYA — air, sky — v·,w/v,ɹ,w, *ʔ, w, W
7	25 RÓMEN — east — r, r, r, r	26 ARDA — region — rd, rd, rh, rh	27 LAMBE — tongue — l, l, l, l	28 ALDA — tree — ld, ld, lh, lh
8	29 SILME — starlight — s, s, s, s	30 SILME NUQUERNA (S reversed) — s, s, s, ч/y	31 ÁZE/ESSE — sunlight/name — z/ss, z/ss, z, ss/ss	32 ÁZE/ESSE NUQUERNA (- reversed) — ss, ss, z, z ·ø(=ö), –
9	33 HYARMEN — south — ç/h, hy/h, h, h	34 HWESTA SINDARINWA — Sindarin HW — –, hw/hwᴍ, hw	35 YANTA — bridge — y i, y·i, i, e	36 ÚRE — heat — w, -u, u, u
10	37 HALLA — tall — ħ—, h—, –, =	VOWELS "1" "" Short Long. VOWEL CARRIERS used for diacritic vowels when no consonant is in the right place. a e i o u y/æ. ·· Long full-vowel ˘ 'Obscure' vw	Nasal + Cons. / Cons. + s / Long cons. / ·· Palatal (soft) ·· consonant	KEY — Std. No. / QUENYA NAME Tengwar, Roman (Old/New) / Blank space / Related Rune(s) / translation of Q. name / WESTRON/BLACK SP. VALUE / QUENYA VALUE Pronun-ciation Spelling SINDARIN VALUE

by.

Long vowels, which occurred both in Quenya and Sindarin, were treated differently in the different types of mode. In 'full' modes, a mark like an acute accent, 43, was placed over the vowel letter; this was called *andaith* 'long mark' (in Sindarin): ɴʄᵧɪᵃᴄ *míriel* Sindarin 'sparkling like jewels'. In the modes in which vowels were written above the consonants, a special 'long carrier' (39) was used for long vowels: ʄᴙʄᴊᴜᴀ *únótime* Quenya 'not countable'; alternatively the sign for the vowel could be doubled: ᴘʄᴘʄᴄᴄ *durbatulûk* Black Speech 'to rule them all'. The doubling was done mostly with the curls ⌢ and ² , less often with ´ , and not with ·· or ·

Signs 47 and 48 do not occur in Tolkien's work, but they have often been used in writing English by those who have developed their own modes for æ, the vowel in *at* ᴘ, ᴐᴘ *fatter* ʙᴘᴢ, ʙᴐᴘᴀᴻ (as opposed to *a*, the *a* of *father* ʙʄᴻ, ʙᴐʙᴀᴻ which is 40-41. But one can also use 40-41 for æ and 42-24 for *a*.

49. Tolkien uses a dot under a consonant to represent an 'obscure' or 'weak' vowel. Presumably in languages like English where unaccented syllables are often obscure this sign would represent the presence of a 'neutral' vowel ə. Tolkien also uses the dot in this semi-orthographic Title Page Inscription to stand for 'silent *e*' in some English words: ʎᶎᴍ *herein*.

OTHER DIACRITICS

In addition to the vowel tehtar, a number of other tehtar were used as diacritical marks:

50, 51. Placing either of these signs over a consonant (usually from rows 1 or 2) inserted the corresponding nasal in front of it: ᴘᴊʙᴄᴘ (Sindarin) *teitha<u>n</u>t*, ᴄᴄᴊᴘᴊᴄ (Black Speech *gi<u>m</u>batul*.

52. This is really a variant of 29 or 30: it represents *s* after another consonant, usually at the end of a word: ʎᶁʄᴙ (English) *hobbits*.

53. Placing this under a consonant made it long or double in length: ʙᴄᴁᴄᴎᴻ (Quenya) *falmali<u>n</u>nar* 'upon many foaming waves', ʎᶁʄᴙ (English) *ho<u>bb</u>its*.

54. Placing two dots under a consonant indicated it was palatalized like the Russian SOFT consonants, or English consonants followed by *y*: ꜞᶎ (Quenya) *elye* 'even thou', ʙᴍᴎᴻ (Quenya) *fanyar* 'clouds'.

SOUND-SHAPE CORRESPONDENCE: A SUPPLEMENT

⌊ETTERS 1-24 are arranged by shape, and the shape corresponds
to the way the sound is produced by the mouth. The rest of
the letters (from 25 on) are not part of this system and have
irregular shapes. Tolkien calls them 'additional' letters.
Most are modifications of the 'primary' letters, except for
27 and 29, which are independent.

The shapes of the primary letters were theoretically
free to represent any set of sounds, according to the convenience of the language. Thus, most of the letters had
slightly different values in the three major languages of
the Third Age of Middle-earth, and the sound-shape correspondence was not quite the same in each language. One general principle was observed.

Each letter consists of two parts: a STEM (*telco*) ı l ȷ,
and a BOW (*lúva*) ∩ ∪. The stem could be SHORT ı, LOWERED ȷ,
or RAISED l; the bow could be OPEN or CLOSED, and at the same
time SINGLE or DOUBLE: ∩ ∪ ⋔ ɯ ٥ ᴑ ထ ಎ.

GENERAL PRINCIPLE

Bow to the right, opening downward: sounds made in the FRONT
of the mouth, like ρ *t*, ℘ *d*, ρ *p*, ℏ *f*.
Bow to the left, opening upward: sounds made in the BACK of
the mouth: ⊄ *ch/k*, ⊄⊄ *j/g*, ૧ *k/kw*, ⊄૧ *g/gw*.

QUENYA

Double bow: NASAL sounds, like ℘ο *nd*, ℔ *mp*, ℔ *n*.
Single bow: sounds which are NOT NASAL: ρ *t*, ℏ *f*, η *r*.
Short stem: sounds in which the AIRSTREAM IS NOT BLOCKED:
℔ *n*, ℔ *v*, ಎ *w*.
Raised and lowered stem: This feature does not correspond
consistently to any type of sound difference.
Closed bow: LABIAL sounds: ρ *p*, ૧ *kw*, ℏ *f*, ಎ *w*.
Open bow: NON-LABIAL sounds.

SINDARIN

Double bow: VOICED sounds, like ℘ο *d*, ℔ *v*, ⊄⊄ *ŋ*, ⊄૧ *gw*.
Single bow: VOICELESS sounds, like ρ *t*, ℏ *f*, ૧ *k*, ૧ *kw*.
Lowered stem: STOP consonants like ρ *t*, ℔ *b*, ૧ *k*, ⊄૧ *gw*.
Raised stem: SPIRANT consonants like ℏ *θ*, ℔ *v*, ⊄ *ch*, ⊄⊄ *gh*.
No stem: these are all NASALS, EXCEPT letters 23 and 24
which are vowels): ℔ *nn*, ℔ *m*, ⊄⊄ *ŋ*.
Closed bow: LABIAL sounds, as in Quenya.
Open bow: NON-LABIAL sounds.

WESTRON/BLACK SPEECH

Double bow: VOICED sounds, as in Sindarin.
Single bow: VOICELESS sounds, as in Sindarin, EXCEPT row 6,
which are voiced.
Lowered stem: STOP consonants, as in Sindarin.

Raised Stem: SPIRANT consonants, as in Sindarin.
No Stem: CONTINUANTS—that is, sounds in which the airstream
is not blocked.
  Row 5 consists of nasal sounds: *m n*, *m m*, *ny*, *ŋ*.
  Row 6 consists of approximants: *n r*, *w*, *y*.
Closed bow: consonants which are acoustically GRAVE (with
a predominance of low frequencies in the sound spectrum):
p p, *m m*, *k*, *kh*.
Open bow: consonants which are acoustically ACUTE (with a
predomiance of high frequencies in the sound spectrum):
t , *dh*, *ch*, *ny*.

THE EVOLUTION OF THE TENGWAR

Jim Allan

TOLKIEN TELLS US that in origin the *tengwar* did not comprise
an alphabet, but were rather a group of related signs that
could be 'adapted at choice or convenience to represent the
consonants of languages observed (or devised) by the Eldar.
None of the letters had in itself a fixed value' (III:397).
It would appear that Fëanor, their inventor, had noticed that
the sounds of a language—its phonemes—tend to be differ-
enced from one another in systematic ways, and so can be
described in terms of their relationship to one another without great difficulty. He wished to indicate this clearly by
divising a writing system in which the characters varied in
shape on a systematic basis, and so the sound relationships
in the spoken tongue could be mirrored by visual relationships in the written language.

As these character were more and more used certain conventions were established. Series I was applied to the
dentals or *t*-series, and Series II was applied to the labials
or *p*-series. In the Eldarin tongues Series III was applied
to the velars or *k*-series, and Series IV to the labialized
velars or *kw*-series. Also, by convention, a lowered stem
was used to indicate a stop, a raised stem to indicated a
spirant, a short stem to indicate a nasal, a single bow to
show voicelessness, and a double bow to show voice. The
characters could also be modified in unsystematic ways to
represent other variations.

If these theoretic assignments of values had been carried through with complete consistency the values of the

K

241

general tengwar alphabet in use in the Third Age of Middle-earth would be as in the chart titled 'Theoretic Eldarin Values' below.

In this chart a preceding *h* indicates voicelessness, and underscoring indicates that the *tengwa* must be supposed to represent some kind of variation on the sound indicated. Except for the use of *ŋ* the roman letter transcriptions of the *tengwar* follows that used by Tolkien in transcribing the Eldarin tongues.

THEORETIC ELDARIN VALUES

	I		II		III		IV	
1	1 p	t	2 p	p	3 cʃ	c	4 q	qu
2	5 po	d	6 pɔ	b	7 ccʃ	g	8 ɔq	gw
3	9 b	th	10 b	f, ph	11 cl	ch	12 cl	chw
4	13 bɔ	dh	14 bɔ	v	15 ccl	gh	16 cd	ghw
5	17 mɔ	n	18 m	m	19 ccʃ	ŋ	20 ɔ	ŋw
6	21 n	hn	22 n	hm	23 cu	hŋ	24 u	hŋw
	25 ɣ	r	26 ʃ	r̲	27 ʒ	l	28 ʃ	l̲
	29 ʓ	s	30 ʔ	s	31 ʒ	z	32 ʒ	z
	33 λ	ch̲	34 cl	chw̲	35 λ	hŋ̲	36 o	hŋw̲

In the chart 'Early Quenya' to be found on page 245 I have shown the values actually assigned in Early Quenya, as revealed by the earliest versions of their Quenya letter names. The consistent theoretic pattern has been greatly modified to adapt it to the peculiarities of Quenyan phonology. Quenya had no voiceless nasals, and so Grade 6, and *tengwar* 35 and 36, were used for the approximants, the consonants closest to vowels. The only voiced spirants possessed by Early Quenya were *v* and *z*, and so Grade 4 was used instead for nasal + voiceless stop combinations which were frequent in the language, and 22 was given the value *v*.

In Quenya *b* and *g* are found only in the combinations *mb* and *ng* [ŋg], and *d* only in the combinations *nd*, *rd*, and *ld*. Hence Grade 2 is used for nasal + voiced stop combinations which and 26 and 28 are used for the combinations *rd* and *ld*.

Note that 7 is *ng* in *finger*—[ŋg], while 19 is *ng* in *singer*
— [ŋ].

Tengwa 23 is given the name *anna*, and could be used to
indicate lack of consonant sound, like the *h* in English *heir*.
Tengwa 36 is named *úre*. It would be used for a *u/w* sound
when this occurred as the second part of a diphthong, and is
so used by Tolkien in his transcription of 'Namárië'. This
may mean that *úre* is to be written $\delta\acute{y}$, rather than $\not{P}\acute{y}$ or $\not{P}\acute{y}$.
Or the earlier form of the word may have been *wúre*. *Tengwa*
35 is available for the second element of *-i* diphthongs.

The sounds of *hr* and *hl* were represented by $l\gamma$ 37 + 25
and $l\widetilde{\sigma}$ 37 + 27. If *hw* existed in this period separate
from *chw* it would similarly have been $l\alpha$ 37 + 24.

The chart titled 'Late Quenya' shows the values of the
tengwar at the end of the Third Age as given in Tolkien's
transcription of 'Namárië'. I have given two entries for
each *tengwa*, first the value it had initially, then its
value medially. If it was not used in one of the two positions the marks -- appear.

It can be seen that certain sounds disappeared altogether. The *z* sound had become *r*, and—since *r* was sufficiently covered by 21 and 25—31 and 32 were now used for
ss (III:401). *Th* became *s*; but Tolkien informs us that in
this case *s* derived from earlier *th* continued to be written
with 9 instead of 29 or 30 (III:392 *TH*). Untrilled *r* had
become trilled (III:392 *R*), but both 21 and 25 remained in
use. In Tolkien's transcription 25 is used preceding a
vowel and 21 is used elsewhere.

Some initial sounds had changed. Initial *ng* [ŋ] had
become *n*, initial *ngw* [ŋw] had become *nw*, and initial *w* had
become *v*.

Tengwa 11 went through more than one change. It had
originally been *ch* in all positions, but initially had weakened to breath *h* (III:401). The sign *halla*, number 37, was
used instead for this initial *h*, and 11 was given the new
name *acha*. (Presumably at the same time initial *chw* became
hw.) Later medial *ch* also weakened to breath *h*, save in the
combinations *acht*, *ocht*, *ucht* where it kept its original [x]
sound. In the combinations *echt* and *icht* it was pronounced
[ç], a sound which was represented initially by *hy* (III:391
H; III:392 *Y*).

It was perhaps at this time that the two underposed dots
were introduced to represent *y*. If not introduced then, they
were certainly used then. The symbol *halla* (37 in the Early
Quenya chart) was replaced by 33 for the value *h*, and the two
underposed dots were used with 33 to indicate its old value
hy. Initial *y* and post-vocalic *y* were no longer represented
by 35, but by 23 with the two underposed dots. *Y* following a

consonant was represented by the two underposed dots and the
tengwa for the consonant. Thus *tengwa* 35 ㅅ, like 36 ᴑ, was
used solely as the second element in a diphthong.

A chart of the *tehtar* is included in the Late Quenya
chart. In Quenya the vowel *tehtar* were placed over the preceding consonant, or failing one, on a vowel carrier. Long
vowels are indicated by placing the vowel *tehta* on a long
carrier, or, more rarely, by doubling the *tehta*, a method
usually only applied to *ó* and *ú*, and less often to *é*. The
equations given for the punctuation marks are only approximate, as the Quenya and English systems do not, of course,
exactly correspond. The first three indicate pauses of
increasing length or intensity. The remaining two indicate
tone, and are used in conjunction with, not instead of, the
first three.

In his transcription of 'Namárië' Tolkien usually places
the vowel *tehtar* above 35 and 36 to represent diphthongs, but
occasionally they are placed above the preceding consonant
instead. Since *hísië* corresponds to S *hith-* one would expect
it to be written ᴕᴊᕼᒿ . But Tolkien writes ᴕᴊᕽᒿ . The two
underposed dots are several times omitted in writings of *ry*.

The only Sindarin mode given by Tolkien in the published
corpus is that of the ancient Mode of Beleriand. It appears
on the Moria West-gate inscription, and is used by Tolkien
to transcribe the 'Hymn to Elbereth' in R. The chart titled
'The Mode of Beleriand' on page 247 shows the values assigned,
fills in some other values to complete the system, and indicates sounds not found in Sindarin by crossing them out.
It is possible that *tengwar* 4, 8, 12, 16, and 20 were not
used at all in this mode, even when there values did occur.
Diphthongs in this mode are normally indicated by the *tehtar*
¨ and ~ , but may be written out in full instead using *tengwar* 38 and 36 (24 may be used for final -*au/aw*) (III:400).
A dot is sometimes placed above 37 and 38 to help distinguish
them from the stems and bows of adjoining characters.

The chart of 'A Mode for Westron & the Black Speech' on
page 247 contains values taken from the Ring Inscription and
that on the title-page of *The Lord of the Rings*, the latter
written from the viewpoint of a man of Gondor. As in Quenya
ᴕ is used immediately preceding a vowel and ᴖ is used elsewhere. In this chart *ch*, *j*, *sh*, *zh*, and *ny* represent [tʃ],
[dʒ], [ʃ], [ʒ], and [ɲ]. *K* corresponds to Eldarin *c*, and *kh*
to Eldarin *ch* [x]. The vowel tehtar are placed above the
following consonants. A dot below the preceding consonant
was used to represent the weak obscure vowels, frequent in
Westron (III:400,404).

This mode, unlike the Eldarin modes, covers all the normal English consonant sounds, and is generally the basis

EARLY QUENYA

	I		II		III		IV	
1	1	t	2	p	3	c	4	qu
2	5	nd	6	mb	7	ng	8	ngw
3	9	th	10	f	11	ch	12	chw
4	13	nt	14	mp	15	nc	16	nqu
5	17	n	18	m	19	ng (ŋ)	20	ngw (ŋw)
6	21	r[1]	22	v	23		24	w
	25	r[2]	26	rd	27	l	28	ld
	29	s	30	s	31	z	32	z
	33	hy	34		35	y, i	36	u
	37	h						

1. untrilled.   2. trilled.

LATE QUENYA

	I			II			III			IV		
1	1	t	t	2	p	p	3	c	c	4	qu	qu
2	5	--	nd	6	--	mb	7	--	ng	8	--	ngw
3	9	s	s	10	f	f	11	--	h	12	hw	--
4	13	--	nt	14	--	mp	15	--	nc	16	--	nqu
5	17	n	n	18	m	m	19	n	--	20	nw	--
6	21	---r		22	v	v	23	--	--	24	v	w,v
	25	r-	r-	26	--	rd	27	l	l	28	--	ld
	29	s	s	30	s	s	31	--	ss	32	--	ss
	33	h	h	34	--	--	35	--	i	36	--	u
		hy	hy		--	lv		y	y		vowel carriers	

·	i	/	e	∴	a	⌢	o	?	u	..	y	s

preceded by corresponding nasal	doubling of consonant

·	,	:	; .	::	.	}	!	ß	?

upon which English modes are created.

A variant of this mode has appeared in a reconstruction of the second page of the Book of Mazarbul which Gandalf read in Moria. This reconstruction was made by Tolkien and published in *The Lord of the Rings 1977 Calendar*, illustrations by J. R. R. Tolkien (London: George Allen & Unwin Ltd., 1976). Christopher Tolkien provides some notes on the last page of the calendar. He identifies the mode used here as the northern variety of the Westron convention. As in the Sindarin Mode of Beleriand the vowels are indicated by *tengwar*.

24. ♉ = a   23. ♋ = o
35. 𝛌 = e   22. 𝚪 = u
  𝟏,í = i   ] = y

The *tehtar* ˙˙ and ˘ are used for diphthongs. A silent *e* is indicated by a dot beneath the preceding consonant.

For *w* 25 𝞬 and 22 𝚪 are both used, so that 𝚪 may be sometimes *u* and sometimes *w*. (Of course, in diphthongs like *ew* and *ow* the *tehta* ˘ is used: 𝛌, ♉.) For *r* 21 𝝂 is used throughout. For *ll* 28 𝚻 is used.

The writing, as on the title page inscription, follows English spelling in part, and English pronunciation in part.

Another variant appears inscribed on a vase in Tolkien's illustration 'Conversation with Smaug' to be found in editions of *The Hobbit* that contain coloured plates, and in several of the Tolkien calendars. The inscription contains two lines, of which the central portions are partially obscured by a ladder leaning against the vase:

[tengwar inscription, two lines]

It can be transliterated as: g dᴶ l d th ? ? ? th r aⁱ n : a k r̄ s t b ī the th ī f; and transcribed in normal English orthography as: *gold th--- Thrain : accursed be the thief*. It follows the northern variety of the Westron convention covered above, save for the use of **o** as *o*. The use of the *andaith* to indicate not only long vowels but a long (= syllabic) *r* is worthy of note.

THE MODE OF BELERIAND

	I		II		III		IV	
1	1	t	2	p	3	c	4	~~gw~~
2	5	d	6	b	7	g	8	gw
3	9	th	10	f, ph [1]	11	ch	12	chw [2]
4	13	dh	14	v, f [3]	15	~~gh~~	16	~~ghw~~
5	17	nn	18	mm	19	ng (ŋ)	20	ngw [4]
6	21	n	22	m	23	o	24	w
	25	r	26	rh	27	l	28	lh
	29	s	30	y	31	ss, ~~x~~	32	5
	33	h	34	hw	35	e	36	u
	37	a	38	i	••	-i [6]	~	-u, w [6]

| ⌒ preceded by corresponding nasal | ╱ indicates a long vowel | • ` | : • |

1. ph represents ␢ derived from ␠,
   final ␣, or ␣␣. (III:392 *PH*)
2. possibly never occurs in Sindarin.
3. final ␣ is transcribed *f*.
   (III:391 *F*)
4. Cf. *certh* 27. Theoretically
should be /ŋw/, but this combination occurs in neither Sindarin nor Quenya. (III:392 *NG*)
5. Perhaps used for ð. Cf. *certh* 52.
6. Used for the final vowels in the diphthongs *ai*, *ei*, *ui*, and *au/aw*

A MODE FOR WESTRON & THE BLACK SPEECH

	I		II		III		IV	
1	1	t	2	p	3	<u>ch</u>	4	k
2	5	d	6	b	7	j	8	g
3	9	th	10	ph	11	sh	12	kh
4	13	dh	14	v	15	zh	16	gh
5	17	n	18	m	19	ny	20	ng (ŋ)
6	21	r	22	w	23	y	24	'
	25	r	26	rh	27	l	28	lh
	29	s	30	s	31	z	32	z
	33	h	34	hw	35	i	36	u

A SURVEY OF SOME

ENGLISH-TENGWAR ORTHOGRAPHIES

Laurence J. Krieg

*An earlier version of this paper was presented in partial fulfil-
ment of the requirements for the course Linguistics 421, The University
of Michigan, 20 December 1971. While working on this paper, the author
received support under Federal grant, C24-808-271.*

ORTHOGRAPHIC THEORIES

GENERAL

THE DEVELOPMENT OF WORKABLE THEORIES of generative phonology
has made it necessary to rethink our theories of what makes
the ideal orthographic system for a language. Orthographic
ideals have changed along with theories of grammar for several centuries; for example, the renaissance in England
brought a revival of interest in the etymology of language,
and it was thought that the ideal orthography should reflect
etymological facts. It was at that time that spellings like
island and *debt* were introduced and standardized, replacing
the spellings *iland* and *dett*. Then too, as the concern for
standardization grew, the attitude became one of accepting
any spelling so long as only one spelling was used for one
word. That is, in fact, the ideal which exists now in practice: it is more important that something be spelled 'right'
(that is, in the standard way) than that it be spelled
according to any purely linguistic principles whatever.

This is an important point; when discussing theoretical
matters like the ideal form of a grammar or the best symbols
to use in a phonological transcription, the only practical

concerns are for the convenience of the linguists. This is not so with orthography, where linguistic principles, in most practical cases, have very little to do with what is actually used. In many cases, writing systems can only be observed, like speech-patterns, and such appears to be the case in English. Social factors are often more important than linguistic factors; but the importance of social conditioning to language development has long been underrated. With the revealing work of such men as Labov in this area, we would be foolish to consider orthography apart from social factors.

Although English orthography is certainly far from the control of linguists, other languages' orthographies are not in the same inviolate position. Most European languages have Language Academies which control, to a greater or lesser extent, the way people 'correctly' spell words. Another situation where linguistic principles have control over orthography is in the designing of orthographies for non-literate languages. The last few decades have seen a great many unwritten languages 'reduced' to writing, and a great deal of linguistic thought has gone into this effort.

STRUCTURALIST APPROACHES

Until very recently the structuralist type of linguistics has been dominant; this is natural, since structuralism was the ONLY theoretical linguistic framework of any practical value and standing for many years. Perhaps the most important work in this area was done by Kenneth Pike and the Summer Institute of Linguistics: Pike's *Phonemics: a technique for reducing languages to writing* (1947) is certainly one of the major works devoted to this subject. I will summarize here the basic principles of Pike (1947) since it is representative of the most important theorizing done before the rise of generative grammar.

Undergirding the whole operation of creating phonemic orthographies is the supposition that truly phonemic orthographies are easiest for native speakers to read. This point has been challenged recently (Venezky 1971), though it is not clear to what extent the evidence submitted to the contrary is what it claims to be.

Designing a phonemic orthographical system for a language involves the phonemic analysis of that language; but it was evident that phonemic analysis cannot be made from phonetic data alone. It must be made with phonetic date plus a series of phonemic premises and procedures, and a knowledge of (at least) the most basic grammatical structures of the language. This point was certainly realized by the practical people at SIL, though the theoretical justification was not completely satisfactory to all the structuralists.

The phoneme was defined (basically) as a sound which contrasts with other sounds to change the meanings of utterances; there was the practical assumption on the part of the structural phonemicists that 'phonemes' exist as a real structure in language, not just 'language' in general, but in all spoken language, and to some extent in the minds of the speakers. The phoneme, as the basic contrast unit, should receive a simple two-dimensional graphic structure to represent it in writing. For practical reasons, it was thought necessary to assume that there is only one accurate phonemic analysis for a specific set of data. When two phonemic conclusions both appear to be justifiable, and each seems to account for all the available facts of all types, that conclusion is assumed to be correct which is least complex, which gives to suspicious data an analysis parallel with analogous nonsuspicious data, and which appears most plausible in terms of the alleged slurs into specific environments. In general, elements which are identifiable as phonetically distinct are assumed to be separate phonemes unless it is evident that they are part of a more inclusive phonemic unit —as is the case in English /tʃ/ which is phonetically two segments, [t + ʃ].

Two segments of speech are proved to be phonemically distinct if they consistently constitute the only difference between two words of different meanings. Often, there is fluctuation between full phonemes; an allophone of one phoneme may be the 'norm' of another, as in the case of English /t/ and /d/, which both have intervocalic allophones of [ɾ] as in *latter* and *ladder*, both phonetically ['læɾəʲ] in rapid American speech. However, once two segments are proved to be phonemically distinct it is assumed that they remain phonemically distinct even if there is fluctuation between them. (It is here that the generative phonologists most strongly object.) In order to be considered submembers (allophones) of a single phonemes, the segments must be (a) phonetically similar, and (b) mutually exclusive as to the environments in which they occur. The 'norm' of a phoneme is that sub-member which occurs most often and is least modified by its environments.

To those who believe in the principles of phonemics and in the underlying principle of phonemic orthography—namely, that the phonemic orthography is easiest for the native speaker to read—English has long been one of the prime examples of how BAD a spelling system can be. It is certainly not necessary to cite any of the details that are cited by those who concern themselves with the reform of English spelling; for a cogent summary of its weaknesses see, for example, James Pitman's *Alphabets and Reading: the Initial Teaching Alphabet* (1969). The difficulties with the system (of lack of system as some claim) are summed up in.the alternate spelling *ghoti* for 'fish'.

GENERATIVE APPROACHES

It comes as no small surprise, therefore, to read in Chomsky and Halle (1968) the following statement:

> There is, incidentally, nothing surprising about the fact that conventional orthography is, as these examples suggest, a near optimal system for the lexical representation of English words. The fundamental principle of orthography is that phonetic variation is not indicated where it is predictable by general rule.... Orthography is a system designed for readers who know the language, who understand sentences, and therefore know the surface structure of sentences. Such readers can produce the correct phonetic forms, by means of the graphic representation and the surface structure, by means of the rules that they employ in producing and interpreting speech. (p. 49)

Chomsky and Halle go on to say that phonemic representation is very good for those who are not familiar with the language, such as actors who are trying to pronounce a passage in a strange language, but that to include all the features present at the co-called 'phonemic' level would involve a great deal of redundancy.

The principle underlying Chomsky and Halle's position is that the ideal orthography is that which is closest to the underlying lexical representation, and that underlying representations would contain absolutely no information which is in any way predictable—to do so would clutter the lexicon, and make it necessary to revise the orthography frequently in order to keep abrest of low-level rule changes. Their aim in analysing the sound structure of English has been to discover a system of rules and underlying forms that has some sort of psychological reality. Whether or not this is possible or even desirable is subject to questions, but the analysis of English phonology has certainly been advanced by this type of work.

It is argued that the lexicon should contain only the roots in a basic form, and that affixes should be added by rule when ever possible. For example, the (compound) root *telegraph* should be available in the lexicon and further compounds such as *telegraphic*, *telegraphy* should be formable from that lexical item and a set of rules. This would not be possible if the basic form were supposed to be in some phonemic form like /ˈtɛləˌgræf/ and the derived forms were

/ˌtɛləˈgræfɪk/ and /təˈlɛgrəfɪ/. This certainly seems like a good idea, and whether or not it has psychological reality it appears theoretically sound.

The question is, how do they arrive at the conclusions that English spelling is so near to the ideal lexical representation?

Their discussion on the form of the lexicon and phonological rules proceeds to show that this is the case by demonstrating the predictability of stress in English. (For some debate on this, see Dwight Bolinger, 'Accent is predictable (if you're a mind-reader)', Lg.48.633-644, Sept. 1972.) It would be beside the point here to recapitulate their arguments (Ch. 2). They also offer evidence from several processes besides stress placement to show that spelling is close to the lexical form. All the old phonemicists' bugbears like double letters and silent final e's are given a place of honor in this system and eliminated from the final phonetic output by rules. Here for example, is the derivation of the pronunciation [mʌsl̩] from an underlying mussel (pp. 46-47):

underlying lexical form:	mussel
u = ʌ rule - applies only in closed syllables	mʌssel
voicing of intervocalic s (does not apply with ss)	
geminate cluster simplification	mʌsel
stress placement	mʌ́sel
unstressed vowel reduction	mʌ́səl
syllabication of l	mʌ́sl̩

In addition to evidence from the phonological structure, I believe Chomsky and Halle decided on the fitness of the orthography as a lexical representation because of two facts: first, they are highly literate speakers of English. It is fundamental to the Chomsky system of grammar that only the 'ideal' speaker-listener' be considered in formulating the structures; if two professor at M.I.T. are the models for English grammar, the orthography is undoubtedly central to the lexical representation psychologically as well as theoretically. The same is probably true of most literate English-speakers: for us, the written forms are much more important than spoken forms; this is due to many complex social, cultural, and psychological factors. We may get into trouble with this model if we try to apply it to English as a whole; the children and illiterates may have rather different grammars and lexicons.

The second reason for Chomsky and Halle's choice of orthography is that they choose to ignore exceptions to the rules as being an obstruction to the production of a useful theory.

...citation of exceptions is in itself of very little interest. Counterexamples to a grammatical rule are of

interest only if they lead to the construction of a new
grammar of even greater generality or if they show some
underlying principle is fallacious or misformulated.
Otherwise, citation of counterexamples is beside the
point. (p. ix)

Excluding exceptions, English orthography is quite a
passable system; the only difficulty with it is that the
rules are many and complex. Once the rules are mastered, if
we are to accept the evidence of Hanna et al. (1966), we
will be able to spell 80 per cent of English words accurately. (This mammoth computer study made use of 17,000 English words, including the most common.) But it is difficult
to imagine why the expression 'near optimal' was chosen to
describe this system. Only in the laxest systems is 80 per
cent success considered near optimal; it is certainly open to
question whether the great complexity of the rules is justi-
fied when so large a percentage of failure is to be expected.

Chomsky and Halle explain what they feel to be the most
likely process by which native speakers of English read
aloud (p. 49). I will summarize this in step-by-step form:

1. The reader is presented with a linear array of symbols
(like this line of writing).
2. He produces a mental array of the lexical representations (underlying forms) of the words he sees written.
3. He does a preliminary analysis of the sentence, using
these resources:
    a. the contents of the syntactic component of his gram-
       mar;
    b. the contents of the semantic component of his gram-
       mar;
    c. extralinguistic information like knowledge of the
       writer and of the context.
4. The reader arrives at an understanding of what the sentence means.
5. He then produces a 'surface structure' corresponding to
his understanding of the sentence.
6. The sentence in its surface structure form is then pro-
cessed by the rules in the phonological component of the
reader's grammatical system, and the sentence is actualized
phonetically.

Although Chomsky and Halle are not entirely convinced,
it seems true to say that understanding is necessary before
(correct) pronunciation is possible in many cases. Yet when
children learn to read, the obviously do not know what a word
or sentence means until they pronounce it, because for them
the spoken form is still basic. One wonders if the primacy
of the orthographic form in the lexicon of literate English
speakers is not the result, rather than the cause of the

reading process. In other words, is it not possible that the lexical form corresponds to the orthographic form because those who read a great deal cannot do so successfully unless they understand the orthographic forms of words without the intermediary of the spoken form?

Let us turn now from the problems of reading, which are beyond the scope of this discussion, to some observations about 'scribal practise'. Robert King, in his *Historical Linguistics and Generative Grammar* (1969) devotes a chapter to speculation on the application of the principles of generative grammar to the orthographic representation of languages by scribes.

King does not go as far as Chomsky and Halle in requiring that the orthography correspond to the ᵩbasic lexical underlying from; rather he suggests a somewhat less radical system of morphophonemic orthography:

> A morphophonemic writing system has for alphabet the set of morphophonemic entities in the language, and the associated rules are the phonological rules which phonetically interpret lexical items spelled in morphophonemes. This kind of writing system is the nearest analogue in practice to a generative phonology that recognizes only two significant levels of phonological representation: the systematic phonemic (roughly equivalent to the morphophonemic level in writing systems) and the systematic phonetic. (p. 204)

(Chomsky and Halle question the existence of the phoneme at any level of reality.) This he contrasts with an 'autonomous (taxonomic) phonemic writing system...composed of the set of autonomous phonemes in the language, and the spelling rules would be the set of process statements about which allophone of a particular phoneme is to be selected in which environment'.

Using two examples from Germanic languages (Old Norse runic development and the representation of umlaut changes in Old High German) King attempts to demonstrate that scribes tend to write not in autonomous phonemic orthographies, as the structuralists believed, but in orthographies which are more nearly morphophonemic, as the generative grammarians would like to suppose is more natural. The runic examples seem inconclusive, but one tends to agree with Lyle Campbell's statement, in his review (1971) of King, that runes are bound to be a poor example, since their primary function was not so much communicative as magical. The OHG case is not entirely conclusive either, and tends to show more of the perversity of scribes than any system they may use; still, they are certainly not so close to the autonomous phonemic system as to the morphophonemic, and King does demonstrate that Twaddell's (1938) treatment of this case is unsatisfactory. Twaddell's article was the first and most precise statement of the theory that scribes tend to write in some sort of phonemic system, and he used the same OHG umlaut changes that King does as examples.

THE IDEAL ORTHOGRAPHY?

It becomes apparent from these generative treatments that the basic question in formulating a theory of the ideal orthographic system is this: what level of the grammar should the ideal orthography attempt to represent? The highest level would be the lexicon in its most abstract form, and the lowest level would presumably be the actual phonetic output of the individual. No linguistically sophisticated spelling reformer has ever advocated this lowest level as the ideal for orthographic representation, since it is far too variable, though reading aloud would require very few (or no) rules aside from correspondence of symbols to phones. The orthography based on the lexical form (NOT English, in spite of Chomsky and Halle's contention) would have great historical and dialectical generality, but the number and complexity of rules needed to read it would be great.

Here then is the problem: we are faced with a continuum of possibilities, the extremes each offering something good and something bad, the middle offering a solution with (apparently) most of the disadvantages of both extremes! In such a situation it would be foolish to attempt to specify a 'solution' on purely theoretical grounds, and some sort of empirical evidence — or evidence from a sample or representative opinions — should tell us something important about the best way to spell a language.

The observation of scribal practices in King (1969) is to some extent helpful. Still,·the answer provided by the scribes of 1000 A.D. is not necessarily applicable to the situation at the present. It would be interesting to observe how English would be spelled in the absence of strong normative and standardizing controls: this would make it possible to compare the attitudes of modern English speakers with those of the old scribes, who also wrote without strong normative controls.

Observation of children who are encouraged to write without emphasizing the need for correctness provides one such opportunity. However, it has been pointed out (by Chomsky and Halle, p. 50, and others) that the language structures of children during the period of intense language acquisition differ considerably from that of adults. In

order to observe adults in a comparable situation, I propose
to examine some examples of English written with tengwar.

TENGWAR SPELLING SYSTEMS

TOLKIEN'S GUIDELINES

BEFORE CONSIDERING ANY of the private tengwar orthographies
it is essential to see exactly what Tolkien says about
using the tengwar for English. The person interested in
doing so will find very little: a short sample (see Sample 1)
and a paragraph of explanation, which I include here:

> There was of course no 'mode' for the respresentation of
> English. One adequate phonetically could be devised
> from the Fëanorean system. The brief example on the
> title-page does not attempt to exhibit this. It is
> rather an example of what a man of Gondor might have
> produced, hesitating between the values of the letters
> familiar in his 'mode' and the traditional spelling of
> English. It may be noted that a dot below (one of the
> uses of which was to represent weak obscured vowels) is
> here employed in the representation of unstressed *and*,
> but is also used in *here* for silent final *e*; *the*, *of*,
> and *of the* are expressed by abbreviations (extended *dh*,
> extended *v*, and the latter with an under-stroke).

Since it is convenient for comparison, I will provide
two kinds of transliteration: one into the traditional orthographic representation corresponding to the text, and another
adhering as closely as possible to the arrangement of the
tengwar. For these close transliterations I will use a
quasi-phonetic Roman transcription whose major principle will
be to represent one Fëanorean character with one equivalent
Roman character. In general, the consonants will correspond
as in the table at the head of the next page, and differences
necessitated by the use of the tengwar will be explained as
they are used. Vowel signs will be transliterated by placing
the Roman vowel letter in the position occupied by the vowel
sign in the tengwar. To avoid confusion with the letters *i*
and *j*, the vowel-carriers (when they occur) will be represented by dashes: - and — respectively. The full-letter vowels will also be represented by equivalent Roman letters, but
they of course will be written on the same line as the consonants rather than above them.

In the transcription of Tolkien's Title-page Inscription the correspondences are as listed: the various supple-
mentary marks are given much as they appear in the text with
the exception of the 'extended stem', which cannot be

Transliteration Correspondences

This table contains Roman letters which are used in transcribing the tengwar in the samples. Remember that these transcription values are not intended to represent phonetic symbols. In particular c, ʀ, ɯ, ʌ and ɥ do not represent their normal phonetic values, and , in the ş and ʒ has no phonetic significance.

CONSONANTS:

ρ	t	ρ̃	p	ᴄɟ	c	ᴄ̃	k
ρ̃	d	ρ̃	b	ᴄɟ	ɟ	ᴄ̃	g
ʮ	θ - ʇ	ʮ̃	f	ᴅ	ʃ		
ʮ	ð	ʮ̃	v	ᴄᴅ	ʒ		
ʍ	n	ʍ̃	m			ʋ	ŋ
ʋ	ɹ	ʋ̃	w	ᴄ	y	ᴄ	ɯ
ʏ	r	ʏ̃	ʀ	ᴄ̃	l	ʒ̃	ʌ
ʟ	s	ʔ	ş	ᴇ	z	ʒ	ʒ
ʌ	h	ᴅ	ʍ - ↓	ᴧ	ɥ	ο	u

VOWELS:

TEHTAR DIACRITICS	ï	î	´	˛ ɟ	´	?	˙	..
FULL VOWEL SIGNS	ʊ	ᴧ	˛ ɟ	ᴄʊ	ο	ᴄ	ꝯ
ROMAN EQUIVALENT	a ɑ	e	i T	o	u	(ə)	y

duplicated with Roman letters and are represented by the capital letter corresponding to the tengwa whose stem is lengthened.

SAMPLE I. TITLE-PAGE INSCRIPTION, THE LORD OF THE RINGS

𝔷 𝓵íⁱ𝔪 𝔭óí 𝕛𝔫 λ𝔭̂ĵʒ:~
a   ee   y   o i
ʒ s--n   b-   Ð h b t_s : ~

as seen   by the Hobbits.

On glancing at the direct transcription, it is immediately obvious that the tengwar graphic system is different
from the Roman in more ways than one. Not only are the symbols different, but they are arranged in space quite differently. Rather than scan in a straight line, the eye must
move in a series of vertical sweeps.

NOT → → → →   BUT RATHER ↓√↓√↓√↓

This is necessary in order to read the vowel signs. Presumably the reader who develops some facility with the system
would be able to scan the line horizontally and get the meaning from the general shapes of the words, as we do with Roman
letters. These differences clearly result from changes in
'low-level' rules (in the generative grammatical framework).

Two further difficulties arise: first, the word boundaries are not at all clear; second a great many abbreviations
are used. Both these problems have nothing to do with tengwar per se, and are encountered in most old manuscripts,
where the writing-surface was at a premium for various reasons, and it was thought unecessary to indicate boundaries and
common words in full. The matter of word-boundary notation
is interesting: in some languages the phonology at some level
erases word boundaries—French and Spanish are examples of
this. In some other languages, such as German, word boundaries (and even certain morpheme boundaries) are represented
in speech. The status of English is not clear; some words
appear to be marked off in the surface phonology, but not
others.

The use of abbreviations for *and*, *of*, *the*, and *of the*
represents a departure from both traditional orthography and
phonemics. It is possible, however, that such function words
are not represented in the lexicon with the same sort of
features as other words; in that case it would make little
difference to the native speaker what symbol is used in representing them. Of these, we do of course use & in traditional orthography, though its use is somewhat restricted.

The status of double letters (marked with an underposed
tilde) is half-way between that of the surface phonology,
which does not indicate them at all, and the traditional
orthography (or lexical representation, if we follow Chomsky
and Halle.)

TRADITIONAL TENGWAR MODES

The English-tengwar orthographies devised by Tolkien enthusiasts may be divided into two broad categories: the phonemic and the traditional. It will be noted that most of the designers classify their own systems as either one or the other type, but few manage to adhere strictly to a consistent representation. I will begin with consideration of the systems based on traditional English orthography.

SAMPLE 2. LOS ANGELES, CALIFORNIA. LETTER TO THE EDITOR OF
PARMA ELDALAMBERON, LATE 1971.

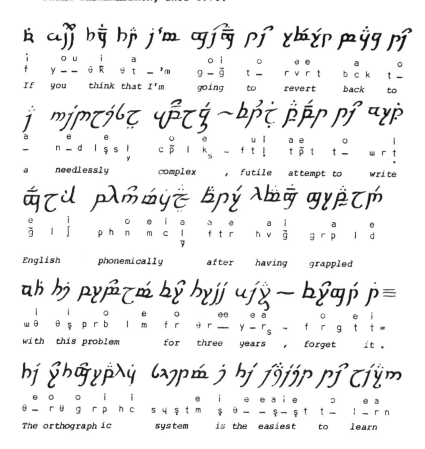

[Tengwar script with interlinear transliteration]

```
      o    i      e   e a    a  i  u o u    ɔ        a      e
t _  w  r  t  ~  θ _  l _ ş t  ɓ  ɕ  _ _ ş  ~  ð   b  f  r  θ _
                                                y
to    write  ,  the  least    ambiguous   ,  and by   far    the
```

```
    i    e     o      a      i e a      i        a   u      o ɔ
s p̃ l ş t    t _    t r n  s l t r t    Ξ  _ ' v   r g _ d   t _ _

simplest    to    transliterate.        I've   argued     too
```

```
     o  e      i i   u e     i    o o    a    o   e u      o
l   g̃     v r   θ ş ş s _ _  y*θ  t _ _  m n    t _  r t r n   t _
                                                 y
long    over   this issue  with too   many   to   return   to
```

```
    e     o i o   o   a     o e  i         e    a   i
θ _   n t _ n    f  _  p h n m c   s ụ ş t ṃ  ð  _

the   notion   of  a  phonemic    system   and  I
```

```
  a*e o     e u    o    a e     e     o    i     a      a
θ  r f r    r f ş  t _   c p t  θ _   m d   n   ʃʃ p   r m  ʃʃ   Ξ

therefore  refuse to    accept  the   mode  in    "Parma".
```

---

* "Scribal error"?

The text of this letter clearly states the position of
traditional orthography supporters. For them the written
word is uncontrovertably basic to the psychological lexicon,
and the phoneme indeed has no psychological reality. They
are unable to read writing which relates directly to sounds;
they would probably have equal difficulty coding and decoding
phonemic representation in Roman-phonetic writing.

This is a mode which uses diacritics rather than full-
letter vowels. The five most commonly accepted vowel signs
are used, and only one sign is placed above one letter or
carrier. Word-final silent *e* is represented by an underposed dot (used for the letter *i* when placed over the tengwa); the tilde is used for preceding homorganic nasal when
over the letter, and for doubling when under the letter.

These are the only exceptions to strict adherence to traditional orthography.

SAMPLE 3. LOS ANGELES, CALIFORNIA. POEM 'THE LORD OF THE RINGS' BY J.R.R. TOLKIEN, TRANSCRIPTION FROM **CARANDAITH** *1:4, 31.*

The Lord of the Rings

Three rings for the Elven - kings under the sky,

Seven for the Dwarf - lords in their halls of stone,

Nine for the mortal men doomed to die,

one for the Dark Lord on his dark throne

in the land of Mordor where the shadows lie.

ɾ̃m̃ ẏȳ ɾ̃ ẏⱡ ⱡm Ⱬ— ɾ̃m̃ ẏȳ ɾ̃ ⱡm̃ ⱡm—

One   ring   to   rule them   all   ,   one   ring   to   find them, ...

---

* Scribal error.
Note that the letter ૫ (which usually has the value *y*) is used for *i*.
Also ʀ = *rd*.

I quote here at length the introduction to this mode by
its author:

> To begin with, I'm advocating an orthographic mode
> of writing English, For the uninitiated, an orthography
> is a particular way of spelling words in a language, gen-
> erally assumed to be the Conventional way. The ortho-
> graphies of English and German are different because
> sounds are represented by different letter-patterns:
> English *oi* and *ts* as opposed to German *eu* and *z*. The
> orthographic mode of writing English is what you're
> reading now.
> The immediate alternatives are phonetics and phonemic
> orthographies. The difference between them is roughly
> the difference between a photograph and a sketch: phon-
> etics is a precise science of recording sounds, whereas
> phonemics is only approximate. ...
> The idea of a phonemic orthography for English is
> not as ludicrous, as it leaves flexibility for accents—
> the letter *r* can be rolled, flapped, 'softened' or
> dropped according to the speaker. The most obvious dis-
> advantage of such a system is that it equates words
> that are pronounced the same but spelt differently—*our*
> and *hour*, *night* and *knight* would be written the same.
> This is countered, and as far as I'm concerned cancelled
> out, by the advantage of distinguishing between pairs
> like *lead* (leed) and *lead* (led). Most of these can be
> figured out from context, but they remain awkward even
> so.
> One marked disadvantage of both the above systems
> [phonetic and phonemic] is that for use with the tengwar
> (or any script other than the Roman) they will never be
> as immediately readable as the orthographic. It's well
> enough of a chore to convert one alphabet to another
> without compounding the effort by then having to convert
> phonemics (or phonetics) into conventional spelling. I
> guess I'm just ƚ̸a̸t̸y̸ practical at heart, and leave out
> steps when I can get away with it.
> I've been trying to think up possible arguments
> against an orthographic mode, but it's much like trying
> to find a hole in the ocean. The only one I've come up
> with so far concerns the English orthography itself.
> It's illogical, inconsistent, and hard for foreigners to
> learn.
> I'll be one of the first to convert to a better

orthography if someone invents one — but in the mean-
time, we're all used to reading this one, and we can
read it faster and easier than any other. Until a
changeover is officially declared by some large group I
will continue to use this system for the sake of my
readers. Ghod only knows it's frustrating enough to
read my prose without it being written in some strange
spelling....

Besides, English written in the tengwar is for those
who already know English — an English primer in the
Elvish script is a pretty far-out idea but just as use-.
less. And what good would tengwar-written phonemic English be for foreigners if they're going to learn it this
way in the first place? As you see, I've managed to
convince myself pretty thoroughly I'm RIGHT. So much
for the insignificant Opposition!

Tengwar such as ᚻ, ᚻᚣ, ᚳᚳᛚ, and ᛏᛞ...represent single
phonemes (units of sound), not combinations thereof, and
they are not represented in English orthography by single
graphemes and are thus not permissable. If you don't
follow my logic here, please ask me to elaborate. I
admit it's a a little complicated, but it works out in
the end. In effect, what I'm saying is, first follow
English orthography per se, and THEN adopt peculiarities
of Tolkien's script.

The tengwa for H (ᚴ) is a little awkward, and after
all it would be EASIER if we could write such common
letter combinations as T+H, C+H, G+H etc. with single
graphemes. So I introduce the gimick [sic] Tolkien
explains on III.398/496 — that of extending the stems
of the tengwar both above and below the line to add +H.

In the transcription of Sample 3, notice that the eye-scan is
from the bottom to the top of the line (→↑\↑\↑\↑). Also note
the extended form for the letters TH. This is explained as
not being phonetically motivated, but based on calligraphic
practices of Renaissance Italy, where frequent letter combinations were expressed as merged digraphs. The same motiva-
tion is given for the special R-form for RD. Use of the
tilde to indicate preceding N was also common during that
period, and is carried over here. Word-final silent E is
treated exactly as all the other vowels are; the alternation
between vowels written with full-letter forms and as diacritics is based on esthetic considerations.

In general, it can be seen that the use of the tengwar
in this case is primarily for artistic satisfaction; this is
not out of line with the original purpose of the tengwar as
devised by Tolkien, who writes (in a personal communication):

> I devised the *tengwar* for a special purpose; and they
> are based as much on knowledge of the art of writing as
> on my moderate knowledge of phonetics.... The *tengwar*
> were developed to fit a (fictional) historical situa-
> tion, and their primary purpose is calligraphic.

The appeal of the tengwar is in its beauty and mystery: the

fact that it is secret and graceful makes it both interesting
and fulfilling, but the potential as a system for reducing
the frustrations of the English spelling system is not interesting to this sort of person.

SAMPLE 4. *LOS ANGELES, CALIFORNIA. DESCRIPTIVE SELECTION.
LATE 1971.*

It is possible that I am the only person

around that even occasionally uses

a full or semi-full mode based on

the mode of Beleriand; and even

I vary my mode on occasion

(cf. the "y" sound in underposed dots

264

[tengwar script]

a b o y   vs.   θ T u ʃ e d   h e ɾ ~   a ð   n o ṭ

above   vs.   the 'j' used   here -   and   note

[tengwar script]

θ   u ṣ V   l ~ l   to   T ð T c a ṭ   n a s a l ₛ   T n   θ

the use of   '—'   to   indicate   nasals   in   the

[tengwar script]

l a s t   f e y *   l T ṇ ₛ ·   a ð   θ   l e l   V   l u s e d l

last   few   lines   and   the 'e'   of   'used'

[tengwar script]

V s.   θ ∴   V   l l T ṇ ₛ l ·)   T   m T j * h t   a l s o

vs.   the '.'   of   'lines'.)   I   might   also

[tengwar script]

o c c a s T o n · a l   œ r T ṭ   l o c a s T o n a l l T l

occasionally   write   'occasionally'
   ỹ

[tengwar script]

T   a ī n t   e c s a c t l   c o n s T s t e ṭ.
                              y
I   aint   exactly   consistent.

---

* Apparently, Series 4, usually used for velars, is not used in this
  mode—so here the letters for c and j stand for k and g. The sample
  does not contain examples of English *ch* and *sh* so we cannot tell what
  they are in tengwar. The similarity of the semi-vowel of Series 3,
  y (here velar, thus w) to the vowel o has caused confusion in the
  word *write*.

Probably one of the most completely orthographic systems, but it is interesting to note the inconsistency with
which Roman letters are assigned to various tengwar conventions, as the writer points out. The fact that several dif-

different tengwar possibilities exist makes it difficult to
arrive at a standard mode for English, even granting that the
orthography, rather than the phonology, should be the base.

It will be noted that in this and other traditional
writing systems (except in Sample 3) the digraphs -*h* are
almost always transcribed as single letters in the tengwar.
This includes *th* (which is usually spelled with the tengwar
þ whether it represents /θ/ or /ð/), *sh*, *ch*, *wh*, and generally (though not as often) *ph*.

PHONEMIC TENGWAR MODES

Before considering the phonemic samples I would like to
quote from the guidelines sheet for one phonemic system of
which (unfortunately) I was unable to obtain sufficient samples. This author has just described a commonly used orthographic system for writing English tengwar:

> Since I am a linguist, I personally use a more linguis-
> tically sophisticated mode. This mode is phonemic,
> which means that every differentiable group of sounds
> is assigned its own letter. (Thus p in *spill*, *pill*,
> *tip* is written the same, even though all three are phon-
> etically distinct. I do not believe that any language
> in the world had a phonetic script in popular use.)
> Tolkien intended the Tengwar to be used in this way,
> since his transcriptions of Elvish are phonemic, and
> since the relation between the series and grades of the
> tengwar is a phonemic one.

Although Tolkien has privately cast doubt on his apparent
intention that English or other real languages should be
represented phonemically, it is difficult to avoid coming to
this conclusion given the phonetic arrangement of the letters
and his statement that they are 'not in origin an alphabet'.

The statement quoted above is typical of the attitude
behind most of the phonemically-based systems. Such systems
are generally devised by people with considerable interest in
linguistics, although it is in some cases questionable
whether the interest in linguistics or in the tengwar came
first. For these people the appeal of the tengwar is primarily linguistic rather than artistic, and is seen at least
in part as a potential excape from the weaknesses of traditional English orthography.

*SAMPLE 5. EAST LANSING, MICHIGAN. PERSONAL LETTER, FEBRU-
ARY, 1968.*

ɱʲʏ pɕɯ,

d T r p a m.

Dear   Pam,

(imŋ ċ λɕɓ ɦɕɱɕʒj ɠɕɾpʌɱ ɕʏ ʒɱ̃ po

s i n ş ̬a h a v f ̬a n a l T g o t ̬e n a r a ̬d t u

Since   I   have   finally   gotten   around   to

ʏ̇ɕṗɪɑ, ċ ɱʲɟɕɱʌp po ɱoc ɠʲoɱ ɕʏ ɕɾpɑ ɕɓ ip:

 ̬r a t ɪ ŋ,   ̬a   d T ş ̬a d e d   t u   d o   a   g u d   j o b   ǝ v   i t :

writing,   I   decided   to   do   a   good   job   of   it:

ɱɕʏoʏɕʒj ċ ɐiʒ ʌ̣pʌʏ c ɦoʒ ʏjpɕʏp ɕɱ

n a c u r a l T ̬a w i l ̰ e k ş p e k ̬a f u l   r i p o r t   o n
                                      [sic]

Naturally   I will   expect   a   full   report   on

ɦɯ ʏjɱ ɕpɐiʒ ipj ɕɓ ɦiʏ ʒʌpʌʏ.

ð ǝ r i d ǝ b i l i t T ̄ ǝv ð i s l e t ̬e r :

the readability   of this letter.

ɕⅼɯ ɕɯ ɯo ʼ ɦɱʌʒ ɠ̣pʌɱ̣ ɕʏ imʌ̣ɠ̣ɠʏ ʏɑʒ ʼ

ʃ ̬e m o n   y u ʃ ð o ʒ g r ̬e d z a r   i n e k ş ̣u z ǝ b l   ʃ

Shame on   you! Those   grades   are   inexcusable   !

dċ, ɯo ɠoɱ λɕɓ ɕp ʒjɟɱ ɠɕɾpʌɱ c [c] ɕʏpo

 ̬m a,   y u   k u d   h a v   a t   I T ş t   g o t ̬e n   a   [C]   o r   t u

Why, you could   have   at   least   gotten   a   [C]   or   two

Inṣted əv səm əv ðoz [A] g redz aˢt ðeʳr

instead of some of those [A] grades I see there.

ᵐaˑ gredz for fɪ̣ṣt tɪm wˑɪ not kwaˑt

My grades for First Term were not quite

az gud, bət ðatₛ laf [ ] ðe wɪ:

as good, but that's life [C'est la vie] **They were:**

eŋliʃ kop̄oziʃon [_] jenral kemistrT [_]

English composition [-] General Chemistry [-]

kemistrT laboratorT[_] kalkuləs[_] animal

Chemistry Laboratory [-] Calculus [-] Animal

hʌẕbaðrT [_] fizikal edukeʃən[-]: v⃰at givz

Husbandry [-] Physical Education [-]. That gives

mT an avˑɹaj əv [---] at ðə mome ʔ:

me an average of [----] at the moment...

---

* Scribal error?

This sample represents the spelling of a group of students enrolled in a seminar on Tolkien. I quote from the

introductions to the guide-sheet for a basic phonemic mode:

> The following mode for the representation of English is
> designed to be straightforward and readily understood by
> anyone familiar with the Tengwar.... This is intended
> as a reasonably phonemic system and does not follow
> English spelling; silent letters and other peculiarities
> of English orthography should be ignored.

The system represented in Sample 5 is fairly good as a phonemic transcription. It is somewhat inconsistent in representing syllabic /r/, sometimes using the combination representing [əɹ] and sometimes the syllabic [ɹ]. The vowel sounds
represented by the letter *o* are rather poorly differentiated;
the writer uses the basic *o* letter for the first two *o*'s in
composition, and also in *on* and *hope*. He uses the symbol for
o^W in *own*, presumably to differentiate it from *on*. Ortho-
graphically doubled letters are represented with a subposed
tilde fairly consistently.

Departures from the idea of one-to-one correspondence
between phoneme and grapheme have also occurred when the
tengwar system offers two variants of one letter (as in the
case of *s* (*6/9*) and *z* (*ʒ/3*), or a standard combination of
two sounds in one letter (such as *rd* ᴪ and *ld* ᴣ).

SAMPLE 6. PORTIONS OF TWO POEMS FROM THE LORD OF THE RINGS,
*CALLIGRAPHIC INSCRIPTIONS IN THE FLY-LEAVES. TAKOMA PARK,
MARYLAND. EARLY 1969.*

6-A. 'TO THE SEA, TO THE SEA...' (FULL-LETTER VOWELS)
ᴐ = ə; ᴈ = æ.

t ū   ð ə   s T ·   t ū   ð ə   s T :   ð ə   ʍ   a*t   g ə l ẓ   a r   k r a l ŋ .

To   the   sea,   to   the   sea!   The   white   gulls   are   crying,

ð ə   w i ð   i z   ɒ l ō i ŋ   æ ð   ð ə   ʍ a l t   f ō m   l ẓ   f l a l ŋ:

The wind is blowing   and   the   white   foam   is   flying.

w e s t ·   w e s t   ə w ē ·   ð ə   r a u ð   s ə n i ẓ   f ā l l ŋ:

West,   West   away,   the round   sun   is   falling.

* Scribal error.

[Tengwar script line]

g r ē ʃ l p· g r ē ʃ i p· d u y u h i r ðem k ā l i ŋ·

Grey   ship,   grey   ship,   do   you   near   them   calling,

[Tengwar script line]

ð ə v o i s e ʒ ə v m a i p i p əl ðæt h æ v g o n b i f o r m T :

The voices   of   my   people   that   have   gone   before   me ?

[Tengwar script line]

a i w i l   l T v· a i   w i l   l T v   ð ə w u d ʒ ð æ t b o r   m i·

I   will   leave, I   will   leave   the   woods   that   bore   me;

[Tengwar script line]

f o r a u r d ē ʒ a r e ð i ŋ æ ðd a u r y i r ʒ a r f ē l i ŋ :

For   our   days   are   ending   and   our   years   are failing.

[Tengwar script line]

a i w i l p æ ʂ ð ə w a i d w ō t ə r ʒ   l ō n l i   s aⁱ l i ŋ:

I   will   pass   the   wide   waters   lonely   sailing.

[Tengwar script line]

l o ŋ   a r ð ə w ē v ʒ o n ð ə l æ s t ʃ o r f o l i ŋ·

Long   are   the   waves   on   the   last   shore   falling,

[Tengwar script line]

s w T t a r ð ə v o i ʂ e ʒ i n ð ə l o ʂ t a i l c o l i ŋ·

Sweet   are   the   voices   in   the   lost   isle   calling,

---

* This error apparently due to confusion.

(tengwar script line)

I n -e-rz--ea- ·in e l v e n h ō m · ð æ t n ō   m æ n k æ n di ş k ə v ə r ·

In Eressea, in Elvenhome,   that   no   man   can   discover,*

(tengwar script line)

м e r ð ə l T v ʒ f a l n ō t .. l æ ð ə v m a i p T p ə l   f o r e v ə r :

Where the leaves fall not: land of my people forever!

---

* Spelled according to the Quenya mode, since it is a Quenya name.

6-B. FROM 'EÄRENDIL WAS A MARINER'. (DIACRITIC VOWELS)

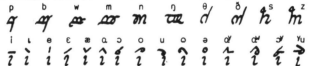

Symbols Used in This Transcription

A specially modified tengwar system is used here. Several letters
are changed in shape and value. In particular, note the following:

p   b   w   m   n   θ   ð   s   z

i   ɪ   e   ɛ   æ   ɑ   ɔ   o   u   ʊ   ə   ɒ   ɔ   ɑ   ʌ   ʸu

This system gives a 'unit phoneme' analysis to some vowels that are
considered compound in other systems. An underposed acute accent
is used to mark stress when it falls on some syllables beside the
penultimate in polysyllabic words (as *'errandless, un'heralded*).

(tengwar script line)

ə   æ ɪ   ə   æ ə   ɑʸ

f r m   n ʃ ŋ   v ð n r w s

From gnashing of the   Narrow Ice

(tengwar script line)

ɛ   æ ə   ɑʸ   o ɛ   ɪ

ɸ r ʃ d -   l z   n   f r z   n   h l z

Where shadow lies on frozen   hills

271

ᴋʏᴀᴇᴍᴀᴛʜʏ ʜᴛ'ᴅ ᴀᴇɴ ᴀᴇʙʀɴŋ ᴡᴇsᴛ

ə	ɛ ə	l	æ	ə	ʟ	e
f r m	n ð r	h t ' s	ð	b r n ŋ		w st

From   nether   heats and   burning   waste

i	ə	ʟ	e æ	ə	o ʟ	ʟ
h-	t r n d	n	h st	ð	r v ŋ	st l

He   turned   in   haste and roving still

ɔ	ɑ ɛ	ə	ɔ ə	ɑ	ɑ	e
n	st r l s	w t r z	f r		st r -	

on   starless waters   far astray

æ	æ	i	e	ɔ	ɑʸ ə	ɔ
t	l st	h-	k m	t -	n t	v n t

At last   he   came   to   Night of Naught

æ	æ æ	ɛ ə	ɑʸ	i	ɔ	
ð	p st. ð	n v r	st	h-	s-	

And passed, and never sight he saw

ə	ɑʸ ʟ	ɔ	ɔ	ɑʸ	i	ɔ
v	ʃ n ŋ	ʃ r	n r	l t	h-	st :

Of   shining shore nor light he sought.

ʟ	ə	æ	e	ɑʸ ʟ	ʟ	
ð	w ð z	v	r θ	k m	d r v ŋ	h m .

The winds of   wrath   came driving   him,

```
 æ       aʸ  i  ɩ        o    i      ɛ
 d    b  l  d l -  n     ð    f m   h-  f l  d
And   blindly     in the     foam   he   fled
```

```
    ə       ɛ    ɒ   i    æ   ɛ æ    ɩ
 f  r m   w  st  ɩ -  st   d   r  d  l   s.
From      west    to east  and errandless,
```

```
 ə    ɛ  ɑ    ɛ   i    o    ɑ        ɛ
 n  h  r  l  d d  h-  h  m   w   r  d   f l  d
Unheralded    he homeward      fled*.
```

* Should read 'sped'.

I quote a significant remark written by the transcriber
of these poems:

> I could not rely on spelling, as some people have done,
> because (and I state this with great feeling), I simply
> do not BELIEVE IN English spelling except as a necessary
> evil.

He continues in this vein, explaining his difficulty in
learning spelling and his contact with Spanish, which provided him with a phonemic ideal. If we are to take him at
his word, we would probably have to say that this person does
not have an underlying lexical representation based on the
orthographic form. The tengwar system he uses certainly
seems to be consistently phonemic, though in 6-A the alternate forms of the *s* and *z* letters are used without implying
phonemic significance; again, the tilde is used for homorganic nasals in 6-A.

PUNCTUATION

I have said nothing about punctuation because it is not
generally treated in discussions of orthographic theories.
This is not to say that it is unimportant; but I have found
that most people who write with the tengwar generally use the
standard orthographic punctuation conventions, simply using
different symbols. In most cases (significantly) the coma is
represented by a single dot or dash and the period by more
than one dot or dash; sometimes by a more complex mark. The
tendency is to make the comma a smaller mark than the period,

L

273

in contrast to the system used in standard orthography.

To my knowledge, no attempt has been made to devise a system of punctuation based on intonation contours and juncture types.

CONCLUSIONS

0PINION IS DIVIDED among tengwar writers as to whether the basis of their system should be the traditional orthography or some sort of phonemic theory. To date, no attempts have made to relate the tengwar to the underlying phonology of English by using the principles of generative grammar and phonology; orthographic systems have tended to follow the irregularities of the traditional system. The frequent use of single tengwa for -*h* digraphs in the spelling suggests that these are psychological units in the underlying representation of traditional orthography for most people.

The most general conclusion that one can reach from this set of data is that most literate speakers of English probably do have underlying psychological-lexical forms which are close to the traditional orthography, or are based primarily on it. There are those who probably do not have a lexicon based on the orthography, but it is difficult to assess the relative number of these or their general level of linguistic sophistication. It is possible that non-linguistically trained literate English speakers would be able to learn to read and write a phonemically-based system of tengwar if one were provided ready-made with standard forms for each word, so that the individuals would not have to generate phonemic forms on their own.

Finally, the fluctuation which is common between types of system and the inconsistent use of various optional letters and marks leads us to agree with the closing statement of King (1969):

> *Scribal practice is not a satisfying field for the linguist. The harder one works with extensive date, the harder scribal practice is to explain in any consistent way.* (p. 213)

Bibliography

Campbell, Lyle. Review of Robert D. King, *Historical Linguistics and generative grammar*. *Language*, 47:1 (1971), 191-209.

Chomsky, Noam, and Morris Halle. *The Sound Pattern of English*. New York: Harper & Rowe, 1968.

Hanna, Paul R., Richard E. Hodges, Jean S. Hanna, Edwin H. Rudorf, Jr.

Phoneme-grapheme correspondences as cues to spelling improvement. Washington, D.C.: U.S. Government Printing Office (U.S. Office of Education Research Project No. 1991), 1966.

King, Robert D. *Historical linguistics and generative grammar.* Englewood Cliffs, N.J.: Prentice Hall, 1969.

Pike, Kenneth L. *Phonemics: a technique for reducing languages to writing.* Ann Arbor: Univ. of Mich. Press, 1947.

Twaddell, W. Freeman. 'A note on Old High German umlaut', *Monatshefte für Deutschen Unterricht*, 30 (1938), 177-81.

Venezky, Richard L. *The Structure of English Orthography.* The Hague: Mouton, 1970.

A PARALLEL TO THE TENGWAR

Jim Allan

ŞEVERAL YEARS AGO, while browsing through the local library,
I chanced to leaf through a short book entitled *Studies in
Phonetics and Linguistics* by David Abercrombie (London:
Oxford University Press, 1965). Suddenly, on page 51, a
chart caught my eye (reprinted on the facing page). It por-
trayed an alphabet very similar in style and organization to
the tengwar of Fëanor. Not only did the characters of the
'Univerfall Alphabet' somewhat resemble them, but they varied
among themselves in somewhat the same way with single bows,
double bows, open bows, closed bows, and variations of the
stems. They were presented in 'ranks' and 'files' answering
to Tolkien's presentation of the tengwar in 'grades' and
'series'. Both systems used diacritics to represent vowels.

The originator of this alphabet was a certain Francis
Lodowick or Lodwick. Abercrombie writes: 'Apart from the
facts that he was a merchant of Dutch origin who lived in
London, was elected a Fellow of the Royal Society in November 1681 and sworn of the Council in December 1686, lived a
long life and knew a great number of people, I have been able
to find out practically nothing about him'.

In 1647 Lodwick published a book entitled in full: *A
Common Writing: Whereby two, although not understanding one
the others Language, yet by the helpe thereof, may communicate their minds one to another*; and, in 1652 he had printed
a pamphlet on the same subject with the title: *The Ground-
Work, or Foundation Laid (or so intended), For the Framing of
a New Perfect Language: And an Vniversall or Common Writing*.
These works outlined a proposed new universal language, like

The Univerſall Alphabet. 137

The Table of Conſonants

The Table of Vowels

The Lords Prayer in Engliſh.

PLATE I, from Francis Lodwick's 'Essay towards an Universal Alphabet',
Philosophical Transactions, 16:182 (June 26, 1686), 137.

Esperanto, and Abercrombie believes it was the earliest such
language to be presented in England. Lodwick also produced,
but never published, a shorthand in both an English and
Dutch version, the latter being, Abercrombie believes, the
first Dutch shorthand.

The *Universal Alphabet*, or 'universalphabeth' as Lodwick
once calls it, was worked out during, or previous to, 1673;
was first published in 'Essay towards an Universal Alphabet',
Philosophical Transactions 182, Vol. 16, 1686; and was
reprinted almost in full in *The Philosophical Transactions
and Collections to the End of the Year 1700 Abridg'd and Dis-
pos'd under General Heads*, by John Lowthorp, London, 1705,
Vol. III. pp. 373-79.

Lodwick intended his alphabet to be capable of representing accurately the pronunciation of any language, and it
is indeed capable of doing a sufficiently accurate job for
most European languages. He devised new characters instead
of using the familiar roman letters and modifications of them
in order to be free of their 'corrupt and differing expressions.'

Using the voiced stops as a base, Lodwick represents
the corresponding voiceless stops by the addition of a
hook, the (voiced) nasals by addition of a double hook
the voiced spirants by a closed hook, and the voiceless spirants by a closed hook crossing the stem in the middle. The
character ƕ in rank 6, file 2, was to be used in transcribing
nasalized vowels; and ⌐ in file 12, as indicated by the
explanatory Hebrew *aleph* (א), for the glottal stop [ʔ], and
perhaps as a vowel carrier for the second vowel in combinations such as *oe* in *coerce* and *yi* in *marrying*. The character η in rank 1, file 3, represents the English *j* sound,
[ʤ], as in *journey*, while ᵇ in rank 4, file 4, represents
the French *j* sound, [ʒ], as in *journée*, and in English *azure*,
rouge, *occasion*. The character ᵐ in rank 4, file 3, transcribed *g̃n*, represents the French *gn*, [ɲ], pronounced somewhat as *ny* in *canyon*.

As for the blank entries, Lodwick says that their sounds
are 'so like in pronunciation to some others in the Table,
that the difference would be too nice for common discern-
ment'. The characters ᵇ and ᵇ in 4:1 and 5:1 would be the
bilabial spirants [β] and [Φ]. The first three characters
in file 5 would be the labio-dental voiced stop [6], the
labio-dental voiceless stop [π], and the labio-dental nasal
[ɱ]. The first three characters in file 6 would represent
varieties of the counterparts in file 2, pronounced with the
tongue farther back in the mouth. (The first three characters in file 2 actually repesent *d*, *t*, and *n* pronounced with
the tip of the tongue on the upper teeth, as in French, not
on the alveolar ridge as in English.)

Stressed syllabes are indicated by underlining.

Lodwick's alphabet is similar to the tengwar in its characters, conceptual framework, and method of presentation. Both use mainly four columns, for in Lodwick's system, files 5 to 12 contain only one or two characters each, and the two in file 5 really fill the two blank spaces in file 1 for most European languages.

Of the two systems, the tengwar is unquestionably the superior. Its modification of the character shapes is more systematic, and provides for unvoiced nasals, aspirates, and other variations if required. Also, since the tengwar do not really compose an alphabet, but are 'a system of consonantal signs, of similar shapes and style, which could be adapted at choice or convenience to represent the consonants of languages observed', it is possible to show the relationship of the approximants to the corresponding stops and spirants by assigning them to characters whose theoretic values are not required by the language. Most important is the readibility of the tengwar. Abercrombie criticizes Lodwick's alphabet: 'It suffers from the same defect as all its "representational" predecessors and successors: the letters are far too like one another, and reading becomes a painful and laborious process.' But I don't find material written in tengwar particularly hard to read, providing the mode used is of a normal kind, and I am, at the time, not out of practice. Nor have I encountered complaints from others that the tengwar characters are too alike. The tengwar system succeeds here, in part, because it takes advantage of the difficulty in showing the relationship of the liquids, semi-vowels, and *s* and *z* to other consonants by its representing them through characters contrasting with the stem-and-bow combinations used for stops and spirants. And the regular variations that occur are ones paralleled in roman letters, and so those who read roman letters are already trained to watch for them. There is the lowering, raising, and shortening of the stem, as in *p/b*; *q/d/a*; *h/n*; *g/o*; *y/u*; *j/l/i*; the rotation of characters, as in *p/d*, *q/b*, *n/u*, *m/w*; doubling, as in *n/m*, *v/w*; and opening, as in *b/h*, *g/y*, *a/c*, *n/r*.

Might Tolkien have known of Lodwick's work? Or, perhaps, might Lodwick too have walked with Elves?

THE RUNES

Jim Allan

OLD ENGLISH RUNES

    In current British editions of *The Hobbit* is printed
a short introduction by Tolkien in which he chiefly talks
about the runes on Thror's Map. He says:

> Runes were old letter originally used for cutting
> or scratching on wood, stone, or metal, and so were
> thin and angular. At the time of this tale only the
> Dwarves made regular use of them, especially for
> private or secret records. Their runes are in this
> book represented by English runes, which are known
> now to few people.

In short, just as we must suppose that the English roman letter script on Thror's map must stand for an original Westron
tengwar script, so we are to suppose that the runes Tolkien
shows on the map are substitutions for the actual *certar*
characters used by the Dwarves.

    Rune is from an old Germanic root meaning 'secret', and
was probably a name given to various marks and signs used by
priests and diviners in their rituals, and to other marks of
various meanings. The RUNIC ALPHABET came later based on
various North Italic alphabets, which were in turn based on
the Phoenician or Canaanite alphabet. The Phoenicians were
the greatest traders of the ancient Mediterranean world and
left behind their alphabet wherever they went. The Phoenician
alphabet was adapted and changed in various local areas to
fit better the local languages, and so arose a number of
slightly differing alphabets all through the Mediterranean

area. The rise of Athens led to its version of the alphabet
gaining primacy in the Greek world, and the slightly varying
alphabets of the rest of the eastern Mediterranean were gradually forgotten. Similarly, the later rise of Rome led to
the version of the alphabet current there becoming the only
acceptable alphabet for the writing of Latin, and the local
varieties with their slightly differing forms of characters
—and even different numbers of characters—died out. But
before they did, sometime about 250 to 150 B.C., a version
of one of these North Italic alphabets was taken up by a
forgotten Germanic tribe, recast somewhat to better express
the sounds of their own tongue, and so gradually spread
throughout the Germanic world.

The Anglo-Saxons developed their own version of this
runic alphabet, notable for its large number of characters.
There were other differing runic alphabets in Germany and
Scandinavia, all sprung from the same source. But in all
countries they gradually fell from use. Runes had become
connected with a great amount of pagan lore and magic, and
so were generally frowned upon by the church. Also, those
who valued reading and writing and the search for knowledge
naturally turned to Latin and to the roman letter where
they could find such. And so the literates of the societies,
those most able to forward the runic alphabet, tended to be
those with the least will to do so. Rune-lore became rustic,
indulged in by the learned only in game. Finally it ceased
altogether to be a part of anyone's daily life. The Latin
alphabet had triumphed.

In the introduction to *The Hobbit* Tolkien remarks
that 'on the Map all the normal runes are found, except Ψ for
X'. He points out that some single runes stand for two of
our modern letters, and that 'other runes of the same kind
(ᛠ *ea* and ᛥ *st*) were also sometimes used. We can add to
this the rune ᛇ *eo* which appears on the original dust jacket
of the British edition of *The Hobbit* in the runic spelling
of the name of its publisher 'George Allen and Unwin'.

Putting all these runes together we arrive at a very
reasonable adaptation of the Old English runes for use with
Modern English. This alphabet appears at the head of the
following page. The characters are listed in their traditional order—the English runic alphabet was known as the
futhorc from an anagram of the values of the first six letters—with their Old English names, translations of those
names, and a listing of letters from the Modern Latin and
Modern Greek alphabets for each rune indicating modern
cognates to the form from which it was probably originally
taken. The source for each of the runes is not so certain
as the table suggests, but the observer should be able to
note the undeniable resemblence in about half the cases and

to see, at least, how there easily could be a relationship in about half the remainder.

ᚠ	f	*feoh* 'cattle'	(F)		ᛋ	s	*sigel* 'sun'	(S Σ)
ᚢ	u	*ūr* 'aurochs'	(U V Y)		↑	t	*tīr*, an old god	(T)
ᚦ	th	*þorn* 'thorn'	(D)		ᛒ	b	*beorc* 'birch'	(B)
ᚩ	o	*ōs* 'god˙'	< ᚫ		ᛖ	e	*eh* 'horse'	(E)
ᚱ	r	*rād* 'journey'	(R)		ᛗ	m	*man* 'Mankind'	(M)
ᚳ	c	*cēn* 'torch'	(C G Γ)		ᛚ	l	*lagu* 'water'	(L Λ)
ᚷ	g	*gyfu* 'gift'	(X Ξ)		ᛝ	ng	*Ing*, an old god	(Q)
ᚹ	w	*wyn* 'joy'	(F)		ᛟ	ee	*ēðel* 'property'	(O)
ᚻ	h	*hægl* 'hail'	(H)		ᛞ	d	*dæg* 'day'	(Θ)
ᚾ	n	*nȳd* 'need'	(N)		ᚪ	a	*æsc* 'ash (tree)'	(A)
ᛁ	i	*īs* 'ice'	(I)		ᚣ	y	*ȳr* 'yew-bow'	< ᚢ
ᛇ	eo	*ēoh* 'yew'	(I)		ᛠ	ea	*ear* 'sea' or 'earth'	
ᛈ	p	*peorð* ???	(P Π)		ᛣ	k	*calc* 'sandal' or chalice'	
ᛉ	x	*eolhx* 'defence'	(Z)		ᛥ	st	*stān* 'stone'	

The rune ᛟ originally had the value *o*, but then ᚫ was devised as a modification of ᚫ to cover the normal *o* sounds, and ᛟ was used for a modified *o* sound (usually the result of *i*-affection) *œ*. But *œ* early changed to *e*, and so the value of the rune was again modified. Tolkien's use of it for *ee* is a reasonable modern development.

Tolkien notes:

> I and U are used for J and V. There is no rune for Q (use CW); nor for Z (the dwarf-rune ᚼ may be used if required.

There was, in fact, an Old English rune for *j* which was sometimes used. It had the form ᛄ , was named *gēr* 'year', and followed ᛁ .

A second normal rune not included by Tolkien is ᚫ , another derivation from ᚫ . As indicated by its name *æsc*, ᚫ actually had the Old English value *æ*. Since *æ* is the most normal sound for our modern letter *a*, the use of ᚫ for *a* in modern English is quite correct. ᚪ represented Old English *a* with the sound [ɑ] as in Modern English *father*. It might still so be used for *a* when it has this sound. The name of the rune was *āc* 'oak', and it followed ᛞ .

In his use of the runes Tolkien spells *when* ᚻᚹᛖᚾ (HWEN), following the Old English method of showing the voiceless *w*.

RUNES

THE *CERTAR* OR *CIRTH*

The Sindar of the First Age developed an alphabet of nineteen characters, which could not have been sufficient to cover all the phonemes of Sindarin. Inspired by the *tengwar* of Fëanor, Daeron the loremaster of King Thingol of Doriah used this old alphabet as the foundations for a new, devising new characters from the old and so reassigning values among the old that, as with the *tengwar* of Fëanor, the relationship between the sounds of the language were mirrored by the relationships between the shapes of the characters. For *t* the symbol ᛐ was used as having the closest resemblance to the *tengwa* p. For *p* the character ᚹ was used from its resemblance to ꝑ, and for *c* was used ᚴ from its resemblance to q. An addition of a second branch to the stem paralleled the doubling of the bow in the *tengwar*. Reversing of the character paralleled the raising of the stem in the *tengwar*.

Because the characters had been originally developed through cutting and scratching upon wood and stone they were angular and simple in design, and so bear a resemblance to the much later Germanic runic alphabet.

This was the Certhas Daeron, the Alphabet of Daeron. It was later expanded into the Angerthas Daeron, the Long Alphabet of Daeron, by the Noldor of Eregion, who wished for further characters to express easily sounds in the languages of Men and the sounds of their own Quenya. For a sound like English *ch* [tʃ] which could be considered halfway between *t* and *c*, they used ᛕ, which had formerly been *h*, but which in shape could be related to both ᛐ and ᚴ. Similarly ᚶ was created for *qu* with features relating it to both ᚴ and ᚹ. Variations on these new characters paralleling those representing the other voiceless stops created two new series.

But a symbol for *ŋw* was apparently not needed, so ᛉ was used instead for the combination *ngw* [ŋgw]. Some new characters, not too well integrated into the systematic variations, were also created for the combinations *nd* and *ng* [ŋg]. In Sindarin *mh* had become *v*, and so ᛄ was given the new value *mb*.

This full expansion of the Angerthas Daeron may be called the Angerthas Eregion, for it occurred in Eregion. It represents the fullest form of the *certar* alphabet used by the Eldar, for after the destruction of Eregion the Elves generally ceased to use the *cirth* at all.

The chart on the following page portrays the characters in this stage of the Angerthas Daeron arranged so as to make the logic of the system clear. I have given the characters values following Tolkien's system of transcribing Elvish. That is, *c* is used instead of *k*, and *y* indicates the Sindarin vocalic *y*, not a consonant.

Angerthas Daeron

CONSONANTS

No.	Value
1	p
2	b
3	f, ph
4	v, -f[1]
5	hw
6	m
7	mh[3], mb
8	t
9	d
10	th
11	dh
12	n
13	ch)
14	j
15	sh
16	zh
17	nj
18	c
19	g
20	ch
21	gh
22	ng, n[2] (ŋ)
23	qu
24	gw
25	chw
26	ghw, w
27	ngw
28	nw
29	r
30	rh
31	l
32	lh
33	ng
34	s
35	s
36	ss, z
38	nd
44	w
54	h
39	i(y)
–	+h

VOWELS

No.	Value
42	u
43	ú, û
45	y
46	e
47	é, e
48	a
49	á, a
50	o
51	ó, ô
52	ö
39	i
II	i, î
–	&

1. final f
2. in the combinations *nc* and *nqu*
3. archaic value

The vowels are also somewhat unsystematic in their
representation of length. It would seem that originally the
vowel letter was written twice, Ⱥ arising from such a double
writing, and only later was the procedure of doubling
part of the letter adopted. Also, originally ⵝ had the
value *m*, but when it was decided that a symbol for *mh* was
desirable, new symbols ß and ⵝ were created for *m* and
mh leaving ⵝ free, so it became *hw*.

Many of these changes are discussed at length in III:
402ff, and so there is no need to go into them further here.
Also discussed are the later developments by the Dwarves of
the Angerthas Moria and the Angerthas Erebor in which many
unsystematic changes were made. But it may be helpful to
have the various sytems laid out neatly, and this is what
the chart 'The Evolution of the Cirith' on the following page
attempts to do. In this chart, just to keep my readers on
their toes, I have used *k* not *c*, and *y* represents consonantal
y. The Sindarin vocalic *y* is indicated by *ü*.

Further information on the Angerthas Erebor was made
available in *The Lord of the Rings 1977 Calendar*, illustrated
by J. R. R. Tolkien (London:George Allen & Unwin Ltd., 1976).
There the first and last pages that Gandalf reads from the
Book of Mazarbul appear in a transcription in the Angerthas
Erebor. It is from this transcription that runes 59-62 are
taken, and whence the value of *ou* for 38 is derived. The
difference between the values of 38 and 60 is not clear.
Rune 38 is used on the first page for all occurrences of *ou*.
Rune 60 is used for *ou* in *out* in the other page. The hand-
writing on the two pages is intentionally different, and it
may be that the variation is a matter of personal choice of
which of two available symbols to use. A single rune is also
used for *oa*, but the page is not clear enough to discern its
form distinctly. The word 'the' is represented by a short
high verticle stroke, thus: ' . 'Of' is simple ⴄ *v*. 'Is'
is often indicated simply by the *z* rune ⵋ .

Some numerals also appear: ⴷ for '3', ⴍ for '4', and ⵍ
for '5'.

Underscoring is used to indicate double consonants and
long vowels in Dwarf-names. But *ó* is Ⱥ , save once when
it is Ⱥ̲ .

THE EVOLUTION OF THE CIRTH

ED = Early System of Daeron; LD = Late System of Daeron; EG = Angerthas Eregion; M = Angerthas Moria; EB = Angerthas Erebor. The original *cirth* are marked by *. Values in parentheses are less common.

#	ED	LD	EG	M	EB	#	ED	LD	EG	M	EB
1*	p	p	p	p	p	34	s	h/(s)	h/(s)	h(s)	s
2*	b	b	b	b	b	35*	s	s/(h)	s/(h)	'	s
3	f	f	f	f	f	36*	ss	ss	z	ŋ	ŋ
4	v	v	v	v	v	37	=	=	=	ng	ng
5*	m,mh	hw	hw	hw	hw	38	=	=	nd	nj	ou
6*	=	m	m	m	m	39*	i,y	i,y	i(y)	i	i
7	=	mh	mb	mb	mb	40	=	=	y	y	y
8*	t	t	t	t	t	41	=	=	hy	hy	hy
9*	d	d	d	d	d	42*	u,w	u	u	u	u
10	th	th	th	th	th	43	=	=	ú	ú	z
11	dh	dh	dh	dh	dh	44	=	w	w	w	w
12*	n	n	n	r	r	45	=	ú	ú	ú	ú
13*	h	h/(s)	ch	ch	ch	46*	e	e	e	e	e
14	=	=	j	=	j	47	é	é	é	é	é
15	=	=	sh	sh	sh	48	a	a	a	a	a
16	=	=	zh	=	zh	49	á	á	á	á	á
17	=	=	nj	z	x	50*	o	o	o	o	o
18*	k	k	k	k	k	51	ó	ó	ó	ó	ó
19*	g	g	g	g	=	52	=	ö	ö	ö	ö
20	kh	kh	kh	kh	kh	53	=	=	=	n	n
21	gh	gh	gh	gh	=	54	=	=	h	s/(h)	h
22*	ŋ	ŋ	ŋ	nn,n	n	55	=	=	=	ə	ə
23	=	=	kw	kw	kw	56	=	=	=	a	a
24	=	=	gw	gw	gw	57	=	=	=	=	ps
25	=	=	khw	khw	kwh	58	=	=	=	=	ts
26	=	=	ghw/w	ghw/w	ghw/w	59	=	=	=	=	ai
27	=	=	ngw	ngw	ngw	60	=	=	=	=	ou
28	=	=	nw	nw	nw	61	=	=	=	=	ea
29*	r	r	r	j	g	62	=	=	=	=	ew
30	rh	rh	rh	zh	gh		=	=	=	+h	+h
31	l	l	l	l	l		&	&	&	&	&
32*	lh	lh	lh	=	=		=	=	=	=	the
33	=	=	ng	nd	nd		=	=	=	=	doubling

THE CORRECT TENGWAR AND
CERTAR VALUES

Jim Allan

THE SUCCESSIVE EDITIONS AND PRINTINGS of *The Lord of the Rings* are marked by various revisions in the text made by Tolkien, but also by errors on the part of typesetters, some of which are not corrected in subsequent printings, but carried on. Appendix E II, where the tengwar and certar are discussed, has more than its fair share of such errors, mistakes that can only confuse and mislead the reader who tries to master the writing systems from the text as found, or wishes to compare Tolkien's assignment of values with those appearing in various places in this book. There has been sufficient argument among Tolkien fans as to assignment of values without the further còmplication of a faulty text at the base of the arguing.

1. The sentence beginning III:398, line 20 (III:496, line 21 in the Ballantine edition) ought to read, following α:

> The doubling of the bow indicated the addition of 'voice': thus if 1, 2, 3, 4 = *t*, *p*, *ch*, *k* (or *t*, *p*, *k*, *kw*), then 5, 6, 7, 8 = *d*, *b*, *j*, *g* (or *d*, *b*, *g*, *gw*).

Texts βγδε incorrectly read '*c*' instead of '*ch*'. This has led many designers of English tengwar modes to similarly use *c* for tengwa 3

2. The sentence following that discussed in 1 should read, following α:

> The raising of the stem indicated the opening of the consonant to a 'spirant': thus assuming the above values for Grade I, Grade 3 (9-12) = *th, f, sh, kh* (or *th, f, kh, khw/hw*), and Grade 4...

Texts βγδε incorrectly read *'ch'* for the first *'kh'*.
Texts γδε incorrectly read *'hk'* for the second *'kh'*.
Text ε reads *'...values of Grade 1, ...'*.

3. The note at the bottom of the same page as the sentences discussed in 1 and 2 ends in the clause *'ŋ is used for ng in sing'* in texts αβ. The clause is absent in γδε. This was a purposeful change made by Tolkien. See number **5** below.

4. A section titled NOTE appears on the following page in βγδε. The second-last sentence should read, following γδε:

> Similarly, Grade 4 was used for the extremely frequent combinations *nt, mp, nk, nqu*, since Quenya did not possess *dh, gh, ghw*, and for *v* used letter 22.

Text β incorrectly reads *'dli, gli, ghio'* for *'dh, gh, ghw'*. It looks as though this NOTE was given to Ballantine in handwritten form, and these letters were misread.

5. In the listing of tengwar letter names the last two names in series 5 appear in α as:

> *noldo* (older *ŋoldo*) one of the kindred of the Noldor,
> *nwalme* torment;

Text β reads:

> *noldo* (older *ŋoldo*) one of the kindred of the Noldor,
> *nwalme* (older *ywalme*) torment;

The form *'ywalme'* is an obvious error for a correct *'ŋwalme'*. A further revision appears in γδε:

> *noldo* (older *ngoldo*) one of the kindred of the Noldor,
> *nwalme* (older *ngwalme*) torment;
> [text ε actually reads *'... nwalme (older* ngwalme) torment;'*]

Here the sound [ŋ] is represented by *ng* in agreement with Tolkien's use elsewhere and his general principle of transribing Elvish words and names into roman letters following

the conventions of Latin spelling so far as is practical.
This revision accounts for the dropping of the clause discussed in **3** above.

6.   The fourth sentence of the second-last paragraph in
this appendix should read, following α:

> The disclocation in values was due mainly to two causes:
> (1) the alteration in the values of 34, 35, 54 respec-
> tively to *h*, ' (the clear or glottal beginning of a word
> with an initial vowel that appeared in Khuzdul), and *s*;

Texts βγδε omit the apostrophe sign indicating the glottal
stop or lack of consonant.
Texts γδε also omit the preceding comma.

7.   In the sentence following that discussed above in **6**
texts αβ read correctly:

> ... and the consequent use of 36 as *ŋ* and the new *certh*
> 37 for *ng* may be observed.

Texts γδε incorrectly read '*n*' for '*ŋ*'

THE WIELDERS OF THE THREE AND OTHER TREES

Paula Marmor

Foreward: I realize that many of the conclusions I leap
to herein are, to say the least, highly debateable; the
degree to which I myself accept their validity is depend-
ent upon my state of spiritual inebriation at the time.
Naytheless, of the accuracy of the basic tenets I have no
doubt; the other material is included to confuse the
issue.

THE INTENT OF THIS CONGLOMERATION of useless trivia is to
   show the bearers of the elf rings—Galadriel, Elrond, and
Gandalf by the end of the Third Age, as well as the older
bearers Gil-galad and Círdan—as archetypal figures of a
Moon-Water Goddess, a Sky-Air-Thunder God, and a Sun-Fire
God (Eliade, Ch. II-IV). This triplicity long reigned in the
Mediterranean and Celtic pantheons, although it is essentially foreign to the northern mythos as we know it; there
the Sea, Wind, and Fire are brothers (Hlér, Kari, Logi
[Grimm: 601,631]), and the Sun is referred to as 'She', with
the Moon being represented as masculine (as in Tolkien (I:
172). However, in general Norse gods of Air and Fire are
men, those of Water women, and Jacob Grimm gives evidence
that at a remote period the Sun and Moon were male and female
among the Germanic peoples as in the other Indo-European
mythologies (882-84).

   There are two areas where parallels between the ring-
bearers and these divinities may be looked for: in the symbolic 'package' which surrounds the bearers in *The Lord of
the Rings*, and in the overall pattern of the history of the
Three. To find the most symbolic passage concerning the
Three, refer to the scene at the end of the work: Sauron is
cast into darkness and the bearers are free to reveal themselves to mortal creatures. But their dominion in Middle-
earth has passed, and they are becoming one with the natures

293

of their rings. They are *fanar* of what they will become in the Uttermost West.

It is here that the most revealing description of Galadriel as the archetypal Moon-Water Goddess occurs:

> But Galadriel sat upon a white palfrey and was robed all in glimmering white, like clouds about the Moon; for she herself seemed to shine with a soft light. On her finger was Nenya, the ring wrought of *mithril*, that bore a single white stone, flickering like a frosty star. (III:303)

Nenya is from the Quenya and Sindarin root NÉN 'water', and this was Galadriel's special province. (For a list of the evidence connecting the Three with the elements Water, Air, and Fire—the alchemical triplicity—I refer the reader to Virginia Dabney's 'On the Natures and Histories of the Great Rings'.) In all mythologies, the Moon is given rulership of water, as creatrix of the tides (Eliade: 159). The whole pattern is Moon-rain-water-woman-serpent-fertility-death-regeneration (Eliade: 107). The Moon Goddess also weaves (Eliade: 181-82): the cloaks woven by Galadriel and her ladies had the hue of 'leaf and branch, water and stone' (I:386), and were in effect identical with the cloaks of invisibility of the fairy tales.

In astrological lore, the solstitial and equinoctal (angular) signs are referred to as Cardinal Signs. The Moon is the ruler of the Cardinal Water Sign: Cancer, the sign of the Summer Soltice. In this position, Galadriel is the Lady of Planting and the Harvest; earth from her land will grow marvelous crops wherever it is sprinkled, and only in her land of Lórien will the mallorn grown East of the Sea and West of the Shire-mallorn, her gift to Master Samwise.

In his book *The White Goddess*, poet-mythographer Robert Graves discusses the Mother Goddess of the Triple Moon (new-full=old = maiden-wife-old woman = Arwen-Celebrían-Galadriel) as she figures in Celtic and Mediterranean mythology (see also James, *The Ancient Gods*: 296ff) and her predominance in ancient cults of tree and forest theophany scattered throughout Europe. She is the Lady of the Trees (Eliade: 280ff); while each month of the lunar calendar (thirteen in all) is represented by its specific tree, the Goddess rules them all. The name *Galadriel* in Sindarin means either 'Lady of the Tree(s)', from *galadh*, or 'Lady of Bright Light', from *galad*. The Quenya form is **Altáriel*: †*alta* may be the archaic form of *alda* 'tree', or the High Elven equivalent of *galad*. (The similarity is intentional; see below.)

In his exploration of the extent of worship of the Goddess, Graves ties the thirteen-month calendar in with various mysteries of ancient Europe: the assorted alphabets and their tree-symbols (specifically the Irish Tree-Ogham, the

beth-luis-nion or *boibel-loth*), the Twelve Tribes of Israel
(a 'solarization' of an original thirteen, including the
tribe of Gad [Graves: 269ff]), and the jewels of the breast-
plate of the High Priest of Yahweh (ibid.). Using J. I.
Myers' identifications of the stones, Graves has reconstructed their arrangement to fit the lunar tree calendar,
the tribes, and his own theories; in his version, the stone
of the Summer Solstice is the white carnelian, which may be
the stone Galadriel wears.

There is not as much evidence for Elrond as a Sky-Air
God. At the Havens he 'wore a mantle of grey and had a star
upon his forehead, and a silver harp was in his hand...'
(III:308). His ring is the blue *Vilya* 'air', and his rulership is over the Autumnal Equinox and the Cardinal Air Sign
Libra. Libra is the sign of justice and judgment; hence
Elrond's role as counselor. Libra's ruling planet is Venus
in her role as Muse; thus he bears the Harp. (The Sky divinity Zeus was the patron of poetry and song [Grimm: 901].)
Elrond's father was Eärendil, the Morning Star (Grimm: 723),
and his daughter is Arwen *Undómiel* 'Evenstar'. If Arwen
were a Celtic divinity her name would mean 'The High White
One'; in reality the Welsh name for the Evening Star is
Gweno 'The White One' (Grimm: 1507), *-wen* and *gwen* being the
same word. The Morning and Evening Stars are both phenomena
of the planet Venus, the one coming before the sun and the
other after. His ring was given him by Gil-galad, whose name
means 'Star of Bright Light' (R:65); this may be another
aspect of Venus. The name *Elrond* is 'Star-(of the)-Vault'.
The element *-rond* is any large high enclosed area; it is
translated 'hall' in *Merethrond* and 'cave' in *Aglarond*.
'Vault' is an Elvish metaphor for 'sky'; Orion is sometimes
called *Telumehtar*, perhaps meaning 'Lord of the Vaults': cf.
telluma 'vault, dome'.

Gandalf is the bearer of *Narya*, the Ring of Fire. In
relating Fire and Sun, recall that the Eldarin words for
'Sun', *Anar*, *Anor*, *Nór-*, are derived from the words for
'Fire', nÁr and naur; nÁr is used for 'Sun' in the month
names *Narquelië/Narbeleth*, *Narvinyë/Narwain*, and *Nárië/Nórui*
('Sun-waning', 'Sun-new', and 'Sunny' in Quenya and Sindarin). The Elves thought of nÁr as red (in the Index *Narsil*
is glossed 'red-and-white flame' γδεIII:438), probably
because the setting sun appeared red over the Undying Lands.

The jewel of Narya is 'red as fire' (III:310), and Gandalf has special dominion over that element. His sign is the
Cardinal Fire Sign Aries, ruler of the Spring Equinox. Aries
is ruled by the 'red planet' Mars, although one contemporary
astrological theory—which I adhere to but will spare the
reader the details of—assigns the rulership of Aries to

Pluto, the planet of death, rebirth, and the underworld, reminiscent of Gandalf's transformation after the battle with
the Balrog on Zirak-zigil.

In the lunar calendar, the Vernal Equinox falls in the
fourth month, that of the alder, a tree connected with fire
in British folklore (Graves: 21). The tribe of this month is
Judah; the stone is—Eureka!—the brilliant red fire-garnet
or pyrope.

To digress for a moment (I have to put in at least one
digression or I'll ruin my reputation), consider the third
month. It began on February 19 and ran through March 18,
with Aragorn's birthday, March 1 (III:370)—the feast day of
St. David, the patron-saint of Wales—, neatly in the middle.
The tribe is Zebulon and the stone is (may I have the envel-
ope please?) the sea-green beryl (Graves: 271), the Elfstone
(I:213)! (By the way, Bilbo calles Eärendil's stone an emerald, but the emerald is a variety of beryl, so consistency is
maintained.) Thus Aragorn's royal name is his birthstone, so
to speak. This month is also the sign Pisces, the sign ruling the sea and usually considered the symbol of Christ, the
King who shall return.

It should surprise no one to learn that *Aragorn* may mean
'Lord of the Tree'. The tree of the third month is the ash,
the same as the great world tree, Yggdrasill (from *Yggr*,
another name of Óðin). Grimm defines *Yggr* as the thrill or
shudder of terror (Grimm: li); Graves connects it etymologic-
ally with the Greek *hygra* 'water or sea', and mentions that
it was sacred to the sea god Poseidon.

A word (or several) on the White Tree: as I indicated
above, it may have been an ash. In the Norse Eddas, the
first man and woman are Askr and Embla, literally 'Ash-tree'
and 'Work-woman' (Grimm: 572) (hmph!). Perhaps this resemblance would indicate that the second of the Two Trees was an
elm; most likely, however, it was the oak, a tree more widely
revered than any other (Graves: 176ff). However, I believe
that the Tree of Gondor was actually the mountain ash, or
rowan, which isn't REALLY an ash tree at all. It is related
to the apple, which brings in Avalon, the Golden Apples of
the West, and all sorts of tempting irrelevancies which I
will avoid at the moment. The rowan, however, has always
been identified with the ash family in popular imagination,
or the name *mountain ash* would not exist at all. In country
England, the rowan is called the *quicken* or *quickbeam*, OE
cwicbēam 'tree of life' (Graves: 167). Now our Quickbeam was
very attached to rowan trees ('Whenever he saw a rowan-tree
he halted awhile with his arms stretched out, and sang, and
swayed as he sang' [II:86]). Tolkien translates Quickbeam's
Sindarin name *Bregalad* as 'quick (lively) tree' (G:172); but

-*galad*—as in *Gil-galad* 'Star-(of)-Bright Light' (see above)
—, ought to mean 'light'. It is *galadh* that, like OE *bēam*,
means 'tree'. Now, there is no etymological explanation this
side of Sigma Draconis for the similarity between *galad* and
galadh except as an intentional word play on the name *Quickbeam*, translateable both as 'fast light' and 'tree of life'.
The prosecution rests.

To digress again (this is fun!), there is one symbol of
Aragorn not covered above: the eagle. In Gondor, he was
known as *Thorongil* 'Eagle of the Star' '...for he was swift
and keen-eyed, and wore a silver star upon his cloak' (III:
335). The Elfstone which Galadriel gave him on behalf of
Arwen, and which had been hers, was set in a brooch in the
form of an eagle (I:391). (I suspect that it was a twin to
the one Eärendil wore into the West—'upon his breast an
emerald' [I:246]—but there is no evidence for this.) Now it
happens that in addition to the thirteen-consonant Tree-
Ogham, there is a bird-Ogham. Graves identifies the eagle
with the sacred bird of the Winter Solstice, the day that
belonged to no month' (Graves: 299). The Winter Solstice is
the first day of the Cardinal Earth Sign Capricorn. (Inter-
estingly enough, while traditionally the eagle is the highest
octave of Scorpio—the cherubim being the angular signs of
about 2000 B.C., Taurus-Leo-Scorpio-Acquarius, that is, Bull-
Lion-Eagle-Man—sidereal astrologer Cyril Fagan has connected
the eagle with Capricorn [*American Astrology*, May 1971, 29]).
I believe the eagle to be the symbol of two people: the
greatest of the Elven Smiths, he who made the Great Jewels,
and his descendant whose name may mean 'Silversmith', he who
forged the Rings of Power: Fëanor and Celebrimbor. These two
created beyond their measure and in their pride gave Morgoth
and Sauron the keys to their power. It is fit that those who
followed Fëanor into exile should bear the eagle of his house
as a sign of their inheritance.

The Three Rings were wrought by Celebrimbor in Eregion
c. S.A. 1590. Originally they were in the possession of the
three highest of the Eldar in Middle-earth: Gil-galad, Círdan, and Galadriel. Before his death on Orodruin, Gil-galad
passed his ring on to Elrond. Círdan gave Narya to Gandalf
upon his arrival at the Havens from the West (I:256;III:364-
-66).

There is evidence in the history of the rings of a pattern corresponding to what Eliade calls 'a movement away from
the transcendence and passivity of sky beings towards more
dynamic, active, and easily accessible forms' (Eliade: 52,
126). Thus Eru, the One, is generally inactive in the
affairs of Middle-earth, and in this reflects the position
of such heavenly deities as Ouranos compared to his active

grandson Zeus. Eru and Manwe, the Lord of the Valar, are
seldom mentioned and never invoked. Like the ancient supreme
sky gods, they have been replaced by beings with closer ties
to Men: the lesser Valar and in turn, the High Elves. This
process continues within recorded history. Círdan has relin-
quished his position to the Wizard Gandalf (who is VERY
involved in the affairs of Men), and the last High Elven
king, Gil-galad, has passed away and been replaced by Elrond
Peredhel, the Half-elf.

Graves outlines the development of Mediterranean mythology from this pantheistic level back to monotheism in three
basic stages. The first consists of the Great Goddess, Queen
of Heaven, a triple lunar deity, whose Star-son becomes her
lover and is slain by the Serpent. The Serpent lays an egg
which the Goddess swallows, becoming impregnated and giving
birth to the Star-son again (Graves: 163-9). This is the
representative myth of the primitive matriarchal (and primarily agricultural) society, depicting the death and rebirth
of the Sun (that is, the vegetational year.)

The second stage sees another son born to the Goddess;
he is Thunder-Storm-Sky-God. He destroys the Star-son and
the Serpent, marries his mother, and begets on her children
who become the assorted gods and goddesses. Among the children are a Sun god and his sister, who becomes the Triple Muse
and effectively takes over the position and devotees of her
mother, the Triple Goddess. This stage is transitional;
Graves interprets the marriage of the Goddess (who before
became lover but never accepted the bonds of matrimony) and
her subsequent dethronement as the sociological or military
conquest of a matriarchal society by a patriarchal one.
Eventually, this patriarchal system conquers completely: the
Sun God gradually absorbs the attributes of the other deities, and the Goddess-cult fades into the background.

The third stage is purely patriarchal (or begins that
way; as far as Christianity is concerned, the Goddess has
made an effective return in the person of the Virgin Mary);
there are no goddesses at all, but one father god (James:
316) who may be seen as a dual or tripartite being, as the
Father, Son, and Holy Spirit of Christianity (Graves: 338-
93). (But the 'spirit that moved on the face of the waters'
was conceived of by the Hebrews and Greeks as female (Graves:
157); so in Gothic, the word for 'spirit, soul' is *saiula*,
derived from *saius* 'sea', and thought of as feminine; it was
perceíved as an 'undulating fluid force' [Grimm: 826]. Again
we have the triplicity male-female-male.)

Now we must apply this historical pattern to the rings.
There was only one bearer of Nenya, Galadriel, and she is the
Goddess. The Star-son who is destroyed by the Serpent is
Gil-galad 'Star of Bright Light' who first bore Vilya and who

was killed by the touch of Sauron (I:266). (It is not coincidental that this name is so similar to the Greek *sauros* 'lizard'—as in *dinosaur*. The serpent has ever been the symbol of the Devil.) Vilya 'sky, air' is then passed on to Elrond 'Star-vault', who becomes the Sky-Thunder God. Instead of marrying the Goddess Galadriel, he marries her daughter, Celerbrían, the Goddess-as-wife. (The name *Celebrían* means 'Silver----'. It would be nice if the second part were 'wheel', as in the Welsh *Arianrhod* 'Silver-wheel', the name of another Moon Goddess. But it probably isn't.)

In the place of the son of the Sky God comes Gandalf, the Sun-and-Fire God, who brings wisdom to Middle-earth as counselor to Aragorn, that is, mortal man aspiring to the love of the muse, Arwen, grandaughter of Galadriel and the Goddess-as-maiden. (The Triple Moon Goddess, by the way, was represented as white, red, and black, for the young, full, and old moon as pictured by the ancients. Galadriel was blond, Arwen brunette. By all rights Celebrían should have been a redhead!)

In most mythologies, the Sun God has a twin brother with whom he battles, their alternate terms of kingship taking the place of those of the Star-son and Serpent as the waxing and waning year. There are two possibilities for this enemy of Gandalf. The first that comes to mind is the Balrog, who defeated Gandalf and cast him down. However, the more likely candidate is Saruman; the myth always specifies a BROTHER (that is, the hero's darker self) as tanist. Saruman is another figure of the man whose thirst for knowledge has led him to the paths of evil. He is to the Third Age what Fëanor and Celebrimbor are to the First and Second.

The third stage of the myth pattern properly belongs to the Fourth Age and lies outside the compass of *The Lord of the Rings*. Then the Rings hold no sway over the hearts and minds of Men; for all of their glory and grace, the time of the Lesser Powers of Middle-earth is passed, and they are forgotten, and Men worship only the One.

References:

Dabney, Virginia. 'On the Natures and Histories of the Great Rings', *Mythcon I Proceedings*. Ed. Glen H. GoodKnight. Whittier, California: The Mythopoeic Society, 1971.

Eliade, Mircea. *Patterns in Comparative Religion*. Cleveland, N.Y.: World, 1963.

Graves, Robert. *The White Goddess*. New York: Noonday Press, 1966.

Grimm Jacob. *Teutonic Mythology*. Trans. James Steven Stallybrass. 4 volumes. 1883, 1888; rpt. New York: Dover Publications, 1966.

James, E.O. *The Ancient Gods*. New York: Putnam, 1960.